Philosophy, Dreaming and the Literary Imagination

Michaela Schrage-Früh

Philosophy, Dreaming and the Literary Imagination

palgrave
macmillan

Michaela Schrage-Früh
University of Limerick
Limerick, Ireland

ISBN 978-3-319-82165-8   ISBN 978-3-319-40724-1 (eBook)
DOI 10.1007/978-3-319-40724-1

© The Editor(s) (if applicable) and The Author(s) 2016
Softcover reprint of the hardcover 1st edition 2016
This work is subject to copyright. All rights are solely and exclusively licensed by the Publisher, whether the whole or part of the material is concerned, specifically the rights of translation, reprinting, reuse of illustrations, recitation, broadcasting, reproduction on microfilms or in any other physical way, and transmission or information storage and retrieval, electronic adaptation, computer software, or by similar or dissimilar methodology now known or hereafter developed.
The use of general descriptive names, registered names, trademarks, service marks, etc. in this publication does not imply, even in the absence of a specific statement, that such names are exempt from the relevant protective laws and regulations and therefore free for general use.
The publisher, the authors and the editors are safe to assume that the advice and information in this book are believed to be true and accurate at the date of publication. Neither the publisher nor the authors or the editors give a warranty, express or implied, with respect to the material contained herein or for any errors or omissions that may have been made.

Printed on acid-free paper

This Palgrave Macmillan imprint is published by Springer Nature
The registered company is Springer International Publishing AG
The registered company address is: Gewerbestrasse 11, 6330 Cham, Switzerland

For David and Frederic

Acknowledgements

This book would have remained a dream without the generous assistance and support of family, friends, colleagues and institutions. First of all, I thank the Johannes Gutenberg-Universität Mainz for their financial support, which allowed me to present papers at several international dream-related conferences, most notably at two inspiring conferences of the International Association for the Study of Dreams in Chicago (2009) and Asheville (2010), respectively.

I am indebted to the Faculty of Arts, Humanities and Social Sciences, University of Limerick, for funding my attendance at the 'Cognitive Futures in the Humanities' conference, University of Durham, in 2014, and for a generous book completion award in spring 2016. Completing this book would not have been possible without the support of my colleagues at the University of Limerick, who have in various ways facilitated and encouraged my research. I would especially like to thank Anita Barmettler, Jean Conacher, Joachim Fischer, Margaret Mills Harper, Gisela Holfter, Marieke Krajenbrink, Cathy McGlynn, Patricia Moran, Tina Morin, Margaret O'Neill, Veronica O'Regan, Orla Prendergast and Maria Rieder.

Further thanks are due to Anja Müller-Wood, Patricia Plummer and Alyce von Rothkirch for their insightful comments on earlier chapter drafts, as well as to the anonymous readers at Palgrave for offering helpful feedback on the manuscript. Likewise, I am grateful to Sibylle Wittek for her excellent research assistance during the early stages of this project. Heartfelt thanks go to Hans-Walter Schmidt-Hannisa, Marie Guthmüller and all members of the DFG-funded network 'The Nocturnal Self' for fruitful discussions on a fascinating topic. Most importantly, I thank Jennifer M. Windt for our inspiring conversations which sparked my interest in the philosophical dimensions of dreaming.

On a more personal note, I am grateful to my mother, Renate Schrage, for being there from afar during difficult times. And finally, above all, I thank my husband Rainer David W. Früh and my son Frederic Samuel Noah Früh for their unfailing encouragement and loving support during the long and sometimes difficult writing process. This book is dedicated to them.

Limerick, June 2016

Contents

1	Introduction	1
2	Towards an Aesthetics of Dreaming	21
3	Dreaming and Waking Imagination	59
4	Dreaming Fictions, Writing Dreams	131
5	Conjuring Up the Dream: Three Literary Case Studies	207
6	Conclusion	261
Bibliography		269
Index		291

1

Introduction

Throughout the ages, dreaming has served as an analogy for the creation of literary fictions to such an extent that this analogy has turned into a metaphorical commonplace, evoked whenever we nonchalantly refer to Hollywood as a *dream* factory or to our nocturnal dreams as a dream *theatre*. Depending on cultural context and individual inclination, the metaphor of fiction as dream has been either negatively or positively connoted, ranging from a view of dreams as meaningless fancies to a view of dreams as divine revelations. Countless writers have, moreover, embraced the notion of a 'dream-and-literature-symbiosis',[1] claiming to find creative inspiration and sustenance in their dreams, while their experiences have in turn inspired philosophical reflections. Thus, the Italian Renaissance philosopher Girolamo Cardano (1501–1576) viewed dreaming and artistic creation as analogous processes, showing 'an awareness that dream and art function as modes capable of extending the imagination's creative powers'.[2] Paracelsus (1493–1541), too, acknowledged the dream's creative potential and its inspirational value for artists: 'Frome

---

[1] Rupprecht (2007), 4.
[2] Primm (1987), 163.

© The Author(s) 2016
M. Schrage-Früh, *Philosophy, Dreaming and the Literary Imagination*,
DOI 10.1007/978-3-319-40724-1_1

time immemorial artistic insights have been revealed to artists in their sleep and in dreams, so that at all times they ardently desired them'.[3] With the rise of Romanticism the aesthetic quality of the dream itself was increasingly emphasized,[4] culminating in Samuel Taylor Coleridge's (1772–1834) view of poetry as a 'rationalized dream'[5] and Jean Paul's (1763–1825) notion of dreaming as 'involuntary poetry'.[6] Even Robert Macnish (1802–1837), a nineteenth-century philosopher firmly rooted in the materialist tradition, marvelled that the imagination could produce dreams 'lighted up with Prothean fire of genius and romance; [...] magnificent poetry; [and] peopled with new and unheard-of imagery'.[7] These ideas still reverberate in present times, for instance in Jorge Luis Borges' (1899–1986) rephrasing of Coleridge and Jean Paul respectively in his references to literature as a 'directed dream' and to the act of dreaming as 'perhaps the most ancient aesthetic expression'.[8]

In *Such Stuff as Dreams: The Psychology of Fiction* (2011), Keith Oatley takes his cue from such analogies, in particular drawing on William Shakespeare's concept of the dream as a 'model world'[9] from which the Bard's 'idea of theater as model-of-the-world',[10] comparable to a dream, could develop. In his stimulating study on the psychology of fiction, Oatley repeatedly refers to this dream analogy:

'Dream' is a good metaphor for fiction because most of us have experience of dreaming and know that dreams are somewhat apart from the ordinary world. We know, too, that they are constructed by ourselves. They are not direct impressions of the world, and they may be meaningful.[11]

---

[3] Paracelsus quoted in Primm (1987), 166. One such example from the Renaissance period is Albrecht Dürer (1471–1528). See Schmidt-Hannisa (2001a), 85.
[4] Hans-Walter Schmidt-Hannisa convincingly argues that the Romantics were the first to establish an understanding of the dream as aesthetic experience. See Schmidt-Hannisa (2001a), 84.
[5] Coleridge, *Notebooks*, vol. 1, 2086.
[6] See Schmidt-Hannisa (2001b).
[7] Macnish, *The Philosophy of Sleep*, 67.
[8] Borges, *Seven Nights*, 40. For other examples of writers inspired by their dreams, see Epel (1993), Townley (1998) and Royle (1996).
[9] Oatley (2011), 2.
[10] Oatley (2011), 3.
[11] Oatley (2011), 16.

Content with metaphorical evocations of the dream, however, Oatley stops short of posing the question that almost inevitably suggests itself: If dreams and fictions are so intimately connected, might not the 'psychology of fiction' be the same as, or at least closely related to, the psychology of dreaming? And, if so, might not his study of 'what happens psychologically when we engage with fiction as readers or audience members, and of what we are doing as writers and performers',[12] infinitely profit from taking into account the findings of contemporary sleep and dream research? After all, both dreaming and waking fictions can be considered as manifestations of the same 'literary mind',[13] to use Mark Turner's much-cited phrase, and the vast majority of dream researchers today emphasize the creative, expressive and imaginative qualities of dreams.

Dreams figure prominently in literary writing,[14] which is hardly surprising given that dreaming is a cross-cultural universal activity.[15] After all, we spend one third of our lives in sleep, and research has shown that during that seemingly passive and restive state, we dream in regular cycles, several times a night, regardless of whether we recollect our dreams or not.[16] Even though more than 95 % of our dreams may go unremembered,[17] those remaining 5 % give evidence of a private and fascinating world of our own, a world that defies natural laws and is all the same experienced as real while the dream lasts. As Lord Byron aptly writes: '...Sleep hath its own world,/And a wide realm of wild reality'.[18] This world is not bound to time and space and can carry us back and

---

[12] Oatley (2011), 18.
[13] Turner (1996).
[14] This is documented by the sheer number of anthologies featuring literary dreams. See De La Mare (1984 [1939]), Hill (1968), Almansi and Béguin (1986b), Brook (2002) and Gidion (2006). For useful overviews on dreams in literature, see Atchity and Atchity (1990), Rupprecht (1991) and Rupprecht (2007).
[15] For the universality of the dream experience, see Bosnak (2007), 9; Parman (1991); and Solomonova et al. (2011), 174.
[16] See Aserinsky and Kleitman (1953). In 1953, Eugene Aserinsky and Nathaniel Kleitman discovered that sleep consists of two cyclically alternating states, REM (rapid eye movement) and NREM (non-rapid eye movement) sleep. During REM sleep, we experience our most vivid and extensive dreams, although dreaming can occur during NREM sleep as well in the early and late hypnagogic stages of sleep, upon falling asleep and upon waking up.
[17] See Hobson (1988), 7.
[18] Byron, 'The Dream' (1816) quoted in De La Mare (1984 [1939]), 386.

forth between distant childhood scenarios and the previous day, taking us in one instant to our present workplace (curiously refashioned) and in the next to a classroom 30 years ago (curiously resembling our present workplace). The next moment, we find ourselves trapped in some hijacked plane, a house under siege, stuck in the middle of a traffic jam or walking on a beautiful Southern beach. Our dreams can be variously populated by people we know or used to know, by people we have never before encountered (though they may bear vaguely familiar traits) or by odd composites. Sometimes, these dream characters undergo transformations before our very eyes, from stranger to friend or from baby to bird. In dreams, we tend to take such transformations in our stride, unblinkingly accepting for real the most outlandish occurrences, such as being chased by humanoid monsters or visited by long-dead relatives. At times we can accomplish things we never could in waking life, like flying unaided; we can live through dramatic situations and intricate plots ranging from the everyday to the extraordinary; and we can experience the entire spectrum of emotions, from overwhelming elation to profound embarrassment to mortal fear. While it lasts, the dream is the only reality we know,[19] but it is a reality that can never be shared at first hand and that tends to evaporate or haphazardly survives in fragmentary glimpses or clumsy dream reports that never quite capture the actual dream experience. Upon waking, the bits and pieces recollected from our dreams often appear bizarre, nonsensical or simply mundane. At other times, they seem to provide spiritual guidance, insights into the hidden depths of our psyches or even prophetic glimpses of the future. On notable occasions, dreams have been known to trigger scientific discoveries, groundbreaking problem-solving as well as aesthetic creations.[20] Finally, dreams can feel 'real' enough to blur the boundaries between waking and sleeping, sanity and madness, truth and delusion, thereby providing a rich source of inspiration for artists and philosophers alike.

The dream, then, is a powerful, if elusive, second reality that has inevitably invited speculation about its origins, functions and meanings. As

---

[19] A relatively rare exception are lucid dreams, in which the dreamer is aware that he or she is dreaming and may even be able to direct and manipulate dream events to some extent. See LaBerge (1993), 338–341.

[20] For examples, see Stevens (1995), 278–291; Barrett (2001); and Bulkeley (2010), 31–46.

Cavallero and Foulkes put it: 'Dreaming is, after all, a manifestation of the human mind, and perhaps the one that has most tantalized and puzzled us throughout our recorded history'.[21] According to William Dement, 'the emotional impact of our dreams can be so powerful that they might as well have occurred', which is one reason why dreams have 'fascinated people since at least the beginning of recorded history'.[22] Attempts to explain the phenomenon of dreaming have ranged from a belief in supernatural visitations and spiritual night journeys on one end of the spectrum to naturalized (somatic, psychological, psychoanalytical or neurocognitive) models on the other. In Gover and Khan's words:

> Dreams have alternately been hailed as messages from the gods and dismissed as random hallucinations. The pendulum of popular opinion has swung from one extreme to the other throughout recorded history and between cultures and camps, with scientists, psychologists, sages, and philosophers all weighing in.[23]

Between the two extremes, however, a great diversity of attitudes to dreams in terms of their origins, functions and value can be detected.

In Homeric times, for instance, dreams were not considered as subjectively generated internal experience, but rather as objectified messengers sent by a deity or by the dead. Their value was determined by their prophetic accuracy and whether they had come through the gates of horn or through the gates of ivory. As Penelope explains to Odysseus:

> For there are two gates of insubstantial dreams; one [pair] is wrought of horn and one of ivory. Of these, [the dreams] which come through [the gate of] sawn ivory are dangerous to believe, for they bring messages which will not issue in deeds; but [the dreams] which come forth through [the gate of] polished horn, these have power in reality, whenever any mortal sees them.[24]

---

[21] Cavallero and Foulkes (1993b), 1.
[22] Dement (1999), 293.
[23] Gover and Kahn (2010), 181–182.
[24] Miller (1994), 15.

While the Homeric conception of dreams implied that the sleeper was *visited* by a dream, in later classical antiquity, this idea was expanded, in that the soul was now believed to leave the body and travel to the spatially envisioned dream world, where it 'could wander at will, free from earthly shackles'.[25] With the emergence of the Judeo-Christian tradition, the concept of true versus false dreams was complicated by the notion of good versus evil dreams. As Parman points out: 'The divine itself was bifurcated into good and evil. Angels and devils populated the eternal realm, fighting for the occult soul. Dreams were still a bridge to the supernatural, but dreamers were encouraged to distrust their dreams, not knowing if they were sent by angels or devils'.[26]

Such supernatural dream beliefs were rivalled by naturalistic ones. Rather than endorsing the Homeric view that dreams are messages from the Gods, Aristotle, for instance, viewed them as 'images produced by interconnecting physiological and psychic processes'.[27] His views on dreams were put forward in three of the treatises of the *Parva Naturalia*, in which he argued that sleep is caused by digestive processes, due to which 'vapours' rise up to the head and cause the mind to dream. Later proponents of the naturalist view differed, in that they considered dreams as either meaningless or valuable for their diagnostic potential or their capacity to provide psychological or moral insight. Thus, in Thomas Hobbes' (1588–1679) *Leviathan* (1651), dreams, 'the imaginations of them that sleep', are reduced to simple mechanical operations resulting from 'the distemper of some of the inward parts of the body'.[28] In contrast, Francis Bacon (1561–1626), in his *Advancement of Learning* (1605), suggested that natural dreams could enable physicians to 'discover the state of the body by the imaginations of the mind'.[29] And finally, Sir Thomas Browne (1605–1682) maintained that 'dreams may be fallacious concerning outward events, yet may they be truly significant at home, and whereby we may more sensibly understand ourselves'.[30]

---

[25] Parman (1991), 27.
[26] Parman (1991), 27.
[27] Miller (1994), 43.
[28] Hobbes, *Leviathan*, 11.
[29] Bacon, *The Advancement of Learning*, 368.
[30] Browne, 'On Dreams,' 344.

The two rival views on dreams as either supernatural or natural phenomena, then, can be traced in countless variations and different evaluations throughout history, frequently overlapping and competing with each other and leading to complex systems of categorization by those believing that dreams can derive from diverse causes and thus require careful individual assessment.[31]

In more recent years, the findings of neurocognitive sleep and dream research have granted unprecedented insight into the physiological processes accompanying our dreams. Yet dreaming ultimately remains resistant to phenomenological analysis and scientific exploration alike, because—beyond the science fiction world of movies such as *Inception* (2010)—as yet there simply is no way to 'enter' another person's dream or to either record or relive the original experience of one's own.[32] What is more, despite the rapid advancement made in the field of neurocognitive dream and sleep research from the mid-twentieth century onward, researchers continue to disagree on the precise origins of and functions fulfilled by dreams. Even though the biochemical and neuronal processes taking place in our bodies and brains during various sleep phases have to some extent been explored and understood, discussion about how to interpret the data has hardly abated. After all, as Gerald Edelman wisely warns us, 'great care must be exercised in relating physiological states to the contents of conscious states in language-bearing animals'.[33] Accordingly, while neuroscience provides us with fascinating insights into the physiology underpinning various dream states, it tells us only half the story; without being complemented by the subjective experience of the dreamer, the scientist's story will always remain incomplete. Thus, when

---

[31] To give just one example, in his *Commentary on the Dream of Scipio*, Macrobius, in the early fifth century, outlined three different types of reliable dreams: in the oracular dream (*oraculum*), the future is revealed by a revered figure of authority; in the prophetic dream (*visio*), the dreamer is shown events that come literally true; and in the enigmatic dream (*somnium*), which can occur in five different varieties, the dreamer is presented with ambiguous images that require interpretation. These dreams were clearly set apart from their insignificant peers, namely the *insomnium*, a meaningless wish-fulfilment and memory dream, and the *visum*, referring to hypnagogic visions and nightmares and considered equally meaningless. See Miller (1994), 96.

[32] One exception here is lucid dreaming, during which the dreamer is able to influence the dream events and even to communicate with dream researchers via predetermined signals. See LaBerge (1988).

[33] Edelman (1989), 212, quoted in States (1993), 42.

John Allan Hobson claims that '[c]onsciousness is the continuous, subjective awareness of the activity of billions of cells firing at many times a second [...] and sometimes so remarkably aware of itself (during dreams) that it recreates the external world in its own image',[34] he clearly conflates the scientist's objective stance with the subjective experience of the dreamer, who could not care less about the 'activity of billions of cells'. For while her cells are firing, the dreamer experiences dream landscapes of unprecedented beauty, thwarted dream journeys full of unexpected impediments or relentless pursuits in a blood-freezing nightmare. Alfred Alvarez, then, is certainly right when he points out that '[u]nderstanding the physiology of the brain, even the physiology of dreaming, is different from understanding the mind'.[35] This view against biological reductionism is clearly endorsed by many cognitive researchers such as David Foulkes, who reminds us that any 'brain-event-to-mind-event correspondences'[36] remain at present highly speculative. In this view, brain science, despite the manifold insights it provides, is ultimately unsuited to fully capturing what Blanchot termed the '*other* night',[37] the night of the dream. Dreaming, then, remains the most private, subjective and elusive of all human experience, although providing, in Gover and Khan's words, 'an alternative form of consciousness and a different way of thinking'[38] that is well worth exploring.

In order to get closer to a genuine understanding of the dreaming mind, then, the scientific approach needs to go hand in hand with an understanding of dream phenomenology in the sense of the qualitative characteristics of the manifest dream content or, in other words, the subjective awareness of the dream state, which can only be experienced 'first hand' in one's own dreams and 'second hand' through dream reports and narrations. And indeed the majority of contemporary dream researchers are 'aiming at an integration of the physiological and phenomenological descriptions of dreaming'.[39] What is more, in order to explore this

---

[34] Hobson (1988), 133.
[35] Alvarez, *Night*, 98.
[36] Foulkes (1990), 41.
[37] Blanchot (1982), 163.
[38] Gover and Kahn (2010), 182.
[39] Schwartz (2000), 56.

'different way of thinking', an interdisciplinary perspective is called for, as no single discipline alone could succeed in illuminating the multifaceted experience of dreaming. As Kelly Bulkeley rightly puts it, in view of the 'infinitely diverse nature of dreaming [...] the best ways to increase our understanding of dreaming is to engage in [a] kind of free-ranging interdisciplinary dialogue'.[40] Don Kuiken, too, has noted the inevitable crossing of 'traditional disciplinary boundaries between physiology and psychology, literature and psychology, psychology and religion, etc.'[41] involved in any scholarly engagement with dreaming. He has particularly stressed the gains of such an interdisciplinary endeavour, emphasizing the richness and complexity of the 'resulting interdisciplinary literature' which 'reflects the diverse factors that shape dream content and structure, [...] reveals the variety of dreamers' reactions to dream experience, and [...] underlines the depth of dreams' influence on human affairs'.[42] In this interdisciplinary dialogue, literary and cultural studies ought to play a central role, not least because, in Herschel Farbman's words, 'only fiction—"fiction" naming here that genre- and media-crossing discourse of strange facts that don't require corroboration to be credited—will ever be able to represent the space that opens up behind the closed eyes of the sleeper'.[43] This is because, radically put, the subjective dream experience remains closed to all but the dreamer and his or her telling of the dream requires an act of faith on the part of the audience, since '[n]o one can corroborate or contest the dreamer's tale'.[44] Viewed thus, the experience of dreaming is not only subjective but also 'essentially literary'.[45]

Accordingly, one central aim of the present study is to lay the groundwork for an aesthetics of dreaming, based on the empirically informed assumption that our dreaming and waking imagination are two sides of the same coin and that by understanding dream physiology and cognition we may gain valuable insights into how and why our minds create and consume literary fictions. Irving Massey understands the term

---

[40] Bulkeley (1999), 5.
[41] Kuiken (1991a), 185.
[42] Kuiken (1991a), 185.
[43] Farbman (2008), 8.
[44] Farbman (2008), 8.
[45] Farbman (2008), 10.

aesthetics as referring to the study of 'the sources of an art object, the characteristics of the art object, and the relation of the art object to its audience'.[46] This object-oriented approach, however, arguably cannot be separated from its subject-oriented counterpart which focuses on 'the affective, cognitive and phenomenological features of a particular mode of appreciation, judgment, or experience'.[47] This is particularly the case when the 'object' in question is dreaming. Brandon Cooke rightly points out that aesthetically appreciated objects need not be limited to art objects but may include 'various non-art artefacts and events', including 'mental objects (such as dreams and fantasies)'.[48] These mental objects, however, per se have no tangible existence outside the dreamer's mind, so that their study independent of their creators'/recipients' affective and cognitive processes is an impossibility. Dreams can have literary and narrative qualities and can be experienced aesthetically, just like a movie, a play or a fictional story in a book. But the aesthetic experience is limited to an audience of one, the dreamer, and a case could be made that not even the dreamer can consciously access the dream experience except through potentially distorting memory and translation processes. Accordingly, in order to study the experience of dreaming and relate it to other aesthetic and imaginative experiences like waking storytelling or reading, we have to rely on dream reports, our own and others' experience of dreaming as recalled and retold upon waking as well as on the data derived from neurocognitive and empirical research. Secondly, we can study aesthetic objects derived from the dream, such as literary texts based on or inspired by dreams or texts that seek to simulate and convey the dream experience so as to evoke a sense of dreamlikeness in the reader. My approach, then, centres not only on the 'mental object' of the elusive dream experience, as illuminated by dreamers' subjective reports and the findings derived from neuroimaging studies, but also on the more accessible art objects related to dreaming as well as the manifold interconnections between both.

This study, then, seeks to explore the intersections between the dreaming and waking imagination from an interdisciplinary perspective, with

---

[46] Massey (2009), 14.
[47] Cooke (2012), 16.
[48] Cooke (2012), 16.

the cognitive sciences providing a particularly suitable, though certainly not the only framework. This is an endeavour which, to my knowledge, few literary critics have so far embarked on. The reason for this lacuna may be twofold. Firstly, many critics interested in literary dreams, oneiric fictions or the aesthetics of dreaming as a matter of course still resort to Freudian or, in more general terms, psychoanalytical paradigms, regardless of the fact that many of Freud's hypotheses regarding the 'dream-work' have been seriously challenged, modified and in some instances downright refuted by the findings of recent sleep and dream research.[49] Secondly, some literary critics and philosophers are still wary of the recently emerged field of the cognitive sciences, which, arguably, offers the best starting point for an empirically informed approach to the subject of dreaming and the literary imagination. The cognitive sciences, an interdisciplinary field exploring human cognitive abilities such as perception, thought, imagination and language, connect scientists and scholars ranging from philosophy and psychology to neurology, anthropology and linguistics. The distrust many literary critics and philosophers still harbour with respect to this vibrant new field may be grounded in the cognitive science model prevalent in the 1950s that has, however, been long superseded by more recent concepts.[50] While the cognitive sciences initially viewed the brain as isolated from the body, as a merely rational, mechanical computer model of the mind, this model has been gradually replaced by the concept of the 'embodied mind'.[51] Mental processes are no longer viewed as dissociated from the human body and its specific environmental location, but rather as interactions with chemical and motor activities, sense perceptions, external and internal influences and the interactions between the brain and other (sense) organs discovered by 'powerful new methods and technologies in neuroscience that are yielding previously undreamed-of knowledge about the physiological underpinnings of the

---

[49] See Domhoff (2001a, 8–13) for a summary of 'the main empirical findings that explain why Freudian theory is not considered viable by most dream researchers' (4). See also Carroll (2004), who criticizes scholars in the humanities for continuing 'to repeat the formulas of Freud, Marx, Saussure, Lévi-Strauss—formulas that have now been obsolete in their own fields for decades' (x).
[50] See Richardson (1999), 158.
[51] Lakoff and Johnson (1999).

"inner world"'.[52] The neurobiological approach as practised, for instance, by Antonio Damasio and Gerald Edelman emphasizes the central role of emotions as well as environmental influences and experiences in cognitive processes. As Solms and Turnbull point out: 'Modern neuroscience is becoming increasingly aware of the role played in brain development by experience, learning, and the quality of the facilitating environment'.[53] In Ellen Spolsky's words, cognitive scientists have come to realize that 'the human epistemological inheritance is pretty much what one would expect from an evolving animal: the brain is not a machine purposely designed for computation in a stable environment, but it is just what is needed for interpretation and adaptation in a constantly changing one'.[54] And as Alan Richardson aptly puts it:

> Recent work in cognitive neuroscience has indeed come to integrate the emotive, instinctive and irrational into its picture of unconscious mental life, often with a respectful nod toward Freud, and has returned to the embodied conception of mind—neither hardware nor software but 'wetware'—more characteristic of neuroscience in the period of its Romantic beginnings.[55]

The awareness of the complex and far from fully explored interplay between biological factors (including the subconscious) and sociocultural influences arguably prevents the cognitive neurosciences from regressing into essentialist modes of thinking or biological determinism. At the same time, the inclusion of (neuro-)cognitive insights in the humanities runs counter to what might be called 'cultural determinism' which reduces the formation of human identity, language and consciousness to mere cultural construction.

Thus, the embodied cognitive sciences in particular provide a variety of potential points of contact with the fields of literary studies and philosophy from which both disciplines could profit. As R.M. Willems and

---

[52] Solms und Turnbull (2002), 5.
[53] Solms und Turnbull (2002), 11.
[54] Spolsky (2001), 7.
[55] Richardson (2001), 63. Richardson here refers to the title of Stephen Kosslyn and Oliver Koenig's *Wet Mind: The New Cognitive Neuroscience* (New York: Free Press, 1992).

A.M. Jacobs put it in a recent article entitled 'Caring about Dostoyevsky: The Untapped Potential of Studying Literature' (2016):

> A full picture of the story-liking nature of the human mind calls for a much more intimate collaboration between cognitive scientists and scholars in the humanities. It requires that scientists not be guided by the traditional division between academic cultures, but to be united in their common goal to understand the workings of the human mind. [...] [C]ognitive neuroscientists should start caring about Dostoyevsky and other ingenious writers, and take advantage of the strong human affinity for narrative.[56]

This claim echoes Patrick Colm Hogan's earlier assertion that '[c]ognitive science can hardly claim to explain the human mind if it fails to deal with such a ubiquitous and significant aspect of human mental activity as literature'.[57] I would extend this claim to include the 'ubiquitous and significant [...] mental activity' of *dreaming*, which has for a long time been neglected by the cognitive sciences—surprisingly enough, if dream images can indeed be understood as 'the embodiment of thoughts' and 'the medium by which a psychological process, cognition, is transformed into a form that can be perceived'.[58] As Foulkes and Cavallero put it in their pioneering essay collection *Dreaming as Cognition* (1993):

> With cognitive psychology, scientific psychology regained its 'mind.' But it did so in a very selective way, leaving out whole areas of mental experience and mental phenomena. Prominent among these omitted areas was one of the most pervasive, impressive, yet puzzling forms of distinctively human experience—dreaming.[59]

However, they also maintain that 'many of the principles and concepts of cognitive psychology can quite easily be mapped onto dream phenomena and that, when this is done the result is a richer and more humanly interesting cognitive psychology'.[60]

---

[56] Willems and Jacobs (2016), 244.
[57] Hogan (2003), 4.
[58] Hall (1953a), 274.
[59] Cavallero and Foulkes (1993b), 1.
[60] Cavallero and Foulkes (1993b), 3.

While dream researchers, too, have repeatedly emphasized the potential benefits of such interdisciplinary endeavours for both the humanities and the cognitive sciences,[61] thus far relatively few literary scholars have followed that call. The majority of recently published studies on literature and dreams tend to repudiate neurocognitive insights as irrelevant to, or inappropriate for, their field of study, sometimes explicitly so.[62] In contrast, my interdisciplinary approach to an aesthetics of dreaming seeks to draw together empirical research in the cognitive sciences and the substantial range of work in the humanities, notably cognitive literary theory, reader-response criticism as well as literary aesthetics and philosophy of mind. Taken together, this range of works provides a plethora of innovative approaches to dreaming that shed new light on imaginative processes and that may serve to enhance our views on aesthetic creation. Most notably, this includes the philosophical works by Colin McGinn, Bert O. States, Harry T. Hunt and Jennifer M. Windt, especially in so far as they explore interconnections between dreaming, consciousness and imagination. Other approaches that have paved the way for this study include, among others, Keith Oatley's work on the psychology of fiction, Richard Walsh's work on dreaming and narrativity, and Don Kuiken's empirical studies on types of impactful dreams on the one hand and readers' emotional responses to literary texts on the other. Irving Massey's book *The Neural Imagination* (2009) likewise provides a useful reference point in its explorations of music and language in dream.

A good number of literary and cultural histories as well as critical studies on literary dream narratives and representations have been published in recent years. Noteworthy examples of cultural histories include Peter-André Alt, *Der Schlaf der Vernunft: Literatur und Traum in der Kulturgeschichte der Neuzeit* (2002), Daniel Pick and Lyndal Roper, eds. *Dreams and History: The Interpretation of Dreams from Ancient Greece to Modern Psychoanalysis* (2004) as well as Helen Groth and Natalya Lusty, *Dreams and Modernity: A Cultural History* (2013). In all three, the Freudian paradigm plays a central role and there is little, if any, reference to recent neurocognitive advances in sleep and

---

[61] See Kuiken (1991a); McNamara (2008), 11; and Barcaro and Paoli (2015).
[62] See Alt (2002), 359–373 and Farbman (2008), 8–10.

dream research. There are also a number of studies centring on particular authors or literary periods, which tend to view literary dream representations and narratives either in light of their cultural and historical contexts or through the lens of Freudian, Jungian or poststructuralist analysis. An example for the first approach is provided by Hodgkin, O'Callaghan and Wiseman, eds. *Reading the Early Modern Dream: The Terrors of the Night* (2008). Examples for the latter approach include Matthew C. Brennan, *The Gothic Psyche: Disintegration and Growth in Nineteenth-Century English Literature* (1997), providing a Jungian reading of nineteenth-century Gothic writings; Ronald R. Thomas, *Dreams of Authority: Freud and the Fictions of the Unconscious* (1990), applying a Freudian approach to Victorian and modernist literature; and Herschel Farbman, *The Other Night: Dreaming, Writing, and Restlessness in Twentieth-Century Literature* (2008), centring on Blanchot and, to some extent, Freud.

In recent years, however, a group of German literary scholars, including Manfred Engel, Bernard Dieterle, Hans-Walter Schmidt-Hannisa, Marie Guthmüller, Susanne Goumegou and Stefanie Kreuzer, have produced relevant publications applying non-Freudian approaches to oneiric writings and dream narratives with a focus on German, French and Italian traditions. Noteworthy recent examples are Susanne Goumegou and Marie Guthmüller, eds. *Traumwissen und Traumpoetik: Onirische Schreibweisen von der literarischen Moderne bis zur Gegenwart* (2011) and Stefanie Kreuzer, *Traum und Erzählen in Literatur, Film und Kunst* (2014). Kreuzer's comprehensive and stimulating monograph explores German-language dream narratives and oneiric texts from three centuries in light of the findings of recent dream and sleep research. However, in its distinctly narratological focus, Kreuzer's approach differs substantially from mine. What is more, the range of dream-related research she draws on is somewhat limited as she mainly takes into account publications in German. She thus excludes some of the findings particularly relevant to my own more wide-ranging approach, including important works by dream researchers and scholars such as G.W. Domhoff, Don Kuiken, Tore Nielsen, Deirdre Barrett, Ernest Hartmann and Bert O. States.

To my knowledge, with the exception of Bert O. States' pioneering monographs in the 1980s and 1990s, this is the first book-length exploration of the intersections between dreaming and the literary imagination to draw together findings from a broad range of neurocognitive, empirical, philosophical and literary sources. The focus of this study is on dreaming and the *literary* imagination rather than on other art forms such as painting, film, music or dance. In the course of the book, these other art forms may occasionally be evoked as reference points, if only to show why the creation and reception of *literary* narratives in many ways comes closer to the experience of dreaming. One concise definition that the majority of contemporary dream researchers would likely subscribe to is that dreams are 'visual scenarios composed of affect-laden images and simulations of events that are perceptually and thematically organized into a narrative typically concerning the self/dreamer'.[63] The empirically informed insight that dreams tend to have a narrative structure explains my focus on narrative literary texts. At the same time, the predominantly visual dream experience, 'composed of affect-laden images', poses interesting problems for the literary writer striving to capture the dream's atmosphere so as to create a dreamlike effect in the reader.

This study, then, is in two parts. While Chaps. 2 and 3 focus on the processes, origins, functions and the subjective experience of dreaming in relation to the waking and, more specifically, the literary imagination, Chaps. 4 and 5 explore the question if and how the 'language' of *dreams* can be translated into a literary language of *dream*. In this sense, my approach also bears on all three areas of study relevant to cognitive narratology as defined by Marie-Laure Ryan: the study of the minds of characters, the mental activity of the reader and narrative as a way of thinking.[64] What it foregrounds first and foremost, however, is the value and importance of the imagination. As Lamarque and Olsen rightly point out:

> A key feature of the pleasure that literature affords is the demands it makes on the imagination. It is through the imaginative reconstruction of a work's content that readers come to see what value or interest the work holds. Literature has long been associated with the imagination, not just as a product of the imagination but also as a prompt for it.[65]

---

[63] McNamara (2008), 83.
[64] See Ryan (2010), 476.
[65] Lamarque and Olsen (2004), 207.

While most studies on dreams and/in literature tend to focus on psychological, often psychoanalytical, readings, the present book, while not wholly disregarding such perspectives, opts to take a slightly different route by exploring the aesthetics of dreaming in relation to the literary imagination.

Chapter 2 outlines the present state of the art of neurocognitive and empirical dream research. It starts out by assessing Freud's waning relevance in light of theories formulated in response to watershed discoveries such as REM sleep and, more recently, the default mode network. These research findings provide compelling evidence that dreaming encompasses a much broader spectrum of dream states than acknowledged by Freud, with REM sleep at one end of the spectrum and waking states such as daydreaming or readerly immersion at the other. This insight paves the way for a comparative analysis of major evolutionary approaches to dreaming and waking fictions. Evidence suggests that dreaming and waking storytelling may share similar adaptive functions. Arguably, both dreaming and the human delight in waking fictions help develop survival-enhancing capacities such as connection-making, blending and theory of mind. There is, moreover, reason to assume that the need to tell stories may have been sparked not least of all by the desire or need to communicate one's dreams.

Chapter 3 discusses whether dreams are sensory perceptions deluding us into false beliefs or manifestations of the same imaginative capacity responsible for our creation of, and immersion in, waking fictions. Drawing on a broad range of empirical evidence, I argue that dreaming erodes any clear-cut boundaries between imagination and perception. On this basis, the chapter goes on to explore the 'paradox of authorship', that is the puzzle how dreams can be simultaneously authored and experienced as lived reality. Comparing and assessing two contrasting approaches by Colin McGinn and Bert O. States respectively, I argue that dreaming is in many ways similar to writerly immersion and creation. The next subchapter discusses the similarities and differences between dreaming and reading stories. Here, the main focus is on visualization processes in dreaming and reading as well as on the much debated 'paradox of fiction', including questions concerning belief, empathy and emotion. In addressing these problems, I draw on work from a broad range of philosophers, reader-response critics and cognitive literary theorists, including Jean Paul Sartre, Victor Nell, Keith Oatley, Wolfgang Iser, Ellen J. Esrock, Patrick Colm Hogan, Jennifer M. Windt and Richard Walsh, among others. I argue that the differences between the dreamer's and the reader's immersion are in degree rather than in kind, corroborating my argument with both empirical evidence and a plethora of examples from literary writers, literary texts and dream reports.

Having established that the processes involved in the creation and reception of literary texts bear striking resemblances to the processes operative in dreaming, Chap. 4 is concerned with the diversity of dream types as well as with the 'language' of dreams and its translation into literary works of fiction. After providing an overview of attempts at dream categorization and how these dream types might mirror, and be related to, literary genres, modes or narrative techniques, I turn to the question of dream phenomenology or the 'language' of the dream. What are the formal properties of dreams? Is there a specific kind of dream 'language'? If so, how can it be translated into the language of literature? Do some elements resist translation? Are some literary genres particularly suited to the creation of dreamlikeness? In addressing these questions, I refer to work by George Lakoff, Don Kuiken, Harry T. Hunt and Bert O. States, among others. Examples drawn on to illustrate my findings include selected nineteenth- and twentieth-century literary texts, with special emphasis on the three genres I consider particularly conducive to the creation of a dreamlike effect in the reader, namely, the ballad, the gothic novel and the short story.

Chapter 5 rounds off this study by drawing together the findings from previous chapters in three in-depth literary case studies. The texts—Kazuo Ishiguro's *The Unconsoled* (1995), Clare Boylan's *Black Baby* (1988) and John Banville's *The Sea* (2005)—have been chosen not only for their diversity but because they span the entire range of dream consciousness from REM-dream-like immersion in Ishiguro's novel to the subtle destabilization of the boundaries between dreaming and waking reality in Boylan's text to the wavelike blurring of memory, imagination and dream in the soliloquy provided by Banville's narrator. In my explorations of what makes these novels 'dreamlike', I analyse not only the narrative strategies and techniques employed by the respective authors to create a sense of dream but also the resulting aesthetic effect on the reader.

Dreaming is a universal psychobiological process shared by humans across all ages and cultures. As indicated by McNamara's concise definition above, dreams primarily deal with emotional ('affect-laden') concerns and the self, which suggests that they 'are more similar than they are different around the world'[66] and that 'the dream experience [may be] less variant than other aspects of culture'.[67] As Calvin Hall claims, 'the world of sleep [...] is a world in which all of mankind speak the same language, the language of imagery and metaphor'.[68] Incidentally, this idea echoes Coleridge's quite similar observation made in 1818: 'The Language of the Dream/Night [...] is a language of Images and Sensations, the various dialects of which are far less different from each other, than the various Day-Languages of Nations'.[69] The universality of 'typical dreams'[70] was also recognized and commented upon by Charles Dickens:

> [H]ow many dreams are common to us all, from the Queen to the Costermonger! We all fall off that Tower—we all skim above the ground at a great pace and can't keep on it—...we all take unheard-of trouble to go to the Theatre and never get in—or to go to a Feast, which can't be eaten or drunk—or to read letters, or placards, or books, that no study will render legible—or to break some Thraldom or other, from which we can't escape—or we all confound the living with the dead, and all frequently have a knowledge or suspicion that we are doing it—we all astonish ourselves by telling ourselves, in a dialogue with ourselves, the most astonishing and terrific secrets—we all go to public places in our night dresses, and are horribly disconcerted, lest the company should discern it.[71]

Dreams may thus reflect 'literary universals' in even more palpable ways than verbal art, that other form of storytelling which, as Patrick Colm

---

[66] Domhoff (2003), 32.
[67] Gregor (1981), 389, quoted in Domhoff (2003), 32. This was Gregor's conclusion after conducting a study of dream reports from a small group of natives in the Amazon jungle.
[68] Hall (1968), xviii.
[69] Coleridge, *Notebooks*, vol. 3, 4409.
[70] See Schönhammer (2004).
[71] Dickens, *The Selected Letters*, 226.

Hogan rightly reminds us, for all its 'national, historical, and other inflections [...] first of all and most significantly [is] an activity engaged in by all people at all times'.[72] Studies about the dreaming and the waking mind clearly ought to join forces in order to arrive at what Rosalind Cartwright calls 'a fuller picture of the human psyche'.[73] The present study on intersections between dreaming and waking forms of imagination hopes to contribute precisely to this endeavour.

---

[72] Hogan (2003), 3.
[73] Cartwright (2010), 6.

2

Towards an Aesthetics of Dreaming

From Freud to Neuroscience

No book has impacted the modern attitude to dreams, their origins and meanings as deeply and enduringly as Sigmund Freud's *Die Traumdeutung* (1899/1900). Arguably, one of the reasons for its success was that Freud ingeniously interwove and remodelled strands from the most important approaches to dreaming prevalent in the late nineteenth century: romantic, rationalist and somaticist. As James Hillman points out:

> From the romantics he took the idea that the dream contained a hidden but important personal message from another world. From the rationalists, Freud accepted the idea that the manifest dream, dream language as it appeared, was a worthless jumble of nonsense—for Freud, however, it was decipherable into a latent value and meaning. With the somaticists, he agreed that the dream reflected physiological processes—for Freud, however, these had mainly to do with sexuality and sleep.[1]

---

[1] Hillman (1979), 8.

At the same time, however, the influence of his psychoanalytical school served to suppress other insights that, in turn, foreshadow current approaches to dreaming based on empirical and neurocognitive findings. As Sophie Schwartz points out:

> There are many striking analogies between the way scientists are studying dreams at the end of the 20th century and the way scientists were studying dreams at the end of last century, whereas during an intermediary period corresponding to the first half of the 20th century, dream research was either dismissed by behaviorist principles or dominated by Freudian ideas.[2]

In fact, Mary Arnold-Forster (1861–1951) noted as early as 1921: 'The principles laid down by Freud [...] have been so unhesitatingly accepted that anyone who should question their universal applicability would find himself in a small minority, for the modern school of psycho-analysis that is based on Freud's teaching has an immense vogue.'[3] Even today, there basically seems no way around Freud's *Traumdeutung*, which is why even a study emphatically not employing a Freudian approach first needs to clarify why certain of Freud's hypotheses no longer hold. In order to do so, I will first briefly outline Freud's concept of the 'dream work' and then assess it in light of the findings of neurocognitive and empirical dream research that inform my own approach.

The idea that the interpretation of dreams is, above all, 'the royal road to a knowledge of the unconscious activities of the mind',[4] as Freud so famously put it, resulted in the fact that dreams were mostly regarded as a means to an end, the psychotherapist's entrance into the patient's submerged world of childhood experiences and repressed infantile desires and drives. Dreams, in this theory, are viewed as 'wishfulfilling hallucinations'.[5] According to Freud, what mattered was not so much what happened ostensibly in the dream, but rather the buried truths that could be excavated through careful interpretation and associative analysis of the dream symbols. This is why he differentiated between the manifest

---

[2] Schwartz (2000), 55.
[3] Arnold-Forster, *Studies in Dreams*, 5.
[4] Freud (1953 [1900]), 608.
[5] Rycroft (1979), 9.

dream content (the dream as we remember and report it) and the latent dream thoughts (that could only be revealed psychoanalytically by means of free association). What Freud called the 'dream work' worked like this: during sleep, our unfulfilled, often libidinal wishes, usually repressed by our ego, threaten to invade consciousness and disturb sleep. In order to guard our sleep, a repressive censorship mechanism disguises these possibly disturbing desires as ostensibly harmless bits of daytime residue. Our wishes are thus secretly fulfilled without disturbing our sleep or destroying our respectable self-image. As Freud himself puts it, 'the content of a dream is the representation of a fulfilled wish and [...] its obscurity is due to alterations in repressed material made by the censorship'.[6] These 'alterations in repressed material' are achieved through the dream work, 'the process by which the latent content of a dream (its original, undisguised text) is translated into its manifest content (the text as actually remembered and reported by the dreamer)'.[7] Its most important tools are displacement, symbol formation, condensation and secondary revision, the latter of which turns 'a sequence of discrete disguise-images' into a more or less coherent narrative.[8]

As Rycroft explains, displacement 'obeys the laws of association and generates figures of speech; displacement from whole to part producing synecdoche, displacement from something to something else which resembles it producing metaphor, and displacement from something to something else associated with it producing metonymy'.[9] The second major mechanism, condensation, 'is the process or device by which two or more images are fused to form a composite image which has meaning derived from both (or all)—or which means that which is common to both'.[10] As Anthony Shafton puts it, in order to ensure maximum disguise, '[a]n image cannot enter the dream unless more meanings than one converge in and complexify it. Every image is thus "over-determined." Condensation is responsible for hybrid imagery'.[11] Accordingly, every

---

[6] Freud quoted in Rycroft (1979), 8.
[7] Rycroft (1979), 20.
[8] Shafton (1995), 58.
[9] Rycroft (1979), 16–17.
[10] Rycroft (1979), 14–15.
[11] Shafton (1995), 53.

dream image has a multiplicity of meanings and numerous referents, as exemplified for instance by the tendency of people to merge into composite dream characters or change their identity in the course of a dream. The latent dream thoughts and repressed desires can only be unravelled by means of the psychoanalytical technique of free association. As Shafton points out: 'The main point upon which Freud insisted is that his upper level of coherence, the manifest dream, is a mere facade and not a direct analog for, not a helpful metaphor for his lower and more essential level of coherence, the latent dream-thought'.[12] Instead, according to Freud, 'we should disregard the apparent coherence between a dream's constituents as an unessential illusion' and view the 'dream [as] a conglomerate which, for purposes of investigation, must be broken up once more into fragments'.[13] Crucially, and of particular relevance in the context of this study, Freud also denied that the dream work was in any way creative or imaginative; its sole achievement was seen as transforming the latent dream thoughts by means of the mechanisms described above.[14] As Ernest Hartmann notes, in the various psychoanalytical schools even today, 'the dream itself is seen as an irrational mental product, which can be discarded as soon as it has been properly analyzed to arrive at the underlying meaning it has disguised'.[15]

According to Freud's view, then, dreams fulfil the biological function of guarding the dreamer's sleep by converting any disturbing thoughts and wishes that may arise into disguised wish-fulfilling hallucinations. They can be put to a therapeutic use because through the method of free association, patient and analyst, in a joint effort, can bring to consciousness the repressed latent dream thoughts. What is more, Freud viewed dreams as repressive mechanisms and thus as 'analogous to neurotic

---

[12] Shafton (1995), 59.

[13] Freud (1953 [1900]), 449.

[14] See Freud's article 'On Dreams' (1914 [1902]) in which he states: 'If we keep closely to the definition that dream work denotes the transference of dream thoughts to dream content, we are compelled to say that the dream work is not creative; it develops no fancies of its own, it judges nothing, decides nothing. It does nothing but prepare the matter for condensation and displacement, and refashions it for dramatization [...]' (71–72).

[15] Hartmann (2000b), 62.

symptoms'[16] and 'constructed by the same psychological mechanisms despite the fact that they occur not only in neurotic but also in healthy persons'.[17] Since he, at the same time, agreed that there 'is some connection between dreams and the waking imagination', it easily followed that 'imagination must also be an abnormal psychic phenomenon'.[18] As David Foulkes laconically puts it: 'Dreams have had a most difficult time escaping the historical accident that they entered scientific psychology via the clinic'.[19] And Bert O. States succinctly sums up the damage done: 'In one master metaphor (the Royal Road) Freud bypassed any possibility that the dream might serve any other than a repressive function.'[20]

It is important, however, to keep in mind Anthony Shafton's warning that 'those dreamworkers who make little of Freud might be faulted for disrespecting the basis for much of what they themselves think about dreams'.[21] In fact, Freud's general description of the processes of condensation, symbol formation and displacement is undeniably appealing and these processes may well be operative in many dreams. Cavallero and Foulkes point out that in cognitive psychology, 'important work on the mnemonic sources of dreams continues to receive inspiration and to borrow methods from Freud's dream-process psychology'.[22] As they argue, 'Freud did discover some of the boundary conditions of dream

---

[16] Rycroft (1979), 4.
[17] Rycroft (1979), 8. In Freud's own phrasing in 'Revision of the Theory of Dreams' (1992 [1933]): '[I]n the construction of neurotic symptoms the same mechanisms (we do not venture to say "processes of thought") are operative as those which have transformed the latent dream-thoughts into the manifest dream' (41). In 'On Dreams' (1914 [1902]), he moreover states: 'In truth, the dream work is only the first recognition of a group of psychical processes to which must be referred the origin of hysterical symptoms, the ideas of morbid dread, obsession and illusion' (78).
[18] Rycroft (1979), 5.
[19] Foulkes (1978), 7.
[20] States (1987), 11.
[21] Shafton (1995), 51. See also Mary Arnold-Forster, whose book *Studies in Dreams* (1921) sets out to contradict the Freudian view that all dreams are symbolic representations of repressed libidinal wishes, yet all the same acknowledges that '[t]he value of Freud's contribution to science would seem to lie, not in these applications to his teaching, or in the deductions that his disciples have drawn from it, but in the new and original point of view which he opened up, and the great stimulus that he gave explorers in the field of psychological research' (5).
[22] Cavallero and Foulkes (1993b), 5–6.

construction'.²³ This view is also corroborated by Don Kuiken, who claims that '[d]espite declining confidence in psychoanalytic theory, especially its drive-discharge components, Freud's classic study of dream formation continues to be an important point of departure in dream psychology'.²⁴ However, there is surely no need to view these dream formation processes as repressive mechanisms disguising libidinal wishes; rather they may be manifestations of the hyper-associative way in which our minds work under the physiologically specific conditions characteristic of various sleep state phases. Moreover, contrary to Freud's claims about the dream work's uniqueness and distinctness from waking forms of thought, it has been suggested 'that the dream-work, if it exists, is an instance of figurative thought'.²⁵ As Domhoff points out, Freud's hypothesis about the existence of day residue in every dream has failed to be confirmed by empirical studies while his claim that speech acts in dreams virtually always repeat remembered speeches (either heard or read) has been proved wrong.²⁶ In fact, after the analysis of hundreds of speech acts in sleep laboratory studies, researchers could show that these speech acts tended to be new constructions rather than reproductions, thereby testifying to the creative potential of dreams.²⁷ Ultimately, as Domhoff sums up, 'standard empirical methods have not been able to show support for any aspect of Freud's theory'.²⁸ Likewise, the vast majority of contemporary dream researchers repudiate the assumption that dreams (and by implication imaginative works of art) are expressions of neuroses. As Palombo concludes: 'Freud's theory remains a powerful and clinically useful statement about the *psychopathology* of dreaming, though no longer [...] a reasonable explanation for the phenomenon of dreaming in its entirety'.²⁹

---

[23] Cavallero and Foulkes (1993b), 6.
[24] Kuiken (1991b), 231.
[25] Domhoff (2003), 139.
[26] See Domhoff (2003), 136.
[27] See Domhoff (2003), 136.
[28] Domhoff (2003), 143.
[29] Palombo (1983), 312, my italics.

Freud's influential theory brought to a halt the study of the manifest content of dreams and 'helped to discourage scientific interest in, and study of, dreaming by more empirical psychologists'.[30] Conversely, 'the psychoanalytic interpretive system undermined any attempt to understand the dreaming mechanisms in neurophysiological terms'.[31] However, both approaches have experienced a powerful resurgence in the past 60 years. The most noteworthy paradigm shift in dream research since Freud's publication of *Die Traumdeutung* was doubtlessly marked by Eugene Aserinsky and Nathaniel Kleitman's discovery of *rapid eye movement* sleep in 1953. With the help of electrodes recording brain waves and eye movements, they initiated 'a whole new field of research that opened the black box of sleep to the light of science'.[32] What they discovered was that '[s]leep is not a state of coma, but rather a period of regular cyclic changes between two distinctive organizations of brain and body activity'.[33] The state now known as REM (for *rapid eye movement*) occurs in regular 90-minute cycles during sleep and is accompanied by especially vivid, visual, narratively complex and intense dreams.[34] The discovery of REM sleep turned upside down much of what had been accepted as self-evident, most importantly the notion that during sleep our brains rest.[35] Sleep could no longer be viewed as one homogeneous state but 'had to be conceived as two distinct organismic states, as different from one another as both were from wakefulness. REM sleep was one state, NREM sleep the other. It also had to be conceded that sleep could no longer be thought of as a time of brain inactivity and EEG slowing'.[36]

---

[30] Cavallero and Foulkes (1993b), 5.
[31] Schwartz (2000), 56.
[32] Cartwright (2010), xi.
[33] Cartwright (2010), xi–xii.
[34] See Domhoff (2001b), n. pag.
[35] As William C. Dement (1993) points out, '[i]n the late 1950s, sleep was widely regarded as a single state. The notion of REM sleep as a separate biological state did not yet exist. The occurrence of the eye movements was quite compatible with the contemporary dream theories that the dream occurred when sleep lightened to prevent or delay awakening; that is, dreaming was regarded as the "guardian of sleep"' (506).
[36] Dement (1993), 507.

In fact, we now know that during REM sleep the brain is 'in a state of heightened activation akin to wakefulness. There is also activation of other bodily systems. You begin to breathe differently, your heart rate increases, and your genitals (in both males and females) become engorged'.[37] At the same time, sleepers are effectively paralysed during REM sleep, which prevents them from acting out their dreams.[38] What is more, with the help of recent neuroimaging techniques, researchers have been able to show that there is 'more activation of brain areas concerned with emotion and with complex visual image generation, and less activation of brain areas concerned with memory, self-reflective awareness, and directed thought'.[39] Because of the latter, the dreamer's short-term memory is inhibited both during and immediately after dreaming, which may explain the perceived incoherence and discontinuity of some dreams as well as our difficulty in directing our will during dreaming and in recalling our dreams upon waking.[40] Conversely, the fact that there is much higher activity in the limbic and paralimbic areas responsible for sensory association and emotion provides evidence that during REM sleep 'we are seeing and hearing things that are not logical but probably have emotional associations'.[41]

The minute analysis of the physiology of the sleep cycle suggests that dreaming cannot be solely concerned with or caused by repressive mechanisms, as Freud had proposed. Thus, 'laboratory studies have revealed that dreaming takes place longer, more frequently, and more regularly than he or any other theorist ever imagined before the serendipitous discovery of REM sleep in 1953'.[42] As John Allan Hobson claims, 'the automaticity and the fixed quality and quantity of dreaming [produced or accompanied by a specific brain mechanism] make dreaming an integral

---

[37] Solms and Turnbull (2002), 183.
[38] See Solms and Turnbull (2002), 183.
[39] Hobson and Wohl (2005), 35. In fact, the dorsal lateral prefrontal cortex and the precuneus in the parietal lobe, both responsible for the functioning of our short-term memory, are deactivated during REM sleep. See Gover and Kahn (2010), 182.
[40] See Gover and Khan (2010), 182.
[41] Cartwright (2010), 27.
[42] Domhoff (2003), 136.

part of vegetative life rather than a mere reaction to life's vicissitudes'.[43] In view of this, Freud's thesis of the dream as the guardian of sleep is no longer cogent.[44] As Alfred Alvarez aptly puts it, the opposite may well be the case: '[S]leep is the guardian of dreams. We don't dream—even if the Freudian censor has done its work and we dream successfully—in order to preserve our sleep; we sleep in order to dream because dreaming is a natural and necessary bodily function.'[45] In a similar vein, Andreas Mavromatis argues that 'one function of sleep must have been, and still is, to provide the conditions necessary for the occurrence of dreaming and at the same time secure the organism's safety during that most vulnerable period when its attention is withdrawn from the immediate physical surroundings'.[46]

Freud's claim that all dreams are wish-fulfilments is qualified by the sheer diversity of sleep states and mentation. As Mavromatis sums up at the end of his groundbreaking study on hypnagogia (hallucinations occurring during the transitional stages between sleeping and waking), this is not to deny 'that dream activity can ever be wish-fulfilling or that some dreams may constitute the mind's reaction in sleep to the experiences of the previous day, as Freudian psychoanalysis holds. However, wish-fulfilling dreams and those involved with the experiences of the previous day constitute only one or two species of the wider genus of oneirosis'.[47] This insight, however, in no way precludes that dreaming deals with psychologically relevant material and may provide access to repressed or forgotten material. In fact, 'oneiric imagery may refer to the present psychophysical state and mental preoccupations of a person (autosymbolic), contain solutions to problems, or point to future resolutions of present conflicts (anagogic)'.[48] Incidentally, Freud's reductive model of dreams as wish-fulfilling hallucinations also fails to account for the nightmare experience, a problem which Freud tried to solve by suggesting that

---

[43] Hobson (1988), 15.
[44] For other reasons contradicting the hypothesis, see Domhoff (2003), 142.
[45] Alvarez, *Night*, 131.
[46] Mavromatis (1991), 275.
[47] Mavromatis (1991), 280.
[48] Mavromatis (1991), 280.

nightmares indicate a failure of the censorship mechanism or even the fulfilment of a masochistic wish.[49] Nightmares, however, are far too universal experiences to be accounted for in such a way, which is especially true for dreams of posttraumatic stress disorder. These dreams are more frequent and more persistent than Freud assumed and thus need to be compatible with any convincing theory on dreams. As Domhoff notes: 'At the very least, traumatic dreams and recurrent dreams show that wish-fulfillment dreams are only a subset of all possible dreams'.[50]

In order to arrive at empirically comparable results, recent dream researchers increasingly rely on dream reports collected in sleep lab awakenings, home-based monitoring using a so-called Nightcap device or personal dream journals.[51] Sophie Schwartz refers to this 'coming back of introspection' as 'a profound epistemological renaissance'.[52] The revived interest in the manifest content of dreams especially in the past three decades has led dream researchers to perceive dreams as experiences which are predominantly visual and subjective experiences as well as expressing sensations in a universally consistent way.[53] As Schwartz points out: 'These epistemological reassessments constitute the basic dimensions upon which contemporary dream research is built'.[54] Most researchers[55] rely on the Hall-Van de Castle system of content analysis developed by Calvin S. Hall and Robert Van de Castle in 1966 to quantitatively analyse the manifest content of dreams in terms of Characters, Social Interactions, Activities, Striving, Misfortunes and Good Fortunes, Emotions, Physical

---

[49] Freud, initially, even went so far as to deny the nightmare full dream status as he found its disturbing effects difficult to reconcile with his theory of wish fulfilment. In his later work, Freud argued that the nightmare was caused by anxiety about forbidden wishes threatening the ego and could ultimately be considered as an example of dream censorship gone wrong. As McNamara (2008) explains: 'Beginning with Freud himself, various attempts have been made to argue that nightmares are really wishes, but masochistic in content[.] [...] But this approach seems forced and nonfalsifiable. Given the fact that many people awaken from a nightmare it seems hard to argue that nightmares protect sleep via hallucinated wish fulfilment.' (106).
[50] Domhoff (2003), 140.
[51] See Domhoff (2003), 107.
[52] Schwartz (2000), 57.
[53] See Schwartz (2000), 57.
[54] Schwartz (2000), 57.
[55] See, for instance, Foulkes (1985), Hobson (1988), Antrobus (1993), Domhoff (1996), Strauch and Meier (1996) and Schredl (2010).

Surroundings, Descriptive Elements, Food and Eating, Elements from the Past.[56] The coding system also has five different emotion categories: anger, apprehension, confusion, happiness and sadness. According to Domhoff, 'the Hall-Van de Castle system of content analysis has the necessary reliability and validity for research that links dream content to the neural network for dreaming, on the one hand, and to waking cognition on the other'.[57] One of the most important insights provided by content analysis studies is that '[p]eople dream most often about the people and interests that preoccupy them in waking life',[58] which confirms the strong continuity between dream content and waking life.

The most influential theory to have emerged from physiological REM sleep findings is arguably Hobson's and McCarley's *activation synthesis model*, introduced in 1977 and initially based on the assumption that REM sleep is the physiological correlate to dreaming. The theory has since been considerably revised and adapted by Hobson, but the basic assumption has remained intact, namely that the brain functions as 'a dream machine'[59] trying to make 'the best of a bad job'[60] by struggling to turn randomly produced sensory data into coherent stories. As Gerald W. Vogel points out, according to Hobson and McCarley's hypothesis,

> [t]he pontine neurons that generate REM sleep send electrical signals to many brain areas. The targets include the forebrain, which involves brain regions responsible for conscious thought, voluntary movement, conscious sensations (such as sight, touch, and hearing), and conscious feelings (such as love, hate, and fear). [...] According to the activation-synthesis hypothesis, the activation of the forebrain areas generates the conscious dream experience. [...] The forebrain also has the higher mental function of synthesizing or integrating different experiences into a coherent whole. [...] Thus, [...] the dream narrative is a forebrain synthesis of a hindbrain acti-

---

[56] See Domhoff (2003), 67. The system is based on Hall's earlier work of thematically classifying the phenomenological characteristics of thousands of dream reports given by ordinary subjects and published in his *The Meaning of Dreams* (1953).
[57] Domhoff (2003), 67. See also Hall and van de Castle (1966) and, for a concise summary of the Hall-Van de Castle system, see Domhoff (2003), 67–94.
[58] Domhoff (2003), 145.
[59] Hobson (1992), 452.
[60] Hobson and McCarley (1977), 1347.

vation pattern—hence the term *activation-synthesis hypothesis*. The narrative is determined by physiological events, not by meaningful psychological events such as the disguised fulfillment of unconscious wishes.[61]

In Hobson and McCarley's view, the electric signals produced by the pontine hindbrain are both random and psychologically unmotivated, which accounts for what they consider the bizarreness of dreams or distortion of dream images. Thus, although the forebrain tries to 'synthesize its random patterns into a meaningful whole' by drawing on 'ordered activation patterns of stored memories',[62] these attempts are not always successful. With this explanation, Hobson and McCarley account for dream bizarreness and occasional dream coherence at one go. At the same time, 'they were able to claim that since the generation of REM is an automatic, preprogrammed process, its unconscious mental correlate [dreaming] is as "motivationally neutral" (Hobson and McCarley, 1977, 1338) as the brainstem mechanism that generates your heartbeat'.[63] Dreaming, according to this view, is the result of the forebrain's more or less successful attempts at coming up with 'the best possible fit of intrinsically inchoate data produced by the auto-activated brain-mind'.[64]

Nevertheless, Hobson, perhaps in a reconciliatory gesture towards those colleagues criticizing his earlier writings for 'biological reductionism',[65] clearly concedes that dreams are far from psychologically meaningless:

> The activation-synthesis hypothesis assumes that dreams are as meaningful as they can be under the adverse working conditions of the brain in REM sleep. The activated brain-mind does its best to attribute meaning to the internally generated signals. It is this synthetic effort that gives our dreams their impressive thematic coherence: dream plots remain remarkably intact despite their orientational disorganization. And it may be that their symbolic, prophetic character arises from the integrative strain of this synthetic effort. The brain-mind may need to call upon its deepest myths to find a

---

[61] Vogel (1993), 3.
[62] Vogel (1993), 3.
[63] Solms and Turnbull (2002), 187.
[64] Hobson (1992), 453.
[65] Rycroft (1979), 36.

narrative frame that can contain the data. Hence, one can continue to interpret dreams metaphorically, and even in terms of the dynamically repressed unconscious, if one so chooses.[66]

The psychological relevance of the dream state is thus confirmed even by a neurological hardliner such as Hobson, who grants that the problems posed or even solved in dreams 'may be perceptual as well as emotional and thus provide hints of interest to both one's aesthetic and one's psychological self'.[67] In more recent publications, Hobson has increasingly emphasized the aesthetic and creative potential involved in dreaming and its interconnectedness with waking states of imagination. Most importantly, he has likened dreams to visual art such as painting: 'Like works of art, dreams may have a narrative or metaphorical character which depends on language, but both are experienced primarily as vision and emotion, and both integrate vision and emotion in compelling, surprising, and meaningful ways.'[68] He also emphasizes the auto-creative originality of the dream process:

> During REM sleep, the brain and its mind seem to be engaging in a process of fantastic creation. It is obvious that our dreams are not simply the reliving of previous experience. On the contrary, we are often actually fabricating wholly novel ones. Thus new ideas and feelings, and new views of old problems, can be expected to arise within dreams. These may be carried forward into the unconscious mind or remain unconscious as part of our deeper creative repertoire. [...] Thus the brain of one and all is fundamentally artistic. [...] Each of us is a surrealist at night during his or her dreams: each is a Picasso, a Dali, a Fellini—the delightful and the macabre mixed in full measure.[69]

In emphasizing the interconnectedness of waking and dreaming imagination, Hobson takes care to set his model of the auto-creative brain-mind apart from Freud's dream work model. Thus, rather than reducing

---

[66] Hobson (1992), 463.
[67] Hobson (1988), 16.
[68] Hobson and Wohl (2005), 16.
[69] Hobson (1988), 296–97.

'creativity to a rehearsal of psychopathological conflict',[70] Hobson views dreaming as an 'intrinsically creative act', designed to 'create rather than to disguise meaning' and characterized by 'the creative unpredictability of the dreaming brain as a source of artistic inspiration'.[71]

Hobson's dismantling of some of Freud's fundamental premises is convincing as far as it goes. However, Hobson's insistence on the *purely* physical origin of dream consciousness has not remained uncontested. Thus, it remains debatable whether dreams are generated in a bottom-up or top-down manner: Do the low-level sensory brain areas automatically produce images that the higher-order areas then try to shape into coherent stories (as Hobson would have it) or is the brain's production of images a visual rendering of cognitive processes such as wishes, thoughts, fantasies and memories during sleep? Thus far, there is no definite proof for either assumption. However, despite Hobson's achievement of rendering 'REM dream properties consistent with physiological events during REM sleep',[72] his activation synthesis model crucially fails to account for the fact that REM sleep can occur without dreaming and dreaming can occur without REM sleep. Even the NREM sleep phases show mental activity, though at times closer to verbal thinking than to the visual dream narratives experienced during REM sleep.[73] What is more, the hypnagogic phases of sleep onset and awakening are also often characterized by complex dream narratives and vivid imagery and have been described as REM-like.[74] Based on this insight, Cavallero and Foulkes, arguing for a cognitive approach to dreaming, suggest that REM sleep may be 'facilitating the occurrence of dreaming, by way of its central nervous system activation, only in organisms that also have certain kinds of mental representations and processing capabilities'.[75] Crucial empirical

---

[70] Hobson and Wohl (2005), 14.
[71] Hobson and Wohl (2005), 15.
[72] Vogel (1993), 3.
[73] As Hobson (1988) points out: 'Not only does dreaming occupy as much as two hours per night, but mental activity of some sort appears to accompany at least half of our sleep. In fact, the most common form of mental activity in sleep is not dreaming but thinking. Sleep thinking is not accompanied by sensory illusions and is not bizarre. It tends to be commonplace, often concerned with real-life events of yesterday or tomorrow, and is usually banal, uncreative, repetitive' (8).
[74] See Foulkes and Vogel (1965) and Mavromatis (2001).
[75] Cavallero and Foulkes (1993b), 9.

evidence for this theory is provided by Foulkes' studies concerning the apparent lack of REM dreaming in young children below age 5, from which he concludes that dreaming may be viewed

> more as a high-level symbolic skill, a form of intelligent behaviour with cognitive prerequisites and showing systematic development over time, than as a relatively low-level, automatized, congenitally-given kind of perception, which routinely takes place during REM sleep in the absence of perceivable objects or events.[76]

Based on this and other empirical evidence, Cavallero and Foulkes conclude that 'the explanation of dreaming ultimately stands on the same ground as that of every other process studied by cognitive psychology—understanding, psychologically, what those mental conditions are in which dreaming becomes possible'.[77]

Even though dreaming is not dependent on REM sleep, vivid and narratively coherent dreams most predictably occur during REM sleep, which is the reason why REM dreams have been most thoroughly researched.[78] As McNamara et al. point out:

> When subjects are awakened from REM sleep, they generally report a 'dream'—a narrative involving the dreamer who interacts with others in ordinary or extraordinary ways in both familiar and strange settings. The emotions in the dream are often unpleasant and the events recounted occasionally involve bizarre and improbable elements.[79]

The story-like structure of dreams was confirmed, among others, by an empirical sleep laboratory study conducted by Cipolli and Poli in 1992. Dream reports collected from subjects after REM sleep awakenings and after morning awakenings were analysed according to a modified version of a formal story-grammar designed for narrative texts (Mandler

---

[76] Foulkes (1993), 120–121.
[77] Cavallero and Foulkes (1993b), 9.
[78] For a detailed description of the physiological stages composing both REM and NREM sleep, see McNamara et al. (2010).
[79] McNamara et al. (2010), 70–71.

and Johnson, 1977). The results confirmed that the formal elements of dreams resemble typical stories in terms of characters, settings and a hierarchical event structure. Since the reports from REM sleep awakenings and morning awakenings showed no significant differences, it was concluded that narrative structure is inherent to the dream experience rather than retrospectively imposed on the dream when recalled in wakefulness.[80]

In a more recent study published in 2015, Cipolli et al. have found that 'the characteristics of structural organization of dream-stories vary along with time of night' and that 'the elaboration of a long and complex dream-story requires a fairly long time and the availability of a great amount of cognitive resources to maintain its continuity and coherence'.[81] Subjects awakened from NREM sleep tend to report less bizarre, less unpleasant dreams that are generally set in more familiar surroundings.[82] However, NREM sleep can be subdivided into three or four descending stages, displaying 'an "ultradian" rhythm through the night',[83] with the duration of REM sleep phases increasing towards the end of the night. It seems likely that,

> [a]s sleep cycles into an REM sleep episode, mentation reports [...] become more dream-like and bizarre, and as sleep cycles into an NREM sleep episode, mentation reports become more thought-like and less bizarre. In short, there is a continuum of mental activity that varies along several dimensions and in tandem with brain activation patterns that fluctuate in a relatively predictable manner across the entire sleep episode.[84]

Nielsen, Kuiken et al. (2001) have compared dream reports from stage REM and stage 2 of NREM sleep and have found that, while reports from both stages 'might not differ with respect to simple presence or

---

[80] See Cipolli and Poli (1992).
[81] Cipolli et al. (2015), 234.
[82] See McNamara et al. (2010), 71. In the context of such findings, McNamara (2008) suggests that 'REM and NREM may exhibit specializations in processing routines for emotional material with NREM preferring pleasant emotional material and REM preferring unpleasant material' (139).
[83] McNamara et al. (2010), 70.
[84] McNamara et al. (2010), 71.

absence of the constituents of a story (characters, scenes, etc.), stage REM mentation would more likely be characterized by the complex story measure of episodic progression'.[85]

The insight that dreaming involves aspects other than the physiological conditions of REM sleep becomes even more cogent when we accept that dreaming not only occurs in other sleep phases but, as Harry T. Hunt points out, also 'under hypnosis (where dreams can be directly suggested), in "daydreaming" as studied under laboratory conditions, and in the "waking dreams" or guided fantasies characteristic of various therapeutic traditions'.[86] This places dreaming in close proximity to waking states of creativity and imagination. Similarly, Andreas Mavromatis, drawing on the scope of hypnagogic experiences in particular, argues that 'there are many kinds of dream not all of which answer the same exact definition, and whose relationship to the parameters of sleep varies widely—so much so that sometimes sleep may be said to be absent'.[87] Such a view is corroborated by an increasing number of researchers.[88] Kuiken sums up some of the 'compelling reasons to expand classificatory efforts beyond the boundaries of sleep' as follows:

> One reason is that the cognitive models of dreaming currently under development emphasize the continuity between sleeping and waking mentation. [...] A second reason is evidence that aspects of dream cognition persist or are reactivated during wakefulness. Beyond demonstrations of an immediate carry-over of REM mentation into waking cognition, there is evidence that some dreams influence waking affect well into the day. We know next to nothing about the dream persistence, spontaneous reminiscence, dream déjà vu, etc., that may mediate dreams' impact on waking thoughts and feelings. The dream-like quality of these moments deserves careful description.[89]

---

[85] Nielsen, Kuiken et al. (2001), 10.
[86] Hunt (1989), 3.
[87] Mavromatis (2001), 108.
[88] See Kuiken (1991a), 198; Cavallero and Foulkes (1993b), 10; Hartmann (2000b), 66; and Hartmann (2011).
[89] Kuiken (1991a), 199.

The most substantial evidence supporting the view that dreaming is a state decoupled from sleep was arguably provided in the wake of what has been called the 'serendipitous discovery'[90] of the default mode network, a network of brain regions that have been found to be more highly activated when we rest, and let our minds wander freely, than when we focus on specific tasks.[91] As Oatley explains, this core network 'supports the psychological processes of autobiographical memory, finding one's way around in the world, imaginative thinking about the future, knowing the perspective of other people, and appear[s] similar to the activity observed in the brain during undirected thought (e.g. daydreaming)'.[92] Arguably, the discovery of the default mode network may prove to be just as revolutionary as the similarly serendipitous discovery of REM sleep half a century before, as it provides strong evidence of overlap between brain activation during dreaming and waking states of undirected cognition such as daydreaming. Thus, several studies have found striking similarities between brain areas activated during dreaming and during waking mind-wandering (daydreaming), with several hubs 'even more active during REM sleep than at rest, augmented by secondary visual and sensorimotor cortices that support sensorimotor imagery'.[93] It is also likely that this augmented default mode network is active during sleep onset and stage 2 of NREM sleep.[94] As Domhoff and Fox point out:

> The main features of the default network [...] include the medial prefrontal cortex (which in turn has several sub-regions), the medial temporal lobe, the bilateral inferior parietal lobule/temporoparietal junction, and the posterior cingulate cortex, with the medial prefrontal cortex (MFPC) and the posterior cingulate cortex (PCC) serving as major hubs.[95]

A research study conducted by Andrews-Hanna et al. (2010) on spontaneous cognition during passive states has established that there are two

---

[90] Buckner (2011).
[91] See studies by Raichle et al. (2001), Buckner et al. (2008) and Pace-Schott (2013).
[92] Oatley (2011), 20–21.
[93] Domhoff and Fox (2015), 343. See Chow et al. (2013) and Fox et al. (2013).
[94] See Domhoff and Fox (2015), 343.
[95] Domhoff and Fox (2015), 345.

sub-systems both of which are activated in states of restfulness: the dorsal medial subsystem is activated when we think about our *present* situation or mental state; the medial temporal subsystem is activated when we think about or *future* situation or future self.[96] Besides, the default mode network shares a number of regions with the network for social cognition.[97] These findings suggest that during waking mind-wandering, 'people tend to engage in self-relevant internal cognition processes predominantly about significant past and future events'.[98] As Domhoff and Fox point out, 'they also fit with the frequent focus on personal concerns and interpersonal interactions during dreaming' and might help 'explain why dreaming as intensified mind-wandering is often focused on the dreamer's concerns about his or her relationships with significant others, regrets about the past, and worries about anxiety-arousing future events'.[99]

The view that the forebrain (cortex) plays a significant role in dreaming is widely shared by contemporary dream researchers. As Domhoff notes: 'For those who want to develop a neurocognitive theory of dreams that encompasses the whole range of dream content, it is now the forebrain network for dream generation that is the real issue'.[100] Acknowledging the need to come up with a theory of dreaming not dependent on the physiological conditions of REM sleep, Ernest Hartmann introduced a model arguably better suited to the accommodation of a broader spectrum of dream states. Even though he concedes that the REM state may be partic-

---

[96] See Andrews-Hanna et al. (2010), 559.
[97] See Domhoff and Fox (2015), 345.
[98] Andrews-Hanna et al. (2010), 559.
[99] Domhoff and Fox (2015), 347. Domhoff and Fox (2015) also note the difficulties in conducting further studies on the default mode network's specific relevance for dreaming. Firstly, neuroscientists researching the default mode network currently are focused on the network's relevance for conditions such as Alzheimer's, schizophrenia or autism. Secondly, 'the type of studies of the default network and its relationship to ongoing mentation that are needed (namely, combined EEG/fMRI studies) are more difficult to conduct during sleep because of the noise of the fMRI scanner, the fact that it takes an entire night to adapt to sleeping in a laboratory in the best of circumstances, and the relatively time-consuming process of awakening participants from sleep and having them attempt to recall often hazy mental experiences' (343). In view of these difficulties, Domhoff and Fox suggest conducting studies during waking mind-wandering, presuming that during restfulness subjects might occasionally slip into the dream state (see 343).
[100] Domhoff (2001b).

ularly conducive to producing 'the critical biology necessary for dreaming to occur', it is clearly not the sole, probably not even the primary, trigger.[101] Basing his model on research evidence by Mark Solms and others, Hartmann, in line with more recent findings, suggests that 'the relevant biology of dreaming is the biology of the cortex—the surface of the brain whose billions of connecting neurons allow us to experience our thoughts and imagery'.[102] The biological state at the cortex underlying the dream experience is 'perhaps most commonly, or most readily, produced by the conditions of REM sleep but [...] can also be produced at other times—frequently at sleep onset and occasionally during wakefulness; perhaps at times of daydreaming or reverie, including "artistic" reverie; and also in psychedelic drug states, among others'.[103]

Hartmann, then, considers dreams as 'obviously meaningful in the sense of dealing with our emotional concerns' and insists that 'they are not random products of a disordered brain'.[104] Dreaming, according to Hartmann's model, is about making connections, both at the neuronal and at the psychological level. As he explains:

> Our minds, based on the structure of the human cortex, consist of the functioning of many billions of units [neurons] which form a kind of net, often called a neural net. [...] All that can happen in a net of this kind is the activation of different portions of the net and the strengthening or weakening of connections. All information is assumed to reside in the connection strengths between units, and what occurs in waking thought, in daydreaming, or in dreaming is that various connections are made. I believe, however, that there are important differences in the style of these connections. Connections are made more broadly and loosely in dreaming. In fact, we can consider a whole continuum of mental functioning ranging

---

[101] Hartmann (2000b), 66. Here, Hartmann refers to studies of brain damage and its effects on dreaming as conducted by Mark Solms, which have shown 'that reported loss of dreaming occurs after a number of different widespread cortical lesions but does not occur after brain-stem lesions that interfere with REM sleep. In fact it is quite possible to continue to have normal REM sleep and yet to experience no dreaming, and it is also possible to have dreams initiated by electrical activity starting elsewhere in the brain (in certain cases of seizure activity) rather than by the usual brain-stem activation of REM sleep' (66).
[102] Hartmann (2000b), 66.
[103] Hartmann (2000b), 66.
[104] Hartmann (2000b), 67.

from focused waking at one end to dreaming at the other, with the dreaming end involving the loosest, or most broadly made connections.[105]

These connections are not randomly made but are emotionally guided, a point especially stressed by Hartmann and in accord with the fact that brain areas involved in the generation and experience of emotions are hyper-activated during the dream state. As Hartmann suggests, 'artistic creativity, exactly like dreaming, involves making new connections broadly, guided by the dominant emotions'.[106] Based on the current state of the art of neurocognitive research, Hartmann's suggestion that dreaming is part of a continuum running 'from focused-waking-thought at one end through looser thought or reverie to fantasy, daydreaming, and eventually to dreaming'[107] is highly compelling. The empirically informed insight that dreaming and waking fictions may well be two sides of the same coin paves the way for the next chapter in which the possible functions of both dreaming and waking fictions are explored from a variety of evolutionary perspectives.

Evolutionary Perspectives on Dreaming and Waking Fictions

In recent years, a number of approaches that might be subsumed under the heading of 'evolutionary' have come up with various explanations regarding the functions of dreaming. Their shared basic assumption is that if dreaming occurs as often and as regularly as it does in all humans (and in most mammals), it very likely serves some crucial function assisting the individual's and the species' survival. The earliest evolutionary theories focused on REM sleep rather than dreaming. As Jerome Siegel puts it:

> Virtually all mammals have REM sleep. In human adults it occupies approximately 90 to 120 minutes of sleep time each night. The intense

---

[105] Hartmann (2000b), 67.
[106] Hartmann (2000b), 73.
[107] Hartmann (2011), 31.

brain activity during this state is mirrored by intense mental activity experienced as dreams. It is difficult to believe that this physiological state does not have some vital survival role.[108]

This assumption is corroborated by scientific evidence: 'Early studies in humans and animals found that [REM sleep] deprivation produces a selective increase in the amount of REM sleep when sleep is allowed after deprivation is terminated', which indicates 'that a need for REM sleep exists and accumulates in its absence, analogous to our need for food and water'.[109] Since REM sleep generally is accompanied by vivid dreaming, many researchers consider it likely that dreams, too, have an adaptive function. Even those who doubt this assumption, notably Owen Flanagan and G.W. Domhoff, tend to concede that dreams have important emergent uses.[110] As Deirdre Barrett puts it, 'dreaming evolved over at least 164 million years of mammalian history and seems to be fine tuned to certain psychological purposes'.[111] This view seems even more pertinent when taking into account that 'REM-deprived subjects […] begin to have more dramatic dreams in the NREM period and hallucinations and "microdreams" in behavioural wakefulness'.[112] These observations clearly support the theory that dreams serve important functions in their own right and are not merely epiphenomena of REM sleep. Assuming that sleeping and waking imagination are two sides of the same coin, the

---

[108] Siegel (1993), 507.

[109] Siegel (1993), 507.

[110] The philosopher Owen Flanagan argues that dreaming may only be an epiphenomenon of REM sleep rather than an adaptive function itself. He views dreams as the 'spandrels of sleep', beautiful architectural spaces in dome and arch design that have no architectural function per se but can be embellished and thereby endowed with meaning and function: 'They [dreams] are mental spandrels, but we can work them into all sorts of useful, creative, and fun things we have learned to do in our lives. If we choose to do so, if we choose to work and play with dreams, it is due to human inventiveness and ingenuity, and it is testimony to our creative capacities to make something out of dreams which are, from a purely biological point of view, epiphenomenal, that are nonadaptations' (124). A similar stance is adopted by Domhoff (2003), who concedes that '[t]he parallels that dreams have with waking figurative thought can be used to explain why dreams have religious and medicinal uses that were invented by people in different cultures in the course of history' (168).

[111] Barrett (2007), 133. For a similar view, see Valli and Revonsuo (2007).

[112] Mavromatis (2001), 274.

insights gleaned from the various evolutionary approaches to dreaming may be equally relevant to, as well as further enlightened by, the inclusion of approaches to the potentially adaptive functions of waking fictions.[113]

The first of these evolutionary theories to be outlined here was provided by Antti Revonsuo. He proposed that dreaming simulates threatening scenarios so that individuals can rehearse for real-life threats without endangering themselves.[114] This hypothesis is supported by neuroimaging data showing that the same brain regions are activated no matter if we actually perform a task or only imagine or dream we do.[115] By being able to rehearse certain scenarios, exercising a part of the brain without having to physically experience potentially dangerous behaviour-eliciting stimuli, we can optimize mental functioning and our response to real-life situations—even more so during a dream whose content is 'perceptually indistinguishable from waking perception'.[116] Incidentally, a similar effect may be true for our reading of stories. Thus, Keith Oatley, referring to the discovery of 'mirror neurons' (neurons firing when an action is observed or imagined rather than actually performed), suggests: 'The importance for reading and understanding of stories is that, perhaps, when we understand an action as we read about it in a novel, our understanding depends on making a version of the action ourselves, inwardly.'[117] The effect, then, would be very similar to dreaming about performing that action.

Drawing on data collected by Hall and Van de Castle in 1966, Franklin and Zyphur suggest that 'the overrepresentation of threatening elements in dreams, which should not occur if dream content is random',[118] clearly

---

[113] See Schrage-Früh (2012).
[114] See Revonsuo (2000).
[115] As Schredl and Erlacher (2008) point out, relevant studies were integrated by Jeannerod (2001) into a theory of neural simulation of action (simulation theory), which postulates that 'covert actions are actual actions' in the sense of sharing 'the same cortical areas' (7). A number of studies subsequently conducted in the field of dream and lucid dream research have resulted in similar findings. For a detailed research overview, see Schredl and Erlacher (2008). Based on this empirical evidence, Schredl and Erlacher (2008) draw the conclusion that 'actions in dreams are represented on higher cognitive levels—equivalent to actual movements—and therefore share, to some extent, the central structures' (7).
[116] Franklin and Zyphur (2005), 65.
[117] Oatley (2011), 19.
[118] Franklin and Zyphur (2005), 66.

supports Revonsuo's threat rehearsal theory. Negative emotions like fear, anxiety and stress have been found to be dominant in our dreams.[119] The threat rehearsal theory also accounts for the fact that during REM sleep, the sleeper's higher-order mental processes needed to intellectually assess situations are deactivated, which may be necessary for the perceived threats to be experienced as real in order to effectively school the individual's survival capacities. Questioning the reality of the dream experience would obviously be detrimental to such a rehearsal effect. All these aspects suggest the adaptive function of dreaming as clearly advantageous to an individual's survival. As Franklin and Zyphur sum up: 'Evidence from mental imagery and dream studies suggest that rehearsal in the dream is treated as a real threat and, therefore, those individuals with these imagery skills to rehearse threatening scenarios should have an improved ability to deal with threat, making them more likely to be the progenitors of offspring'.[120] Quite obviously, this hypothesis has far-reaching implications also for our assessment of both actual nightmares and their cultural and literary representations in the form of, for instance, horror fiction, an imaginative genre that can trigger very 'real' reactions of fear in the reader.

However, as Deirdre Barrett rightly notes, the threat rehearsal theory 'falls as far short of explaining all dreams as did Freud's opposite but analogous theory of "wish fulfilment"'.[121] Accordingly, Revonsuo's model of threat rehearsal has been expanded and complemented by other researchers such as Michael S. Franklin and Michael J. Zyphur, who argue that 'the fitness-enhancing benefits of dreaming is [sic] not restricted to threat rehearsal, and the evolution of other higher-order cognitive faculties has

---

[119] See Payne (2004), 124 and Hartmann (2010), 198. Some researchers, such as Inge Strauch and Barbara Meier (1996), have claimed that positive emotions in dreams are more frequent than previously assumed (see 27). However, on closer examination, there still is an overall dominance of negative emotions to be detected. As Hartmann (2010) points out: 'Interestingly, this group finds "joy" to be the most common emotion among the 12 emotions they consider. However, if their negative emotions—"anger," "fear," "stress"—are combined, it would lead to a much larger total than "joy"' (198). Domhoff (2003), too, confirms the predominance of negative emotions in dreams, noting that 'only 20 % of all emotions in dreams fit into the happiness category, a finding that has been replicated three times (Hall et al., 1982; Roussy, 2000; Tonay, 1990/91)' (70).
[120] Franklin and Zyphur (2005), 66.
[121] Barrett (2007), 337.

been strongly influenced by a dreaming mechanism'.[122] Interestingly, during REM sleep, there is an activity increase in those brain regions implicated in decision making, conflict resolution and social cognition, suggesting that cognitive faculties concerned with the processing of social information are strongly activated. This might account for the large number of dreams involving us in social interaction with other people.[123] According to Franklin and Zyphur, not only the rehearsal of life-threatening scenarios, but also the rehearsal of social situations may play a significant role for an individual's survival. Their theory that during REM sleep we practise and rehearse social scenarios is supported by the fact that REM sleep occurs most frequently in new-borns and decreases throughout the life span. This would suggest that children learn or at least consolidate their social cognitive abilities to a large extent during REM sleep.[124] Franklin and Zyphur conclude that 'the experiences that we accrue from dreaming across our lifespan are sure to influence how we interact with the world and are bound to influence our overall fitness, not only as individuals, but as a species'.[125]

In a similar vein, fiction has been found to be 'about a relatively specific area of knowledge, of selves in the social world'.[126] This implies that fiction might have a socially adaptive function, as suggested by Joseph Carroll when he writes that literature not only provides us with simulated situations through which to 'guide our own behaviour' but also serves as 'a medium for cultivating our innate and socially adaptive capacity for entering mentally into the experience of others'.[127] Elsewhere he notes: 'Literature and the other arts help us live our lives. [...] In all known cultures, the arts enter profoundly into normal childhood development, connect individuals to their culture, and help people get oriented in the

---

[122] Franklin and Zyphur (2005), 66.
[123] See Franklin and Zyphur (2005), 69.
[124] Interestingly, this theory might also at least partly account for the condition of autism. As Franklin and Zyphur (2005) note: 'Autism has been likened to a TOM-deficit and is associated with disrupted sleep patterns.' In light of this, they propose the hypothesis that 'a portion of the deficits observed in autistics may be due to their lack of REM sleep' (72).
[125] Franklin and Zyphur (2005), 73.
[126] Oatley (2011), 158.
[127] Carroll (2004), 116.

world, emotionally, morally, conceptually.'[128] Based on the findings of several empirical tests conducted by his own team, Oatley claims that the skills we learn when engaging 'in the simulations of fiction' indeed 'transfer to the everyday social world'.[129] For instance, avid readers of fiction (as opposed to non-fiction) showed 'better abilities in empathy and theory of mind'.[130] Oatley accounts for these findings by arguing that readers of fictional works 'tend to become more expert at making models of others and themselves, and at navigating the social world'.[131] Ultimately, they are thus better equipped for dealing with everyday social constellations. Obviously, the tests conducted by Oatley and his colleagues are not definite proof of the hypothesis that fiction 'can improve our understanding of other people and of ourselves'[132] and has a potentially beneficial effect accordingly. Their findings, however, are certainly also corroborated by the findings of dream researchers who have suggested similar functions for dreams. Both dreaming and waking fictions can be described as 'mental simulations',[133] and in view of all evidence available, it seems likely that they can achieve similar fitness-enhancing effects.[134]

It is by now widely accepted that both REM and NREM sleep play an important role in processes of memory consolidation as well as the assimilation of new personally significant experience into the structure of memory, with dreams being 'a reflection of the memory consolidation process'.[135] Many researchers even hold the opinion that dreams are crucial to, rather than merely a reflection of, this process.[136] According

---

[128] Carroll (2012), 60.
[129] Oatley (2011), 158.
[130] Oatley (2011), 159.
[131] Oatley (2011), 160.
[132] Oatley (2011), 162.
[133] Oatley (2011), 162.
[134] Obviously, the idea that all kinds of fiction are beneficial is misleading. Oatley (2011), for instance, points out that certain kinds of fiction, for instance those portraying violence, can have a harmful effect, especially on children (see 167). The adaptive value of fiction, then, may be limited to certain themes as suggested by Oatley (2011): 'exploration of the minds of others, investigation of relationships, dynamics of interactions in groups, and grappling's [sic] with the problems of selfhood' (167). Needless to say, there may also be certain kinds of dreams, such as posttraumatic nightmares, that can have a potentially harmful effect.
[135] Payne (2004), 103.
[136] See Palombo (1980), 197; Kuiken (1991), 239; Schwartz (2004), 29; Cartwright (2010), xiii, 8.

to Cartwright, 'hard evidence supports those assumptions, that adequate sleep is essential to physical health, and that dreaming is important to mental health'.[137] Based on her own research findings, Cartwright suggests that in addition to the process of filing the day's significant experience into our memory system, 'while dreaming we are also down-regulating any disruptive emotions attached to those new experiences and modifying the software program of the self on the basis of this new information'.[138] As she explains: 'What we experience as a dream is the result of our brain's effort to match recent, emotion-evoking events to other similar experiences already stored in long-term memory [...] to defuse the impact of those feelings that might otherwise linger and disrupt our moods and behaviors the next day'.[139] Ultimately, in Cartwright's view:

> [S]leep contributes to balancing our emotional lives by modulating the negative emotion invoked by those waking experiences that threaten the present organization of our self-structure. This process, continuously and creatively, overlays images of the new and older memories in REM sleep, threading them into new patterns that literally change our minds. These images may be hard to understand—not because they are forbidden, but because they are blends, more like complex paintings than linear texts. When all goes well, we wake refreshed and with a modified strategy for guiding our behavior toward fulfilling our now somewhat revised conception of ourselves. We are always works in progress. Dreams are a window onto the ongoing work of the mind during its essential night-shift.[140]

In a similar vein, Hartmann points out that '[b]ecause of its broader connection making, dreaming is especially good at noting similarities and creating metaphor. Dreaming makes use of our visual/spatial picturing abilities and provides an *explanatory metaphor* for the dreamer's emotional state of mind'.[141] Accordingly, dreaming 'does not simply consolidate memory, but interweaves and increases memory connections. These new

---

[137] Cartwright (2010), 8.
[138] Cartwright (2010), xvi.
[139] Cartwright (2010), 5.
[140] Cartwright (2010), 178.
[141] Hartmann (1998), 4.

connections, or increased connections, are what make dreaming useful in problem solving, as well as in scientific and artistic creation'.[142] One possible function of dreaming, then, might be the 'broadening of memory through cross-connections, which may be useful in increasing adaptation for future functioning'.[143] Also traumatic events are worked through and assimilated in dreams, especially in nightmares. Referring to post-traumatic dreams in particular, Hartmann suggests: 'As connections are made between the terrible recent event and other material, the emotion becomes less powerful and overwhelming and the trauma is gradually integrated into the rest of life.'[144] In this view, then, the connection-making process in dreams has a therapeutic or healing function inherent in the process of dreaming itself and independent of dream recall or retrospective dream analysis. This function may well have also been adaptive, for, as Hartmann points out:

> Some of us living in relatively peaceful developed world countries may think of trauma as a rare, exceptional event, but in much of the world, there is almost constant trauma. And it is likely that our ancestors—thousands of years ago when we were developing the relevant forebrain structures—lived far more traumatic lives than we do now.[145]

Similarly to Cartwright and Hartmann, Stanley Palombo regards dreaming as an 'intermediate step in the overall process through which new experience is assimilated into the structure of memory. Condensation is not primarily a defensive operation, as Freud suggested, but a test of congruence that determines which associative links will bind the new experience into the structure of the dreamer's past'.[146] As he points out: 'If the

---

[142] Hartmann (1998), 4.

[143] Hartmann (1998), 123.

[144] Hartmann (1998), 13. Interestingly, in dealing with the dreams of traumatized persons, Hartmann has noted that initially their posttraumatic dreams tend to re-enact the trauma in a very literal fashion. As the healing process sets in, their dreams become more and more metaphorical and increasingly associative.

[145] Hartmann (2010), 201. As Tore Nielsen and Ross Levin (2007) point out, despite a number of 'promising theoretical advances, however, there is still no evidence that the CIs [central images] identified in dreaming serve to facilitate emotional adaptation in the manner postulated by Hartmann' (298).

[146] Palombo (1983), 306.

opportunity for new combinations arises repeatedly, as we now know it does in the regular cycles of dreaming sleep, then the emergence of novel forms and qualities becomes inevitable'.[147] Moreover, he emphasizes that the matching process is able to 'go beyond the narrow logical categories of waking thought to reach deeper levels of experience otherwise inaccessible to the dreamer' and suggests that this ability explains 'the important role played by dreaming in the creative process'.[148] Ultimately, elaborating on the inherent creativity of the dream process, Hartmann, too, suggests similarities between dreaming and waking processes of creative imagination: 'If we consider the artist as someone who can see things a bit more broadly or can make connections a bit more easily than most, we can see this as a developed form of an ability we all possess in dreams.'[149] Deirdre Barrett, citing a number of relevant experimental studies, likewise sees the creative potential of dreams as one of their adaptive functions, arguing that 'dreams are thinking or problem solving in a different biochemical state from that of waking'.[150]

Attempts to highlight and explore the dream's creative rather than its pathological potential have led recent dream researchers to become more interested in what Freud termed the manifest dream content and to explore the aesthetic value of our dream experiences.[151] Accordingly, they view dreams as products of play rather than work and as creative visions rather than neurotic symptoms. In Kelly Bulkeley's words:

> What the play metaphor clearly highlights is the genuine creativity that is involved in dream formation. Whereas Freud repeatedly depreciated the creativity of dreaming, the vast majority of contemporary dream researchers insist that creativity is an essential, integral part of the dream formation process.[152]

---

[147] Palombo (1983), 307.
[148] Palombo (1983), 312.
[149] Hartmann (1998), 164.
[150] Barrett (2007), 140.
[151] A similar view was stated by Jung as early as 1931 in his lecture 'The Practical Use of Dream Analysis' where the author claims that '[t]he manifest dream picture is the dream itself and contains the whole meaning of the dream' (Jung quoted in Rupprecht [1999], 79).
[152] Bulkeley (1999), 64.

Dreams, then, are seen as expressive, rather than repressive, as offering metaphorical expressions of emotional content and metaphorical solutions to unsolved problems and conflicts rather than distorted symbols of repressed wishes. If viewed, in Montague Ullman's phrase, as 'metaphors in motion',[153] dream images are not distorted, but they simply express many things at once, much like literary metaphors, uncovering analogies in at first glance unrelated objects or activities that tend to be overlooked by our more rationally oriented waking minds. This is, of course, a property they share with waking fictions. As Oatley explains:

> Metaphor contributes to the enjoyment of fiction because we like to be discoverers. We are genetically predisposed to enjoy the new thoughts that can occur when a this becomes a that. Such discoveries are continuations of those made in pretend play, in which we can discover that a table can become a house.[154]

They are also continuations of the creative abilities we all share in dreams.

Michele Stephen's model of the 'imaginal mind' is particularly suited to accounting for the creative, transformative and visionary potential inherent in many dreams. Her model suggests the co-existence of two separate memory registers, the 'semantic/language register of memory', which is usually available to waking consciousness, and the 'emotionally-coded memory register',[155] which catalogues experience according to its emotional significance and operates outside consciousness.[156] Stephen associates dreaming primarily with the older processor or memory register of what she calls the 'imaginal mind'. According to Stephen, one major function of REM sleep and dreaming 'is to review the day's sensory input and relate it to, and encode it in, the emotional memory system. [...] This process of storing in memory [...] involves linking new sensory

---

[153] See Ullman (1969).
[154] Oatley (2011), 35.
[155] Stephen (2003), 97.
[156] This model is very similar to the model of the 'hybrid mind' as proposed by Andy Clark, which assumes the co-existence of two mental processors, the older of which is intuitive, non-verbal and works by association, whereas the newer one can be conceived of as a 'linguistic processor'. See Oatley (2011), 76.

information to existing emotional categories or schemas'.[157] Dreaming, in this view, 'represents a different way of apprehending and evaluating the world'.[158] Freed from our semantically constructed conceptions of the world, dreams can provide us with insights occluded in everyday life by representing 'the incomprehensible, the unthinkable—unthinkable, that is, in language and words'.[159] As Stephen points out, '[t]he creativity of the imaginal system is of a special kind that arises from its capacity to represent information and express things which cannot be represented or expressed verbally, and thus are not registered in the verbal memory system. It steps in where language fails'.[160] This, according to Stephen, accounts for the central role attributed to dreams in prophecy and, I would suggest, links the roles of prophet/dreamer and poet/writer, both of whom are enabled to 'transcend the semantically created world of society and culture, and thus [are provided with] the means of formulating a new vision which can be translated into language at a later date'.[161] In David Kahn and Tzivia Gover's words:

> Dreaming, it can be argued, is, in fact, a no-holds-barred form of thinking that is often visually rich, emotionally charged, creative, associative, and seemingly boundless in its content and creative configurations. In particular, dreaming consciousness affords us the ability to be a part of and experience a world unconstrained by the realities of the wake physical world—and, when awake, to use the images and stories we have created while dreaming. Although easy to dismiss as meaningless hallucinations, and although easily forgotten, dreams allow us to experience things beyond our abilities in waking reality, and beyond the laws of physical science and nature. Dreams give us the opportunity to bring into the physical world the insights and the creative and original perspectives contained within them.[162]

---

[157] Stephen (2003), 98.
[158] Stephen (2003), 110.
[159] Stephen (2003), 110.
[160] Stephen (2003), 111.
[161] Stephen (2003), 110. Stephen's model can be usefully employed to a more 'shamanic' conception of the cultural uses of dream and poetry. For a detailed discussion of this model in relation to the contemporary Irish poet Paula Meehan, see Schrage-Früh (2009).
[162] Gover and Khan (2010), 194.

Accordingly, quite a few literary philosophers have turned their attention to the interconnectedness of dreams and fictions, most notably among them Bert O. States. According to States, not only are 'the roots of art'[163] in the dream, but 'the dream [...] is the ur-form of all imaginative thought'.[164] He argues: 'The dream precedes art both in the history of the race and the history of the individual psyche.'[165] To States, then, dreams are 'naked fictions' and fictions are 'dreams in street clothing'.[166] In other words, a dream can be compared to a first rough draft of fiction, developing according to the same compositional rules as a work of literature and deriving from a similar innate need to structure the world by turning our experience into narrative. What is more, as Irving Massey notes, '[g]iven the indications that dream developed before language appeared on the evolutionary or the mental screen' it may well be that '[p]erhaps dream tells us a little about what the mind was like before it came to be dominated by language; it may afford us a glimpse into our prehistory'.[167] Referring to occasional instances of seemingly bizarre and disjointed language (in the sense of speech acts) in dreams, he points out that while appearing defective from the waking point of view, 'dream language can be seen as often successful in expressing inchoate, blurred, or overlapping thought-moods that ordinary, syntactically complete, monosemantic language could not even begin to deal with'.[168] This type of dream language thus shares some of the inherently polysemantic properties of literary language. Both dreams and fictions, then, can be viewed as adaptive functions because the capacities they school such as condensing 'emotions and abstractions into images and [finding] resemblances in categories that are miles apart [...] are what enable the organism to adapt to unexpected changes in its environment'.[169]

This view ties in with John Tooby and Leda Cosmides' hypothesis that the human delight in fictions and other products of the imagination

---

[163] States (1987), 79.
[164] States (1993), 85.
[165] States (1987), 78.
[166] States (1997), 236.
[167] Massey (2009), 60–61.
[168] Massey (2009), 61.
[169] States (1987), 95.

serves an adaptive function. As they point out: 'Involvement in fictional, imagined worlds appears to be a cross-culturally universal, species-typical phenomenon'.[170] Of course, the same is true of the cross-culturally universal activity of dreaming, which David Mitchell aptly describes as being 'near the genderless feet of the totem pole of *Homo sapiens*' common denominators'.[171] A further similarity is that 'fictional worlds engage emotion systems while disengaging action systems (just as dreams do)'.[172] Both dreams and fictions may be instrumental in reliving and assimilating emotional experiences we might otherwise have difficulty coming to terms with by providing us with what Oatley calls 'appraisal patterns'.[173] As he explains with respect to fictions:

> Prompted by defamiliarization, we bring ourselves and our past experience to these patterns and we actively encourage ourselves to experience the literary emotions in imagination. A remembered emotion is now experienced in a new context, so the range of our experience of it is increased. In turn we may focus on the text, on a memory, and on the timeless quality of the emotion in a way that can take us out of ourselves.[174]

Drawing on the Indian *rasa* theory of literary emotions, Oatley argues that we enjoy fictional stories precisely because we recognize 'patterns of emotions that we have experienced ourselves (in life or literature) in a new context'. Our emotional involvement becomes possible because we 'project ourselves imaginatively into this context, and experience the emotions in a way that enables us to understand them more deeply, and in the process perhaps to make some changes in ourselves'.[175]

In contrast to all other species, humans seem to be uniquely equipped with the capacity to distinguish between actual truth and imagined or contingent truth. As Mark Turner points out: 'Running two stories mentally, when we should be absorbed by only one, and blending them when

---

[170] Cosmides and Tooby (2001), 7.
[171] Mitchell, 'What Use Are Dreams in Fiction?' 437.
[172] Cosmides and Tooby (2001), 8.
[173] Oatley (2011), 122.
[174] Oatley (2011), 122.
[175] Oatley (2011), 124.

they should be kept apart, is at the root of what makes us human'.[176] While Turner further notes that we do not know how and when 'this advanced human ability for blending evolved', it is all the same 'tantalizing that it was preceded phylogenetically by both dreaming and memory, each of which requires that the brain differentiate between the immediate environment and a different story'.[177] Dreams and consciously created fictions alike, then, serve the purpose of broadening our scope of experience in an almost unlimited way. As Oatley puts it: 'In the branch of imagination called fiction, we can enter in imagination many more situations than a lifetime could contain. In doing so we undertake mental enactments. We become for a while people who we are not, and have feelings for people we would not otherwise know'.[178] In addition to contributing to our theory of mind, the ability to 'read' another individual's feelings and thoughts, we may learn to know ourselves better:

> In art [...] our conception of our selfhood can change, for instance towards understanding in ourselves certain potentialities that we might not normally admit to ourselves, which we might think belong only to others. We discover that we too, as members of the family of human beings, are at least mentally capable of emotions that are not very creditable'[179]

Needless to say, throughout history, dreams, too, have repeatedly been viewed as potential mirrors to our hidden or 'true' selves.[180]

Fiction and, I would argue, dreams, then, have the powerful and highly advantageous effect of 'unleashing our reactions to potential lives and realities [so that] we feel more richly and adaptively about what we have not actually experienced. This allows us not only to understand others' choices and inner lives better, but to feel our way more foresightfully to

---

[176] Turner (2003), 120.
[177] Turner (2003), 121.
[178] Oatley (2011), 30.
[179] Oatley (2011), 117.
[180] To give just one example, as early as the seventeenth century, Owen Feltham (2005 [1661]) in his essay 'Of Dreams' remarks: 'Dreams are notable means of discovering our own inclinations. The wise man learns to know himself as well by the night's black mantle, as the searching beams of day. In sleep, we have the naked and natural thoughts of our souls [...] Surely, how we fall to vice, or rise to virtue, we may by observation find in our dreams' (16).

adaptively better choices ourselves'.[181] In this way, Tooby and Cosmides account for the fact that as human beings we spend much of our time immersed in recreational activities involving aesthetic enjoyment that has no ostensible survival value in the outside world. As they argue, both aesthetically driven behaviour and dreaming may have been selected for to 'cause fitness-enhancing changes to the brain/mind'[182] and hence

> may be driven by adaptations operating in their organizational mode. According to this analysis, aesthetically driven behavior only appears non-utilitarian because our ordinary standards of function are focused on the struggle to achieve adaptive changes in the external world, such as caring for children, acquiring a mate, foraging, and so on. When we recognize that for many actions the goal is instead to make adaptive changes in the immense and subtle internal world of the mind and brain, then the puzzle of how natural selection could build complex systems to produce pointless behaviors (potentially) evaporates.[183]

In this context, the recently emerged view that the dream state is not necessarily restricted to sleep may be illuminating. The human ability to immerse oneself in what Mavromatis calls 'oneiric activities during wakefulness, such as daydreaming, doing art, doing creative science, being creative in general, letting go without falling asleep (hypnagogizing)' might thus account for the fact that 'man needs less sleep than any other mammal which has been studied'.[184] According to this argument, the functions fulfilled by dream sleep have their analogues in the functions fulfilled by creative waking activities and it may well be that the human ability 'to relax and engage in oneiric activities may have as a result an overall reduction in the need to sleep and have sleepdreams'.[185]

The need to tell stories may have been sparked not least of all by the desire to communicate one's dreams. Thus, the earliest documents of written-down stories actually record and interpret the author's dreams,

---

[181] Cosmides and Tooby (2001), 23.
[182] Cosmides and Tooby (2001), 14.
[183] Cosmides and Tooby (2001), 16.
[184] Mavromatis (2001), 276.
[185] Mavromatis (2001), 277.

for example, the Sumerian dream text *The Epic of Gilgamesh*, inscribed on a clay tablet over 5000 years ago.[186] This example shows that 'from the beginning, storytelling and dreaming overlapped and were seen as having meaningful affinities'.[187] In Bulkeley's words, there clearly is 'a core connection between the primal human experience of dreaming and the cultural wonders of creative inspiration'.[188] What is more, an interesting suggestion regarding nightmares as adaptive functions has been offered by Patrick McNamara:

> Nightmares are frightening experiences and to survive a nightmare and live to tell about it may elicit respect from others. Though less true in modern society this is what I believe occurred among our ancestral populations. In conditions of tribal living before the advent of evidence-based science or modern comforts hearing about a nightmare would have been tantamount to listening to a terrifying religious vision. The individual telling the tale would have been treated as marked or sacred in some sense.[189]

This hypothesis is corroborated by studies of premodern tribal cultures which suggest that 'nightmare sharing was linked with changes in identity and social status. For example, a child who shared a nightmare in some compelling way might be marked for later training to become a shaman, with the nightmare serving as evidence for the child's worthiness for such training'.[190]

There is ample evidence to assume, then, that dreaming and waking storytelling not only share similar adaptive functions but have been inextricably entwined from an early age. And indeed, as Carol Schreier Rupprecht notes: 'Rarely in any culture can one find a poet, playwright, novelist, or short story writer with a significant body of work who does not include dreaming in some form'.[191] Incidentally, empirical research supports the hypothesis that a rich and vivid dream life frequently coin-

---

[186] See Rupprecht (2007), 2 and Oatley (2011), 134.
[187] Rupprecht (2007), 2.
[188] Bulkeley (2010), 45.
[189] McNamara (2008), 94.
[190] McNamara (2008), 95.
[191] Rupprecht (2007), 21.

cides with heightened creativity. Thus, Hartmann has found that persons with thin boundaries, 'in whose minds, things are relatively fluid',[192] thoughts and feelings tending to merge and overlap, are both more likely to experience frequent vivid dreams (often nightmares), to recall their dreams and to be creative in their waking lives.[193] This claim is corroborated by writers throughout the ages who have testified to their own rich dream life which many of them see as indispensable to their waking imagination. As Schreier Rupprecht sums up: 'Although the hypothesis about dreaming as the origin of all human creativity will always remain unprovable, we can hear in the voices of these writers an unassailable conviction that their dreams enable them to create. And their voices echo through centuries and across cultures'.[194] Arguably, studying these writers' dreams in conjunction with their consciously created fictions may not only shed new light on these works but may also provide clues to the creative process itself. Taking its cue from these insights, the following chapter sets out to explore in how far the processes at work in dreaming can be usefully compared to the processes at work in waking states of creative and imaginative immersion such as writing and reading fictions.

---

[192] Hartmann (1998), 220.
[193] See Hartmann (1998), 220. For further studies confirming the link between 'thin boundaries', vivid dreams and creativity, see Levin et al. (1991), Hartmann et al. (2001) and Schredl and Erlacher (2007).
[194] Rupprecht (2007), 7–8.

3

Dreaming and Waking Imagination

The Spectrum of Imagination

Most of us will intuitively agree that dreams are in some ways akin to our waking imaginations. Metaphorically describing Hollywood as a *dream* factory or our nocturnal dreams as a dream *theatre* already suggests that we perceive an analogy, if not a deep-rooted similarity, between our waking and sleeping fictions. Artists, filmmakers and writers have for a long time fruitfully explored this link and dream researchers have confirmed it: 'Dreams can be considered as a kind of imagination. Both dreaming and imagination are a simulation of the real world on a higher cognitive level.'[1] However, at the phenomenological level, dreaming arguably *feels* more 'real' than imagined, which is why philosophers and scientists have sometimes drawn attention to the *deceptive* rather than the *imaginative* qualities of dreaming. René Descartes (1596–1650) may be the most prominent example: 'How often does my evening slumber persuade me of such ordinary things as these: that I am here, clothed in my dressing gown, seated

---

[1] Erlacher and Schredl (2008), 7.

next to the fireplace—when in fact I am lying undressed in bed!'[2] Dreams, here, are described as sensory hallucinations simulating our waking perception so accurately that we find it almost impossible to be completely certain whether we are asleep or awake at any given moment in time.[3]

In contrast to Descartes' example of an unspectacular dream of sitting quietly by the fireplace, other dreams may 'deceive' the dreamer into taking for reality the most extravagant, outlandish or impossible situations. The dreamer's largely uncritical stance vis-à-vis dream bizarreness has in turn given rise to the view that the dream state may equal a form of temporary mental derangement. This view is elaborated in Charles Dickens' humorous short piece 'Night-Walks' in which the novelist claims that dreams are 'the insanity of each day's sanity':

> Are not the sane and the insane equal at night as the sane lie a dreaming? Are not all of us outside this Hospital [Bethlehem Asylum], who dream, more or less in the condition of those inside it, every night of our lives? [...] Do we not nightly jumble events and personages and times and places, as these do daily? [...] Said an afflicted man to me, when I was last in a hospital like this, 'Sir, I can frequently fly.' I was half ashamed to reflect that so could I—by night. Said a woman to me on the same occasion, 'Queen Victoria frequently comes to dine with me, and her Majesty and I dine off peaches and macaroni in our night-gowns [...].' Could I refrain from reddening with consciousness when I remembered the amazing royal parties I myself had given (at night), the unaccountable viands I had put on table, and my extraordinary manner of conducting myself on those distinguished occasions? I wonder that the great master who knew everything, when he called Sleep the death of each day's life, did not call Dreams the insanity of each day's sanity.[4]

---

[2] Descartes, *Meditations*, 14.

[3] Eventually, Descartes came to the conclusion that 'waking life was more consistent than dreams' (Dreisbach [2000], 33). This insight is mirrored by Hobbes, who, though likewise emphasizing the wake-like sensory quality of dreams, all the same held that dreams 'are not only less constant, but also less coherent and more absurd than waking life' (Dreisbach [2000], 34). As he argued: 'For my part, when I consider that in dreams I do not often nor constantly think of the same persons, places, objects, and actions that I do waking, nor remember so long a train of coherent thoughts dreaming as at other times; and because waking I often observe the absurdity of dreams, but never dream of the absurdities of my waking thoughts, I am well satisfied that, being awake, I know I dream not; though when I dream, I think myself awake' (Hobbes, *Leviathan*, 11).

[4] Dickens, 'Night-Walks', 131–132.

Dickens here eloquently foreshadows the stance taken by a twenty-first-century neuroscientist like Hobson, who argues that dreams are more akin to delusional than to imaginative states. Basing his view on neuroimaging findings on the activation of visual cortical areas responsible for heightened and enriched visual-sensory perception,[5] Hobson claims that dream images provide us with 'a convincing simulacrum of reality'.[6] He goes on to argue that these 'visual, auditory, tactile, and postural sensory illusions of dreams are as formally impressive as any schizophrenic patient's hallucinations'. This, according to his argument, is why 'dreaming could [...] be the mental product of the same *kind* of physiological process that is deranged in mental illness'.[7] Elaborating on what they consider our inevitable delusion during the dream state, Hobson and Wohl write accordingly:

> Telling a psychotic patient that the accusing voice that is heard or the fantastic insect that is seen crawling up the wall of his room are not real at all, but merely symptoms of his illness, is every bit as much a fool's errand as trying to convince ourselves during our dreams that we are not really awake but only experiencing the symptoms of sleep. Delusion goes hand in hand with hallucination precisely because there is no more convincing subjective experience than vivid perception. In our dreams we believe, indeed, we cannot but believe what we see and hear.[8]

The consequences of such a view are far-reaching in that dreams, the '*symptoms* of sleep' (my italics), are viewed as a form of (temporary) mental delusion. 'What is the difference between my dream experience and the waking experience of someone who is psychotic, demented, or just plain crazy?' Hobson asks in *Dreaming as Delirium* (1999), only to provide the answer himself:

> In terms of the nature of the experience, there is none. In my New Orleans dream I hallucinated: I saw and heard things that weren't in my bedroom.

---

[5] See Hobson (1988), 16.
[6] Hobson (2002), 53.
[7] Hobson (1988), 9.
[8] Hobson and Wohl (2005), 20.

I was deluded: I believed that the dream actions were real despite gross internal inconsistencies. I was disoriented: I believed that I was in an old hotel in New Orleans when I was actually in a house in Ogunquit.[9]

The question ostensibly at stake here is whether dreams are nocturnal sensory hallucinations deluding us into false beliefs or whether they are manifestations of the same imaginative and creative faculties that make us invent, and immerse ourselves in, daytime fictions. As Richard Walsh notes:

> [T]he narrativity of dreams depends on the assumed sources of dream material. Is the selection of dream material itself a cognitive process, drawing purposively upon episodic and semantic memory? Or is the input to dream cognition an effect of other determinants (instinctual drives, sensory stimuli, recency effects, random brain activity), in which case the cognitive phase of the dream-work is the effort to make sense of this material, which is functionally equivalent to sensory data? The ambiguity is between fiction and illusion, or narrative and experience.[10]

Colin McGinn and Jonathan Ichikawa, who are among the most vigorous proponents of what might be called the 'imagination view', have tried to settle this question in favour of the narrativity of dreams. Both have made strong claims supporting the view that dreams consist of mental images (derived from episodic and semantic memory and/or imagination) rather than percepts (derived from sensory data) and that accordingly they are imaginative experiences rather than sensory hallucinations deluding us into false beliefs. In this, they have a famous predecessor in

---

[9] Hobson (1999), 5. It should be noted that Hobson's equation of dreaming with waking hallucinations is highly problematic. In the introduction to *Hallucinations* (2012), Oliver Sacks explains that, 'in general, hallucinations are quite unlike dreams' (xiii). With specific reference to Charles Bonnet Syndrome hallucinations, he notes: 'Dreams are neurological as well as psychological phenomena, but very unlike CBS hallucinations. Dreamers are wholly enveloped in their dreams, and usually active participants in them, whereas people with CBS retain their normal, critical waking consciousness. CBS hallucinations [...] are remote, like images on a cinema screen in a theater one has chanced to walk into. The theatre is in one's mind, and yet the hallucinations seem to have little to do with one in any deeply personal sense' (27). At a later point in the book, he outlines similar differences with regard to hallucinations occurring in patients of Parkinsonism (80).
[10] Walsh (2007), 129.

Sartre, who, in his *Psychology of Imagination* (1940), devotes one entire chapter to the exploration of the imaginative status of dreaming, arguing that 'in the dream consciousness *cannot perceive*, because it cannot emerge from the imaginative attitude in which it has enclosed itself. [...] It does not perceive, nor does it seek to perceive, nor can it even conceive what a perception is'.[11] Sartre's view ties in with McGinn's claim: 'If we speak of the dream as constructing an imaginary world, then we must regard it as consisting of images, since percepts don't create imaginary worlds (as opposed to illusory ones).'[12] This approach, then, challenges Hobson's view according to which dreaming involves both percepts (the same kind of sensory experience we have during waking) and a delusional belief in these percepts' presence.

In what follows I will argue against such a rigid binary conception of imagination as opposed to perception. In this approach, I concur with Jennifer M. Windt, who rightly argues that 'dreaming blurs any sharp boundaries one may want to introduce between imagining and perceiving'.[13] Accordingly, while I would certainly not subscribe to the view that all dreams are hallucinatory delusions, there is at the same time no point in denying that the dreamer typically experiences his dream environment as though it was perceived and real rather than imagined and fictitious. In fact, as Cavallero and Foulkes point out, dreaming gives us 'whole worlds which, as they are typically experienced, are as vivid as waking perception' and yet these worlds 'are generated entirely from within the mind'.[14] While dreaming clearly consists of mental images, it 'probably constitutes for most of us [...] the most vivid form of mental imagery that we experience'.[15] This view is corroborated by Nancy Kerr:

> In perception we record the characteristics of the environment, and in imagery we recreate them. The imagery we experience while dreaming is

---

[11] Sartre (1972 [1940]), 192–193.
[12] McGinn (2004), 179.
[13] Windt (2015), 252. Calling the 'dichotomous conception of imagining and perceiving [...] a philosopher's construction', Windt comes to the convincing conclusion that '[i]t is empirically implausible, creates more problems than it solves, and is best rejected' (251).
[14] Cavallero and Foulkes (1993b), 13.
[15] Cavallero and Foulkes (1993b), 13.

perhaps even more similar to perceiving, in that the visual, auditory, and other sensory qualities of the dream are hallucinatory in quality and are taken by the dreamer to represent reality.[16]

And yet, as Kerr further points out, 'visual imagery in dreaming is not a mere reflection of current visual perceptual capabilities, but instead represents an at least partially autonomous cognitive processing system capable of recreating at night a visual aspect of the world *that cannot be directly perceived in wakefulness*'.[17]

In this view, dreams, rather than being sensory hallucinations deluding us into false beliefs, can be considered as particularly vivid manifestations of the same imaginative faculties that allow us to create, and immerse ourselves in, waking fictions. Again, however, there is no reason to view perception and imagination as diametrically opposed. On the contrary, according to the 'continuum theory', as elucidated by Nigel J.T. Thomas, images and percepts can be viewed as 'varieties of the same species, differing in degree rather than in kind, and lying at opposite ends of a continuous spectrum with many varieties of imaginatively informed perception, such as *seeing as*, hallucination, and perceptual errors of various sorts, filling in the continuum between them'.[18] With the following example about the 'anthropomorphic transformation' of trees, Hobson and Wohl in fact propose quite a similar view:

> In waking a tree is just a tree. We have to squint and let our minds fall into the twilight zone to see it as a person. Yet all trees do have trunks (torsos) and roots (limbs) which can become the building blocks of anthropomorphic transformation. In dream generation and in phantasmagoric art, the associative rules that govern such transformations are loosened with the result that the continuity between persons, times, places, and actions is ruptured and the contextual wholeness of dream scenes is fragmented.[19]

This example aptly illustrates the permeable boundaries between perception, hallucination and imagination. For *even in waking*, we may imagine

---

[16] Kerr (1993), 18.
[17] Kerr (1993), 31, my italics.
[18] N. Thomas (2014), 135.
[19] Hobson and Wohl (2005), 22.

3 Dreaming and Waking Imagination   65

that a tree turns into a person (or a person into a tree); we may temporarily be deluded into believing that the tree in the distance *is* a person; we may metaphorically describe the tree as a person in a poem or depict it as such in a painting; and finally we may witness the tree's literal metamorphosis from tree to person (or person to tree) in a bizarre nocturnal dream, which might, in turn, inspire the myth about a girl (Ovid's Daphne) turning into a tree or a horror story in which trees turn into humanoid monsters. To illustrate the range of possibilities, let us consider a few literary examples.[20] In the following account, Walt Whitman describes what he calls a 'dream-trance': 'I had a sort of dream-trance the other day, in which I saw my favourite trees step out and promenade up, down and around, very curiously—with a whisper from one, leaning down as he pass'd me, *We do all this on the present occasion, exceptionally, just for you.*'[21] This account of a waking dream might easily have inspired a fantasy story or a poem, and, indeed, literature and myth are replete with illustrations of the permeable boundaries between perception and imagination. One fictional story involving an episode with trees is Edgar Allan Poe's 'The Narrative of Arthur Gordon Pym' (1838). Halfway through the text the narrator describes an anxiety dream in which 'the strange trees seemed endowed with a human vitality, and waving to and fro their skeleton arms, were crying to the silent waters for mercy, in the shrill and piercing accents of the most acute agony and despair'.[22] While this description refers to the narrator's nightly dream, in Daphne du Maurier's short story 'The Pool' (1959), a walk through the gloomy woods at nighttime unleashes the young protagonist's imagination so that she feels genuinely threatened by the anthropomorphized trees surrounding her: '[T]he tall trees were watching. Any sign of turning back, of panic, and they would crowd upon her in a choking mass, smothering protest. Branches would become arms, gnarled and knotty, ready to strangle, and the leaves of the higher trees fold in and close like the sudden furling of giant umbrellas.'[23] All

---

[20] Interestingly, one of the earliest dream poems in Old English, 'The Dream of the Rood', makes use of the anthropomorphic associations suggested by Hobson, in that it narrates the poet's dream encounter with a tree that tells him about Christ's crucifixion.
[21] Whitman, 'Thoughts under an Oak—A Dream', 116.
[22] Poe, 'The Narrative of Arthur Gordon Pym', 446.
[23] Du Maurier, 'The Pool', 143.

these examples testify to the gradual rather than sharp contrast between perception and imagination whose range is creatively explored in these and other works of literature and visual art.

While these examples may provide only anecdotal evidence, the contrast between perception and imagination is further eroded by empirical findings suggesting similarities in the biochemical and mechanical processes that enable us to both perceive objects and to form mental images in these objects' absence.[24] This evidence is in line with Simon Baron-Cohen's broad definition of imagery as 'a picture in your head' which is 'usually the product of one of the five senses (though it can also be generated without any sensory input at all, from the mere act of thinking or dreaming)'.[25] As he elaborates, 'the products of the imagination are derived from imagery, following some transformation of the basic imagery'.[26] Baron-Cohen thus defines basic imagery as encompassing mental images either generated by sensory input or in the absence of sensory input and allowing for transformations that in turn facilitate imaginative creation. This definition paves the way for Harry T. Hunt's view that 'we must distinguish between imagery as detached perception—essentially part of perceptual functioning—and imagery as rearrangement, which merges with symbolic cognition'.[27] While some dream imagery may be based on 'detached *perceptual* schemata', our more interesting dreams are facilitated by our capacity for '"schematic *rearrangements*", [...] necessary for the higher mental processes involved in self-reference, creative imagination, and language'.[28] Descartes' dream of a quiet evening by the fireplace would thus fall into the first category, while a dream in which the philosopher suddenly found himself in a crowded dining room full of strangers demanding he give a formal speech in his nightdress would fall into the second. This insight also potentially settles the controversial issue of whether animals and infants experience dreams (which would only be possible if dreams were based on percept-like reproduction or anticipa-

---

[24] See Antrobus et al. (1964) and Andrade et al. (1997).
[25] Baron-Cohen (2007), n. pag.
[26] Baron-Cohen (2007), n. pag.
[27] Hunt (1989), 41.
[28] Hunt (1989), 41, my italics.

tion of reality without requiring the capacity for imaginative reorganization) or whether dreaming is a higher cognitive ability depending on the cognitive symbolic capacity that only develops in humans from the age of five years onwards.[29] As Hartmann notes with reference to research findings by Foulkes, 'our typical adult dreams develop only gradually and slowly over the course of childhood, and [...] there is a similar development of fantasies, daydreams, and story-telling'.[30] According to Hunt's model, animals', infants' and possibly some adults' dreams may belong to the first category, displaying the capacity to image in the absence of concurrent stimulation. In these dreams, situations from everyday life are simply replayed. However, it is those dreams dependent on the 'self-referential capacity, uniquely developed in man [sic], potentially present in higher primates and dolphins, indexed by novel recombinations of past experience'[31] that are spontaneously recalled, considered worth telling and occasionally remembered for a lifetime (or beyond, if passed on to later generations). According to Hunt, then, this theory leads us back to

> the more organismic-holistic traditions of cognitive psychology and their insistence that symbolic intelligence ultimately rests on and reorganizes the senses. We are back at the point of having to regard flying in dreams as both a sensory expression of vestibular activation and an imaginative metaphor. Dreaming thus becomes *the* focus for any study of the functional continuity and interrelations of percept and image.[32]

This view renders the debate on whether dreams are delusions or imaginations somewhat redundant by suggesting that both faculties—perception and imagination—are involved in the process to varying degrees.

In the remainder of this chapter, then, I will sound out potential similarities between the processes of dreaming and waking forms of imagination with special emphasis on attention dependence, volition and belief. In doing so, I will draw on empirical evidence and take my cue

---

[29] See Hunt (1989), 47.
[30] Hartmann (2011), 76.
[31] Hunt (1989), 48.
[32] Hunt (1989), 41–42.

from Thomas' model of the 'multidimensional spectrum of imagination', according to which 'percepts, dreams, hallucinations, and waking mental images, as well as all the various types of imaginative perception, are all products of the imagination'.[33] By mapping out not only the similarities but inevitably also 'the various dimensions along which imaginative experiences differ from one another',[34] I hope to lay the foundations for a meaningful, nuanced and empirically informed discussion of dreaming and waking forms of imagination in terms of each other.

One often noted similarity between dreaming and waking forms of imagination is that both are largely attention-dependent. While the physical world around us will not evaporate simply because we close our eyes or are preoccupied with dreaming or daydreaming, both the dream and the daydream tend to come to an abrupt end once the physical world intrudes and demands our attention. Colin McGinn certainly has a point when he argues that being engaged in a dream more or less precludes other imaginings. Our mind is completely focused on the dream images, because as soon as (or at least not long after) our attention wavers, the dream images tend to dissolve:

> Just as your mind cannot wander from your daydreams and expect them to proceed by themselves, so it cannot wander from your dream images—and the reason in both cases is the attention-dependence of the imagination. This explains the *enthralling* character of dreams, the single-mindedness of the dream state. [...] It can never be hard to pay attention to one's dreams simply because they have no existence independently of the attention.[35]

---

[33] N. Thomas (2014), 159.
[34] N. Thomas (2014), 159.
[35] McGinn (2004), 79. Interestingly enough, writers have often played with the notion that dreams have precisely that: a reality independent of the dreamer's attention. This notion has accordingly given rise to fantastic stories of parallel worlds with the dreamer leading a hidden double life or being increasingly claimed by or lured into the alternative dream existence. Occasionally, this idea also comes up in dream reports. Thus, writer Stephen Laws describes a recurrent joyful dream in which he visits a place full of friendly strangers he never met in waking life but who seem to know him and welcome him back to their world. As he notes, '[t]here are times when it seems that the real world might be the dream place and the place I sometimes go to when I sleep is the reality' (Royle [1996], 138).

In this view, dreaming is ultimately closer to daydreaming and other states of waking imagination than it is to ordinary perception or hallucinatory states which do not necessarily block out additional sensory perceptions and thought processes. Thomas, however, draws our attention to the phenomenon of 'inattentional blindness', arguing that we need to actively attend to our visual surroundings in order to actually perceive them.[36] Even more crucially, McGinn's claim is qualified by a number of dream phenomena that tie in with the continuum theory rather than the strictly binary view of imagination versus perception. For instance, while in most sleep dreams the actual surroundings of the sleeper are blanked out and dreamers find themselves in an imaginary spatiotemporal realm largely closed off from the 'real' world, during hallucinatory sleep paralysis, typically experienced upon awakening from a nightmare, 'elements of rapid eye movement (REM) sleep [...] intrude into wakefulness producing a particular and paradoxical reality. During these episodes, experients are usually aware of the surroundings, often can hear people or televisions on in the next room, yet cannot move and may have extremely intense hallucinations'.[37] Such an experience is vividly recalled by the American novelist Siri Hustvedt:

> Some years ago in a rented house in Vermont, I couldn't sleep and lay awake listening to the sounds of mice in the walls, bears that sounded like owls calling to each other in the woods and the wind in the trees. I then dreamed I was lying awake on the very bed where in fact I was sleeping, but someone had broken into the house. Because the room where I actually was and the room I dreamed were identical, the threshold between waking and sleeping had blurred and, when I woke up, I thought I heard the burglar moving around downstairs. It was a frightening experience, a temporary loss of the boundaries between waking experience and the illusions of dreams.[38]

Secondly, at times sensory perceptions can intrude and be incorporated into our dreams, at least temporarily. The ringing of a phone or an alarm

---

[36] See N. Thomas (2014), 152.
[37] Solomonova et al. (2011), 174.
[38] Hustvedt, 'What Is Sleep?', n. pag.

clock may in such instances briefly enter our dreaming consciousness as, say, a school bell or a siren, depending on the dream context. In such cases, '[t]he external stimulus gets incorporated in to the dream by way of an interpretation of it that fits the content of the dream' and is thus a 'clear case of imaginative hearing: the imagination has imposed an "aspect" on the stimulus that is partly constrained by its acoustic character and partly pure fancy'.[39] As the early twentieth-century dream researcher Havelock Ellis puts it: 'Whatever the stimuli from the physical world that may knock at the door of dreaming consciousness, that consciousness is apart from them, and stimuli can only reach it by undergoing transformation'.[40] An amusing description of the phenomenon of imaginative hearing is provided by Charles Dickens in 'Early Coaches', included in *Sketches by Boz* (1836). In this sketch, Dickens describes the restless night of a business man who is awaiting and eventually experiencing his early morning call after having fallen asleep in the small hours:

> [...] At last you fall into a state of complete oblivion, from which you are aroused, as if into a new state of existence, by a singular illusion. You are apprenticed to a trunk-maker; how, or why, or when, or wherefore, you don't take the trouble to inquire; but there you are, pasting the lining in the lid of a portmanteau. Confound that other apprentice in the back shop, how he is hammering!—rap, rap, rap—what an industrious fellow he must be! You have heard him at work for half an hour past, and he has been hammering incessantly the whole time. Rap, rap, rap, again—he's talking now—what's that he said? Five o'clock! You make a violent exertion, and start up in bed.[41]

These examples suggest that imagination and perception differ in degree rather than in kind and are linked by a broad spectrum of forms of 'imaginative perception'. Besides incorporating sense perceptions into dream contexts, the phenomenon of 'imaginative perception' includes, but is not limited to, seeing human faces in the clouds or the foliage of a tree, mistaking the nocturnal outlines of the furniture in our darkened

---

[39] McGinn (2004), 86.
[40] Ellis, *The World of Dreams*, 18–19.
[41] Dickens, 'Early Coaches', 156–157.

bedroom for a scary monster, 'recognizing' a friend in what turns out to be a complete stranger or discovering animal shapes in random ink blots. These examples vary according to the degree to which the respective percepts constrain our imagination. At one end of the continuum we have 'reliable, veridical perception (seeing things as just what they are) [occurring] when good seeing conditions and an intent not to be deceived converge to ensure that our experience is maximally constrained by what is present'.[42] At the other end, 'when we choose to set aside the constraints of the current deliverances of our senses almost entirely, our imagination is free to construct what imagery it will'.[43] Significantly, as Thomas points out, this form of free imagination, like perception, can still be conceived as 'a form of seeing as, but it is unconstrained seeing as: it is seeing nothing (which, being nothing, imposes no constraints) as whatever we may want it to appear to be'.[44] Or, as Rodolfo R. Llinás and Denis Paré provocatively put it, wakefulness may be '*nothing other than a dreamlike state modulated by the constraints produced by specific sensory inputs*'.[45]

One characteristic often considered typical of dreams is that they are more difficult to control and manipulate at will than our waking imagination. While we are to some extent in control of our waking imagination, most of us are neither able to direct or deliberately terminate our nocturnal dreams. In this respect, dreams may appear closer to percepts than to images. We can banish images, or at least make an effort to do so, but we cannot banish visual impressions, unless we close our eyes or change our spatial position.[46] Accordingly, it could be argued that, since ordinarily we cannot control our dreams or wake up at our own bidding if a dream fails or ceases to suit us, dreams do not consist of images in the conventional sense. In contrast to this, Ichikawa claims that dream

---

[42] N. Thomas (2014), 158.
[43] N. Thomas (2014), 158.
[44] N. Thomas (2014), 158.
[45] Llinás and Paré (1991), 525.
[46] See Ichikawa (2009), 5. However, as Nigel Thomas (2014) notes with respect to the implicit distinction between direct and indirect control drawn here, 'it is not at all clear that any sharp and principled distinction can be drawn between mental acts and bodily acts' (140). Thus, willing an image to go away through mental control or blocking out a percept by closing one's eyes or turning one's head, again, may imply a difference in degree rather than in kind.

experiences are, at least to some extent, subject to our will. As he argues, 'dreams appear to show evidence of design' to such an extent that it 'is natural and reasonable to speak of ourselves as unconsciously authoring our dreams'.[47] In lucid dreams, this unconscious authorship even becomes conscious. As Stephen LaBerge and Howard Rheingold put it: 'Empowered by the knowledge that the world they are experiencing is a creation of their own imagination, lucid dreamers can consciously influence the outcome of their dreams. They can create and transform objects, people, situations, worlds, even themselves'.[48] It should also be added that writers often report that their fictions seemingly write themselves, their characters taking on a life of their own and not always behaving according to their creator's plans. Similarly, what about the tune haunting us for hours no matter how hard we try to get it out of our heads? The fact that our efforts to control our wakening imaginings are by no means always successful is perfectly illustrated in Charles Dickens' short piece 'Lying Awake' (1860). Here, he vividly describes his rambling thoughts and memories, including distractions from unwelcome ideas when, for instance, his pleasant reminiscence of a day in the Alps is disrupted by the intrusion of a frightening figure from his childhood days: 'Now see here what comes along; and why does that thing stalk into my mind on the top of a Swiss mountain!'[49] This anecdote ties in with Hartmann's findings that 'thin boundary' people prone to frequent nightmares tend to experience frightening daydreams—or 'daymares'—as well. According to Hartmann: 'These daymares obviously have the scary and out-of-control characteristics of the dreams we know as nightmares'.[50] All this suggests that dreaming and waking imagination are anything but diametrically opposed when it comes to the criterion of agency or control.

    Another argument that has been used against the view that dreams are similar to waking imaginative experiences is that dreamers tend to uncritically believe in the dreamworld into which they are thrown. Arguably, this is not usually the case when we daydream, read a novel or watch a

---

[47] Ichikawa (2009), 19.
[48] LaBerge and Rheingold (1997), 3. For a contrasting view, see Windt (2015), 262–263.
[49] Dickens, 'Lying Awake', 432.
[50] Hartmann (2011), 36.

movie. In contrast, Ichikawa takes the stand against the view that dreams involve false beliefs when he claims that these 'belief-like states we take toward the content of our dreams while dreaming are not beliefs, but rather imaginings'.[51] Thus, it may be true that while being enthralled by a dream, we tend to uncritically accept all kinds of unrealities, inconsistencies and irrationalities. However, in most cases, we are immediately able to detect these upon awakening. What is more, dream 'beliefs' (or 'imaginings') ordinarily do not tend to impact our real beliefs. In my dream, I may temporarily 'believe' that I am an actor living in Hollywood, but as soon as I wake up from my dream, this imagination will be discarded, and in most cases simply forgotten, without ever affecting my firmly held long-term belief that I am a lecturer in Europe and have never been to California (except in my dreams). However, again there are exceptions to the rule well suited to the blurring of such seemingly clear-cut boundaries. In fact, not only can some dreams have a powerful emotional effect on dreamers that lasts long after awakening, but 'reality dreams, identifiable by their expressions of intense somatic imagery'[52] can lead to temporary, and on occasion permanent, confusion of dream and reality. Tore Nielsen refers to the 'oneirogenic effects' such dreams can have on 'our waking animistic beliefs',[53] convincingly arguing that such dreams may 'have been implicated in the development of beliefs in malevolent other-than-human beings'[54] as well as in 'benevolent spiritual forces'.[55] These and other cases of 'retrospective dream deception'[56] clearly testify to the strong 'reality sense'[57] of some dreams.

These special cases aside, however, the argument that we are deluded because while dreaming we fail to grasp the inconsistencies of a dream might be based on the false premise that the same day time rules of consistency and reason inevitably also apply to the dream state. Generally, I would argue that 'reality testing', that is viewing the dream experience

---

[51] Ichikawa (2009), 10.
[52] Nielsen (1991), 23.
[53] Nielsen (1991), 233.
[54] Nielsen (1991), 250.
[55] Nielsen (1991), 234.
[56] Windt (2015), 487.
[57] Nielsen (1991), 233.

with reference to the physical everyday world, may not necessarily be the most fruitful approach. Andreas Mavromatis rightly argues that waking imaginative experiences, such as watching movies, may provide better points of reference:

> [W]hen we watch a movie we do not as a rule dissect it in terms of camera angle, lighting, direction, acting, etc., or in terms of realistic temporal continuity. On the contrary, having accepted certain conventions we think it quite natural that one hundred years may be condensed in the space of a few minutes, and not infrequently we become moved to anger, tears, exhilaration, and so on by the film's contents, knowing full well that the whole thing is fictitious—not to mention our intellectual elasticity in implicitly accepting the conventions of a cartoon movie.[58]

Similarly, when immersed in a dream, we tend to go with the flow of the dream plot unfolding around us, unquestioningly accepting the dream's *conventions* while the dream experience lasts, without necessarily being deceived as to its reality status. This seems to be the case in the following excerpt from a dream experienced by writer Dave Rimmer:

> Penguin and whisky tumbler merge into one and metamorphose into a queer-looking bird. It reminds me of a 'badly drawn bird' from an old John Glashan cartoon. It is reddish brown and has a huge beak with rows of sharp, pointy teeth. It never seems to be anything more than two-dimensional, literally an animated cartoon.[59]

That dreamers immersed in a dream scenario are not necessarily deceived as to its reality status becomes even more obvious in lucid dreams, in which dreamers are aware of the fact that they are dreaming. Some lucid dreamers train themselves to look out for bizarre elements in a dream which will alert them to the fact that they are dreaming. In some cases, it is then possible for the dreamer to maintain this precarious state of dream immersion/critical awareness for an extended period of time and to even manipulate the dream setting and plot to a certain extent.

---

[58] Mavromatis (2001), 108.
[59] Royle, *The Tiger Garden*, 199.

In other words, these dreamers maintain their imaginative immersion in the dreamworld without being deceived as to its reality status. As testified by numerous dream reports, these lucid dreamers' emotional and sensory responses to the dream events are in no way diminished by their lucidity, but often even enhanced. This phenomenon has been described by Mary Arnold-Forster, an early twentieth-century lucid dreamer and recorder of dreams, with regard to one of her favourite flying dreams, which she was able to make 'recur more or less at will', while 'greatly [increasing] its pleasurable features'.[60] Similarly, attempts at influencing the dream content can result in a more faded or constructed character of the dream setting that challenges the claim that dreams are necessarily experienced as percept-like or realistic. Thus, in his short text '*Dreamtigers*', Jorge Luis Borges describes his unsuccessful attempts at re-creating the tigers from his illustrated childhood 'encyclopedias and books of natural history' in his grown-up lucid dreams:

> Childhood passed away, and the tigers and my passion for them grew old, but still they are in my dreams. At that submerged or chaotic level they keep prevailing. And so, as I sleep, some dream beguiles me, and suddenly I know I am dreaming. Then I think: this is a dream, a pure diversion of my will; and now that I have unlimited power, I am going to cause a tiger.
>
> Oh, incompetence! Never can my dreams engender the wild beast I long for. The tiger indeed appears, but stuffed or flimsy, or with impure variations of shape, or of an implausible size, or all too fleeting, or with a touch of the dog or the bird.[61]

Unless lucid dreaming is viewed as a state of consciousness completely unrelated to dreaming, a description like this clearly suggests a gradual—rather than a sharp—distinction between the creation of images in waking and dreaming. As Windt convincingly suggests: 'Perhaps one reason why the imagination and the quasi-perceptual view have seemed so attractive to different thinkers is that dream imagery occasionally conforms to

---

[60] Arnold-Forster, *Studies in Dreams*, 35.
[61] Borges, '*Dreamtigers*', 294.

both: some dreams indeed involve vivid, wakelike visual imagery, while others may take on a faded, washed-out quality'.[62] It is important to note that the lucid dreamer producing 'flimsy' or non-wakelike images or performing acts like flying unaided is still unquestioningly immersed in his or her dream. This suggests that neither dreaming nor waking fictions necessarily require belief to be immersive and powerful.[63]

Given the above considerations, a number of useful insights may be gleaned from exploring dreaming in relation to waking imagination. This view is shared by Windt, who, in view of recent empirical findings, concludes that 'the comparison between dreaming and waking imagination is a fruitful project'.[64] Here Windt refers specifically to the groundbreaking discovery of the default mode network and research findings concerning the network's role in waking mind-wandering. A recent empirical study by Fox et al. (2013) has found strong evidence that daydreaming and dreaming not only involve the same brain mechanisms but also share similar content and thought processes. Systematically examining first-person reports about waking mind-wandering and dreaming, the researchers found that 'in both states, content is largely audio-visual and emotional, follows loose narratives tinged with fantasy, is strongly related to current concerns, draws on long-term memory, and simulates social interactions. Both states are also characterized by a relative lack of meta-awareness'.[65] They then compared data from neuroimaging studies of the default mode network (with high chances of mind-wandering) and REM sleep (with high chances of dreaming) and found significant similarities in the activation patterns of the cortical regions (especially in the medial prefrontal cortex and medial temporal lobes). At the same time, they also noticed a number of interesting differences, for instance that during REM sleep more regions beyond the default mode network are activated, which might account for the more intensely visual and bizarre character of most REM dreams as compared to daydreams. As they further point out, in contrast to waking mind-wandering, in dreaming 'external

---

[62] Windt (2015), 274.

[63] For an in-depth discussion of the problem of belief in dreams and fictions, see Sect. 'The Dreamer as Reader, the Reader as Dreamer'.

[64] Windt (2015), 285.

[65] Fox et al. (2013), 11.

sensory inputs are almost entirely blocked, and the audio-visual content can take on the aspect of an immersive, three-dimensional simulated reality'.[66] They therefore conclude that dreaming might be viewed 'as an intensified version of waking spontaneous thought—or conversely, that MW [mind-wandering] during wakefulness could be seen as an attenuated, waking form of dreaming'.[67]

One important difference between dreaming and waking mind-wandering as highlighted by Fox and his colleagues is that 'dreams appear to be temporally extended, fairly cohesive narratives spanning several minutes or longer, whereas waking MW thoughts typically only last for several seconds'.[68] It is precisely in view of this difference between waking mind-wandering and dreaming that I suggest dreaming might be even more fruitfully compared to waking forms of narrative immersion such as writing and reading stories. And in fact, a recent study using functional magnetic resonance imaging (fMRI) confirmed that the default mode network not only 'showed significant increases in activity during story-reading compared with resting baseline' but also that 'engagement of the network grew from the beginning of the story to the end of the story'.[69] Together with a number of other findings about the default mode network's relevance in regard to social cognition,[70] internally directed time travel[71] and mental time travel,[72] these are cogent indications that the network might be even more strongly implicated in the processing—and possibly constructing—of narratives rather than in aimless mind-wandering. This, in turn, suggests that dreaming and engaging with waking fictions might be strongly related activities; in other words, dreaming means 'experiencing a narrative process: a reciprocal process of creation and reception'.[73] In this process, the dreamer is not only simultaneously creator and recipient of the dream, but in most cases also plays an active, even central part within

---

[66] Fox et al. (2013), 11.
[67] Fox et al. (2013), 11.
[68] Fox et al. (2013), 11.
[69] Kaplan et al. (2016), 5.
[70] See Mar et al. (2012).
[71] See Immordino-Yang et al. (2012).
[72] See Ostby et al. (2012).
[73] Walsh (2010), 142.

the dream narrative. The dream state, then, may well provide us not only with the 'purest form of imagination',[74] but also with the strongest form of reader identification as well as with the strongest form of narrative immersion. Accordingly, the next two sections will explore similarities and differences between dreaming and writerly immersion and between dreaming and readerly immersion, respectively.

The Dreamer as Author, the Author as Dreamer

In his autobiographical essay 'A Chapter on Dreams' (1888), Robert Louis Stevenson traces his trajectory from oversensitive child prone to and frightened by frequent vivid nightmares to professional writer purposely exploiting his nocturnal dreamworld for fictional plots, episodes and images that would sell. His anecdote of how a dream sparked two central scenes of his most famous tale, *The Strange Case of Dr. Jekyll and Mr. Hyde* (1886), is by now classic: 'For two days I went about racking my brains for a plot of any sort; and on the second night I dreamed the scene at the window, and a scene afterwards split in two, in which Hyde, pursued for some crime, took the powder and underwent the change in the presence of his pursuers.'[75] Of even greater interest in the context of this chapter is his account of a dream that provided him with a full-fledged plot so intricately designed and crafted that he, the dreamer, was completely taken aback by its carefully prepared final revelation: '[N]ot only was the secret kept [from the dreamer], the story was told with really guileful craftsmanship. The conduct of both actors is [...] psychologically correct, and the emotion aptly graduated up to the surprising climax.'[76] Such an apparently artfully crafted dream is bound to raise questions about dream authorship. Who is the author of the dream? If the dreamer himself has authored the dream, how can we account for his surprise at its denouement? Then again, if the dreamer is *not* the author of the dream,

---

[74] Nir and Tononi (2010), 95.
[75] Stevenson, 'A Chapter on Dreams', 104.
[76] Stevenson, 'A Chapter on Dreams', 102.

who else could it be? Stevenson proposed his own tongue-in-cheek theory, crediting the 'Brownies' or 'little people' in his brain, '[w]ho do one-half my work for me while I am fast asleep, and in all human likelihood, do the rest for me as well, when I am wide awake and fondly suppose I do it for myself'.[77] Casting his dream-self as audience to the nocturnal dream-workers, he describes himself as sitting 'idly taking his pleasure in the boxes, [as he is given] better tales than he could fashion for himself'.[78]

Countless writers throughout the ages have highlighted the aesthetic, creative and narrative qualities of their dreams, which occasionally seem to surpass the dreamer's own waking imagination and aesthetic abilities. Such accounts are too numerous to ignore or relegate to the realm of myth. Samuel Taylor Coleridge, who famously remarked that in certain sorts of dreams 'the dullest Wight becomes a Shakespeare',[79] commented on one of his own particularly 'fantastic' dreams, claiming that he 'would have required tenfold the imagination of a Dante to have constructed it in the waking state'.[80] Thomas Browne writes in his *Religio Medici* (1643): 'I am in no way facetious, nor deposed for the mirth and galliardize of company, yet in one dreame I can compose a whole Comedy, behold the action, apprehend the jests, and laugh myself awake at the conceits thereof.'[81] Another example is provided by Dostoyevsky, who notes in *Crime and Punishment* (1866) that in some dreams '[m]ost monstrous pictures are put together, but all the circumstances are so subtly interwoven, the details so artistically harmonious in every minute respect, as to defy human imitation, be the artist a Pooshkin or a Tourgeneff'.[82] Stevenson, referring to himself in the third person, reported how he not only enjoyed the Brownies' theatrical performances but also used to read in his dreams: 'tales, for the most part, and for the most part after the manner of G. P. R. James,

---

[77] Stevenson, 'A Chapter on Dreams', 103.
[78] Stevenson, 'A Chapter on Dreams', 100. Stevenson's essay is embedded in a lively nineteenth-century popular dream discourse, and his diligent Brownies are an image for what was known as 'unconscious cerebration', a term coined by the physician William Carpenter and popularized by Frances Power Cobbe in two influential essays. See Cobbe (1870) and Cobbe (1871).
[79] Coleridge, *Friend* I, 145.
[80] Coleridge quoted in Ford (1998), 8.
[81] Browne, *Religio Medici*, 98.
[82] Dostoyevsky, *Crime and Punishment*, 44.

but so incredibly more vivid and moving than any printed book, that he has ever since been malcontent with literature'.[83] Katherine Mansfield claimed she had dreamed an entire short story,[84] while W.B. Yeats commented on his poem 'The Cap and Bells' (1899) as follows:

> 'I dreamed this story exactly as I have written it, and dreamed another long dream after it, trying to make out its meaning, and whether I was to write it in prose or verse. The first dream was more a vision than a dream, for it was beautiful and coherent, and gave me the sense of illumination and exaltation that one gets from visions, while the second dream was confused and meaningless. The poem has always meant a great deal to me, though, as is the way with symbolic poems, it has not always meant quite the same thing.'[85]

And finally, H.P. Lovecraft, who enjoyed (and suffered) a vivid dream life that often fuelled his stories, at one point half-jokingly asked: 'I wonder, though, if I have a right to claim authorship of things I dream? I hate to take credit, when I did not really think out the picture with my own conscious wits. Yet if I do not take credit, who'n Heaven *will* I give credit tuh?'[86]

This 'paradox of authorship', that is how a dreamer can simultaneously 'author' a dream and experience it as though it was externally created, still preoccupies dream researchers even today, a century after Stevenson's account of his subconscious creative abilities, imaginatively anthropomorphized as helpful little fairies. As David Foulkes puts it: 'How can it be that, with no deliberation at all, we effortlessly create with a sleeping mind delicate scenarios of a sort which forever elude the best intentions, the most elaborate preparations, and the most diligent efforts of our waking mind?'[87] There have been quite a few attempts at solving this puzzle,

---

[83] Stevenson, 'A Chapter on Dreams', 97.
[84] See Mansfield, *Letters*, 161. Mary Arnold-Forster provides a similar account related to her by an unnamed writer friend who dreamed 'an original and very dramatic story' which, when writing it down, 'seemed to be like a tale that was told to him rather than a thing of his own creation' (*Studies in Dreams*, 60).
[85] Yeats quoted in Hayter (1969), 74.
[86] Lovecraft, *Dream Book*, 11.
[87] Foulkes (1978), 4.

with more or less satisfactory results. Here, I will briefly outline and discuss two recent attempts at solving the mystery of dream authorship. The first is Colin McGinn's in many ways problematic 'psychic split' and 'time lag' theory. The second is Bert O. States' arguably more promising approach which focuses on dreaming as creative process. Critically reviewing both approaches in light of phenomenological evidence and relevant neurocognitive findings will also provide some first insight into why dreaming can more usefully be compared to imaginative states of writerly and readerly immersion than to the more commonly referred to activity of watching movies.

In Colin McGinn's approach, Stevenson's Brownies turn into what McGinn calls an 'internal creative dream designer'.[88] In a fashion quite similar to Stevenson, McGinn proposes distinguishing between the audience and the unconscious author of the dream, thus presupposing what he calls 'a "psychic split" in the dreaming mind'.[89] As he rightly notes: 'Dreams often have plot-like structures, with surprises and revelations; they seem shaped to suit the emotions and concerns of the dreamer; they draw upon recent experiences, as well as old memories. They seem, in short, very like a fictional genre—a certain type of story-telling'.[90] According to McGinn, then, it is the dream's storytelling quality that justifies the assumption of the dreamer's agency despite the illusion of passive reception. As he points out:

> [D]reams can be chaotic and baffling, but they generally have some sort of temporal progression and sense of connectedness; they are not just a series of random images. And since we know that human brains house agent-like entities in the production of day-time images, there is no reason of principle not to suppose that the images of dreams have a similar type of causation. The difference is that in the dream the actions of the agent are hidden; but the production process is essentially the same.[91]

---

[88] McGinn (2004), 84. At various points in his work, McGinn (2005) discusses the dreaming process in clearly anthropomorphic terms, making it clear, however, that he considers this analogy as a useful tool to illustrate the complex processes involved in the act of dreaming (see 191).
[89] McGinn (2004), 89.
[90] McGinn (2004), 90.
[91] McGinn (2004), 90–91.

The question remains, however, why the dreamer's agency and authorship are concealed from the dreamer in the first place. After all, when daydreaming, are we not ultimately aware of being our daydream's own creator? Why should this be different in our nocturnal dreams? A Freudian answer might be that the dreamer's agency is hidden by the censorship mechanism so as to ensure their psychological stability and thus 'guard' their sleep. As McGinn argues, however, one need not resort to Freudian theory in order to account for his 'psychic split' theory. According to his argument, it is necessary for the dreamer to experience such a split simply because otherwise 'dream belief and its associated emotions' could not be guaranteed and, as McGinn claims: 'For some reason, we have a *need to believe* during the dream, and this requires the illusion of passivity'.[92] However, as we will see in the next chapter, the question whether belief is indeed required for imaginative immersion is highly debatable. Also, McGinn's answer still falls short of explaining *how* the 'internal dream designer'—whoever he or she may be—should manage to come up with seemingly spontaneous and yet more or less skilfully constructed dream plots several times a night.

Acknowledging this problem, McGinn proposes a rather speculative and ultimately not very convincing time lag model based on the analogy between film and dream production. More specifically, he suggests that 'the brain contains a library of potential dreams, waiting to be shown on a given night, instead of dreams being projected off the cuff each night'.[93] As he points out: 'There is really no reason to believe that the entire creative process behind the dream took place on the night of the dream, the moment before the dream entered my dreaming consciousness'.[94] Rather, in McGinn's view:

> Dreams are a reworking of experience, so it makes sense to suppose that they are reworking it all the time. When a dream refers to the past, then, it is likely that at least some of the initial dream work was done at or

---

[92] McGinn (2004), 91.
[93] McGinn (2005), 186.
[94] McGinn (2005), 186–187.

around the time referred to. [...] As with film production, there is a considerable time lag between the early stages of production and the final viewing.⁹⁵

McGinn's time lag model, however, is in no way backed up by phenomenological or scientific evidence. On the contrary, the fact that dreams often draw on past experience is arguably more convincingly accounted for by the brain's associative matching of new and old experience according to emotional and psychological categories. What is more, comparing the dreamer's experience to a 'final viewing' of a film whose considerable production work has happened behind the scenes fails to do justice to the complexity of the dream state. As Barbara Meier astutely notes:

> Dreamers are not merely uninvolved spectators of some external dream action, they are related to what is going on before and around them in different ways. On the one hand, they are participants in the dream play, incorporating various roles, leading parts, supporting roles, serving as extras. On the other hand, their reactions to the dream events are manifested in accompanying reflection, deliberation, consideration, and inferential intentions. Thus, analogies of dreams as movies or dramatic plays are adequate metaphors for the dream, if they are not limited to the film or the play *per se*, but comprise the performance of these products in front of an audience, or rehearsing in front of the director.⁹⁶

---

⁹⁵ McGinn (2005), 187. McGinn's model draws on the cassette theory of dreaming, first introduced in Daniel Dennett's article 'Are Dreams Experiences?' (1976). In this article, Dennett aims to come up with a plausible rival theory to challenge what he calls the 'received view' which takes for granted the unproven claim that dreams are subjective experiences. Using anecdotal evidence about dreams whose narrative rather inexplicably leads up to an ending determined by waking sensory stimulus, he suggests that 'our "precognitive" dreams are never dreamed at all, but just "spuriously" recalled upon waking' (159). While also briefly suggesting that there might be a dream library full of dreams composed and recorded during our waking hours, he is quick to discard this possibility for what he considers to be the more likely one: that even though dream production takes place during sleep, it is just an 'unconscious composition process and unconscious memory-loading process' (161), which turns into a subjective experience only upon awakening and consciously recalling the dream. His main argument is that the average sleeper would never be able to say for certain if a recalled dream was actually experienced or if a dream cassette (of a possibly never experienced dream) was instantaneously inserted into his or her memory upon awakening. He thereby draws into doubt the validity of dream reports and makes a strong case for scientific dream research. See also Windt (2013).

⁹⁶ Meier (1993), 63.

Ultimately, then, McGinn's model fails to convince. It remains highly speculative and is in parts contradicted by empirical findings that confirm most dreamers' intuitive sense that their dreams develop spontaneously and can even to some extent be manipulated. The most important evidence in this regard is research carried out with experienced lucid dreamers able to communicate their dream experiences in real-time via previously determined eye movement signals or to perform certain previously determined movements and actions in their dreams.[97] Also the impact that waking sensory stimulus can have on the dream narrative speaks against McGinn's theory.[98]

In his article 'Authorship in Dreams and Fictions' (1994), Bert O. States offers an arguably more compelling model by tackling the paradox of authorship from a different angle. Pondering the 'compositional similarities of dreams and fictions', both of which 'recreate human experience in narrative form', his central question is, 'how does a dream plot a sequence of events that never occurred but is simultaneously experienced as an occurring reality?'[99] Who authors the dream and according to which principles? States' approach most significantly differs from both Stevenson's and McGinn's in that he views the dreamer not only as audience of the dream but as active participant in the dream plot: 'To me this is the deepest enigma of dreaming: how is it that one can be within a dream, as one is within waking reality, and simultaneously produce the world one is in—rather like the mollusk which secretes its own house and then lives in it.'[100]

In trying to get a grip on this 'enigma', States, from the outset (and rightly so, I think), rejects the 'psychic split' theory. As he wryly puts it: 'The last thing I want to suggest is the notion of a two-part brain, in one part of which there is a little author sitting at a tiny neuron processor writing stories for the other part'.[101] Instead, he sets out to explore possible similarities between the actual creative processes at work in dreaming and waking storytelling, suggesting that, 'while creating a story the

---

[97] See LaBerge (1990), LaBerge and DeGracia (2000) and Erlacher and Schredl (2008).
[98] For an overview of relevant contemporary studies, see Windt (2015), 358–360.
[99] States (1994), 238.
[100] States (1994), 238.
[101] States (1994), 239.

storyteller is, in a manner of speaking, really dreaming under different, if more controlled, circumstances'.[102] According to this view, the process of creating a story is like an altered state of waking consciousness and 'is to waking consciousness, perhaps, what lucid dreaming [...] is to normal dreaming'.[103] To back up his theory, States points to anecdotal evidence from writers' accounts of their own creative process:

> Fiction writers will commonly tell you two things that occur in the composition process: first, that the story, when it is going well, 'writes itself'— meaning, I gather, that the writer becomes more like a *secretary* than an author: in this happy state, the story unfolds as fast as one can write it down, and the awareness of authoring these events is mixed with a sense of actually watching them *taking place* while authoring them: writing and experiencing interpenetrate each other, as in a dream.[104]

In *On Moral Fiction* (1978), John Gardner confirms this suggestion when he writes that 'everyone who has ever seriously attempted a long fiction knows how remarkably similar writing is, in some respects, to dreaming'.[105] This rather sweeping statement is corroborated in Naomi Epel's collection *Writers Dreaming* (1993), in which various American writers describe the creative process at work in fiction-writing in strikingly similar terms. One of these writers is Stephen King, who elaborates on the similarities between writing and dreaming as follows:

> Part of my function as a writer is to dream awake. And that usually happens. If I sit down to write in the morning, in the beginning of that writing session and the ending of that session, I'm aware that I'm writing. I'm aware of my surroundings. It's like shallow sleep on both ends, when you go to bed and when you wake up. But in the middle, the world is gone and I'm able to see better. Creative imaging and dreaming are just so similar that they've got to be related.[106]

---

[102] States (1994), 239.
[103] States (1994), 239.
[104] States (1994), 239–240. For a similar account of how writers often feel they are following instructions (rather like readers) in creating their works, see Scarry (2001), 245.
[105] Gardner (1978), 179.
[106] Epel (1993), 141.

King goes on to suggest that in such a 'semidreaming state' he is able to retrieve long forgotten memories and that he has come to treasure 'the ability to go in [that state] when one is awake',[107] quite accurately surmising that 'whether you're dreaming or whether you're writing creatively the brainwaves are apparently interchangeable'.[108] King's observations and intuitions about the similarities between dreaming and creative writing are echoed by numerous other writers' accounts throughout Epel's collection. Some of these accounts stress the extent to which writers lose themselves in the fictional world they are in the very process of creating. Thus, Anne Rice describes how '[w]riting for me is being in the illusion of the novel. It's just sailing right into it. I don't sit there conscious of striking keys and making words. I'm just seeing the action. It's very much like daydreaming or dreaming'.[109] Similarly, Maya Angelou compares the state in which she finds herself while writing to an 'enchantment',[110] and Amy Tan confirms that the 'kind of writing [she does] is very dreamlike'. She explains that she often plays music to help her block out 'the rest of my consciousness, so I can enter into this world and let it go where it wants to go, wherever the characters want to go'.[111] Other writers use similar techniques, like sticking to specific rituals, so as to induce what John Barth calls 'a kind of trance state'[112] or to find, in King's words, 'a way of saying to the mind: you're going to be dreaming soon'.[113] James W. Hall sums up the perceived similarities between dreaming and writing as follows: 'I don't see that the dream state that we have at night is that much different in some ways from the dream state that writers learn to put themselves into as they're writing. I know that sounds like kind of a romantic notion but it's very true for me and I've heard other writers say similar things.'[114] The fact that some writers indeed 'learn to put themselves into' a dreamlike trance state is confirmed by British writer

---

[107] Epel (1993), 141.
[108] Epel (1993), 141.
[109] Epel (1993), 212.
[110] Epel (1993), 27.
[111] Epel (1993), 284.
[112] Epel (1993), 44.
[113] Epel (1993), 142.
[114] Epel (1993), 110.

Clare Jay, who refers to what she calls 'the writer's trance' as a consciously induced state, 'a waking version of lucid dreaming, where we sink as deeply as we can into our unconscious minds while remaining awake, allowing ideas to flow freely and rapidly as dream imagery mingles with our imagination'.[115]

Such accounts suggest that, rather than assuming a binary distinction between waking and sleeping consciousness, it makes sense to propose a continuum along the lines of Thomas' multidimensional spectrum of imagination model. In a similar vein, States proposes a continuum including hybrid states such as lucid dreaming and 'this bracketed state of focused attentiveness'[116] in which the writer seems to create in a dream-like trance: 'just as the lucid dreamer is slightly awake, slightly *outside* the dream, while being largely *inside* it, so the waking author is slightly asleep, or slightly *inside* the fiction while being largely *outside* it.'[117] A good example of this is provided by Coleridge's poem 'Christabel', in which the reader seems to witness the creation of the poem, its process of coming into existence, in this sense sharing the narrator's dream-in-progress. This becomes most obvious in the first part of the poem when the narrator repeatedly asks and answers questions about, for instance, the setting: 'Is the night chilly and dark?/The night is chilly, but not dark' (14–15) or about the plot: 'What sees she there?//There she sees a damsel bright [...]' (57–58). Tellingly, the narrator is not presented as having complete control over the events narrated in the poem. Thus, for instance, later in the poem he entreats Sir Leonile not to 'wrong' (634)

---

[115] Jay (2011), 15.
[116] States (1994), 240.
[117] States (1994), 240. It goes without saying that this dreamlike state of composition, which has much in common with Freud's concept of the primary process, is only part of the authorial craft. In the same way that dreams do not usually come as full-fledged pieces of art, such drafts often require thorough revising, which typically takes place in the author's more wake-like stages. As States (1994) points out: 'One of the things we commonly find in writers' descriptions of how they work is that they write best when they let their imagination dictate the flow, but that the results must often be adapted, or retrofitted, to waking standards of intelligibility' (240). In this context, it may also be interesting to take into account S.T. Coleridge's notion of poetry as a 'rationalized dream' (*Notebooks*, vol. 1, 2086), 'which suggests that the creation of poetry requires the magnitude of loss of volition as experienced in dreams, with the crucial qualifier that there is still some reason present. This is a rationalising presence, which is not discernible in other states of dreaming' (Ford [1998], 35–36).

his only child, a plea that is, however, to no avail. In this sense, the narrator is like a dreamer: emotionally immersed in the storyworld and yet unable to deliberately change its outcome or effectively influence the narrative's or dream's course of events.

In view of the above evidence, it seems plausible to assume that 'the dreamer does compose the dream as it unfolds' in the same way that an author lets his or her imaginative flow run its course.[118] The fact that dreams, daydreams and fictional first drafts often tend to occur as more or less coherent narratives can be accounted for by Keith Oatley's suggestion that the initial stages of composition draw on long-term working memory 'in which longer lasting connections are generated between the verbal and intuitive layers. In writing this might be the process in which knowledge of style, tropes, and literary sentence generation is drawn on, to elaborate the dream of a story'.[119] The story drafts of dreams are thus generated through recourse to the imaginal memory register. Drawing on several neurocognitive studies, Pace-Schott demonstrates that dreaming, waking mind-wandering, 'pathological states such as delirium or confabulation' and what he refers to as 'normal narrative production'[120] all display a narrative structure, which indicates that 'story structure may also be the basic manner in which the brain organizes experience'.[121] The research he cites is supportive of his hypothesis that the human mind harbours an innate '"story-telling instinct" or module'.[122]

The above anecdotal as well as empirical evidence supports the claim that 'narrative structure is not an artful invention but rather a natural process of the mind',[123] so that for a narrative structure to occur, conscious preplanning on the dreamer's part is in no way necessary. Rather, the dream plot develops according to the interaction of emotional concerns and an evolving scenario of different dream characters, setting, objects and occurrences. In States' words:

---

[118] States (1994), 241.
[119] Oatley (2011), 147.
[120] Pace-Schott (2013), 2.
[121] Pace-Schott (2013), 2.
[122] Pace-Schott (2013), 1; see Mar 2004.
[123] Kilroe (2000), 136.

The dream is a cumulative process whose developments are not controlled by the dreamer but originate in the dreamer's thought about the experience in progress. Very much like waking thought, dreaming is something of a discovery process. It is a matter of thought being converted to imagery whose sum effect thereupon constitutes a point of 'orientation' from which future possibilities must be drawn. Thus the dreamer dreams the dream without suspecting that he or she is the efficient cause of what is going on. In the waking world, one might say to oneself in a similar situation, 'Is there an exit here?' and there would or wouldn't be an exit, as conditions empirically dictated. In a dream, to ask if there is an exit is already to posit the possibility of an exit. [...] Whether it will become a true exit will depend on the nature of the emotional incentive to which the dream is in thrall.[124]

Unlike McGinn's view, then, dreams are not completely preplanned by an intelligent dream designer and are not 'screened' for us as finished nightly movies. Instead, what is happening is basically what happens in waking: We are faced with a particular situation or constellation of things in conjunction with a particular prevailing emotional mood. During our dream, we deal with and react to the given situation as best we can. The main difference is that in dreaming, in contrast to waking, our thoughts are instantly converted into images that lead the way forward and are typically arranged in a narrative way. To illustrate this, it may be useful to focus for a moment on an actual dream by Jorge Luis Borges. In his essay collection *Seven Nights* (1984), he recounts his dream of an encounter with a friend (unknown to him in real life), who seemed much changed, his face being marked by illness or possibly guilt. The friend keeps his hand hidden inside his jacket until eventually he withdraws it to reveal the claw of a bird. As Borges comments: 'The strange thing is that from the beginning the man had his hand hidden. Without knowing it, I had paved the way for that invention: that the man had the claw of a bird and that I would see the terrible change, the terrible misfortune, that he was turning into a bird'.[125] However, according to States' model, there is no need to assume that the bird metamorphosis was in any way preplanned

---

[124] States (1994), 242.
[125] Borges, *Seven Nights*, 35.

and prepared from the dream's beginning. Rather, speculating about a reason for the friend's hidden hand, the dreaming mind proposed the option of some hideous secret such as a disease and, for reasons impossible to grasp without further contextual knowledge, suggested the bird metamorphosis as an explanation for the friend's tragic secret. A different emotional context or mood might have led the dreamer to envision a hidden weapon, a stolen piece of jewellery, an ugly wound or mark, all of which might have pushed the dream plot into an entirely different direction.

States' model echoes Sartre's view that '[i]n an imaginary world there is no dream of *possibilities*, since possibilities call for a real world on the basis of which they are thought of *as* possibilities. Consciousness cannot get perspective on its own imaginations in order to imagine a possible sequence to the story which it is representing to itself: that would be to be awake'.[126] Accordingly,

> it is not by conceiving other possibilities that the sleeper is reassured [...]. It is by the immediate production of reassuring events in the story itself. He does not say to himself: I could have had a revolver, but suddenly he does have a revolver in his hand. But too bad for him if at that very moment a thought should occur to him which in the waking state would assume the form of 'what if the revolver had been locked!' This 'if' cannot exist in the dream: this rescuing revolver is suddenly locked at the very moment when it is needed.[127]

This is because, as States aptly puts it, 'story writers have the opportunity to revise or to "test drive" their events before buying them outright, whereas in dreams all first thoughts are final sales'.[128] The idea that dreams are only just preliminary drafts does not necessarily render them useless though. As Oatley aptly notes: 'For all of us, an imperfect draft or a piece that did not come out right can be a portal of discovery'.[129] It can also be redrafted, enhanced and turned into a successful final draft in a state of

---

[126] Sartre (1972 [1940]), 198.
[127] Sartre (1972 [1940]), 199.
[128] States (1994), 243.
[129] Oatley (2011), 143.

waking creativity. As the British fantasy fiction author John Gordon puts it: 'The usefulness of dreams is that they subvert our waking state, but it can only be wakefulness that makes them into something more than mere dreams'.[130]

Occasionally though (and this leads us back to the beginning of this chapter and Stevenson's anecdote about the creation of *Jekyll and Hyde*), writers have pointed out how dreams provided them with ideas, images and even experiences that fuelled their writing or with imaginative solutions when they were stuck in the writing process. One example is Elizabeth Gaskell's account of Charlotte Brontë's conscious uses of her dream life whenever she wanted to describe experiences out of her range:

> [S]he had thought intently on it many and many a night before falling to sleep,—wondering what it was like, or how it would be,—till at length, sometimes after the progress of her story had been arrested at this one point for weeks, she wakened up in the morning with all clear before her, as if she had in reality gone through the experience, and then could describe it, word for word, as it had happened. (413)

Likewise, Bharati Mukherjee describes how the endings of some of her stories and novels came to her in dreams, often taking her 'by surprise' and completely contradicting her original intentions or expectations.[131] Amy Tan notes how '[s]ometimes, if I'm stuck on the ending of a story, I'll just take the story with me to bed. I'll let it become part of a dream and see if something surfaces'.[132] And last but not least, Stephen King recounts how a dream furnished him with a crucial scene for his novel *It* (1986) when he was stuck in his writing to the point of desperation: 'I woke up and I was very frightened. But I was also very happy. Because then I knew what was going to happen. I just took the dream as it was and put it in the book. Dropped it in. I didn't change anything.'[133] These examples vividly illustrate how in dreams the creative process continues,

---

[130] Royle, *The Tiger Garden*, 91.
[131] Epel, *Writers Dreaming*, 161.
[132] Epel, *Writers Dreaming*, 285.
[133] Epel, *Writers Dreaming*, 138.

how waking and dreaming permeate each other and how the boundaries between our waking and sleeping imagination constantly blur.

There is, then, no reason to assume that dreams are random, chaotic or even meaningless creations just because they have not been preplanned in detail, especially taking into account that numerous writers of fiction (such as King, Tan or Mukherjee) do not necessarily tend to preplan their works down to the last detail either.[134] What is more, States draws our attention to the 'concept of scripts as the major extrinsic factor in dream construction' in the sense of 'patterns of acquired and recurrent behavior'[135] according to whose principles dreams (and first drafts of waking fictions) may unfold. As States points out, 'when dreams tell stories they are inescapably bound up with scripts of some kind, exactly like literature itself', and he concludes: 'If [...] there are certain involuntary and intrinsic capabilities for producing dream and fictional narratives, they are given additional direction and probability by the way experience in the waking world teaches us its patterns of probability.'[136] This view is corroborated by Owen Flanagan, who, in regard to a selection of his own dreams, argues:

> My brain was able to construct these particular dreams out of memories and experiences stored in my mind. [...] The construction of the narrative works, as best it can, with emotions, desires, thoughts and memories stored in our mind-brain and cast in a way that is affected by our way of telling stories, by culturally available genres of storytelling, as well as by whatever spin our self-conception contributes to the structure and trajectory of the narrative.[137]

Since we only have conscious access to the dream by remembering or retelling it, the extent to which narrative conventions are inherent in

---

[134] See, for instance, Bharati Mukherjee: 'I'm the kind of writer who in the very first draft really doesn't know what adventures the characters will get into' (Epel [1993], 161) or Stephen King: 'When I'm working I never know what the end is going to be or how things are going to come out. I've got an idea what direction I want the story to go in, or hope it will go in, but mostly I feel like the tail on a kite' (Epel [1993], 137).
[135] States (1994), 248.
[136] States (1994), 248.
[137] Flanagan (2000), 143.

the dream experience itself or are drawn on retrospectively to translate the dream experience into a coherent story is, of course, difficult to determine.[138] What is more, dreamers are not only the authors of their own dreams, but simultaneously the recipients of, as well as characters within, their emerging dream narratives. This insight paves the way for the next chapter which will be concerned with the similarities and differences between dreaming and reading fictions.

The Dreamer as Reader, the Reader as Dreamer

Writing and reading are activities rarely performed in dreams.[139] One possible explanation for this may well be that dreaming is precisely a form of writing/reading, or, to put it differently, a form of narrative immersion involving mental processes similar to those implicated in, for instance, readerly immersion. What if a dreamer were to read a novel in a dream? Arguably, before long, the dream setting and plot would morph into that of the novel, the words on the page coming visually alive in the virtual reality surrounding the dreamer. This is precisely what happens in the following dream recorded in Havelock Ellis' *The World of Dreams* (1911), a rare dream report featuring prolonged readerly activity:

> Again I dreamed that I was coming up the Thames (apparently in a steam boat), reading a novel, written by a friend, which was the history of some one [sic] who arrives in England coming up the Thames to London, by what I felt to be an extraordinary coincidence, in exactly the same way as I was at the moment. Then I found myself seemingly at the end of a London pier, with the river rippling at my feet, and in front the superb panorama of London; exactly the scene which, in less detail, was described in the book.[140]

---

[138] The problem of 'translating' dream experiences into literary language is dealt with in Sect. 'Translating the "Language" of Dreams' in Chap. 4.
[139] See Hartmann (2000a).
[140] Ellis, *The World of Dreams*, 53.

This dream report arguably accentuates what is implicit in all dream experiences: that the dreamer is simultaneously writer and reader, creator and recipient of his dream. It is impossible to determine whether the descriptions in the novel prompt the dream setting or whether the dream setting triggers the descriptions in the novel. In either case, both have emerged from the same mind, for the 'novel, written by a friend' is, after all, a product of the dreamer's mental activity just like the rest of the dream. Arguably, a dream in which the dreamer reads about, say, a secluded cabin in the Alps, but simultaneously finds himself 'at the end of a London pier' would be difficult to maintain, simply because the 'single-minded' dreamer would be unable to uphold two different parallel strands of mental activity—immersion in the dreamworld *and* in the book's storyworld—for any extended period of time.[141] The attempt would most likely result either in the collapsing of one scenario into the other, the emergence of a new amalgamated scenario or in the dreamer's awakening.

While dreams are characteristically solipsistic experiences,[142] literature, in Sartre's definition, 'exists only for and through other people', with '[t]he combined efforts of author and reader [bringing] into being the concrete and imaginary object which is the work of the mind'.[143] However, even though the dream experience is limited to one subjective dreamer, this dreamer combines both writer and reader in his imaginative dream construction and reception. Thus, as Patrick McNamara rightly points out, the dreamer, unaware of having created the dream character he is interacting with, 'watches how that character's subsequent actions and interactions with others unfold over time. Even

---

[141] Interestingly, in a letter from 1805 Robert Southey (1881) commented on his inability to read in his dreams and reached a similar conclusion: 'This impossibility of reading is perfectly explicable; the mind cannot form its associations and embody or print them co-instantaneously. One operation must precede the other, and it is as impossible in dreams to read what is passing as it is to overtake your own shadow' (370). The 'single-mindedness' of dreams has been explored by Allan Rechtschaffen (1978), who notes in dreaming 'the strong tendency for a single train of related thoughts and images to persist over extended periods without disruption nor competition from other simultaneous thoughts and images' (97). For a more in-depth discussion of this dream characteristic, see Sect. 'The "Language" of Dreams' in Chap. 4.

[142] See Engel (2004), 113.

[143] Sartre quoted in Iser (1980), 108.

when a dreamer dreams that he is being pursued by strangers, animals, or demons that intend to do him harm, he is attributing mind to those pursuers'.[144] Like the reader, then, the dreamer (whose mind has dreamed up the dream characters) is generally unable to control these characters' actions and constantly speculates about what they might be up to. Or, as Charles Dickens more eloquently puts it in his short piece 'Lying Awake' (1860), in dreams it is common for us to 'hold, with the deepest interest, dialogues with various people, all represented by ourselves; and to be at our wit's end to know what they are going to tell us; and to be indescribably astonished by the secrets they disclose'.[145] If my suggestion that the dreamer is simultaneously creator and recipient of his dream is accepted, then reader response theory is bound to provide crucial further insights into the similarities between dreaming and reading. Accordingly, the remainder of this chapter will focus on some core concerns at the heart of both reader response theory and dream research, including world simulation, visualization, spatiotemporal immersion and questions concerning identification, emotional involvement and belief.

At the phenomenological level, dreaming may arguably be closer to *reading* than to *writing* stories. Ordinarily, the dreamer experiences herself as passive recipient or as character engaged in the dream plot rather than as author or director of her dream. As Victor Nell points out: 'Whatever work takes place in reading and dreaming [...], it is *subjectively* effortless. The cognitive passivity reading and dreaming share is markedly different from the closely related activity of fantasy production as in storytelling'.[146] Of course, this sense of passivity is an illusion since even the most ordinary act of perception depends on 'the active, purposeful, attentive seeking out of environmental information'.[147] The creation of mental images without sensory input surely requires an even higher degree of activity on the reader's or, arguably, the dreamer's part. More crucially, reader response theories have increasingly emphasized

---

[144] McNamara (2008), 136.
[145] Dickens, 'Lying Awake', 433.
[146] Nell (1988), 201, my italics.
[147] N. Thomas (2014), 152.

the reader's active role in the creation of the literary text, which only ever comes into being through the reader's completion of the creative process. As Wolfgang Iser puts it in his seminal work *The Act of Reading* (1980), 'the text is a "structured prefigurement", but that which is given has to be received, and the *way* in which it is received depends as much on the reader as on the text'.[148] Iser's insistence on the reader's active role has, more recently, been confirmed by Oatley, who argues that 'even in the most passive readings, we write our own versions of what we read'.[149] Oatley elaborates that as readers we engage in a world-creating process in the same way the dreamer does: 'We create our own version of the piece of fiction, our own dream, our own enactment. We run a simulation on our own minds. As partners with the writer, we create a version based on our own experience of how the world appears on the surface and of how we might understand its deeper properties.'[150] This view is corroborated by research on the phenomenon of mirror neurons, neurons that fire no matter if an action is performed or only observed. As already discussed in Chap. 2, various experiments employing functional neuroimaging techniques have shown that the same brain areas are activated whether we perform a physical task or whether we read or dream about that task.[151] As Oatley points out: 'These experiments indicate that, based on their experience, readers construct an active mental model of what is going on in the story, and can also imagine what might happen next'.[152] Or, as he puts it elsewhere, 'the relation of text to world is a kind of dream or simulation, that the reader constructs from the kit of parts supplied by the writer'.[153] Thus, when

---

[148] Iser (1980), 107.

[149] Oatley (2011), 62.

[150] Oatley (2011), 18.

[151] See Speer et al. (2009) and Erlacher and Schredl (2008).

[152] Oatley (2011), 20.

[153] Oatley (2003), 167. This concept of a reading process in which the reader takes an active and creative rather than a passive and receiving part is in stark contrast to earlier phenomenological approaches such as Georges Poulet's (1969), in which the reader is depicted as becoming 'prey' to what he reads: 'The consciousness inherent in the work is active and potent; it occupies the foreground; it is clearly related to its *own* world, to objects which are *its* objects. In opposition, I myself, although conscious of whatever it may be conscious of, I play a much more humble role, content to record passively all that is going in me. A lag takes place, a sort of schizoid distinction between what I feel and what the other feels; a confused awareness of delay, so that the work seems first to

Nell views storytelling and dreaming as respectively the prototypes of active and passive fantasy,[154] this difference ought to be understood as one of degree. Moreover, he disregards the often blurred boundaries between the respective states when he claims that dreaming 'is nearer to primary process and therefore syntactically primitive, illogical, and unreal, whereas active fantasy is produced by an act of conscious will in response to an externally imposed task, with full reflective awareness'.[155] Creating a work of literature clearly requires the constant interplay between alternating active and passive fantasy modes. As Nell realizes, 'daydreaming lies midway between waking and dreaming and may easily shade off into one or the other'.[156] However, the same is surely the case for other states of consciousness along the multidimensional spectrum of imagination such as creative writing or reading.

Fantasy production (in the sense of storytelling) may indeed be experienced as comparatively effortful, while dreaming is 'a passive cognitive product [which] arises spontaneously with a feeling of drifting rather than one of responsible effort'.[157] According to this view, reading and dreaming are closely related (though not identical) states. As Nell puts it:

> [T]he book is an active fantasy product, logical and with explicit connections, reflective, and publicly available. But the story unfolding in the reader's mind is a passive product, making use of what Freud calls 'ready-made phantasy'. The reader's experience is therefore that an active-fantasy product produces a passive cognitive experience which may be described in exactly the terms that Holt uses for reverie or daydreaming—effortless, dreamy, abstracted, drifting—and yet, paradoxically, continually under the sway of an active input.[158]

---

think by itself, and then to inform me what it has thought. Thus I often have the impression, while reading, of simply witnessing an action which at the same time concerns and yet does not concern me. This provokes a certain feeling of surprise within me. I am a consciousness astonished by an existence which is not mine, but which I experience as though it were mine' (59–60).

[154] See Nell (1988), 205.
[155] Nell (1988), 205.
[156] Nell (1988), 205.
[157] Robert Holt quoted in Nell (1988), 205.
[158] Nell (1988), 206.

Reading can thus be viewed as 'a form of consciousness change',[159] and the reader's 'effortless, dreamy, abstracted, drifting' state varies according to the kind of reading matter he or she is consuming. Like dreaming or daydreaming, *ludic* reading, in the sense of reading for pleasure and recreation, in particular, may put us under a 'spell of entrancement' surpassing mere absorption as well as 'transporting us to other places and transfiguring our consciousness to make other people of us'.[160] In turn, the experience of 'guided dreaming'[161] that is fiction can help us discover new aspects of ourselves or, as Oatley puts it, 'the Forms that we understand, and partially create, can become newly recognized aspects of ourselves'.[162] Interestingly, the kind of literature that comes closest to representing the actual dream state may be less suited to inducing such entrancement in the reader. Referring to experimental literary works such as Joyce's *Finnegans Wake* (1939) or Barnes' *Nightwood* (1936) as 'the kind of mimetic literature that is in many respects closest to primary-process material', Nell points out that '[i]n these and similar literary products, connections are implicit, word use is neologistic, and the logic is more autistic than rational. [...] In other words, there are some reasons to think that a work of art's proximity to primary process reduces its utility as a ludic reading input'.[163] In contrast to this, it is formulaic and less difficult mimetic literature that may most easily enable the reader to lose herself in an imaginary story to the extent of 'sinking through the page into the world of the book'.[164]

This 'world-creating process'[165] is enhanced by the reader's capacity for transforming the words on the page into mental images or, in other words, the reader's visualization of the narrative they are immersed in. As John Gardner puts it in *The Art of Fiction* (1983), reading can evoke

---

[159] Nell (1988), 199.
[160] Nell (1988), 199.
[161] Borges, Foreword, *Brodie's Report*, 346.
[162] Oatley (2003), 165.
[163] Nell (1988), 207.
[164] Nell (1988), 216.
[165] Nell (1988), 216.

'a rich and vivid play in the mind' so that 'suddenly we find ourselves seeing not words on a page but a train moving through Russia, an old Italian crying, or a farmhouse battered by rain. [...] Fiction does its work by creating a dream in the reader's mind'.[166] A similar view is expressed in Virginia Woolf's short essay 'Reading', in which Elizabethan travel literature is described as 'lull[ing] us asleep' while visually bringing to life exotic places:

> And so, as you read on across the broad pages with as many slips and somnolences as you like, the illusion rises and holds you of banks slipping by on either side, of glades opening out, of white towers revealed, of gilt domes and ivory minarets. It is, indeed, an atmosphere, not only soft and fine, but rich, too, with more than one can grasp at any single reading.[167]

Accordingly, Ellen J. Esrock takes issue with earlier reader response theories that tended to dismiss the relevance of readerly imaging. In her book *The Reader's Eye: Visual Imaging as Reader's Response* (1994), she makes a convincing case for the significance of visual image production during the reading process, which can serve both cognitive and affective functions.[168] In doing so, she particularly stresses how, for instance, '[e]rotic or bizarre material arouses the kind of readerly interests that are habitually associated with vision. When such interests are aroused and the material is narrated with sufficient coherence and detail, the reader is prompted to image'.[169] Incidentally, Esrock's reference to 'erotic or bizarre material' provides an interesting link to dream vividness and dream recall, both of which are particularly heightened by this kind of material. However, Esrock further notes that 'even without such affective prompts, readerly imaging is encouraged when fictional characters are engaged in specifically mentioned acts of visual perception. Verbs like *saw*, *gazed*, and *looked* all suggest

---

[166] Gardner, *The Art of Fiction*, 30–31.
[167] Woolf, 'Reading', 21–22, quoted in Lamarque and Olsen (2004), 202.
[168] See Esrock (1994), 179.
[169] Esrock (1994), 183.

there is something to see. A verb like *behold* practically commands the reader to take a look'.¹⁷⁰ As Renate Brosch elaborates:

> It appears that close scrutiny and intense observation by fictional characters, often described as affected viewing, provide an emulative visualisation on the part of the reader. Lasting impressions are also produced by a prolonged eye contact or by one character watching another closely with the intent of finding out that character's mood, motivation or personality.¹⁷¹

Accordingly, recent reader response theories increasingly stress the central role of visualization in the processing of narrative texts. Visualization during reading is triggered by a text's visuality, including all components of a narrative that prompt visualization in the reader's mind and, as Brosch puts it, 'visuality is necessary and visualisation unavoidable in processing narrative'.¹⁷²

In her groundbreaking study *Dreaming by the Book* (2001), Elaine Scarry suggests, and analyses, various ways of authorial instruction that facilitate such visualization in the reader. According to Scarry, the mental images generated in daydreaming tend to remain 'feeble and impoverished' but imagining under authorial instruction is more vivid and 'sometimes closely approximates actual perception'.¹⁷³ While Scarry offers some fascinating insights into authorial strategies facilitating visualization, I would still argue that the reader's visualization of the narrative significantly differs from actual visual perception. Thus, the images prompted by authorial instruction can indeed be 'extraordinarily vivid and affecting',¹⁷⁴ but they are at the same time less stable and saturated than perceivable images. They are, in fact, more dreamlike. As Brosch—partly drawing on Colin McGinn—rightly notes: 'In visualising a textual narrative in the reading process, the images never become concrete as in a movie but remain transient and evanescent, always potentially adapt-

---

[170] Esrock (1994), 183.
[171] Brosch (2013), 176–177.
[172] Brosch (2013), 169.
[173] Scarry (2001), 6.
[174] Brosch (2013), 169.

able and emendable to new knowledge presented by the narrative'.[175] At this point, it should be noted that, despite the traditional analogy drawn between actual and cinematic dreams, dreamers and spectators quite obviously find themselves under totally different conditions. While the dreamer generates internal 'world-creating' images, the spectator, as Christian Metz points out, 'receives images and sounds offered as the representation of something other than themselves, of a diegetic universe, but remaining true images and sounds capable of reaching other spectators as well, whereas the dream flux can reach the consciousness of no one but the dreamer'.[176] In Metz' view, then, '[t]he film image belongs to that class of "real images" (paintings, drawings, engravings, etc.) which psychologists oppose to mental images. The difference between the two is what separates perception from imagination in the terms of a phenomenology of consciousness'.[177]

It goes without saying that the process of mental visualization not only varies from reader to reader but that its description and analysis pose challenges to even intensely visual readers. Again, it may be necessary to resort to literary writers in order to capture the sense of what it is like to be gradually, imperceptibly and irresistibly drawn into the world of the book, to become visually immersed in the storyworld. In this context, Peter Schwenger quotes the opening of Italo Calvino's novel *If on a Winter's Night a Traveller* (1986) whose first chapter playfully describes how the novel's reader ('you') starts reading and gradually visualizing the 'misty' images materializing behind and around the words, signs and paragraphs he or she perceives on the page:

> The novel begins in a railway station, a locomotive huffs, steam from a piston covers the opening of the chapter, a cloud of smoke hides part of the first paragraph. In the odor of the station there is a passing whiff of station café odor. There is someone looking through the befogged glass, he opens the glass door of the bar, everything is misty, inside, too, as if seen by nearsighted eyes, or eyes irritated by coal dust. The pages of the book are clouded like the windows of an old train, the cloud of smoke rests on the

---

[175] Brosch (2013), 170.
[176] Metz (1977), 109.
[177] Metz (1977), 109.

sentences. It is a rainy evening; the man enters the bar; he unbuttons his damp overcoat; a cloud of steam enfolds him; a whistle dies away along tracks that are glistening with rain, as far as the eye can see.[178]

While this description prompts the reader to image by repeatedly drawing attention to the act of seeing and to visual details of the setting, it likewise 'mimics the process of settling into a novel's world' during which we are still vaguely aware of the words on the physical page while the images taking shape inside our minds are 'reluctant to come into fully focused realization'.[179] The misty, foggy and blurred details of the fictional world described here (which in turn might be likened to a dream-like state) are at the same time adequate 'metaphors for the properties of visual imaging'.[180] The passage cited by Schwenger minutely illustrates the gradual and fragile process, ending with a reference to the reader's 'eye that is no longer muffled, myopic, blurred, but one focused on a clearly delineated space'.[181]

Even after the reader has thus fully entered the storyworld and has adjusted his vision to its imaginary realm, his mental images remain unstable, amendable and in continual need of renewal. For instance, the image of a fictional character formed in our mind may undergo numerous metamorphoses in the course of the reading process, as new information becomes available or our emotional response to the characters and the plot changes. A similar observation is made by Iser, who points out that there is a striking difference between reading a novel and watching a film, the latter of which provides us with percepts rather than mental images:

> When we imagine Tom Jones, during our reading of the novel, we have to put together various facets that have been revealed to us at different times—in contrast to the film where we always see him as a whole in every situation. This process of compilation, however, is not additive. The different facets always contain references to others, and each view of character

---

[178] Calvino quoted in Schwenger (1999), 64–65.
[179] Schwenger (1999), 65.
[180] Schwenger (1999), 65.
[181] Schwenger (1999), 66.

only gains its significance through being linked to other views which may overlap, restrict, or modify it. [...] Our image is therefore constantly shifting, and every image we have is duly restructured by each of its successors.[182]

This description inevitably evokes the typically unstable dream images of composite or metamorphosing characters and places. Iser's analysis of the act of reading further suggests that, even though the medium of film is most often credited with a unique affinity to the dream state, it may really be the fictional text that best allows for the recipient's near-dreamlike immersion.[183] This is because as observers we 'always stand outside the given object [such as the film or the painting], whereas we are situated inside the literary text'.[184] As Brosch notes: 'Readers are able to mentally map the fictional world and to not only place things and people into it but to shift around in it and take up different positions in it'.[185] This unique relationship between text and reader, which transcends the subject–object relationship, necessitates 'a moving viewpoint which travels along inside that which it has to apprehend'.[186] It can be argued, then, that we are 'situated inside the literary text' not unlike the way in which we are situated inside the dream. We are 'grasping' the dream and the text as we are moving through it, engaging with shifting places and characters and having to adapt our viewpoint accordingly. Wandering through the

---

[182] Iser (1980), 139. It should be noted that this argument is only convincing as long as we are concerned with cinematic realism. A filmmaker certainly might use cinematic effects to evoke similarly 'shifting images' on screen.

[183] On the other hand, as McGinn (2005) argues, there is a sense of uniqueness to the cinematic experience that distinguishes it from other forms of visual art and may render it closer to the dream experience. Thus, while we look *at* paintings, drawings, theatrical performance and other visual art objects, we do not really look *at* the 'light-constituted movie image' (36) projected onto the screen, but rather we look *into* or *through* it. Explaining the 'complex visual relationship' constituting the cinematic experience, McGinn (2005) points out that 'the image on the screen is seen but not looked at; the actor is seen and looked at; the fictional character is neither seen nor looked at, but imagined' (41). According to McGinn (2005), it is this kind of '*imaginative seeing*', enabling us 'to connect the world of imagination and the world of perception' that is responsible for the pleasure we derive from the specific cinematic experience (53). For detailed analyses of how film and dream experiences are related, a topic that is beyond the scope of the present study, see Metz (1977), Eberwein (1980), Eberwein (1984), Dieterle (1998), McGinn (2005) and Kreuzer (2014).

[184] Iser (1980), 109.

[185] Brosch (2013), 170.

[186] Iser (1980), 109.

storyworld of the novel/dream, we constantly revise our conception of characters and situations as we gain new information that may contradict or correct earlier ideas.

Iser's wandering viewpoint can also be usefully connected to the reader's capacity for conceptual blending. As Brosch argues: 'In processing sophisticated literary texts, blending means a simultaneous awareness of different possibilities which can be merged into a third. Conceptual blending is not just a linguistic or propositional process, it can fuse images as well'.[187] A similar kind of blending occurs in the dream process which modifies and connects memories and future possibilities in a more literal sense, for instance by metamorphosing or merging dream characters and settings. In so doing, the dreaming consciousness often draws on memories from the distant past continually dug up by the associative matchmaking process, in a way similar to what is going on in the reader's consciousness as he or she is confronted with new bits of resonating information. In Iser's words: 'The pointers and stimuli therefore evoke not just their immediate predecessors, but often aspects of other perspectives that have already sunk deep into the past'.[188] In addition to the reader's gathering and blending of information and visual images, however, it is important to keep in mind that the reading process is also influenced by our own idiosyncratic associations and images that are not necessarily in line with the author's instructions. The reading process clearly also implicates an element of mind-wandering or, as Schwenger puts it: 'Our absorption in the words of the page is never, can never be, complete; our attention often wanders, and does so arbitrarily'.[189] If we could consciously retrace the twists and turns taken by our minds in the reading process, the result might often resemble the ostensibly incoherent and strange meanderings of our dreams. Finally, a reader's visualization of a fictional text usually surpasses the prompts provided by its author in that the reader engages in 'the fantasmatic filling-in'[190] of visual details not described in the text, thus rendering the experience more dreamlike.

---

[187] Brosch (2013), 174.
[188] Iser (1980), 116.
[189] Schwenger (2012), 29.
[190] Schwenger (1999), 2.

3 Dreaming and Waking Imagination 105

Given the importance of visualization in the reading process, then, reading in bed before turning out the light mentally prepares us for the hypnagogic and early sleep stages, both of which are image-dominated.[191] Mary Arnold-Forster describes these 'borderland visions' as consisting of 'pictures which seem to be external to ourselves and which we look at; not pictures which are simply remembered'. She also notes that 'it is the essential nature of these "visions" that no exertion of will can summon them at our pleasure, and that, as far as we can tell, they are wholly independent of our control, and not consciously dependent upon memory'.[192] Hypnagogia are typically distinguished from full-fledged dreams (into which they can develop) by the dreamer's observing and detached stance.[193] The dreamer adopts the position of an observer *looking at* rather than being *situated in* or *interacting with* the hypnagogic imagery. These images are projected into external space rather than occurring inside one's 'head', which adds to their perceived sense of reality and vivacity. The same goes for voices that are heard as though coming from the outside. What is more, hypnagogic images are usually not characterized by narrative cohesion or 'the representation of self typical of dream experience'[194] but tend to consist of images or a succession of images, often experienced as static, sometimes as moving miniatures comparable to 'the constantly changing slides of a magic lantern'[195] or 'a succession of lovely forms on a cinematograph screen'.[196] Alfred Alvarez describes similar experiences in terms of 'a freak show, a zoo of distorted faces, voices talking at full pitch but just out of focus, explosions of light and colour, strange images dissolving into each other, shifting and reassembling themselves'.[197] As Foulkes points out, many reports of hypnagogic experiences lack the visual, almost movie-like

---

[191] For a useful overview of the critical literature on the hypnagogic state, see Schacter (1976).
[192] Arnold-Forster, *Studies in Dreams*, 107.
[193] Some researchers, such as David Foulkes (1974), have argued that sleep onset dreams can have a REM-like quality. For the sake of clarity, however, I will refer only to the type of hypnagogic visions that are experienced as in some sense different from dreaming.
[194] Hunt (1989), 182.
[195] Mavromatis (2001), 19.
[196] Mavromatis (2001), 14–15.
[197] Alvarez, *Night*, 153.

coherence of REM dreams, in which the dreamer 'imagines himself moving about or scanning the scenery. As he walks up a flight of stairs, for example, the imagery changes as would the scene in the continuous movie sequence produced by a cameraman holding his camera at eye level as he climbed the stairs'.[198] In contrast, even hypnagogic experiences displaying some degree of narrative cohesion tend to present the 'story' of the dream not as a visually continuous movie but rather as a series of '"still" shots, with the continuity integrated in an ideational, or conceptual, rather than a perceptual, way'.[199]

The majority of hypnagogic reports stress the apparent autonomy of imagery which 'appears and undergoes transformation before the eyes of the subject and in spite of any efforts he might make to preserve it unchanged: faces change expression, figures, animals, as well as inanimate objects, move, and events develop seemingly of their own accord'.[200] In many cases, the dreamer is not only spatially but also emotionally detached from these images, adopting the role of a passive spectator, 'the images present[ing] themselves as spectacles of the reality in which one does not believe, but one contemplates it, in most cases, with curiosity and sometimes with a real pleasure'.[201] These visions often have a comic quality, though they can sometimes be frightening as well.[202] What is more, even though the hypnagogic 'dreamer' is not necessarily emotionally involved, the images (particularly those of faces or persons) may sometimes embody a particular emotion or mood, as seems to be the case in the following example cited by Mavromatis:

> Out of the whirl of uncouth figures to which I was accustomed, a big stout man, in a grey suit and Homburg hat, emerged, and came up (apparently) so close to me, staring pointedly at me, that I expected him to touch me. The movement and the figure were both so aggressive that I mentioned it to my family the next morning.[203]

---

[198] Foulkes (1974), 323.
[199] Foulkes (1974), 323.
[200] Mavromatis (2001), 28.
[201] Leroy quoted in Mavromatis (2001), 89.
[202] See Mavromatis (2001), 33.
[203] Mavromatis (2001), 16.

3 Dreaming and Waking Imagination

The nineteenth-century writer Frederick Greenwood (1830–1909) notes the originality of these 'visions' or 'faces in the dark' that he frequently marvelled at, comparing them to Blake's visionary poetry:

> As they appear one after another at broken intervals of succession, I often ask myself who was ever like that, or that, and I find no answer except in a fancied resemblance to some historical or mythical personage. They strike the view as entirely strange, surprisingly original, and above all intensely meaning. Blake's visions were some such phantoms as these presented to his eyes in broad daylight.[204]

Quite clearly, at least occasionally, these images assume a symbolic or metaphorical quality not unlike the bizarre visual imagery of REM sleep dreams.[205]

As Mavromatis points out, 'in hypnagogia a person may observe his imagery turning into a full-blown dream without a break in consciousness [which] offers the opportunity of experiencing simultaneously wakefulness and dreaming'.[206] This suggests that in the hypnagogic state the creative processes underlying the dream state may be particularly observable. It is thus not surprising that writers in particular have been fascinated with this phenomenon. Edgar Allan Poe (1809–1849) describes hypnagogia as arising 'in the soul [...] only at its epochs of most intense tranquility [...] and those mere points in time where the confines of the waking world blend with those of the world of dreams. I am aware of these "fancies" only when I am upon the very brink of sleep, and with the consciousness that I am so'.[207] Like Greenwood, Poe, too, emphasizes the originality of these visions as well as the almost supernatural 'awe', 'ecstasy' and 'delight' they create in the recipient, who seems to be granted 'a glimpse of the spirit's outer world'.[208] Hypnagogic experiences have been described

---

[204] Greenwood, *Imagination in Dreams and Their Study*, 18.
[205] See Mavromatis (2001), 28.
[206] Mavromatis (2001), 88.
[207] Poe, 'Marginalia', 494.
[208] Poe, 'Marginalia', 495.

by numerous other writers, but arguably one of the most vivid and poignant descriptions is provided by Katherine Mansfield:

> I couldn't get to sleep last night. When I shut my eyes *gardens* drifted by—the most incredible sort of tropical gardens with glimpses of palaces through the rich green. Trees I've never seen or imagined—trees like feathers and silver trees and others quite white with huge transparent leaves passed and passed. My heart just fluttered: I scarcely had to breathe at all. It was like a vision brought about by drugs. I couldn't stop it and yet it frightened me; but it was too beautiful to stop. One is almost in a state of coma—very strange. I've often got *near* this condition before, but never like last night. Perhaps if one gives way to it and gives way to it one may even be able to get there…Oh, I don't know, but it *was* a vision, not a memory.[209]

The difference between this hypnagogic vision and a full-fledged dream is that instead of moving around in that beautiful landscape, touching and possibly smelling the flowers and trees, Mansfield sees the gardens *drift by* rather like a scene in a movie from which she is spatially detached. Even though Mansfield describes herself as being emotionally and physically affected by the imagery ('My heart just fluttered'; 'I couldn't stop it and yet it frightened me'), she remains outside the scene. On the other hand, the knowledge that she might have stopped the vision had she so chosen ('but it was too beautiful to stop') suggests that she is more than a passive observer. The seemingly external imagery has its origin in her own creative imagination. Even though, her perspective may be rather that of an omniscient narrator who watches over the occurrences from a detached position without really entering the world created or else that of a reader deeply immersed in the fascinating passage of a book.

As documented by numerous accounts, 'the passivity of the reader's experience, which so closely resembles the passivity of the hypnagogic state, may literally bridge reading and sleep by inducing a sleep-related state'[210] and sometimes images and ideas from a text just read can be carried over to these stages. In some cases, the dreamer literally rewrites

---

[209] Mansfield, *Letters*, 417.
[210] Nell (1988), 208.

and completes the author's imaginative work. In Mary Arnold-Forster's words:

> There are, for instance, many dreams whose central idea is gathered from a book, generally a book that has lately been read, or that we are reading at the time. The book, like everything else that the dream mind makes use of, will be completely metamorphosed; but some leading idea or some character taken from it will be carried on into the dream.[211]

As Rupprecht and Bulkeley note, the idea of '[r]eading yourself to sleep [...] is a process familiar to many dreamers in literary texts'. Two famous examples include Leo Tolstoy's Anna Karenina, who 'drowses over a novel, reading herself in and out of a reverie of liminal consciousness' and Emily Brontë's character Lockwood in *Wuthering Heights*, who, 'reading Catherine Earnshaw's diaries and the titles on the bindings of sermon pamphlets, drifts off into not one but two powerful nightmares'.[212] Another interesting example is the conclusion of Edgar Allan Poe's 'The Fall of the House of Usher' (1839), in which the narrator reads aloud from a second-rate romance so as to calm down his agitated friend, only to find that what he reads materializes into a dreamlike reality.[213] The idea that romance-reading in particular can heighten and lead astray the reader's imagination is also drawn on in Henry James' *The Turn of the Screw* (1898), in which the narrator, an avid reader of romances, encounters several apparitions. The first occurs while she is taking a walk in the park, daydreaming about a romantic script involving herself and her employer and vividly recalling 'his handsome face'.[214] Becoming suddenly aware of a figure on one of the towers, she sees 'with a stranger sharpness',[215] perceiving the unknown intruder 'as definite as a picture in a frame'.[216] At a later point, she stays up at night in the library, reading

---

[211] Arnold-Forster, *Studies in Dreams*, 110.
[212] Schreier and Bulkeley (1993), 1.
[213] Poe, 'The Fall of the House of Usher', 213–216.
[214] James, *The Turn of the Screw*, 170.
[215] James, *The Turn of the Screw*, 170.
[216] James, *The Turn of the Screw*, 171.

Fielding's *Amelia*, 'wholly awake',[217] when a sense of premonition causes her to go out on the landing only to discover 'there was a figure on the stair'.[218] While these apparitions are not presented as hypnagogic hallucinations, their descriptions as mutely staring at the onlooker, whose visual imagination has been aroused by her reading matter and near-dreamlike state, are certainly striking.

Several writers claim to have derived inspiration from hypnagogic visions that, in turn, were inspired by their reading matter. For instance, Christa Wolf has described how her novel *Kassandra* (1983) was inspired by a hypnagogic experience which Schwenger describes as 'the prolongation of her bedtime reading'.[219] Thus, an account of Greece's partisan history, which she was reading on her journey to Crete, merged with Wolf's current interest in Aeschylus' *Oreista*, which she was also reading during the voyage. Falling asleep over her reading matter, she had a hypnagogic vision of the face of a young partisan merged with the Greek hero at the heart of her future novel:

> A youthful head, which I knew belonged to a man named Aeneas, was floating on smooth, oily water, surrounded by the petals of water lilies and other verdure. He was looking at me, painfully demanding. And I knew of course, without expressly having to think it, that this Aeneas was also the young partisan whose assuredly ghastly end I had not wanted to know.[220]

However, the arguably most famous example illustrating how the activity of reading can shade into that of dreaming is provided by S.T. Coleridge's account of his creation of 'Kubla Khan'. In his preface to the poem, written 20 years after its actual composition, Coleridge claims to have fallen asleep over a book while reading the following sentences from 'Purchas's Pilgrimage':

> 'Here the Khan Kubla commanded a palace to be built, and a stately garden thereunto. And thus ten miles of fertile ground were inclosed with a

---

[217] James, *The Turn of the Screw*, 197.
[218] James, *The Turn of the Screw*, 198.
[219] Schwenger (1999), 40.
[220] Wolf (1988), 185. For a more detailed account of the novel's genesis and the relevance of (hypnagogic) imagery, see Schwenger (1999), 40–46.

wall.' Kubla Khan's pleasure dome then occurred to him in vivid images, as he composed the poem during 'three hours of sleep, at least of the external senses [...] if that indeed can be called composition in which all the images rose up before him as things, with a parallel production of the correspondent expressions, without any sensation or consciousness of effort.[221]

Whether or not we are prepared to accept this account at face value, Coleridge supplies an accurate example of how the hypnagogic and dream stages may take their cue from our current reading matter, especially if perused while on the brink of falling asleep. Incidentally, an interesting additional twist is provided by Jorge Luis Borges in his short piece 'Coleridge's Dream' (1951) in which the author claims that, unbeknownst to Coleridge, Kubla had his palace built 'according to a plan he had seen in a dream'.[222] This chain of dreams, in turn, is extended by the anecdote of an eminent Coleridge scholar, John L. Lowes, who, in his *The Road to Xanadu* (1957) describes how Coleridge's poem triggered a comparably vivid vision of 'the stately pleasure dome' in one of his own dreams. His dream report is an impressive example of how literature can come to life, or rather take on a life of its own, in the reader's dreams, which makes it worth quoting in full:

> Five years ago, while I was giving the substance of this book as lectures and so had the matter of it much in mind, I came home from New York, after one of the talks, with a feverish cold, and passed a wild night of fantastic dreams. After I had spent some time in taking 'Kubla Khan' out of a clothes basket in successive layers like stiff and freshly laundered shirts, the dream abruptly shifted from its impish travesty of my waking efforts to a vision so lucidly clear that after the lapse of five years, as I write, it is as fresh as when I actually saw it. It was, I knew (as one knows in a dream), the stately pleasure dome of Kubla Khan. But it hung like a mirage on the remote horizon of an endless plain. And there, far and distinct as if seen through the reverse lens of a field-glass, on the crest of a high white cliff rose a shimmering golden dome, with tall, feathery palms, delicate as a spider's tracery, on either side of it. And down the cliff fell, slim and stationary in the distance,

---

[221] Coleridge, 'Kubla Khan', 156.
[222] Borges, 'Coleridge's Dream', 371.

a cataract of foam which sent up a luminous golden mist that bathed the whole landscape in unfathomable amber light. And over it all one felt what one could not see—the profound stillness of a summer noon. To me, as the spectator of the dream, it was, as I say, the sunny dome in Xanadu, and the deep romantic chasm, and the sacred river, and the incense-bearing trees. Yet not the faintest hint of what I saw had ever entered into any conscious visualization of the setting of the poem.[223]

It is particularly interesting how Lowes compares his 'waking efforts', travestied in the dream as domestic household chores, to the effortless dream creation of his own imaginative version/vision of Kubla's/Coleridge's pleasure dome. The description of himself as 'spectator', detached from the 'mirage' arising in the distance, also seems to suggest a hypnagogic dream vision, perhaps experienced shortly before waking, rather than a full-fledged dream.

Fascinating as these accounts of hypnagogic visions are, it needs to be kept in mind that they lack some of the defining characteristics of the dream 'proper'. Thus, Sartre, who believes that dreams consist of hypnagogic rather than mental images,[224] still emphasizes that 'in the dream each image surrounds itself with a worldly atmosphere',[225] providing the dreamer with a sense of spatiotemporal location within a dreamworld which the hypnagogic image lacks:

> [T]he hypnagogic image never occurs as being somewhere. [...] But the person of the dream is always somewhere, even if the place where he is figured schematically as in the Elizabethan theatre. And this 'somewhere' is itself situated in relation to a whole world which is not seen but which is all about it. Thus the hypnagogic image is an isolated appearance 'in the air', while the dream, we might say, is a world.[226]

While Sartre compares the fictionality of this world to the fictional world of a story, recent dream researchers have emphasized that there is an

---

[223] Lowes (1957), 369.
[224] See Sartre (1972 [1940]), 91.
[225] Sartre (1972 [1940]), 196.
[226] Sartre (1972 [1940]), 194–195.

important difference which may help account for the deeper sense of immersion we experience in a dream. As noted before, while in dreams we experience mental imagery of a predominantly visual kind, we not only behold this imagery but are also three-dimensionally immersed in it, moving around in it and interacting with other dream characters. Unlike novels, then, dreams build imaginary or 'possible worlds'[227] which are experienced in spatiotemporal dimensions. Accordingly, Coleridge aptly described dreams in terms of a 'Somnial or Morphean Space'[228] and 'the experience of falling asleep as requiring the dreamer to enter into the physical and psychological space of the dream'.[229] In one notebook entry, he writes: 'O then as I first sink on the pillow, as if Sleep had indeed a material *realm*, as if when I sank on my pillow, I was entering that region & realized Faery Land of Sleep—O then what visions have I had, what dreams—'.[230]

The spatial dimension of dreams as suggested by expressions such as *to fall asleep* or *to enter a dream* is more than a metaphor; rather, it can be considered their most basic characteristic. Accordingly, the dreamer's immersion in the dreamworld surpasses the reader's immersion in the storyworld precisely because the dreamer is *always* also spatiotemporally immersed. In fact, Windt argues that the heterogeneous phenomenon of dreaming can be minimally defined by the sleeper's spatiotemporal immersion in the dream.[231] While it may be common to imaginatively 'enter' the storyworld of a book or film, the '[w]orld-creating power'[232] of dreaming provides us with the illusion of actually and physically being located inside, moving around and interacting with others within the virtual reality of the dreamworld. In this context, Kahn and Gover also draw attention to an often overlooked fact: the curious circumstance that in the majority of dreams we have a dream body which, '[d]espite the fact that our physical eyes are closed, our senses "asleep", and our body in bed

---

[227] See Ryan (1991).
[228] Coleridge, *Notebooks*, vol. 4, 5360.
[229] Ford (1998), 39. According to Ford, '[t]he two terms Coleridge uses, "Somnial or Morphean", are interchangeable: "Somnial" simply meaning of or relating to dreams, and "Morphean" deriving from Ovid's name for the god of dreams, Morpheus' (43).
[230] Coleridge, *Notebooks*, vol. 1, 1718.
[231] See Windt (2015), 516.
[232] Bosnak (2007), 9.

is paralyzed, [...] can see, hear, taste, smell, move, and feel'.[233] Dwelling on this astounding fact, they go on to wonder:

> Why do we have a body at all when we are dreaming? After all, the dream is a form of thinking; it is constructed of images, memories, thoughts, and attitudes. Yet not only do we have a body in our dreams, but we have a highly attuned body that can feel texture, taste, run, and make love. It functions very much like our awake body and in some ways even surpasses it. For instance, we can fly in our dreams, fall from tall buildings without getting hurt, disarm powerful opponents, and squeeze through narrow passageways or pedal bicycles up near-vertical inclines. It seems that in dreaming we project our consciousness into the dream body and fully inhabit it.[234]

As Bosnak points out: 'The most absolute and unmediated form of embodied imagination is a dream. It instantaneously presents a total world, so real that you are convinced you're awake'.[235] This can be explained with research evidence confirming that '[d]reams are related [...] to orientation in space'.[236] They are also 'strongly motoric [and] are regarded as the undisguised read-out of the visuomotor brain. The dreamer is not simply beholding a scene, he is always an active protagonist in a scenario'.[237]

Arguably then, dreaming surpasses readerly immersion because it always also involves spatiotemporal immersion and mostly also a sense of embodiment. Again, however, this difference may be one in degree rather than in kind. Windt, for instance, draws attention to the empirically informed observation that in many dreams bodily perception

---

[233] Gover and Kahn (2010), 189.
[234] Gover and Kahn (2010), 189.
[235] Bosnak (2007), 9.
[236] Bosnak (2007), 37. For instance, persons whose forebrain brain area responsible for the derivation of abstract concepts from spatially organized information has been impaired, cease to have 'subjective experience of dreaming whatsoever' (37). Also, topical damage to the right hemisphere of the brain responsible for visuo-spatial working memory 'comes with a global cessation of the subjective experience of dreaming' (37).
[237] Hobson and Wohl (2005), 182. Hobson and Wohl therefore view dreaming as akin to virtual reality rather than to any other medium such as film, since in virtual reality 'the subject's actions influence his or her perceptions' (182).

is quite weak or partial, and that occasionally dreamers report lacking a dream body altogether.[238] Conversely, Anežka Kuzmičová has explored the 'embodied mind of the reader and the ways in which it spontaneously responds to the sensorimotor qualities elicited by literary narrative'.[239] As she points out, 'the reader's body participates in the world(s) of the story to such a degree that bodily movement is frequently emulated from an enactive first-person perspective rather than visualized from the perspective of a passive beholder'.[240] Differentiating between verbal and direct presence, she argues that 'direct presence is a fully reciprocal phenomenon—the reader becomes as physically present in the imaginary world as the imaginary world becomes physically present in front of and around the reader'.[241] Kuzmičová's argument is supported by a number of neurophysiological studies confirming her hypothesis 'that motor imagery and actual movement literally form one experiential continuum and that motor imagery lacks an overt execution phase'.[242] Literary texts, then, trigger covert movement in their readers by means of specific verbal cues, thus contributing to spatiotemporally transporting the reader into the storyworld and rendering the experience more dreamlike accordingly. However, further and more elaborate studies on sensorimotor simulation are needed, especially as it has been shown that 'sensorimotor simulation is stronger during reading of a full narrative as compared to reading unconnected phrases from the same narrative'.[243]

Despite this lacuna, the existing evidence clearly supports the claim that dreams provide us with an imaginary world not unlike the fictional world of a story. Sartre even claims: 'Because of the fact that a dream carries us suddenly into a temporal world, every dream appears to us *as a story*.'[244] The dream, then, is not 'an apprehension of reality' but 'primarily a *story* and our strong interest in it is of the same sort as that

---

[238] Windt (2015), 333–338.
[239] Kuzmičová (2013), 107.
[240] Kuzmičová (2013), 108.
[241] Kuzmičová (2013), 113.
[242] Kuzmičová (2013), 116. For empirical evidence, see Speer et al. (2009) and Taylor et al. (2008).
[243] Willems and Jacobs (2016), n. pag.
[244] Sartre (1972 [1940]), 195.

of the naive reader in a novel. It is lived as a fiction and it is only in considering it as a fiction which happens as such that we can understand the sort of reaction it arouses in the sleeper'.[245] While being immersed in the fictional world of the dream/story, the dreamer's/reader's consciousness temporarily and unquestioningly accepts its reality, despite the fact that it lacks a spatiotemporal existence outside the imaginary realm.[246] As Sartre claims, in order for this to happen, the dreamer needs to merge with one of the dream characters and become a self in the fictional dreamworld. Here, Sartre detects a difference between dreamer and reader. In order to be gripped by a story, the reader usually identifies with one or more characters, often the first-person narrator, developing feelings of sympathy and empathy in view of their fictional destinies. According to Sartre, *complete* identification between reader and character can never occur, though, because—unlike dreaming—a literary work per se establishes aesthetic distance and allows for the possibility of reflective consciousness. However, Sartre's assumption that a dreamer necessarily lacks such reflective consciousness is contradicted by numerous dream reports in which dreamers critically assess the dreamworld or take on the role of observer of, rather than participant in, the dream plot. Moreover, while it is nevertheless true that the majority of dreams seem to involve an autobiographical sense of self, I would still argue that what Oatley refers to as the reader's 'empathetic identification' comes very close to our quasi-autobiographical experience in the dream state. As Oatley points out: 'Empathetic identification occurs when we insert the character's goals, plans, or actions, into our own planning processor, and we come to feel in ourselves the emotions that occur with the results of actions that we perform mentally as if in the place of character'.[247] Something similar occurs in the dream state, in which our dream-self is often lifted out of our immediate real-life contexts so as to experience imaginary dangers, relationships and crises. As we will see below, in some dreams, the dream-self even adopts a fictional identity that seems completely unrelated to the dreamer's

---

[245] Sartre (1972 [1940]), 205.
[246] See Sartre (1972 [1940]), 197.
[247] Oatley (2011), 116.

waking self. Such dreams testify to the indeterminacy and unstableness of the dream-self that is not necessarily identical with the dreamer's waking self. As Windt perceptively puts it:

> Perhaps dreams of being someone other than oneself—of occupying a body other than one's own, of being an animal, a different person, or even just a younger version of oneself—arise from a vague sense of *not* being quite one's waking self, of some passing awareness of a discrepancy from the way one habitually experiences one's body.[248]

As Sartre further argues, dream immersion is inevitably deeper than readerly immersion because, even though the reader may temporarily be drawn into the world of the novel and live through the protagonist's adventures as though they were his own, briefly glancing up from the letters on the page reestablishes a sense of his or her own identity and existence in the 'real' world.[249] In the 'imaginary world of the dream', on the other hand,

> in which one must be unreal if one is to enter it, an unreal me represents me, suffers, is in danger, even risks an unreal death which will put an end at once to me and to the world that surrounds me. [...] Now this condition of trance which cannot be completely realized in the reader (and which interferes with the aesthetic appreciation of the book) is just what realizes itself in the dream. Once an unreal self occurs in the fascinating world of the dream the imaginary world is at once closed; it is no longer an *imaginary spectacle* which is *before* me because of the fact that I am viewing it: now I am represented in it, I am 'in danger' in it, I have my place in it and it closes in on me.[250]

According to Sartre, then, the imaginary status of both dream-self and dream-perspective is unique and can never be approximated by readerly fictional immersion. Sartre demonstrates this by referring to the example of a dream that starts out as an observation of impersonal scenes (occa-

---

[248] Windt (2015), 330.
[249] See Sartre (1972 [1940]), 200.
[250] Sartre (1972 [1940]), 200–201.

sionally in such cases the dreamer at first believes that he or she is *reading* the story of the dream) until the imaginary person dreamed about merges with the dream-self. Similarly, the following intriguing dream report by Mary Arnold-Forster illustrates this process, while also testifying to its unstableness:

> I was sitting in an arm-chair turning over the leaves of a largish book. [...] I turned over the pages and saw that it contained three stories—'All rather morbid subjects,' I thought—and as I read on my dream changed and I became one of the characters in the first story. It was about a husband and a wife and was rather a prosy narrative, but I remember little of the events of it or of the part I played in it, for I thought it dull, and in my capacity as reader I turned over the pages to read the second story. This was concerned with a murder—a murder that had taken place before the story opened. The man who had committed it was convinced, for reasons that seemed to him wholly adequate, that he was guiltless, and merited no blame for what he had done. I slipped then and there into the person of this man. I remember passionately justifying to myself and to God the righteousness of the act that I had committed. [...] It was all intensely real to me. I remembered the murderer's haunted journey described in *Oliver Twist*. 'People who write about a murderer's mind can know very little about it,' I thought. Again I turned over a page—'Oh, but these stories are very morbid,' I was saying when I woke.[251]

This unusual dream about readerly immersion and identification demonstrates the dreamer's flexibility as she slips into the role of various dream/story characters, even those alien to her waking self (such as the murderer), to the point of completely identifying with their fictional identities and fates. It is interesting that the dreamer throughout maintains her curious double perspective of reader *and* story character, at once detached and emotionally involved. The murderer whose position she adopts and defends reminds her of an actual character in *Oliver Twist*, which further illustrates the permeable boundaries between waking and dreaming imagination; however, her identification with the character of the murderer runs deeper; *her dream-self* committed the act and experiences 'the

---

[251] Arnold-Forster, *Studies in Dreams*, 42.

murderer's mind' in such an intense way that fictional descriptions such as Dickens' seem to her shallow and contrived.

Another example is provided by S.T. Coleridge, who coined the term *dreamatis personae* to indicate that his dreams comprised a vast array of dream characters ranging from friends and daytime acquaintances to historical, fantastical or fictional characters.[252] While his dream-self would sometimes adopt the role of observer or spectator, emotionally detached from the entanglements of his dream-cast, at other times it would merge with one or even several of these *dreamatis personae* and fully identify with them. This is illustrated by the following dream report recorded in a diary entry from 1803:

> Nov. 10th, ½ past 2 o'clock, Morning. Awoke after long struggles & with faint screaming from a persecuting Dream. The Tale of the Dream began in two *Images*—in two Sons of a Nobleman, desperately fond of shooting—brought out by the Footman to resign their Property, & to be made believe that they had none/they were far too cunning for that/as they struggled & resisted their cruel Wrongers, & my Interest for them, I suppose, increased, I became they—the duality vanished—Boyer & Christ's Hospital became concerned—yet still the former Story was kept up—& I was conjuring him, as he met me in the Streets, to have pity on a Nobleman's Orphan [...].[253]

In this dream, Coleridge starts out as passive observer. However, with 'growing interest', he not only merges with the 'two Sons of a Nobleman' ('I became they—the duality vanished'), but the locale of the dream is transformed from an indefinite space into a biographically more resonant environment involving places (Christ's Hospital) and characters (Reverend James Boyer, the school's headmaster) familiar to Coleridge from his childhood.

The formerly 'representative' relationship between dreamer and dream thus turns into what Sartre describes as 'a relationship of *emanation*'.[254] The dreamer can only enter the imaginary and hence

---

[252] See Ford (1998), 36–37.
[253] Coleridge, *Notebooks*, vol. 1, 1649.
[254] Sartre (1972 [1940]), 201, original italics.

non-existent world of the dream by identifying 'with one of the objects of that world', by 'being invaded by the belief that such an imaginary object, which already possesses his being-in-the-unreal-world, is himself: and at the same time he can produce this object and the belief that it is he'.[255] This gives rise to the dreamer's unique perspective that, if anything, resembles more the author's than the reader's fictional immersion, namely, in Sartre's words, 'that curious trait of the dream when everything is seen and known from both a superior point of view, which is that of the sleeper representing a world to himself, and from a relative and limited point of view, which is that of the imaginary me plunged into the world'.[256] Here, Katherine Mansfield's account of how she dreamed her short story 'Sun and Moon' may serve as an example. In the letter to a friend, she describes her dream experience as follows: 'I didn't dream that I read it. No, I was in it, part of it, and it played round invisible me. But the hero is no more than 5. In my dream I saw a supper table with the eyes of 5. It was awfully queer—especially a plate of half-melted ice-cream…'.[257] Even though Mansfield's dream-self was 'invisible' she felt that she had a part in the story and her perspective was clearly that of a five-year-old boy. It is precisely this dream-inherent uniqueness of a double perspective that makes Sartre conclude that 'a dream could in no way be represented in the world of perception'.[258] Again, I do not concur with Sartre's absolute stance, not least of all because his binary model fails to accommodate in-between states such as lucid dreaming, hypnagogia or waking trance. What is more, a reader immersed in a novel told from an omniscient narrative perspective may well experience a similar double perspective, identifying with one of the characters and in this regard sharing their limited perspective, while at the same time partaking of the omniscient narrator's superior knowledge and point of view. That said, it is surely the

---

[255] Sartre (1972 [1940]), 202.
[256] Sartre (1972 [1940]), 202.
[257] Mansfield, *Letters*, 61.
[258] Sartre (1972 [1940]), 202. Similar claims have been made for the reader's immersion in a narrative told from an omniscient point of view. As Brosch (2013) suggests, one could argue that 'omniscient narratives offer readers an unusually privileged vision impossible outside the realm of fiction' (172). It is, however, a perspective at least occasionally achieved in the dream state.

case that dream immersion as experienced, for instance, during REM sleep constitutes the most extreme or 'pure' form of imaginative immersion possible, which can only be approximated but never *fully* realized in an aesthetic experience like reading. The difference, however, seems to be in degree rather than in kind.

Ultimately, both the fictional text and the dream can carry us into imaginary worlds of such transformative power that both have been compared to temporary states of possession or madness. While the following quote by Iser refers to the reader's momentary self-abandonment to the imaginary world of the novel, it equally evokes the dreamer's 'being lifted out of time' into a dream temporally liberating him from his real-life existence:

> In thinking alien thoughts, the subject has to make himself present to the text, and so leave behind that which has hitherto made him what he is. [...] 'Presentness' means being lifted out of time—the past is without influence, and the future is unimaginable. A present that has slipped out of its temporal context takes on the character of an event for the person caught up in it. But to be truly caught up in such a present involves forgetting oneself. And from this condition derives the impression readers sometimes have of experiencing a transformation in reading. Such an impression is long established and well documented. In the early days of the novel, during the seventeenth century, such reading was regarded as a form of madness, because it meant becoming someone else. Two hundred years later, Henry James described the same transformation as the wonderful experience of having lived another life for a while.[259]

However, it is important to note that even in the eighteenth and nineteenth centuries, there was an increasing sense that novel reading was what Terry Castle describes as a 'phantasmagorical process', involving fears that 'excessive reading—and especially reading books of a romantic or visionary nature—could send one into morbid hallucinatory states'.[260] One of the numerous literary examples illustrative of this belief are the

---

[259] Iser (1980), 156.
[260] Castle (1988), 56.

apparitions occurring to the romance-reading narrator of James' *The Turn of the Screw* as mentioned earlier in this chapter.

This equation of fictional immersion with madness brings to mind the controversy over whether dreams are delusional or imaginative experiences and aptly illustrates the way in which dreaming and fictional immersion differ in degree rather than in kind. It also touches upon the question of belief and emotional identification, in short 'the paradox of fiction', that is the puzzle why, as readers, we should emotionally respond to as well as identify and empathize with characters of whose purely fictional status and nonexistence we are perfectly aware. As James Dawes points out:

> Philosophers have tried to resolve this paradox in three ways [...]: first, and most familiarly, by arguing that the belief-requirement of emotions is not violated in my fictional experience; second, by arguing that emotions do not have belief-requirements; and third, by arguing that my self-described feeling [...] is not in fact an emotion.[261]

In the following, I will briefly review and assess these models as well as their respective implications for the view of dreaming as imaginative experience.

The question of whether belief is necessary to trigger emotion is relevant also to the question if dreams are fictions or delusions. Some researchers, such as Hobson, have argued that in the dream state we are deluded and believe in the dream's reality. Here, he finds an early predecessor in Erasmus Darwin (1731–1802), who expressed similar ideas in *The Botanic Garden* (1789):

> [W]e are perfectly deceived in our dreams: and that even in our waking reveries, we are so much absorbed in the contemplation of what passes in our imaginations, that for a while we do not attend to the lapse of time or to our own locality; and thus suffer a similar kind of deception, as in our dreams. That is, we believe things present before our eyes, which are not so.[262]

---

[261] Dawes (2004), 447.
[262] Erasmus Darwin quoted in Ford (1998), 23.

In contrast, S.T. Coleridge argued that rather than *believing* in the reality of dream occurrences or fictional events in a novel, the dreamer/reader experiences a 'suspension of disbelief', willingly so on the reader's part, involuntarily so on the dreamer's. As he notes in his *Lectures on Literature*:

> [I]t is laxly said that during Sleep we take our Dreams for Realities; but this is irreconcilable with the nature of Sleep, which consists in a suspension of the voluntary and therefore of the comparative power. […] Our state while we are dreaming differs from that in which we are in the perusal of a deeply interesting Novel in the degree rather than in the Kind.[263]

Coleridge's idea of the reader's 'willing suspension of disbelief for the moment, which constitutes poetic faith'[264] anticipates Sartre's stance that fictional immersion involves fascination rather than belief:

> The reading is a sort of fascination and when I am reading a detective story I believe in what I am reading. But this does not mean in the least that I fail to look upon the adventures of the detective as imaginary. What happens is simply that a complete world appears to me as an image by means of the lines of the book. […] And this world closes on my consciousness; I cannot free myself from it, I am fascinated by it. It is this sort of fascination without existential assumption which I call belief.[265]

This sense of absorption during the act of reading is also emphasized by Wolfgang Iser, who argues that the reader is actively involved in producing the fictional world of the novel and thus 'cannot help being affected by his own production'.[266] Describing as 'irrealization' the reader's entrance into the world of the 'non-given or the absent', Iser draws an apt analogy to the dream state by comparing the moment of putting down the book, and thus leaving the imaginary world we have helped to create, to 'a kind of "awakening"'.[267]

---

[263] Coleridge, *Lectures on Literature*, vol. 2, 266.
[264] Coleridge, *Biographia Literaria*, vol. 2, 6.
[265] Sartre (1972 [1940]), 197.
[266] Iser (1980), 140.
[267] Iser (1980), 140.

The 'paradox of fiction' has been used by philosophers such as Ichikawa to support their claim that, even though dreamers are emotionally affected by their dreams, they do *not* necessarily believe in the dream events: 'Fictions arouse emotions in us without causing belief; we seem to be happy that *p*, even though we do not believe that *p*.'[268] However, philosophers of literature hold highly controversial views on how precisely to explain the 'paradox'. Thus, for Levinson, the idea that readers willingly suspend their disbelief for the duration of their reading activity 'unacceptably depicts consumers of fiction as having both a rather tenuous grip on reality and an amazing ability to manipulate their beliefs at will'.[269] It also fails to account for the fact that emotional responses, such as a sense of sadness or grief caused by a character's death or misfortune, often linger much longer than the actual reading experience and can lastingly impact our mood. What is more, as Dawes points out with respect to the sense of fear experienced while we are being immersed in a horror movie or gothic novel: 'With frightening fictions, we never believe we are in danger, on *any* level; we *always* disbelieve. And yet, somehow we are afraid'.[270] Accordingly, another theory aiming to account for the paradox of fiction suggests that, similarly to phobias, emotions do not necessarily require belief at all: 'You do not *really* think bugs are dangerous, but when you see a bug in your basement you are nonetheless overwhelmed by fear.'[271] However, the analogy between phobias and fictional experience quickly loses its plausibility when we consider the respective reactions triggered by the two states. In the case of a phobia, one's belief that there is no real danger is contradicted by the simultaneous belief that there is: a belief that causes one to avoid the perceived threat. As Dawes reminds us, when immersing yourself in a gothic novel, however, 'you *never* believe there are any risks; and in sharper contrast, you inappropriately seek out rather than avoid threatening fictions precisely *because* of the sensations of fear they provide. In a gothic novel, fear is what you want; with a phobia, fear stops you from doing what you want'.[272]

In a more promising approach, Walsh has convincingly argued that '[i]ssues of belief and disbelief are not germane to the mind's capacity for

---

[268] Ichikawa (2009), 22.
[269] Levinson (1997), 23.
[270] Dawes (2004), 449.
[271] Dawes (2004), 449.
[272] Dawes (2004), 450.

narrative elaboration in itself, and of limited importance to the affective salience of such narratives'.[273] In fact, dream lucidity provides important evidence that fictions do not require belief to be effective: 'The fact that dreams may be lucid in varying degrees, and still be dreams, requires us to think of fictive narration as an act that can be directly owned by the creative imagination without being conflated with delusion or (self) deception.'[274] Admittedly, this realization still runs short of explaining *why* characters and events in whose existence we do not believe have the power to make us feel happy, sad or horrified. The question that needs to be addressed is whether the happiness, sadness or horror we experience while being immersed in a fictional narrative is the same kind of emotion we experience in real life or whether it is perhaps not quite as real. Proponents of the make-believe, or imaginary, solution propose that the feelings we harbour for fictional characters and situations are make-believe emotions experienced quite independent of belief. The notions of 'quasi-fear' and 'quasi-elation' produced by engagement with fictional characters and situations account for 'the absence of existential endorsement and motivational upshot vis-à-vis the fictions that are feared or embraced'.[275]

Drawing on ancient Indian theories on emotion and fiction, Patrick Colm Hogan differentiates between an 'aesthetic feeling' (or *rasa*) and the 'real' emotion: 'That aesthetic feeling is, roughly, an empathic version of an emotion or bhāva. When the hero is faced with a dragon, we do not fear the dragon, experiencing the bhāva or emotion itself, and therefore running from the theater. Rather, we fear for the hero.'[276] While these quasi-emotions or aesthetic feelings may not completely correspond to our actual real-life emotions, they need not be considered unreal or illusory. Instead, 'to classify our emotions for fictions as imaginary is to say that they are ones we *imagine* ourselves to be having, on the basis of experiences, contributory to emotion, that we are *actually* having'.[277] Perhaps one could even go further and suggest that fictions occasionally introduce their recipients to certain emotions, enabling them to rehearse

---

[273] Walsh (2010), 154.
[274] Walsh (2010), 154.
[275] Levinson (1997), 26.
[276] Hogan (2003), 81.
[277] Levinson (1997), 27.

emotional states, such as romantic love, *before* actually experiencing them in real life. Here, Gaskell's account of how Charlotte Brontë used to 'rehearse' unfamiliar situations and emotions in her daydreams and dreams before being able to write about them may be a case in point.[278] Dawes elucidates this approach by comparing the recipient's response to that of a child engaged in make-believe play: 'We shrink from the myriad horrors of *The Exorcist* just as a child shrieks when the person assigned to be Monster in the game A Monster Is Chasing Me approaches. But in neither case is anyone really afraid, and the physiological response that each would identify as fear is in fact only feigned or quasi fear.'[279]

A similar, though intensified, fictional immersion may take place in a dream in which emotions can gain a particularly strong grip on us without necessarily outlasting the dream state. As McGinn puts it:

> The basic idea is that the dream is a story—a piece of fiction—told in sensory terms (images), in which the reader becomes unusually deeply immersed. [...] The dreamer becomes so absorbed in the dream story that his responses mimic what he would think and feel if really witnessing the events in question. This notion of absorption or immersion is familiar to us in more diluted forms, as in our response to fictional works of different types—theatrical productions, films, novels, and so on. The idea, simply put, is that the attitudes we have in dreaming are just an extreme case of this.[280]

As mentioned above, the emotions experienced during the dream may gain a stronger grip on us than when we are immersed in a novel or a film. And it is certainly true that, while a dream may cause us to wake up in a cold sweat, reading a crime novel usually will not have quite such an unsettling effect. This is because in the case of novel reading, the words on the page, one's own bodily posture and other external perceptions 'constitute a kind of limit on how immersed you can become'.[281] In contrast to this, when immersed in a dream, '[t]he sole intentional objects are the objects dreamed about; your mind is wholly occupied in representing

---

[278] See Gaskell, *The Life of Charlotte Brontë*, 413.
[279] Dawes (2004), 454.
[280] McGinn (2004), 103–104.
[281] McGinn, (2004), 105.

those objects. [...] It is as if you could read a novel without having to look at marks on a page, or experience a movie without having to gaze at a screen'.[282] As McGinn argues: 'This feature of the dream marks an important distinction between dream immersion and the ordinary waking kind of fictional immersion, and enables us to see how much deeper the immersion might go in the dream case'.[283] And yet, readerly immersion can come close to the dreamer's immersion, as suggested by Rita Felski's evocative description of the reader's enchanted state: 'Literature seems akin to sorcery in its power to turn absence into presence, to summon up spectral figures out of the void, to conjure images of hallucinatory intensity and vividness, to fashion entire worlds into which the reader is swallowed up.'[284] A similar process of absorption is indicated by Peter Handke's comical description of readerly absorption: 'The reader's eyes [...] show that it is not he who is digesting the book but the book that is digesting him; little by little, he is passing into the book, until—his ears have visibly flattened—he vanishes into it and becomes all book.'[285]

Despite Handke's suggestion that the act of reading can draw the reader physically into the book, this sense of embodiment and spatiotemporal immersion is even heightened during the dream state and may also account for the comparatively stronger impact of dream emotions. In fact, the impact dream emotions such as anxiety and fear can have on waking life is well-documented.[286] This insight, however, does not necessarily contradict the idea that both dreaming and waking fictions might involve make-believe rather than real emotions. Thus, even with respect to waking fictions, the bodily reactions of make-believe emotions (such as accelerated heartbeat etc.) are all but indistinguishable from 'authentic' emotions. We can fall deeply in love with a dream character unknown to us in real life for the duration of a dream. The experience may be as intense as it is in waking life, and yet we would be hard-pressed to describe it as 'real' in the sense that our object of love is entirely fictitious and would in many cases utterly fail to attract our attention in waking life—not unlike Titania's infatuation

---

[282] McGinn, (2004), 106.
[283] McGinn (2004), 106.
[284] Felski (2008), 54.
[285] Handke, *Absence*, 53.
[286] See Nielsen (1991), Kuiken and Sikora (1993), Kuiken and Busink (1996), Blagrove, Farmer and Williams (2004).

with Bottom in Shakespeare's *A Midsummer Night's Dream*. What may happen in the dream is that we remember and imaginatively relive an emotion we have experienced in waking life and the underlying physiology of that emotion is the same as if the emotion was real. As Dawes puts it with regard to frightening fictions: 'Our fear may not be a real emotion, but the physiology of a non-incoherent quasi fear is as mystifying as the physiology of an incoherent fear'.[287] In order to account for the very real 'feel' of such 'quasi' emotions, it is useful to draw on recent neurobiological findings suggesting that 'emotions are our experience of precognitive bodily reactions to stimuli'.[288] This means that rather than serving as props in a game of make-believe, fictional (and possibly dream) characters and situations serve as 'props for presenting stimuli to trigger actions and emotions that we wish to experience or cause others to experience. [...] We can will our emotions and cognition no more effectively than we can will away the sensation of itching'.[289] Fictional emotion, then, can in part be viewed as a 'coercive corporeal reaction [...] that alters our cognition and action in the *absence* of belief'.[290] In dreams, of course, this reaction may even be heightened, not least of all because dreaming is clearly less stimulus-constrained than fictional immersion, with the dreamer experiencing a stronger sense of spatiotemporal immersion.

Keith Oatley offers yet another noteworthy solution to the much discussed 'paradox of fiction'. Firstly, readerly empathy can be explained in terms of mirroring:

> It has been found, too, that when people read words that indicate emotional expressions such as 'smile,' 'cry,' and 'frown,' they activate in themselves the facial muscles for making the corresponding expressions. Experiments of this kind indicate that recognition of an emotion in someone else, and also when we read about it in a story, or see something of emotional significance in a film, typically involves mirroring. Mirroring involves empathy. We can recognize emotion by activating our own comparable experience and expression of a similar emotion.[291]

---

[287] Dawes (2004), 454.
[288] Dawes (2004), 455.
[289] Dawes (2004), 457.
[290] Dawes (2004), 457.
[291] Oatley (2011), 113.

Secondly, the emotions a reader experiences during the reading process are not at all 'alien' emotions we temporarily adopt or imitate, but as readers we 'experience emotions mediated by memories, in [our] own personal enactments of stories. Patterns of emotional appraisal provide cues for memory: so that we can bring emotions forward in time and apply them to new contexts, so that they may be better understood and perhaps modified'.[292] In view of this, the process of identification as described by Iser in terms of living 'another life for a while' becomes possible only through the reader's own 'inner enactment'.[293] As readers, we do not simply discard our own life and identity, as it were losing ourselves to the character we identify with, but we bring our own 'personal set of schemas to which we assimilate a work of fiction, and in the personal memories, emotions, and thoughts (Ms, Es and Ts) prompted by reading'.[294] As Oatley further points out:

> The dream model when it is externalized into text [...] exists in an intermediate place, halfway between the world and the mind. When we as readers [...] take up this intermediate object we construct from it our own mental performance, based on our own mental models. We connect what goes in the model to aspects of our own selves, to our own memories, to our own concerns.[295]

Most importantly, we are emotionally involved: 'In watching a film, or indeed engaging with any fiction, we experience a flow of emotion in relation to events. It is we who put these events together, constructing them into something meaningful to ourselves, and experiencing the resulting emotions.'[296]

In this sense, the reader is not all that different from the dreamer thrown into imaginary dream realms constructed out of their own autobiographical experience, memories and emotional concerns. Rosalind Cartwright, for instance, draws our attention to the way in which dreams function to

---

[292] Oatley (2011), 123.
[293] Oatley (2011), 73.
[294] Oatley (2011), 72.
[295] Oatley (2011), 19.
[296] Oatley (2011), 112.

maintain our own self-concept by not only 'constructing models of the world we live in that allow us to anticipate events'[297] but by continuously modifying these models or schemas from experience.[298] Ultimately, the processes involved in engaging with fiction, as described by Oatley, are strikingly reminiscent of those involved in dreaming, with the one difference that, in dreaming, writer and reader fuse into one and the same consciousness. As Oatley notes: 'Fiction has been often thought of as a creation of the writer. Really, it's a joint creation of writer and reader (or viewer), the joint creation of an imaginary, but conscious, world *that has emotion* [...] *at its center*'.[299] Accordingly, it is not necessary for readers to actually *believe* in the story they are immersed in as their emotional responses are really triggered by memory processes activated by 'cues' given by the text. As Schwenger aptly puts it, 'when we put down the story we are in the position of someone who has dreamed and whose waking is disconcertingly incomplete; a fictive reality has seeped into our real body and altered its psychological metabolism. This is the common aftermath of reading'.[300]

---

[297] Cartwright (2010), 157.
[298] See Cartwright (2010), 158.
[299] Oatley (2011), 132, my italics.
[300] Schwenger (2012), 90.

4

Dreaming Fictions, Writing Dreams

The Diversity of Dreams

'Dreams differ very much in character as well as in significance; probably in origin too.'[1] This view expressed by Frederick Greenwood in 1894 foreshadows the insight shared by many dream researchers today: that there exists a 'multiplicity of dreams'[2] which requires careful study and classification. While Freud narrowed down the range of dream types to the wish-fulfilment dream, grudgingly acknowledging the anxiety dream or nightmare as acts of censorship gone wrong,[3] from the publication of his *Traumdeutung* onwards, there have always been critical voices advocating a more diverse and inclusive view on dreaming. A particularly interesting case is Mary Arnold-Forster (1861–1951), a well-read laywoman who, drawing on both her personal, often lucid, dream experience and her informed knowledge of the existing literature on dreams, couched her criticism of Freud's theory in surprisingly outspoken terms.

---

[1] Greenwood (1894), 39.
[2] See Hunt (1989).
[3] According to Freud (1962), '[a] dream without condensation, displacement, dramatization, and, above all, without wish-fulfilment, surely does not deserve the name' (208).

She maintained that 'dreams are of such infinite variety that no theory of their mechanism, even when formulated by the greatest of teachers, will adequately account for the whole of this wide field of human experience'.[4] In her book *Studies in Dreams* (1921), which is based on a careful recording of her own dreams over several years, she emphasizes the diversity of dreams:

> To class them all together into one or two categories is nearly as absurd as to do the same thing with regard to thoughts, each dream being an intensely individual operation of the mind; so that whilst some pass through strange and confused transformations, many others are as logical and consecutive as an ordinary history of travel or adventure.[5]

Arnold-Forster's book is supported by a foreword contributed by the American physician and neurologist Morton Prince (1854–1929). Welcoming Arnold-Forster's approach to the topic, Prince phrases the need to collect as many accurately recorded dreams as possible and to correlate the dream experience with what he calls 'identical phenomena occurring in certain other states of the waking mental life'. As he suggests: 'If this were done, we should be surprised to find what a great variety of forms and structure dreams have, how greatly they differ in type, and in the mental processes involved'. Ultimately, he concludes that 'there must be as many different types of dreams as there are types of organised mental systems: even the Freudian mechanisms, of which I believe I have seen examples, should occur'.[6]

Contemporary researchers largely concur that dreams are experientially diverse and that 'it would be grossly misleading to speak of dreaming as if it were a singular and uniform activity admitting of no variations or species within the boundaries of its definition'.[7] Harry T. Hunt's

---

[4] Arnold-Forster, *Studies in Dreams*, n. pag.

[5] Arnold-Forster, *Studies in Dreams*, 11. Compare also Havelock Ellis' (1911) view: '[I]t is impossible to follow Freud when he declares that all dreams fall into the group of wish-dreams. The world of psychic life during sleep is, like the waking world, rich and varied; it cannot be covered by a single formula. Freud's subtle and searching analytic genius has greatly contributed to enlarging our knowledge of this world of sleep. We may recognise the value of his contribution to the psychology of dreams while refusing to accept a premature and narrow generalisation' (174–175).

[6] Prince, Foreword, n. pag.

[7] Mavromatis (2001), 96.

approach, for instance, is based on such a 'multiplicity of dreams', whose scope he outlines as follows:

> [...] relatively mundane dreams that seem to be based on mnemic consolidations and reorganizations; Freud-type relatively fantastic, pressure-discharge dreams, often based on complex rebuslike wordplay; dreams based on somatic states and illness; dreams based on aesthetically rich metaphor; dreams based on problem-solving and deep intuition (perhaps extra-sensory?); lucid-control dreams; the varieties of nightmare; and a Jung-type archetypal-mythological form of dreaming. These forms potentially overlap, and all may have in common some background mnemic reorganization, but each also has its prototypical exemplars.[8]

It is noteworthy that the same dream types recur throughout history, even though '[w]e find in each historical era and phase of culture a shift in relative importance across a common spectrum of dream typologies'.[9] The 'natural order of dream forms'[10] as identified by Hunt ranges from the archetypal and prophetic to the medical and personal-mnemic. While in classical antiquity the most highly valued type was the prophetic dream, in recent times this dream type has been marginalized in favour of psychologically resonant dreams of a personal-mnemic nature. In light of this, Patrick McNamara's concise definition of dreams as 'visual scenarios composed of affect-laden images and simulations of events that are perceptually and thematically organized into a narrative typically concerning the self/dreamer'[11] is useful only up to a certain point. The need for an empirically informed classification of natural dream types has been repeatedly voiced, but so far the results have been tentative and isolated.[12] Clearly, further studies of the precise characteristics of various dream types are needed. In what follows I will briefly sketch some of the current approaches to dream categorization that might usefully be related to corresponding literary modes, genres and narrative techniques.

---

[8] Hunt (1989), 76.
[9] Hunt (1989), 90.
[10] Hunt (1989), 90.
[11] McNamara (2008), 83.
[12] See Hunt (1989), 97; Kuiken (1991a); and Nielsen (2010).

When empirical sleep lab researchers started to systematically collect dreams from subjects awakened from REM sleep, they came up with a rather surprising and counter-intuitive discovery: Most of the dreams reported were relatively mundane, consisting of more or less coherent episodes from everyday life that showed few of the features traditionally attributed to dreams, such as visual bizarreness or emotional intensity.[13] As Hartmann remarks:

> [T]he clinical literature, involving dreams reported in psychotherapy or psychoanalysis, etc., seems to be full of much more exciting, vivid dreams, compared to the research literature, which consists of relatively dull material. And within the research literature, the dream from laboratory awakenings seem even less exciting than the dreams reported at home (for instance 'the most recent dreams').[14]

How can this result, clearly discouraging for those researchers who view dreams as psychologically and aesthetically meaningful objects of study, be accounted for? Firstly, it seems that the vast majority of our nocturnal dreams can indeed be classified as 'generally realistic and mundane, rather than fantastic and bizarre'.[15] These dreams tend to be 'built around relatively realistic situations, and [are] surprisingly coherent, with well-formed imagery and plausible plot sequences'.[16] Our scripts for everyday situations and scenarios are run without noticeable deviations, with little sense of creativity, innovation or emotional impact. These 'mundane dreams' arguably comprise the largest group of dreams.

Mundane dreams, however, do not often find their way into the dreamer's waking consciousness and memory, unless that dreamer is awakened in the dead of night by a sleep lab worker asking her to report her otherwise forgotten dream. According to Hartmann, 'only a fraction of the dreams of a night are ever remembered, and evidence suggests that more emotionally intense dreams are better remembered'.[17] The same

---

[13] For an overview of relevant studies, see Hunt 1989.
[14] Hartmann (2010), 211.
[15] Foulkes (1990), 39.
[16] Cavallero and Foulkes (1993b), 11.
[17] Hartmann (2010), 212.

may be true for problem-solving dreams as studied by Deirdre Barrett. Drawing on anecdotal evidence, she notes that 'it may be that the most important dream insights wake us up and, therefore, are retained'.[18] Such emotionally intense and insightful dreams are part of the group of dreams that, although occurring at a statistically lower rate, have influenced traditional notions of dreaming—what Foulkes calls 'dream stereotypes'[19]— much more powerfully than mundane dreams ever could. This is because they are spontaneously recalled, especially if their impact has been strong enough to awaken the dreamer in the first place. These dreams are experienced as 'typical' in that they are 'particularly emotionally engaging, particularly unrealistic, or particularly odd in their imagery or thematic sequence'.[20] They are of interest to us precisely because of their bizarre and therefore 'dreamlike' character.

According to Owen Flanagan, dream bizarreness comprises three major elements: incongruities, uncertainties and discontinuities:

> Incongruity (I) refers to mismatches—the blue Caribbean waters viewed from the restaurant in Montreal; Socrates in a business suit. Uncertainty (U) refers to actual persons, things, and events that are not specified in a dream, one's geographical location, the person herself—maybe Beth or maybe Jane. Discontinuity (D) refers to an abnormal shift in person, place, or action—Clinton becomes Reagan: I am in New Jersey one second and I am with the same people in Paris the next.[21]

One possible way of categorizing our nocturnal dreams, then, might be according to their level of bizarreness.[22] Meier, for instance, suggests the categories 'realistic', 'fictitious' and 'fantastic':

> 'Realistic' dreams depict situations that could be taken for a credible description of a waking experience, which seem possible, probable, and without being limited to exact replications of previously experienced wak-

---

[18] Barrett (2007), 145.
[19] Foulkes (1990), 40.
[20] Foulkes (1990), 39.
[21] Flanagan (2000), 148.
[22] For such an approach in the context of German-language literature, see Kreuzer (2014).

ing events. 'Fictitious' dreams give the impression of being 'made-up' stories, introducing new elements in the dream, and combining elements from the waking experience in an unexpected manner. 'Fantastic' dreams show little resemblance to waking life situations; their script deviates in all respects from what we might expect in our waking life.[23]

These dream types can, of course, be further categorized by means of their precise deviations and bizarre elements. Empirical dream researchers have developed complex scales for measuring bizarreness in dreams. One example is the rating scale developed by Haas et al. (1988) which rates bizarreness according to formal and content elements. The category of formal elements is further subdivided into words/neologisms, syntax and plot structure, whereas the content category is subdivided into cultural deviations and deviations from natural law. Deviations from cultural norms can concern setting, characters, objects, plot, speech and emotions/perceptions/feelings; deviations from natural law can concern actions like flying or identity transformations.[24] However, if dreams are characterized merely by a sense of bizarreness, they arguably will not stay in our consciousness for long but will easily be dismissed as curiosities resulting from the mind's deficient properties during the dream state[25] or from the mind's failed attempts at world simulation.[26] It is important to remember, then, that in many cases an increased sense of dream bizarreness tends to coincide with emotional intensity, impact and insight, which turns these dreams into personally meaningful experiences and might also link them to corresponding literary genres or modes.

Bert O. States usefully suggests that different dream types may share 'certain organizational tendencies of the literary forms we refer to as dramatic, epic, and lyric'.[27] From action-packed thriller to adventure tale to imagistic poem, a great variety of literary genres may be accommodated by our nocturnal repertoire. However, 'these modes rarely occur in pure form. We might speak of lyric moments within epic or dramatic structures,

---

[23] Meier (1993), 64.
[24] See Haas et al. (1988), 239–240.
[25] See Hobson (1988), 271.
[26] See Nielsen (2010), 595.
[27] States (1993), 84.

or of confusions of form such as dramatic lyric'.[28] According to States, the most common type is the 'epic' dream, which can be described as 'episodic or picaresque', with the dreamer passing 'successively from adventure to adventure bound only by the loosest of themes or common denominators'[29] and typically involving characters, places and situations familiar from our waking lives. As States puts it, '[o]f all the fictional forms that might be said to fall into the epic class, dreams are probably closest to the soap opera, which is to say that your dreams are the continuing saga of your imaginary life'.[30] In contrast, 'dramatic' dreams, typically involving a sense of danger and tension, are 'marked by strong contingency, surprise, reversal of fortune (as Aristotle would say), and crisis'.[31] Lastly, the 'lyric' dream would be less action-centred and more image-based, with the dreamer 'momentarily [coming] to rest in an emotion made graphic by an astounding image'.[32]

These three modes occur to varying degree in the group of dreams that dream researchers and psychologists have increasingly focused on in recent years, attempting to understand the processes that turn some dreams into what Hartmann calls 'memorable or "big" dreams'[33] and what Kuiken terms 'impactful' dreams.[34] This group is comprised of dreams we remember upon awakening and tell to others not only because of their bizarreness but also because of a perceived sense of emotional intensity, significance or depth. As Kuiken puts it, '[t]he "depth" of personal understanding that dreams facilitate may be more like the "depth" that is nurtured in experiences of art. A significant dream, like aesthetic experience, may involve the expression of feelings, the facilitation of subtle recognitions, the realization of multileveled meanings'.[35] The umbrella term 'impactful', then, accommodates all dreams that continue 'to influence the dreamer's thoughts, feelings, or actions even after awakening'.[36]

---

[28] States (1993), 91.
[29] States (1993), 90.
[30] States (1993), 90.
[31] States (1993), 85.
[32] States (1993), 89.
[33] See Hartmann (2010), 212.
[34] See Kuiken (1995), 133.
[35] Kuiken (1995), 131.
[36] Kuiken (1995), 133.

In traditional terms, these would include 'nightmares, titanic dreams, retrieval dreams, archetypal dreams, prophetic dreams, reality dreams etc.'.[37] Kuiken, however, takes issue with the arbitrariness and fuzziness of these categories. As he points out:

> Unfortunately, the vocabulary and methods usually used to distinguish among dream types is rather impoverished. Some researchers identify dream types by reference to one specific, noteworthy attribute; so, there are studies of nudity dreams, flying dreams, lucid dreams, etc. This is like classifying animals according to color: precise but arbitrary. Other researchers distinguish dream types by reference to broad, vaguely conceived attributes; so nightmares can be nearly any emotionally unpleasant dream that awakens the dreamer from sleep late in the night. This is like classifying plants according to whether they grow quickly: imprecise although somewhat more suggestive of fundamental differentiating properties.[38]

Instead, based on a number of empirical classificatory studies, Kuiken has identified four major types of impactful dreams: 'anxiety dreams', 'transcendent dreams', 'existential dreams' and 'alienation dreams'. These partly correspond to and/or overlap with the more traditional types referred to by Hunt and others, but are more precisely characterized 'according to similarities among their profiles of attributes involving sensory phenomena, movement characteristics, feelings and emotions, motives and goals, and dream endings'.[39] Since the class of impactful dreams is obviously most likely to impact on, and show correspondences to, waking fictions, it is useful to focus on the types identified by Kuiken and his colleagues in some more depth.

Transcendent dreams are 'marked by feelings of ecstasy and awe, graceful and vigorous movement, magical accomplishments, and enhanced awareness of spiritual possibilities'.[40] Even though Kuiken and Busink are wary of such an equation, this class of dreams shows strong resemblances

---

[37] Kuiken and Busink (1996), 98.
[38] Kuiken and Sikora (1993), 133.
[39] Kuiken (1995), 133.
[40] Kuiken and Busink (1996), 100.

to what is known as archetypal dream (in Jungian terminology) or culture pattern dream (in anthropological terminology). Indeed, the examples gathered by Kuiken and Busink, focusing mainly on the dreamer's superhuman achievements and resulting positive emotions, are only weak versions of the visionary forms such dreams can take according to Hunt. For the purposes of this overview, it seems useful to include the rare group of dreams traditionally termed 'archetypal', which comprises 'uncanny numinous emotion, geometric and mandala-like patterns, flying, mythological/metaphysical thinking, encounters with mythological beings, monsters, or strange animals, and those transformations of character [...] characteristic of classical mythologies'.[41] Hunt stresses the visionary quality of these dreams that is very different from 'the patchwork mnemic reorganizations of ordinary dreaming'.[42] In fact, in such dreams, 'mnemic activation is deemphasized' and its 'place is taken by a process of self-referential awareness centered not on verbally mediated symbolism but on increasingly abstract cross-modal visual-kinesthetic fusions'.[43] As Hunt further notes:

> These dreams may be rare in the dream lives of most people, yet they surely occur to many as memorable exceptions. Some, like Jung and tribal shamans, seem to dream in an archetypal style characteristically. The major defining feature of these dreams, part and parcel of their uncanny-numinous quality and aesthetically rich structure, is the powerful sense of felt meaning and portent conveyed directly within the dream. [...] What stays with the dreamer is the fact of having had a powerful, nonverbal and relatively ineffable experience that 'presents' major existential life themes.[44]

States refers to this type of dream as 'lyric', arguing that, while the lyric dream can take many forms, it is mainly characterized by 'a non-narrative mode that expresses a state of mind or feeling in an orderly

---

[41] Hunt (1989), 128.
[42] Hunt (1989), 127.
[43] Hunt (1989), 131.
[44] Hunt (1989), 129.

way'.[45] Thus, while in a certain sense in dreams the self 'always speaks to and of itself',[46] in the lyric dream this autoreferentiality becomes more pronounced as there is little or no evidence of interpersonal exchange. Instead, the dreamer experiences an intense emotion, often visualized by a single strong image, such as a sublime landscape, a mandala pattern or the sensation of dream flight. Such dreams are often described by the dreamer as eliciting feelings of awe, elation, fulfilment or, occasionally, deep spiritual insight. As Kuiken and Busink note, these dreams also often 'distinctively involve journeys',[47] which might link them to mythological tales of heroic quests.

Occasionally, transcendent dreams are accompanied by dream lucidity, which Hunt likens to a state of spontaneous meditation characterized by 'the attitude of detached receptivity' as well as a 'sense of clarity, exhilaration, and openness—an experiential "sense of Being"'.[48] As Green and McCreery point out:

> In addition to the general positive emotional quality of lucid dreams and their tendency towards elation and exhilaration, some people experience a sense of convincing significance in connection with both lucid dreams and ecsomatic experiences, and may even describe them as 'more real than any previous experience.'[49]

Lucid dreams have also been described as '"highly significant" [...] "mystical" or "transcendent"'.[50] An example of a transcendent dream is provided by Gordon Globus, who describes one of his own dreams as follows: *'I am swimming out of the ocean into a rocky grotto. I gaze up, and against the dark vaulted ceiling I perceive a starry display of luxuriant, green, luminous growth, which I experience with a feeling of pleasurable awe'.*[51] This dream captures a moment of intense and overwhelming beauty resulting in, or giving visual

---

[45] States (1993), 88.
[46] States (1993), 89.
[47] Kuiken and Busink (1996), 117.
[48] Hunt (1989), 120.
[49] Green and McCreery (1999), 49.
[50] Green and McCreery (1999), 49. It should be noted that, according to Kuiken and Busink (1996), neither spirituality nor dream lucidity are linked to any specific group of impactful dreams but can occur independent of dream type (117).
[51] Globus (1987), 93.

expression to, the dreamer's *'feeling of pleasurable awe'*. In fact, disentangling the image from the emotion is as impossible as determining which comes first. Although Globus goes on to contextualize and analyse his dream in its autobiographical context, the sense of transcendence or the sublime so intensely experienced is thus difficult to pin down in language.

There are numerous literary examples that correspond to this type of dream, ranging from visionary or prophetic prose writings to poetry of the Sublime to passages in longer works that capture moments of transcendence and thereness. Virginia Woolf's 'moments of being' are a particularly good example. The term, never really defined by Woolf but illustrated with numerous examples both in her fiction and non-fiction, refers to sudden flashes of awareness and insight, to moments of fully and consciously being in the world. Although Woolf does not make this connection, they might well resemble moments of lucidity in the dream state. At the beginning of her memoir 'A Sketch of the Past', Woolf recalls one of her earliest moments of being which shares the convergence of visual intensity and radiance as described in Globus' dream report. Woolf recalls a memory of her infant self in a nursery at St. Ives, 'half asleep, half awake', of hearing the sound of the waves and of seeing them break 'behind a yellow blind, [...] and feeling, it is almost impossible that I should be here; of feeling the purest ecstasy I can conceive'.[52] This moment of an infant's 'pure ecstasy' may be difficult to reproduce in an adult's life but finds expression in a variety of states ranging from deep immersion to glimpses of meaning and connectedness, in which we sense that 'the whole world is a work of art; that we are parts of the work of art'.[53] One literary example of such a moment of being is provided in Woolf's *Between the Acts* (1941), when, towards the end of the novel, Lucy Swithin experiences an instance of transcendent insight when watching the colourful shapes of fish moving just below the water's surface: '"Ourselves," she murmured. And retrieving some glint of faith from the grey waters, hopefully, without much help from reason, she followed the fish; the speckled, streaked, and blotched; seeing in that vision beauty, power, and glory in ourselves.'[54]

---

[52] Woolf, 'A Sketch of the Past', 64–65.
[53] Woolf, 'A Sketch of the Past', 72.
[54] Woolf, *Between the Acts*, 205.

Similarly, in Katherine Mansfield's short story 'Bliss' (1920), the protagonist and focalizer Bertha Young shares precisely such a moment of being with her dinner guest Miss Fulton as they gaze at Bertha's pear tree in full bloom in the moonlight. It is hardly a coincidence that this moment is framed by references to sleep and dream. Thus, Miss Fulton's question if Bertha has a garden, which initiates the scene, is asked in a 'cool, sleepy voice'.[55] After the moment is over, there is an instance of doubt as to whether Miss Fulton really uttered the words 'Yes. Just *that*' or whether Bertha just 'dream[ed] it'.[56] Even though the moment of transcendent 'bliss' is ironically subverted at the end of the story, the experience is described as an almost mystical revelation triggered by the tree in full bloom, which Bertha turns into a symbol of her own life:

> And the two women stood side by side looking at the slender, flowering tree. Although it was so still it seemed, like the flame of a candle, to stretch up, to point, to quiver in the bright air, to grow taller and taller as they gazed—almost to touch the rim of the round, silver moon.[57]

After this shared moment of lucidity, Bertha not only feels elated but 'for the first time in her life [she] desire[s] her husband'.[58] The dreamlike moment of being has thus effected a subtle change within Bertha or has revealed to her a new insight about a hitherto hidden part of herself. Another example of a transcendent dream is Doris Lessing's dream series about a journey northward with a seal, incorporated in her novel *The Summer Before the Dark*, which will be analysed in some depth in 'Translating the "Language" of Dreams'.

The second dream type is the existential dream, which typically involves feelings of distress as well as 'the emergence of feelings the dreamer had been reluctant to acknowledge'.[59] In Kuiken and Businks's research study, dreamers described how they experienced often unsettling moments of self-awareness, including subtle transformations of feelings.

---

[55] Mansfield, 'Bliss', 102.
[56] Mansfield, 'Bliss', 102.
[57] Mansfield, 'Bliss', 102.
[58] Mansfield, 'Bliss', 103.
[59] Kuiken and Businks (1996), 100.

They, for instance, reported that 'they became aware of themselves "as if from the outside", also noting that their own actions within the dream seemed "strange and unfamiliar"'.[60] The existential dream typically shows high emotional intensity, with the range of feelings experienced including discouragement, agony, guilt, anger, and, to a lesser extent, sadness, confusion, disgust and fear.[61] Existential dreams are also characterized by remarkable sensory vividness and clarity as well as by 'affectively intense dream endings, resulting in a sense of the dream's continuing "reality" even after awakening'.[62] This type of dream mainly includes characters familiar from the dreamer's waking life, occasionally deceased friends or family members, and often revolves around themes of loss and separation.[63] In some cases, dreamers also noted the presence of 'mysteriously animated figures possessing spiritual significance'.[64] According to Kuiken, the relatively infrequent occurrence of existential dreams seems 'compensated by their considerable influence on waking thoughts and feelings'.[65] In States' typology, this type of dream might be linked to the dramatic dream, which is characterized by a sense of endangerment and tension.[66] This type of dream may be the one most commonly reflected in literature dealing with existential issues such as death, grief, loss, separation and guilt and is clearly not restricted to a particular kind of genre. However, stories of initiation and moments of epiphany may be particularly associated with this dream type. A good example might be James Joyce's short story 'Araby', a coming-of-age story in which the young protagonist experiences an epiphanic moment of disillusionment after his failed 'quest' and dreamlike, hopeful train journey to the eponymous Araby: 'Gazing up into the darkness I saw myself as a creature driven and derided by vanity: and my eyes burned with anguish and anger.'[67] Another text to be fruitfully read in terms of the existential dream might

---

[60] Kuiken and Busink (1996), 104–105.
[61] See Kuiken and Busink (1996), 103.
[62] Kuiken and Busink (1996), 105.
[63] See Kuiken and Busink (1996), 103.
[64] Kuiken and Busink (1996), 116.
[65] Kuiken (1995), 135–136.
[66] States (1993), 85.
[67] Joyce, 'Araby', 26.

be S.T. Coleridge's poem 'The Rime of the Ancient Mariner', which will be analysed in some depth in 'Translating the "Language" of Dreams'.

Though sharing some characteristics with existential dreams, anxiety dreams are marked by 'intense fear, vigorous activity, repeated avoidance of harm'[68] as well as often 'ineffectual movement'.[69] This type of dream is also characterized by the dreamer's 'relatively limited awareness of the strangeness of [their] own actions' as well as by 'affectively intense dream endings, often precipitating wakefulness, with continuing vigilance about the dream's frightening "reality"'.[70] The dreamer typically encounters hostile strangers, who elicit intense fear by threatening the dreamer's (or, occasionally, other dream characters') 'physical survival'.[71] This dream type is further characterized by 'vivid sensory impressions of environmental threats', often including 'unusual auditory phenomena', as well as by 'frequent physical metamorphoses of dream objects or figures'.[72] The anxiety dream (or nightmare) has impacted on, and corresponds to, the gothic and horror modes.[73] The fact that Henri Fuseli's painting *The Nightmare* (1781) is the stock image of anthologies of gothic and horror fictions is a case in point. Moreover, authors of these fictions from Horace Walpole to Mary Shelley to Bram Stoker have testified to having been inspired by their own nightmares. The first part of Bram Stoker's *Dracula* about Jonathan Harker's journey and sojourn in the vampire's Transylvanian castle may be a particularly good example to further illustrate the manifold generic affinities and will be analysed in some more depth in 'Translating the "Language" of Dreams'.

A fourth type of impactful dreams is the alienation dream. Although this dream type, too, shows a number of similarities with the existen-

---

[68] Kuiken and Busink (1996), 100.
[69] Kuiken and Busin (1996), 107.
[70] Kuiken and Busink (1996), 108.
[71] Kuiken and Busink (1996), 107.
[72] Kuiken and Busink (1996), 107.
[73] As Kuiken and Busink (1996) point out, the group of anxiety dreams shows strong resemblances to traditional nightmare reports, but since the term 'nightmare' is often confusingly used to describe 'any distressing dream resulting in awakening, an approach that conflates anxiety dreams with the quite different attributes (and consequences) of existential dreams' (115), it is useful to avoid the term for clarity's sake.

tial dream, alienation dreams 'expressed a narrower range of emotions',[74] with the emotion of guilt typically missing. This resulted in the dreamer's 'physical expression' of the anger experienced and 'seems consistent with these dreamers' reported lack of fear and of concern about their own mortality within the dream'.[75] What is more, the emphasis in these dreams was more strongly on 'interpersonal efficacy (as opposed to personal integrity in existential dreams)'.[76] Reported 'shifts in feeling' were mainly 'in response to somewhat changed situations'[77] but did not necessarily include the kind of deep personal insight facilitated by existential dreams. Given their relatively weak impact and comparatively narrow emotional range, this type of dream can also occasionally be difficult to tell apart from the group of mundane dreams, which is 'mainly characterized by the *absence* of many of the features that were present in the other clusters'.[78] It may also be linked to States' category of the epic dream, which is characterized by a succession of partly inconsequential episodes and settings. Arguably, the alienation dream might find its literary equivalent in the genre of absurdist fiction as exemplified by the dreamlike world of Franz Kafka's texts, whose protagonists find themselves metamorphosed into insects ('Metamorphosis'), spend all their lives waiting for permission to enter the gate of 'the Law' only to find in their final throes that the gate was intended only for them ('Before the Law') or are put on trial for a crime they have no memory of committing, whose nature is never revealed to them and for which they feel no sense of guilt accordingly (*The Trial*).[79] Kazuo Ishiguro's novel *The Unconsoled*, too, shows many traces of this type of dream and will be analysed in depth in Chap. 5.

According to Kuiken, all types of impactful dreams are characterized 'by visual discontinuities (i.e., explicit "looking", visual anomalies, and sudden shifts in location)' as well as by 'intense affect, especially at the

---

[74] Kuiken and Busink (1996), 112.
[75] Kuiken and Busink (1996), 112.
[76] Kuiken and Busink (1996), 113.
[77] Kuiken and Busink (1996), 113.
[78] Kuiken and Busink (1996), 111.
[79] For the notable absence of a sense of guilt in both Kafka's literary texts and his own dream reports, see Hall and Lind (1970), 86–88.

end of the dream' and by the dreamer's strong reality sense 'even after awakening'.[80] However, the various types also differ with respect to the precise impact they have on the dreamer. As Kuiken reports with regard to the three main types:

> Upon awakening, the 'intensity' of nightmares alerted dreamers to hints of environmental danger, the 'intensity' of transcendent dreams increased dreamers' readiness to express their spiritual inclinations; and the 'intensity' of existential dreams involved feeling transformations that somehow deepened self-perception.[81]

Impactful dreams are generally characterized by narrative discontinuities which occur not randomly but are 'meaningful transformations from more to less prototypic meanings'.[82] These occur in several forms and 'more frequently included explicit looking behaviours (e.g., looking more closely), visual intrusions (e.g., inexplicably appearing objects), and scene shifts (e.g., inexplicable changes in location)'.[83] As Kuiken notes, 'each type of impactful dream tended to present transformations in a different domain. Anxiety dreams portrayed transformations of the physical identities of external objects or characters [...]; transcendent dreams portrayed transformations in primary visuo-spatial perspective [...]; and existential dreams portrayed transformations of personal feelings'.[84] In view of these findings, the study of impactful dream types, especially in conjunction with literary genres, modes and narrative techniques as tentatively sketched in this chapter, is a promising endeavour that would deserve more attention from dream researchers and literary theorists alike. An awareness of the diversity of impactful dream types also both complicates and enriches the notion of a 'language' of dreams and its 'translation' into a literary language of dream, as will be explored in the next two sections.

---

[80] Kuiken (1995), 134.
[81] Kuiken (1995), 134–135.
[82] Kuiken (1995), 137.
[83] Kuiken (1995), 137.
[84] Kuiken (1995), 141.

The 'Language' of Dreams

This section will explore what might be called, with reservations, the 'language'[85] of dreams, focusing on the interplay of visual imagery and narrative structure in particular. According to Coleridge, writing in 1818, '[t]he Language of the Dream/Night [...] is a language of Images and Sensations'.[86] Some 150 years later, Montague Ullman echoed these reflections in his groundbreaking article 'Dreaming as Metaphor in Motion' (1969) in which he described dreaming as 'thinking in a sensory mode'[87] and emphasized the physiological conditions during sleep which force the dreamer 'into a concrete sensory mode and, hence, the need to manipulate visual presentations toward the goal of a metaphorical explication of an inner state'.[88] Cognitive researchers today largely agree that dreaming is a form of thinking under altered circumstances or, to put it differently, the form our consciousness takes in the dream state. However, from the dreamer's perspective, dreaming is not usually experienced as thinking at all. Instead, it is experienced as a very concrete physical and spatiotemporal being-in-the-world, often characterized by a strong 'reality sense'.[89] As Craig puts it, 'what encounters us while dreaming appears to us as tangibly, palpably present' and 'we are hard pressed to find a reliable basis for saying that dreaming experience is in any way less real for us while dreaming than our waking experience while awake'.[90]

---

[85] As Engel (2004) rightly points out, the dream language metaphor is not only inadequate but often serves as a strategy to annihilate the potentially disturbing otherness of the dream (cf. 108). In a similar vein, States (1987) calls the dream a kind of thinking that employs 'strategies of thought that if traced upward into language would eventuate in the master tropes. So dreams are a kind of proto-rhetoric, not yet a language' (6). The term 'dream language' is further confusing because of its possible conflation with the occurrence of speech acts in dreams. For lack of a better term, I will therefore put the term 'language' in inverted commas and will strictly use it in the sense of dream phenomenology.

[86] Coleridge, *Notebooks*, vol. 3, 4409.

[87] Ullman (1969), n. pag.

[88] Ullman (1969), n. pag. Sophie Schwartz (2004) reviews several studies confirming the uneven representation of sensory modalities in dream reports. On the basis of these, she concludes that 'dreaming is primarily a visual experience, but many dreams also have an auditory component. Tactile or motor sensations are less frequent, and dreams have almost no taste and no smell.' (59).

[89] Nielsen (1991), 234.

[90] Craig (1987), 38.

In Cavallero and Foulkes' words, 'being in a dream is like acting out a story or experiencing life itself. Until one wakes, and often even after, taken purely on its own terms and given its own premises, the dream is a momentarily and sequentially coherent universe'.[91] This 'creative transformation of inner experience in perceptible reality'[92] is, of course, in no way adequately captured by metaphorically referring to the dream as having a language or as being a form of thinking. And yet, our dream environment is *not* real; it functions according to its own rules and logic. In States' words, 'the dream stands midway between life and fiction, having some of the characteristics of both'.[93]

One of the most peculiar characteristics of dreams is their self-centredness. Not only are dreams 'consistently self-referential',[94] with the dreamer occurring in about 95 % of all REM dreams, but they are almost exclusively centred on the dreamer's personal life. As Hall notes, they 'have little or nothing to say about current events in the world of affairs', but are instead concerned with the 'whole world of the personal, the intimate, the emotional, and the conflictful'.[95] Accordingly, the dream environment

> may be invested with animistic qualities which reflect the dreamer's conceptions of the world. It may be viewed as benign, hostile, turbulent, sorrowful, lonely, or degraded depending upon the mood of the dreamer. These world-conceptions are often conveyed by the character of the dream setting. If the dreamer feels that the world presents a cold, bleak face, he may materialize this conception in the form of a cold climate and a bleak, rocky setting. A dreamer who feels that his world is one of turbulence and agitation, may dream of thunderstorms, raging seas, battles, milling crowds, and traffic jams. A feeling that the world is benign and peaceful can be scenically represented in dreams by serene natural settings.[96]

---

[91] Cavallero and Foulkes (1993b), 6.
[92] Meier (1993), 63.
[93] States (1993), 98.
[94] Kuiken (1991b), 226.
[95] Hall (1953), n. pag.
[96] Hall (1953), n. pag.

4 Dreaming Fictions, Writing Dreams

In this respect, dreams, while providing us with a seemingly real environment, are comparable to symbolically charged fictional storyworlds which 'make thoughts thinkable and feelings apprehensible by using words [...] to give, among other things, a kind of physical immediacy to the mental and emotional world'.[97] In Eva Brann's words, dreams are 'world-analogues', revealing 'not the speaker's psyche directly but the world as invested by the dreamer's feelings'.[98]

During REM sleep the brain areas responsible for the creation of visual images and emotions are hyper-activated. It is therefore hardly surprising that the 'language' of REM dreams in particular is often emotionally charged, strikingly visual and physically immediate. In order to capture the difference between the language of waking thought and that of dreaming, Rosalind Cartwright resorts to the familiar but apt shorthand of 'speak[ing] prose while awake and poetry in sleep'.[99] This is most obviously the case in 'memorable or "big" dreams'[100] but visible in other more common dream types as well. Based on this insight, Ernest Hartmann has advanced an influential hypothesis aimed at 'relating the dream imagery to the dreamer's underlying emotion'.[101] Studying dreams occurring in times of 'emotional arousal, or heightened emotion: for instance after trauma, at very stressful times, at times of loss',[102] Hartmann and his team arrived at substantial findings about the interconnectedness between dream imagery (especially what he terms the 'central image' of a dream) and the dreamers' underlying emotional concerns. According to his model, 'the central imagery of the dream seems to be picturing, very clearly, though metaphorically, the emotions of the dreamer'.[103] This is best illustrated by the paradigmatic 'tidal wave dream', in which the dreamer, traumatized by an event, experiences his or her sense of helplessness in metaphorical terms: being swept away by a powerful tidal wave. In line with these

---

[97] Alvarez, *Night*, 174.
[98] Brann (1991), 347.
[99] Cartwright (2010), 157.
[100] Hartmann (2010), 198.
[101] Hartmann (2010), 197.
[102] Hartmann (2010), 200.
[103] Hartmann (2010), 202.

findings, Hartmann maintains that there is a 'hierarchy of dreams based on their powerful imagery':

> This hierarchy of image intensity and underlying emotional power is also relevant to the 'meaningfulness' of dreams. Someone examining a collection of lab-awakening dreams, or a collection of 'most recent dreams' from unknown dreamers, may initially come to the conclusion that dreams are random nonsense. However, no one looking at a powerful dream, such as the 'tidal wave' dream, knowing it came from a man whose house had recently burned down, would be likely to call the dream random nonsense. Such a dream is obviously meaningful in relation to the underlying emotion.[104]

Hartmann's example refers to the most impactful and emotionally intense type of the posttraumatic dream, but similar metaphorical contextualization of emotional concerns is visible in other dream types as well. Accordingly, cognitive researchers have suggested that 'some of the unusual and not immediately understandable features of dreams may be the product of figurative thinking—conceptual metaphors, metonymies, ironies, and conceptual blends'.[105] Dreams, in this view, are the product of 'emotional thinking'.[106] Since emotions are often conceptualized in spatial terms, it seems likely that so-called typical dreams such as dreams of flying, falling or nudity in public, which almost everyone experiences at some point in their lives, are shaped by primary metaphors such as 'happiness is up' or 'embarrassment is exposure'. This notion goes back to George Lakoff and Mark Johnson's theory of metaphor according to which even the most abstract concepts are ordered by a complex, unconscious system of conceptual metaphors based on our physical positioning in space and time.[107] Typical flying dreams, for instance,

> may be instances of the primary metaphor 'Happiness is Up', as found in such expressions as 'high as a kite', 'walking on air', and 'floating on cloud nine'. This speculation also fits with the fact that people sometimes become

---

[104] Hartmann (2010), 212.
[105] Domhoff (2003), 33.
[106] States (1993), 79.
[107] See Lakoff and Johnson (1980) and Lakoff and Johnson (1998).

apprehensive about falling during their positive flying dreams, just as people worry that they may 'crash' or 'have the air let out of their balloon' when they are too elated in waking life.[108]

While this model was originally established in the context of waking consciousness, Lakoff has convincingly shown that dreams are likewise shaped by an underlying system of conceptual metaphors. As he argues, 'most thought is unconscious and most thought makes use of conceptual metaphor. Dreams are also a form of unconscious thought that makes use of conceptual metaphor', expressing 'desires, fears, solutions to problems, fantasies, and so on', in accordance with 'the general metaphors used by the dreamer'.[109] Lakoff's model radically modifies Freud's exclusive concern with tabooed metaphors of repressed meanings in dreams. Without denying that such tabooed metaphors can occur in dreams and be usefully analysed in therapy, he argues that everyday conventional metaphors as studied by cognitive linguists are at least equally important for a comprehensive understanding of dreams.[110] This view ties in with Rycroft's assessment that the 'imagination is a normal, universal function or faculty, [...] dreaming is its sleeping form, and [...], if people have neurotic conflicts, these will manifest themselves in their dreams and their waking imaginative products'.[111]

Lakoff, then, suggests a revised notion of the unconscious in terms of conceptual systems, 'the largely unconscious systems of thought in terms of which we think and on which ordinary everyday language is based'.[112] These conceptual systems facilitate 'ontological mapping

---

[108] Domhoff (2001b), n. pag.
[109] Lakoff (2001), 274.
[110] See Lakoff (2001), 284.
[111] Rycroft (1979), 39.
[112] Lakoff (2001), 272. In doing so, he clarifies the way the term 'unconscious' is used in cognitive science as opposed to Freudian usage: 'Freud used the term to mean thoughts that were repressed but might in some cases be brought to consciousness. But the term "unconscious" is used very differently in the cognitive sciences. Most of the kinds of thought discussed in the cognitive sciences operate like the rules of grammar and phonology, below a level that we could possibly have conscious access or control over. [...] The system of metaphors, although unconscious, is not "repressed"—just as the system of grammatical and phonological rules that structure one's language is unconscious but not repressed. The unconscious discovered by cognitive science is just not like the Freudian unconscious' (8–9).

across conceptual domains'.[113] Using the conceptual metaphor 'love is a journey' as an example, Lakoff explains that this metaphor refers to more than just a linguistic expression. Rather, the term 'metaphor' here is used as 'a mnemonic for a set of ontological correspondences that characterize a mapping'.[114] It is thanks to this 'mapping' that we can meaningfully refer to love relationships in terms of journeys, expressing abstract truths in concrete terms grounded in physical experience. This includes not only poetic metaphors but ordinary linguistic expressions such as 'The relationship isn't going anywhere', 'We're at a crossroads. We may have to go our separate ways', 'The marriage is on the rocks' etc.[115] Metaphor, then, is deeply embedded in our everyday thinking and language usage. As such, it is what our 'unconscious' thinking during the dream state rests on as well. Based on this insight, Lakoff proposes the following hypothesis:

> The metaphor system plays a generative role in dreaming—mediating between the meaning of the dream to the dreamer and what is seen, heard, and otherwise experienced dynamically in the act of dreaming. Given a meaning to be expressed, the metaphor system provides a means of expressing it concretely—in ways that can be seen and heard. [...] The dreamer may well, of course, not be aware, upon waking, of the meaning of the dream since he did not consciously direct the choice of dream imagery to metaphorically express the meaning of the dream.[116]

To Lakoff, 'our metaphor system might be seen as part of a "grammar of the unconscious"—a set of fixed, general principles that permit an open-ended range of possible dreams that are constructed dynamically in accordance with fixed principles'.[117]

---

[113] Lakoff (2001), 268.
[114] Lakoff (2001), 266.
[115] See Lakoff (2001), 266.
[116] Lakoff (2001), 273.
[117] Lakoff (2001), 275.

It is interesting to note that Lakoff's concept of conceptual metaphor was in many ways preceded by Frances Power Cobbes' (1822–1904) theory of a 'mythmaking instinct' which she saw at work both in our dreams and in the creation of myth. As formulated by the Victorian journalist:

> At the very least half our dreams (unless I greatly err) are nothing else than myths formed by unconscious cerebration on the same approved principles, whereby Greece and India and Scandinavia gave to us the stories which we were once pleased to set apart as 'mythology' proper. Have we not here, then, evidence that there is a real law of the human mind causing us constantly to compose ingenious fables explanatory of the phenomena around us—a law which only sinks to abeyance in the waking hours of persons in whom the reason has been highly cultivated, but which resumes its sway even over their well-tutored brains when they sleep.[118]

This insight, which is of vital importance to a study of intersections between dreaming and waking fictions, is echoed by Lakoff more than 100 years later, when he writes that 'because of the large range of possibilities permitted by the metaphor system, one person's dreams can have powerful meanings for other people. Other people's dreams hold for us the same fascination as myth and literature, the same possibility for finding meaning in our lives'.[119]

As Domhoff has noted, more complex dreams may make use of 'conceptual blends that often start with basic conceptual metaphors and then are elaborated into highly novel thoughts'.[120] What is more, '[t]he possibility that some dreams are based on figurative thinking provides a way for a neurocognitive theory of dreams to incorporate the idea that past experiences are sometimes used as personal metaphors to express current conflicts that have similar emotions and feelings at their core'.[121]

---

[118] Cobbe (1871), 338. For an in-depth discussion of Francis Power Cobbes' influential theory, see Groth and Lusty (2013), 43–49.
[119] Lakoff (2001), 275.
[120] Domhoff (2001b), n. pag.
[121] Domhoff (2001b), n. pag. As Domhoff (2001b) points out, a focus on metaphorical implications of dreams without thematic content analysis could easily be misleading because 'many resem-

Domhoff also notes that Lakoff's model explains the appeal C.G. Jung's theory of the collective unconscious holds for many people despite its scientifically refuted assumptions that archetypes can be 'inherited'. As he claims: 'In fact, all of the "functional" or "subjective" symbols said by Jungians to represent the psyche, or aspects of it, can be linked to one or more of several conceptual metaphors'.[122] For instance, Jung's idea that houses in dreams represent the human psyche ties in with the conceptual metaphor 'The mind is a container'. In this view, 'Jungian dream theory boils down to the idea that dreams can be understood in terms of waking conceptual metaphors'.[123]

Dreams, however, do not solely consist of metaphors. On the contrary, recent empirical findings have corroborated the intuitive sense that dreams are stories, albeit at times rather inconclusive ones. As Kuiken points out, 'dreams, especially REM dreams, typically have an episodic structure in which dream events initiate dream actions and in which those actions cause certain dream consequences'.[124] However, early attempts by cognitive scientists such as Foulkes to subject dream narratives to a 'story grammar', regardless of semantic elements, are arguably doomed to failure. As Hunt points out: 'It is not just that a story worth telling includes the unexpected, as do the more interesting dreams; ordinary language use is also the wrong model because it misses the way dreaming resembles a phase of creative imagination'.[125] John Barth corroborates this insight from a writer's perspective:

> All dreams, even humdrum dreams, are somewhat out of the ordinary, but give me the surprising twist or the sensation I remember when I don't remember the plot but I remember the odor. [...] If there is significance, not deep psychological or symbolic significance but a kind of narrative

---

blance metaphors and most conceptual blends are likely to be unique to the dreamer. In addition, several different primary metaphors use the same source domain, such as "vertical orientation", so contextual analysis would be necessary to decide among such possibilities as "Happy is Up", "More is Up", and "Control is Up" (Lakoff and Johnson, 1999, pp. 50–53)' (n. pag.).

[122] Domhoff (2003), 145.
[123] Domhoff (2003), 147.
[124] Kuiken (1991b), 227.
[125] Hunt (1989), 165.

imaginative significance, it would reside in that kind of arresting momentary vividness or incongruity.[126]

To understand the narrative structure of dreams, cognitive psychologists like Kuiken have resorted to contemporary theories of memory, and script theory in particular, which 'suggests that people categorize events in their lives according to resemblances between the ordered sequence of actions in those events'.[127] The various script categories according to which the scripts are filed in our memory registers are determined by 'affect associated with goal conditions' so that '[t]he cognitive structures organizing personally significant memories may be called affective scripts'.[128] It is likely that '[i]f an affective script is activated by presleep events with the goal properties and affective qualities that identify the script, and, if that script remains activated during sleep, script instantiating memories will be combined to form the dream'.[129] The novelty of the dream results from the fact that 'elements from a specific remembered event' are combined 'with probable elements inferred from script knowledge'.[130] Ultimately, then, Kuiken's approach suggests that

> dreams combine elements from recent and remote personally significant memories, that dreaming is the implicit comparison of presleep memories with exemplary instances of a class of such memories, and that dreaming influences the waking availability of presleep events which match exemplary instances of such memory classes.[131]

This might account for the typically high level of bizarreness in emotionally intense impactful dreams in which elements from affective scripts are recombined with elements from newly experienced situations which, in turn, activate similar emotionally charged memories. The effect of such

---

[126] Epel, *Writers Dreaming*, 52–53.
[127] Kuiken (1991b), 228.
[128] Kuiken (1991b), 229.
[129] Kuiken (1991b), 232.
[130] Kuiken (1991b), 230. As Kuiken suggests, the processes presumably at work here bear strong resemblances to the dream work mechanisms Freud called condensation and displacement.
[131] Kuiken (1991b), 240–241.

'mnemic superimposition'[132] may well be described as discontinuous, distorted or bizarre, since the emotional connection is not always obvious at first glance. It is precisely this element, however, which turns a mundane dream into an emotionally impactful and aesthetically as well as psychologically remarkable experience.

In a similar vein, Hunt, too, emphasizes the necessary interplay between narrative and imagery in the dream formation process. Most dreams, according to Hunt, are not genuine stories in Ricoeur's sense of the term, including narrative structure, temporal organization and point of view, but instead they 'remain truncated, mundane, and inconclusive, lived out in immediate action sequences, and lack even a hint of narrative voice'.[133] However, in some cases, especially those that Hunt calls 'imaginative-intuitive' dream types, dreaming 'comes closer and closer to Ricoeur's sense of story as an ur-organizational principle of the human mind. It is as though dreams (like lives?) are *trying* to become stories'.[134] Drawing on Ricoeur's notion that a genuine story includes surprising situations and turning points to hold our attention, Hunt suggests that in dreams this element of surprise is achieved by the predominantly visual element of dream bizarreness. According to his argument, 'it is just these image-based transformations of experience that introduce the unexpected into the dream narrative and push the dreamer toward some response (whether during the ongoing dream or upon awakening)'.[135] According to Hunt, then, 'unexpected visual-spatial transformations do not so much disrupt narrative continuity as provide the dramatic sense that fulfills and completes it'.[136] In this sense visual dream bizarreness, far from being randomly disruptive, can be considered 'the very fabric of dream semantics'[137] by means of which a trivial action sequence may be

---

[132] Hunt (1989), 100.
[133] Hunt (1989), 177.
[134] Hunt (1989), 177.
[135] Hunt (1989), 166. The predominance of the visual element in many dreams is further evidenced by the fact that children have visual dreams before the narrative element is introduced. Also, as Hunt (1989) points out, 'the early development of dreams in childhood (and good dream recall among adults) is correlated with visual-spatial, not verbal, abilities' (166).
[136] Hunt (1989), 166.
[137] Hunt (1989), 167.

turned into a potentially meaningful and coherent story. What is more, 'ostensibly bizarre imagery often directly conveys insights that go qualitatively beyond any previous formulation',[138] thus adding dimensions of novelty, creativity and originality to memory-based conceptions of dreams. This is most certainly the case with 'dreams associated with creative discoveries in science, art, and personal dilemmas [which] express an autonomous capacity for visual metaphor that becomes "insight" only when finally articulated'.[139]

This claim is corroborated by several experimental studies which clearly link dream bizarreness and creative imagination, so that 'what has widely been taken as most "primitive" about dreaming, its "bizarreness", turns out to express capacities related to imagination and aesthetic ability'.[140] While normative dreaming often seems to display a narrative deep structure which determines the visual surface of the dream, 'the more subjectively striking and impressive experiences associated with archetypal-titanic dreams'[141] are generally characterized by the predominance of powerful visual-spatial imagery. This imagery 'constrains the subsequent dream grammar and/or redefines the point of the grammar that precedes its intrusion'.[142] As Hunt concludes: 'We arrive then at a picture of two systems, both self-referential and creatively recombinatory expressions of the human symbolic capacity, interacting in different measures to produce both normative dreaming and its imagistically predominant variations'.[143] Ultimately, this leaves us with a model based on 'two distinct cognitive processes in dreaming: a sequentially directed narrative component and a simultaneous visual-spatial component, each of which interacts with and may "entrain" the other'.[144]

---

[138] Hunt (1989), 167.
[139] Hunt (1989), 100. In this context, Hunt (1989) refers to Kekulé's famous dream of snakes biting their tails, which made him discover the structure of benzene rings, as well as to Howe's dream of native warriors carrying spears with holes in them, which suggested to him the correct position for thread placement in the first sewing machine (see 108).
[140] Hunt (1989), 13. Hunt (1989) cites several studies all of which document the connection between high levels of dream bizarreness and creative abilities (12–13).
[141] Hunt (1989), 168.
[142] Hunt (1989), 168.
[143] Hunt (1989), 168.
[144] Hunt (1989), 172. This model is corroborated by neurophysiological findings suggesting that both the left and the right hemispheres are equally involved in generating dreams (cf. 170).

Hunt's bifocal model is particularly well-suited to the accommodation of different dream types as outlined in the previous chapter. According to this model, dreams rely on continual interaction between the narrative and the visual-spatial mode, while one or the other may dominate in different dream types:

> [N]arrative structure and visual-spatial imagery will interact variously in dream formation—each will be capable of leading and entraining the other. The dream is an imagistic experience occurring in a creature who structures its ongoing experience in the form of 'stories' to be told and understood. [...] The interaction of imagery and narrative form constitutes the story of the dream, and there is ample evidence that dream stories can be primarily determined by either dimension.[145]

Hunt's definition of bizarreness as visual-spatial imagery is extended by States with respect to plot structure. As States argues, bizarreness in dreams 'is everywhere and in everything, unquantifiable and pandemic; it is the enzyme that causes the dream image to shimmer with instability and otherness. And this level of bizarreness is precisely what does not survive in dream reports'.[146] Likewise, as mentioned in the previous chapter, Kuiken and his colleagues have found that narrative discontinuities (such as inexplicable change of location or transformation of characters) mostly occur in impactful dreams as opposed to mundane dreams. These dream narrative discontinuities are far from random but 'frequently transform narrative themes to provide non-prototypic variations on those themes', which, in turn, facilitates 'deepened self-perception'.[147] This is the case, for instance, when the anonymous hotel room the dreamer finds himself in suddenly turns into a specific hotel familiar from his childhood vacations. Like Hunt, then, Kuiken views the element of bizarreness (or narrative discontinuity) as constructive of personal meaning.

While dream images may appear bizarre, nonsensical and distorted as compared to our waking experiences, their way of capturing not just

---

[145] Hunt (1989), 160.
[146] States (1993), 39.
[147] Kuiken (1995), 137.

one incident in our lives and its emotional impact but rather a complex and condensed emotional trajectory is arguably very similar to how literary images work. States draws a useful analogy between dream images and cubistic images, explaining that the dream's business is 'to enact the emotion in its entirety as a psychic state that can only be represented cubistically—that is, as a fusion of past and present experience. Cubism is the all-at-onceness of an object; the dream is the all-at-onceness of an emotional history'.[148] When comparing the images that appear distorted and incongruous in dreams to literary images, one realizes that very similar processes may be at work. Referring to Macbeth's evocation of 'virtues' that '[w]ill plead like angels trumpet-tongued', States explains that 'the most naive of readers is double-mindedly able to deliteralize it. [...] The poetic context tames or anesthetizes the visual reality of the passage and we think of it, in our state of reflective double-mindedness, as being beautiful and densely meaningful rather than bizarre or grotesque'.[149] The dreaming mind, in contrast, lacks this 'literary competence', so that the combined metaphor/simile might be literally (and thus grotesquely) presented as actual angels with actual trumpet-shaped tongues. In such a literal metaphor, then, the 'tenor has collapsed into the vehicle and is lost', which accounts for the dreamer's retrospective sense of dream bizarreness or absurdity.[150]

Another noteworthy difference is that, unlike readers of literary texts, dreamers tend to experience dreams without a narrative voice to guide them. In that sense, dreams are 'authorless, unmediated by language, and they unfold intrepidly in a world no different from the waking world with respect to the authenticity of the experience'.[151] While readers require writerly 'instructions to world-making that will help make the simulation run and sustain itself',[152] dreamers find themselves in a virtual world both effortlessly sustained and devoid of authorial guidance. As States points out: 'Transitions or bridges between events are unnecessary in dreams

---

[148] States (1993), 102.
[149] States (1993), 25.
[150] States (1988), 134.
[151] States (1993), 29.
[152] Oatley (2011), 18.

because dreams, unlike waking fictions, require only a felt intelligibility. Unlike the reader of a story, the dreamer does not require transitions, because each new event is all-emersing—as it were, a new thrownness into a complete world'.[153] Accordingly, there is no narrator to inform the dreamer that she is now about to flash back or forward in time or that a change of scene is about to happen. This is why dream characters and settings may undergo seemingly bizarre transformations like the ones described by Mary Arnold-Forster:

> Just as a magic lantern picture fades away on the screen and another instantly takes its place, so our actual individuality changes into another, and so also does the individuality of the other actors in the dream. A. starts with me, but B. insensibly takes his place. I may not even know when the change has happened, and though the dream may work out into a coherent and rational story, the dreamer may in the course of it be two or three persons with different histories, characters and associations. The scene and surroundings of the dream may also change in the same fashion: my Wiltshire home fades into the semblance of another house, a house whose threshold I have not crossed for twenty years, and it in turn may give place to the unfamiliar rooms of a strange mansion that I have never seen.[154]

The dream presents us with such shifts and transformations because it 'cannot deal in flashbacks'.[155] The sense of bizarreness resulting from this may well

> mark the site of a transition, that is, a place where the dream is reminding itself of a related content, much as fiction might shift to a subplot. All fiction has to do to accomplish this is to offer some variation of the 'Meanwhile ...' idea, and we are smoothly transported to another part of the forest. Moreover, a fiction always knows its way back to the point of origin. But the dream has no such locution and consequently shifts in scene are considered to be violations of probability, even though the dream may be reacting to associational urgencies every bit as natural as those of fiction.[156]

---

[153] States (1993), 99.
[154] Arnold-Forster, *Studies in Dreams*, 41.
[155] States (1993), 24.
[156] States (1993), 27.

What seems bizarre in the retelling of a dream from a waking perspective may be experienced as perfectly natural while the dreamer is immersed in the actual dream experience. It is only retrospectively that the 'shifts in scene' are considered as discontinuous and thus bizarre by waking standards.

A dream report by British writer Peter Atkins may serve as an example. Atkins describes how his dream-self walks in London at night-time and 'very near Christmas', noticing without surprise how 'Oxford Street, without ever actually ceasing to *be* Oxford Street, became Leicester Square. The sidewalks outside the big cinemas were packed with people'.[157] His surprise at bumping into Buster Keaton's monochrome self ('unlike everybody and everything else, he was in black-and-white') is immediately allayed by the dream-self's realization that he 'was meant to meet him'.[158] After formally shaking hands, the dream-self succumbs to an emotional outburst, in which he hugs young Buster Keaton and informs him of all the tragic events to come in the actor's life, '[t]he divorces, the alcoholism, the collapse of his career', but also reassures him that 'his genius would be rediscovered and his works revered by generations yet to be born'.[159] After this emotionally charged scene, the actor, whose 'face remained the impassive melancholic mask of his screen persona',[160] shakes the dream-self's hand and gives him gratefully received silent directions to cross the street, which causes another change in the dream setting: 'By the time I reached the other side I was no longer on Oxford Street nor in London. It was daylight and I was on a narrow road that wound among sandhills. I knew without seeing it that somewhere behind me there was a seaside town.'[161] Here, the dream-self discovers a 'clapboard shop' full of long-wished for collectibles and thus very much in accordance with the spirit of Christmas: 'I was very excited to see it and very grateful to Buster for giving me directions. [...] This was the store whose existence I had long suspected, the store where you could find all the things the world pre-

---

[157] Royle, *The Tiger Garden*, 7.
[158] Royle, *The Tiger Garden*, 7.
[159] Royle, *The Tiger Garden*, 7.
[160] Royle, *The Tiger Garden*, 7.
[161] Royle, *The Tiger Garden*, 7.

tended didn't exist.'[162] Unfortunately, he wakes up before finding these anticipated treasures.

This dream encompasses all three elements of dream bizarreness as outlined by Flanagan: incongruity (Young 'black-and-white' Buster Keaton in a late twentieth-century London setting); uncertainty (the unknown purpose of the meeting; a seaside town of unknown location); discontinuity (sudden changes of scene, such as from a busy London Square to a small coastal town and from night to broad daylight). It also contains several other typical dream elements such as the dream-self's 'just knowing' certain things (that there is a coastal town behind him; that he was supposed to meet Buster Keaton; that the shop contains all kinds of collectibles) as well as an emotionally charged atmosphere (the dream-self is highly agitated at meeting his hero Buster Keaton, hugging him and crying as he breaks the distressing news to him; later he feels elated at discovering the dream shop including collectibles in which his idol lives on). It is not that the dream-self fails to notice the transformations of time and place during his dream, but rather there is no need to reflect upon or question them since within the dream they fulfil their necessary emotional and narrative function. Moreover, in a dream revolving around film (the cinemas on Leicester Square, Buster Keaton, the shop containing collectibles such as rare 1920s films), it is all the more fitting that jump cuts should occur abruptly and in accordance with cinematic conventions. Finally, repeated references to 'just knowing' imply an emotional coherence of dream elements that may well appear bizarre or arbitrary from a waking perspective but are perfectly comprehensible to the dreamer's intuitive knowledge.

Occasionally, the dreamer may fail to notice transformations that should appear bizarre even within the dream's conventions. Here, Ellis provides an interesting example illustrating how '[i]t sometimes happens that the dream image is slowly transformed without the dreamer realizing the transformation':

> Thus an image of a doll may take on the character of a human being. In a dream of this kind [...] I imagined that a lady of my acquaintance (whose

---

[162] Royle, *The Tiger Garden*, 8.

identity I could not recall on awakening) had taken a fancy to possess an artificial woman, constructed with cast ingenuity and at enormous expense. The skin and hair seemed real as I noted with a certain horror on observing the breasts and armpits, but in places—I noticed especially one arm—the creature was as defective as an ill-made doll. It was, however, able to walk with a little support, and, most remarkable of all, it gave intelligent answers to questions; this alone it was that caused me a certain surprise. What at the beginning of the dream had only been an artificial image was evidently becoming a real human being, and one can readily believe that such stories as that of Pygmalion's statue may have been suggested by dream experiences.[163]

While the dream experience is 'undisturbed', the dreamer tends to unquestionably accept the strangest and most bizarre occurrences such as the numerous metamorphoses characteristically undergone by dream characters and settings. However, as soon as dreams are verbally shared with others, 'they are submitted to the constraints of grammar and public speech and in the process lose their emotional base and become bizarre'.[164] As Meier notes: 'Dream content elements are considered "bizarre" if they are unlikely, improbable, or impossible in reference to the commonplace waking perspective [...] violating social, logical, or experiential standards'.[165] In fact, the concept of bizarreness is adequate only when viewed from the perspective of waking consciousness, whereas 'during dreaming, all kind of dreamed situations are usually experienced as real, as actually taking place, and not merely being "just a dream"'.[166] Therefore, as States rightly reminds us, 'where dreams are concerned, we are attaching the words *bizarre* and *distorted* to a form of mental experience that strikes us as perfectly normal, however frightening, while we are having it'.[167]

One explanation for this may be that '[a]s dreamers we have lost a crucial capacity of waking thought—reflective awareness, the capacity

---

[163] Ellis, *The World of Dreams*, 46–47.
[164] States (1994), 241.
[165] Meier (1993), 65.
[166] Meier (1993) 64.
[167] States (1993), 14.

to stand back and assess our experience as we have it'.[168] This uncritical acceptance of our dream environment has been explored in some depth by Alan Rechtschaffen, who coined the term 'single-mindedness' in order to refer to what he considered one of the most important properties of the dream: 'the strong tendency for a single train of related thoughts and images to persist over extended periods without disruption or competition from other simultaneous thoughts and images'.[169] Because of this, we tend to uncritically accept for real whatever comes our way in a dream: transformations of space, time and the dream characters inhabiting this forever shifting and changing world in which we 'rearrange the contents of the real world according to a nonhistorical, extratemporal, and subjective directive'.[170]

However, this is not to say that in dreams we are never astonished about unexpected transformations or changes. In fact, as LaBerge and DeGracia have shown experimentally, 'reflective consciousness exists in all dreams and can be measured on a continuum with "lucidity" and "non-lucidity" representing two ends of a spectrum'.[171] Taking his cue from such findings, Richard Walsh concludes:

> Metacognition can occur in all dreams, but whereas in most dreams it is articulated with reference to the dream context itself, in lucid dreams proper it includes waking contexts as well, providing for an awareness of contrasts between the two. Even the latter form of metacognition is not wholly exclusive to lucid dreams, however: a tacit awareness of such contrasts is a general feature of dream experience, being latent, for example, in the sense of strangeness that accompanies many dreams.[172]

In such cases, the dreamer usually comes up with impromptu explanations that make incongruous events appear plausible within the confines of the dream's storyworld. In retrospect, however, this reasoning according to 'dream-logic' often leads to an even heightened sense of bizarre-

---

[168] States (1993), 29.
[169] Rechtschaffen (1978), 97.
[170] States (1993), 29.
[171] LaBerge and DeGracia (2000), 269–270.
[172] Walsh (2010), 148.

ness. As Ellis points out: 'The things that happen to us in dreams [...] are a perpetual source of astonishment and argument to the dreamer. A large part of dreaming activity is concerned with the attempt to explain and reason out the phenomena we thus encounter'.[173] He illustrates this 'logic of dreams' with one of his own dreams:

> I dreamed that I was at the theatre, and that the performers were acting and dancing in a more or less, in some cases completely, nude state, but with admirable propriety and grace, and very charming effect. At first I was extremely surprised at so remarkable an innovation; but then I reflected that the beginnings of such a movement must have been long in progress on the stage unknown to me; and I proceeded to rehearse the reasons which made such a movement desirable.[174]

The dreamer does not completely lose his ability of reflection, but often critically assesses incongruous dream events in an 'on-line evaluation',[175] which can, in turn, regulate the subsequent dream events. Still, it is important to stress that 'dream thinking' differs from its waking form in that it is less complex and less enduring. As Meier points out:

> Dreamers do not constantly evaluate their on-going experience in dreams on the background of their biography, their past history, their future designs. Dreamers, rather, tend to be involved in the dream state without the critical stance they would take while awake. A constant regulatory function of self-evaluation does not seem necessary in the personal private dream world, because it does not have to be shared with others and others' conventions.[176]

It is important to note that the critical awareness which at times surfaces in the dream state does not necessarily lead the dreamer to question or doubt the global reality of the dream events. Here, an example from one of Coleridge's journal entries is illuminating. In 1802, Coleridge wrote

---

[173] Ellis, *The World of Dreams*, 61.
[174] Ellis, *The World of Dreams*, 62.
[175] Meier (1993), 63.
[176] Meier (1993), 63–64.

down the following observations: 'October 3—Night—My Dreams uncommonly illustrative of the non-existence of Surprize in sleep'.[177] One of the dreams he recorded was about Dorothy Wordsworth, 'altered in every feature, a fat, thick-limbed and rather red-haired—in short, no resemblance to her at all—and I said, if I did not *know* you to be Dorothy, I never should *suppose* it/[...] Why, says she—I have not a feature the same/and yet I was not surprised—'.[178] This dream demonstrates that it is possible to gain a level of critical awareness in dreaming without in the least questioning the global reality status of the dream. It is as though the dreamer accepts that he is immersed in an alternative, yet equally potent reality operating according to its own peculiar rules. Globus refers to this circumstance as the 'peculiar *persistence of the dream horizon*', pointing out that '[r]eflection while dreaming is not relevant to our "actual" conditions—that we are "actually" lying in bed—but to our dream conditions'.[179] Despite our occasional recognition of, and our reasoning about, incongruous dream events, then, the reality status of what Ellis aptly calls 'the pseudo-external world that is presented to sleeping consciousness'[180] is hardly ever questioned by the dreamer. The special case of lucid dreaming aside, '[d]reaming consciousness never realizes that the universe that confronts it springs from the same source as itself springs'.[181]

Translating the 'Language' of Dreams

If the dream translates our emotions, sensations and thoughts into what Bert O. States calls 'their imagistic equivalents',[182] it is the writer's task to translate these back into verbal images as well as to capture the dreamlike atmosphere in a dream's literary rendering. What the dreamer experiences in a first-hand and unmediated way must be translated into

---

[177] Coleridge, *Notebooks*, vol. 1, 1252.
[178] Coleridge, *Notebooks*, vol. 1, 1252.
[179] Globus (1987), 82.
[180] Ellis, *The World of Dreams*, 61.
[181] Ellis, *The World of Dreams*, 64.
[182] States (1987), 71.

language to induce similar experiences and emotions in the reader. In this context, Denise Levertov usefully differentiates between being taken over by the imagination in a dream as opposed to taking control of the imagination in creating art.[183] In order to turn the rough draft of a dream into a piece of writing relevant beyond the dreamer's own subjective experience, the 'author's gloss'[184] as well as authorial instruction and guidance are indispensable. It is only then that the dream text is 'more than recapitulation, [becomes] of one substance with the dream; and its power has a chance to extend beyond the limits of the artist's own life'.[185]

From the outset, however, this act of translation poses a number of problems. First of all, it needs to be clarified that the term translation, here, is not used in the Freudian psychoanalytical sense.[186] Rather than taking apart what Freud called the manifest content by 'translating' the dream symbols back into their underlying latent dream thoughts, the writerly act of translation aims to preserve and literarily convey the dream itself, that is precisely the manifest content, as experienced by the dreamer. This act of translation, then, is by no means concerned with demystifying and domesticating the otherness of the dream as would be the psychoanalyst's aim. On the contrary, its object is to *aesthetically* capture and retain this very otherness in a language arguably not its own.

Secondly, the question arises not only how but *if* the nocturnal dream experience can actually be transferred into waking consciousness, *if* oneiric 'language' can be translated into the language of waking narrative in the first place. In their introduction to *Theatre of Sleep: An Anthology of*

---

[183] See Levertov, 'Interweavings', 114.

[184] Levertov, 'Interweavings', 109.

[185] Levertov, 'Interweavings', 119.

[186] According to Freud, '[t]he dream-thoughts and the dream-content are presented to us like two versions of the same subject-matter in two different languages. Or, more properly, the dream-content seems like a transcript [Übertragung in the original] of the dream-thoughts into another mode of expression, whose characters and syntactic laws it is our business to discover by comparing the original and the translation. The dream-thoughts are immediately comprehensible, as soon as we have learnt them. The dream-content, on the other hand, is expressed as it were in a pictographic script [Brill says hieroglyphics], the characters of which have to be transposed individually into the language of the dream-thoughts' (Freud quoted in Rupprecht [1999], 76).

Literary Dreams, Guido Almansi and Claude Béguin pinpoint what they perceive to be the essential problem inherent in any attempt at capturing or recreating the dream experience:

> We know everything about dreams as they are told or written down afterwards, since by then they belong to the common world of the awake. We know nothing about dreams as they are dreamt since they belong to the dreamer's private world, with the possible exception of our own oneiric experience. And perhaps we do not even know our own dreams, since when we recount them to ourselves, or reflect upon the events of the previous night using the autonomous circuits of our memory and thought-processes, we are forced to remodel, modify and adapt our dream experience according to the narrative conventions we are familiar with. These do not necessarily coincide with the narrative conventions of sleep.[187]

According to Almansi and Béguin, then, there is no way of consciously experiencing what they term 'this sixth, oneiric sense': 'The minute we wake up our dream becomes something else; the tale of a dream that follows the laws of story-telling and the conventions of our sight, hearing, taste, smell and touch.'[188] Likewise, as Ian Hacking claims: 'All the dreams that we tell, we tell according to the genres of our time and place'.[189] In view of this, it may well be impossible to decide whether the dream experience itself is shaped by the books we read, the films we watch, the dream beliefs we harbour—or whether these cultural conventions simply shape our acts of remembering and telling. 'To tell a dream is to begin its transformation into a waking narrative',[190] writes Thelma Greenfield. And Bert O. States reminds us: '[T]he telling is not the dream.'[191] Nevertheless, one could argue that every single perception

---

[187] Almansi and Béguin (1986b), 6.
[188] Almansi and Béguin (1986b), 7.
[189] Hacking (2001), 246.
[190] Greenfield (1998), 336.
[191] States (1987), 2. In a similar vein, Engel (2004) points out: 'Schon unmittelbar nach dem Erwachen ist unsere Erinnerung höchst flüchtig, und je mehr wir sie durch bewußtes Memorieren, Erzählen oder Aufzeichnen zu stabilisieren suchen, desto mehr verfälschen wir den Traum, da Operationen wie Reflexion, Versprachlichung, Nach-Erzählung unsere Träume den Ordnungs-

4 Dreaming Fictions, Writing Dreams 169

or feeling is inevitably filtered through culturally modified media and modes of telling. There arguably is no pure, unmediated experience of the world. After all, then, the memory of the dream is all we have to go by, even though we need to be aware that this is what it is: a culturally filtered memory. As Almansi and Béguin put it:

> Where dreams are concerned the absurd distinction between natural and cultural discourse disappears because everything is culture, in the memory as well as in the verbal reproduction of the dream experience. [...] The dream of the 'natural' sleeping dreamer is entrusted to the awakened dreamer, who is *per force* a cultural being, submitted to the conventions of language and narrativity.[192]

The third problem arises from the fact that dreams are arguably our most elusive experiences and rarely find their way into our long-term memories. Mary Arnold-Forster aptly describes how, as soon as we awaken from a dream, '[a] thick mist of oblivion seems to come between us and the memory that we want to recall and literally blots it out. A sea-fog rolling in over sea and land, and obliterating every outline, is the best image of the mist of forgetfulness that nature often interposes between our dreams and our waking consciousness'.[193] In a similar vein, Nathaniel Hawthorne muses on the ephemeral of the dream experience that, upon awakening, we may just about grasp for a fleeting moment before it is irretrievably lost:

> What a singular moment is the first one, when you have hardly begun to recollect yourself, after starting from midnight slumber! By unclosing your eyes so suddenly, you seem to have surprised the personages of your dream in full convocation round your bed, and catch one broad glance at them

---

und Eindeutigkeitsregeln der Wachwelt unterwerfen. [From the very moment of awakening our recollection is highly elusive and the more we seek to stabilize it by means of conscious memorizing, narrating or recording, the more we distort the dream, since operations such as reflection, verbalization and retelling submit our dreams to the waking world's rules of order and disambiguation]' (108, my translation). And Barbara Tedlock (1991) notes: 'While dreams are private mental acts, which have never been recorded during their actual occurrence, dream accounts are public social performances taking place after the experience of dreaming' (249).

[192] Almansi and Béguin (1986b), 9.
[193] Arnold-Forster, *Studies in Dreams*, 38.

before they can flit into obscurity. Or, to vary the metaphor, you find yourself, for a single instant, wide awake in that realm of illusions, whither sleep has been the passport, and behold its ghostly inhabitants and wondrous scenery, with a perception of their strangeness, such as you never attain while the dream is undisturbed.[194]

Even if the dreamer should indeed manage to retain his memory of the dream by writing it down immediately, he can never be sure not to 'half unconsciously fill in those blanks'[195] that are missing, thereby unwittingly falsifying the actual dream experience. The process of translation thus takes place from the moment of waking and remembering the dream.

More crucially, the *essence* or the particular *feel* of the dream experience is frequently lost. Most dreamers who have experienced personally meaningful and intense dreams will be familiar with the sense of frustration caused by the impossibility of preserving their dream in written form and conveying its atmosphere and significance to others to whom the account is like 'a second-hand summary of a fiction one hasn't read'.[196] In Arnold-Forster's words: 'We have all suffered at times from having to listen to the recital of dreams, which, though of scanty interest to the hearer, doubtless still possess for the teller some of the humour and the charm that they seemed to have in the night'.[197] Likewise, Schreier Rupprecht comments on 'the surprising flatness often found in the prose of a dream report when the original dream appears to have been one of great intensity: exotic adventure, bizarre inversion of waking life realities, deep affect' and she concludes: 'On the whole, dream reports tend to be drastically deflated versions of their often powerfully expressive antecedents.'[198] Eva Brann, too, reminds us that 'dreams are dreamed and told in different worlds, whence dream-reports are infected with the hermeneutic difficulties analogous to those

---

[194] Hawthorne, 'The Haunted Mind', 186.
[195] Arnold-Forster, *Studies in Dreams*, 39.
[196] States (1993), 53.
[197] Arnold-Forster, *Studies in Dreams*, 46.
[198] Rupprecht (1999), n. pag.

that anthropological accounts have with alien cultures. The waking report may, after all, simply miss the inwardness of the dream-event'.[199] For this reason, some writers, such as Hermann Hesse, shy away from what they consider to be a futile task impossible to achieve. As Schmidt-Hannisa points out, Hesse, deeply fascinated with his own dream life, perceived an insurmountable discrepancy between his dream experience and the narrated dream. In his view, the dream reached its aesthetic fulfilment only in the process of being experienced, in a performance that could best be compared to the art form of dance, but certainly not to the written word. Trying to capture and piece together the fragmented memory traces of the dream by means of language, to him, resulted in an inevitable loss of meaning as well as in a sense of alienation from the actual experience of interiority.[200]

Other writers, however, take on the challenge of trying to come up with a language of dream, simulating for the reader that which is always already lost upon waking. While dream reports hastily scribbled down by the just awakened dreamer inevitably fail to convey the 'authentic' experience since they are of necessity based on a 'story [...] we summarize from memory', always already 'translated into non-oneiric language',[201] it is arguably the *literary* writer who can come closest to verbally rendering the sense of otherness at the heart of the dream experience: the 'utter discontinuity between the two worlds—the familiar world the waking dreamer opens his eyes to and the distorted, disoriented fantasy land of dreams, populated by strange and vivid presences, where time implodes and impossible events seem perfectly normal'.[202] At least, this is precisely what John Banville postulates in his essay 'Fiction and the Dream' (2005). This essay starts out with the story of a man whose retelling of a clearly impactful dream, 'freighted with a mysterious weight',[203] in which '[s]ome great truth has been revealed to him',[204] utterly and disappointingly fails

---

[199] Brann (1991), 342.
[200] See Schmidt-Hannisa (1998).
[201] Almansi and Béguin (1986b), 8.
[202] Alvarez, *Night*, 112–113.
[203] Banville, 'Fiction and the Dream', 21.
[204] Banville, 'Fiction and the Dream', 22.

to capture his wife's attention. Taking his cue from this story, Banville proceeds to ask:

> But what if, instead of accepting the simple fact that our most chaotic, our most exciting, our most significant dreams are nothing but boring to others, even our significant others—what if he said to his wife, *All right, I'll show you, I'll do more than show you, I'll sit down and write out the dream in such an intense and ravishing formulation that when you read it you, too, will have the dream; you, too, will find yourself wandering in the wild wood at nightfall; you, too, will hear the dream voices telling you your own most secret secrets.*[205]

While our conscious experience of the dream per se is based on memory, it is by means of literary writing that the dreamlike quality of this experience can be reawakened and recreated. What is more, even though it is unclear to what extent our narrative conventions impact our dream recall, shaping and modifying the nocturnal experience according to familiar structures and modes of thinking, 'narratizing processes are at work as the dream is created; they are not simply imposed by the linguistic constraints of the dream report'.[206] Accordingly, there are also undeniable 'compositional similarities of dreams and fictions',[207] both of which emerge from the same 'literary mind'.[208] The literary strategies at the author's disposal, then, are 'put in place not to control the dream but to evoke it in themselves and their readers'.[209] In the remainder of this chapter, without laying any claim to completeness, I will discuss some of the authorial pitfalls and strategies of creating a sense of dream in fictional narratives as well as outline three literary genres arguably most conducive to this endeavour.

Literary dreams have always been a popular tool in the author's workshop. These dreams can have various narrative functions such as foreshadowing or even prophesying future events, facilitating plot twists,

---

[205] Banville, 'Fiction and the Dream', 23, original italics.
[206] Kilroe (2000), 130.
[207] States (1994), 238.
[208] See Turner (1996).
[209] Schwenger (2012), 88.

providing insight into the characters' psyches and motives, creating psychological credibility and symbolic depth or simply reinforcing the narrative's themes. It is important to note, however, that incorporating functionalized dreams in a literary text tends to run counter to the creation of a dreamlike effect. This is because one of the effects of clearly demarcated dreams in longer works of fiction is often to provide a clear-cut line between waking and dreaming reality. The dream is remembered or narrated as a *dream*, and though it can have an impact on the plot—triggering actions or foreshadowing events—it is still strictly set apart from, and not to be confused with, the storyworld's waking reality.

To briefly illustrate this, from the plethora of examples available, let us consider Doris Lessing's *The Summer Before the Dark* (1973), which includes a dream series 'with the feel of a legend or a myth' that, by her own account, the author herself dreamed in the early 1970s:

> [...] I was carrying a seal northwards, through a difficult landscape, very dark, and cold and dangerous, full of storms of snow and ice. The sea, where I had to take the seal, was a long way ahead, and the seal was weak, and perhaps dying. [...] I waited for the final dream of the series, but there wasn't one, so I used the dreams in my novel *The Summer Before the Dark*, and gave the series a happy ending, which is what the novel required. The 'dark' of the title matched with the dark atmosphere of the dream, but the dream ended well and so the story of the novel did too. The seal was playing in a warm and sunlit sea and the cold and the dark had gone.[210]

In the novel, this dream series is used to accompany middle-aged Kate Brown's quest for her true self, gone astray after more than two decades of married life in which she fulfilled a variety of social roles such as wife, housewife, mother, neighbour and host. The novel tells the story of one long summer in which Kate goes through the process of re-defining herself in the absence of her family, her four children having fled the nest and her husband away on business. While the novel could best be described as a realist novel of ideas, in which the intelligent protagonist reflects on her life choices and future direction, the dream series lends her search a

---

[210] Royle, *The Tiger Garden*, 139.

sense of psychological depth and mythological timelessness it might otherwise lack. The dreams are freighted with symbolic significance, guiding and accompanying her search for meaning, identity and healing. In the dream series, she is travelling northward in order to save the ailing seal that clearly represents some part of herself (her soul?). Without changing direction, she miraculously leaves behind the cold and rough winter setting for what appears to be a second spring: 'Immediately in front of her there was a glimmer, like candlelight, and there all by itself in the snow, was a silvery-pink cherry tree in full bloom. Kate pushed through deep snow to the tree and pulled off a flowering twig, and held it in her frozen fingers as she walked on past the tree into the dark ahead.'[211] In Kate's final dream of the series, the snow has turned into spring grass as she reaches the ocean where the seal is finally set free and, after a last look of farewell, joins his fellow seals in play. Kate's dream-self not only realizes that '[h]er journey [is] over' but also that the sun, which she had seemed to leave behind, is now facing her: 'She looked at it, a large, light, brilliant, buoyant, tumultuous sun that seemed to sing'.[212] Kate's dream journey, replete with archetypal symbols and metaphors of renewal, culminates in this moment of transcendent beauty and insight.

While Kate's dreams both complicate and symbolically enrich her psychological journey, its symbols, characters and landscapes are firmly contained by the dreamworld, never bleeding into the storyworld's waking reality. The contours of the dream are framed by clear markers: 'Kate dreamed again about the seal. [...] She told Maureen this new stage of the dream.'[213] Or: 'That night Kate dreamed as soon as she was asleep. [...] She turned, knowing that she had finished the dream. She woke.'[214] For the purposes of this chapter, it may suffice to note that the dream series provides a clear-cut line between waking reality, including Kate's conscious memories, reflections and thoughts, and the deeper levels of her psyche that cannot be consciously reached other than through the realm of dream. While the novel employs the dream series as a structural

---

[211] Lessing, *The Summer Before the Dark*, 219.
[212] Lessing, *The Summer Before the Dark*, 230.
[213] Lessing, *The Summer Before the Dark*, 219.
[214] Lessing, *The Summer Before the Dark*, 230.

device lending depth to the protagonist's psychological journey at a critical moment in her life, the reader looks at these dreams from the outside rather than experiencing the dreamer's temporary immersion in the dream state or any confusion as to the dream's reality status.

One way of achieving a dreamlike effect, then, is to present the dream as waking reality rather than as clearly demarcated dream. As States points out: 'What is missing from most so-called dream literature is precisely the reality of the dream experience, that is, the dreamer's complete conviction in the exclusivity of the dream *Umwelt*'.[215] In the same way that the non-lucid dreamer does not tend to question the global reality of her dream environment, the story's focalizer or narrator may never seriously doubt that the storyworld and the events experienced within it are real—despite the sense of dreamlike bizarreness pervading the text. In other words, the waking fiction needs to 'imitate the single-mindedness of dreams'[216] in which 'bizarreness is the constant behavioral norm'.[217] This is not so say that a story needs to accumulate a myriad of bizarre occurrences and images in order to be experienced as dreamlike. As Meier explains, even if the dream elements typically considered bizarre such as 'strange settings, incongruent characters, objects out of place, inappropriate or impossible actions, perception deviating from normal experience [...] do not comprise a substantive amount of all the dream elements, they may color a whole dream, giving it its touch of strangeness'.[218] The opening paragraph of Edgar Allan Poe's 'The Fall of the House of Usher' (1839) illustrates what States refers to as '*literary* single-mindedness'[219]:

> During the whole of a dull, dark and soundless day in the autumn of the year, when the clouds hung oppressively low in the heavens, I had been passing alone on horseback through a singularly dreary tract of country. At length I found myself, as the shades of evening drew on, within view of the melancholy House of Usher.[220]

---

[215] States (1993), 34.
[216] States (1993), 33.
[217] States (1993), 37.
[218] Meier (1993), 65.
[219] States (1993), 36, my italics.
[220] Poe, 'The Fall of the House of Usher', 199.

This passage depicts what States calls 'a certain monochromatic quality that is the hallmark of the Poe world'[221] and that is also reflected in the monotonous rhythm of the two opening sentences as well as reinforced by the striking use of alliteration and dark assonance. The morbid mood created and reinforced by means of adjectives such as 'dull', 'dark', 'soundless', 'oppressive' and 'melancholy' is passively and unconditionally accepted by the narrator.[222] It is not broken by memories of, or hopes for, brighter days. As States notes, '*singularly* dreary suggests that days are always dreary though not quite *this* dreary'.[223] Like a dreamer, '[t]he Poe narrator creates and then inhabits a Poesque world where only Poesque things can happen. [...] Overall, there is a collusion between world and the self encountering it'.[224]

What does all this imply for the reader's reaction to the text though? According to States, the single-minded mood and perspective created in the fiction is contagious and atmospherically prepares the reader for the uncanny and incongruous events to come.[225] Just like the dreamer is immersed in the dream, the story's reader, too, is temporarily convinced that the 'touch of strangeness' pervading the text is in perfect accordance with, and an integral part of, the storyworld's waking reality. The reader's suspension of disbelief is further reinforced by means of what States calls a 'factual tone of the narrative voice'.[226] This is a quality that also characterizes many of the writings of Franz Kafka, whose stories have often been described as dreamlike. In Selma Fraiberg's words, with reference to Kafka's texts, 'a narrative which attempts to simulate the experience of dreaming or to evoke the "uncanniness" of the dream must deceive the critical and judging faculties of the ego through a prose which apparently sustains logic and belief at the same time that it affirms the delusion'.[227] Gregor Samsa in Kafka's 'Die Verwandlung [Metamorphosis]', for instance, shows little surprise at waking up to find he has been transformed into a

---

[221] States (1993), 35.
[222] See States (1993), 35.
[223] States (1993), 35.
[224] States (1993), 36.
[225] See States (1993), 36.
[226] States (1993), 34.
[227] Fraiberg (1956), 54.

4 Dreaming Fictions, Writing Dreams

giant insect. While in a less dreamlike text Gregor's sense of alienation, isolation and dehumanization might have been expressed in metaphorical terms—J. Alfred Prufrock's exclamation 'I should have been a pair of ragged claws/Scuttling across the floors of silent seas'[228] comes to mind—here the metaphor is presented in a literalized way, as an actual metamorphosis. The narrative's first sentence informs the reader about this nocturnal transformation in such a matter-of-fact way that the reader's surprise, too, is kept at bay and his readiness to believe in the 'delusion' is facilitated: 'Als Gregor Samsa eines Morgens aus unruhigen Träumen erwachte, fand er sich in seinem Bett zu einem ungeheuren Ungeziefer verwandelt [When Gregor Samsa woke from unquiet dreams one morning, he found himself transformed in his bed into a monstrous vermin]' (56, my translation). The striking lack of surprise on Gregor's part, his quiet, passive acceptance of his new insect state and his very pragmatic worries about how to be on time for work despite his clearly indisposed state all contribute to lending the story the 'literary single-mindedness' which is a characteristic feature of the Kafkaesque and can indeed best be described as dreamlike.

However, even though the reader's critical faculties may to some extent be manipulated or even numbed, I would still argue that they are not fully asleep; instead, a certain degree of aesthetic distance and critical awareness on the reader's part is always maintained. Arguably, to create a dreamlike effect, Kafka skilfully plays precisely with this tension between the narrator's uncritical acceptance vis-à-vis incongruent events and the reader's perception of this incongruence. Thus, by referring to Gregor's 'unquiet dreams' in the story's opening sentence, the narrator deliberately arouses the reader's suspicion that Gregor might still be asleep and dreaming. A few lines later, however, this possibility is categorically ruled out once and for all: 'Es war kein Traum [It was no dream]' (56, my translation). Accordingly, rather than being explained by either natural or supernatural causes, 'the initial transformation functions in a way similar to a hypothesis that is not questioned'.[229] It is precisely this sense of ontological instability that triggers a sense of dreamlikeness in the reader, who,

---

[228] Eliot, 'The Love Song of J. Alfred Prufrock', 73–74.
[229] Porter (1993), 43.

unlike Kafka's protagonist, single-mindedly trapped within his own oneiric fiction, can never be quite certain where waking reality ends and dream begins.[230] This moment of 'hesitation', achieved by a deliberate blurring of boundaries, arguably links the dreamlike mode to Todorov's definition of the 'fantastic'[231] and is at the heart of what Susanne Goumegou aptly terms 'oneiric realism'.[232]

Arguably then, in Kafka's work the dreamlike effect emerges from the tension between the narrator's single-mindedness and the reader's perception of incongruence, which in turn results in a moment of hesitation, uncertainty or disorientation on the reader's part. This is a precarious balance as the dreamlike effect would be destroyed as soon as the reader's sense of uncertainty were to turn into outright disbelief. However, as we have seen, dreamers immersed in the dream state, too, can reach varying levels of awareness, ranging from uncritical acceptance to a vague sense of surprise to a high degree of meta-awareness. In this sense, Todorov's definition of the 'fantastic' as dependent on 'that hesitation experienced by a person who knows only the laws of nature, confronting an apparently supernatural event',[233] situated between belief ('the marvellous') and disbelief ('the uncanny') and always on the verge of turning into one or the other, could be said to describe the narrator's as well as the reader's varying levels of critical awareness.

Dreams are uncanny—in Freud's definition of 'that class of the terrifying which leads back to something long known to us, once very familiar'[234]—precisely because in them we encounter figments of our own imagination as though they were real or present and creations of our own mind as though they were other. As Freud points out, in waking fictions a similarly uncanny effect can be achieved 'by effacing the distinction between imagination and reality, such as when something we have hitherto regarded as imaginary appears before us in reality'.[235]

---

[230] See Goumegou (2011), 216.
[231] Todorov (1975), 41.
[232] See Goumegou (2011), 222. For a detailed analysis of the dreamlikeness of Kafka's 'Die Verwandlung', see Kreuzer (2014), 409–437.
[233] Todorov (1975), 41.
[234] Freud (1919), 1–2.
[235] Freud (1919), 15.

The uncanny, then, is generated when encountering our 'supposedly surmounted superstitiousness'.[236] This is clearly the case in stories in which the boundaries between sleeping and waking reality are deliberately blurred or figments from dreams haunt the characters during their waking hours. However, as Freud makes clear, in order to retain an uncanny effect in fiction, it is crucial that 'the writer pretends to move in the world of common reality' so that 'everything that has an uncanny effect in reality has it in his story'.[237] A fairy tale will inevitably fail to produce such an uncanny effect, because its genre conventions rule out the necessary 'conflict of judgement whether things which have been "surmounted" and are regarded as incredible are not, after all, possible'.[238] While the supernatural is an integral part of genres like the fairy tale or the fantasy story, corresponding to what Todorov calls 'the marvelous', a supposedly realistic story in which the author skilfully 'oversteps the bounds of possibility [...] presents more opportunities for creating uncanny situations than are possible in real life'.[239]

Moments of surprise or 'hesitation' on the narrator's/focalizer's or on the reader's part, then, can occur most powerfully in texts which blur the boundaries between dreaming and waking. This effect can be achieved, for instance, by carrying elements from the dream world over into the storyworld's waking reality or by deliberately obscuring the transition from waking to dreaming within the text. In the latter case, this transition can be revealed retrospectively, for instance when the protagonist is depicted as waking up at the end of the dream/story. While it could be argued that this type of dream belongs to the category of clearly demarcated dreams, it has quite a different effect on the reader, an effect that comes close to the dreamer's awakening from a dream she has been taking for reality. Alternatively, the ambivalence between dreaming and waking can be maintained throughout the narrative without being clearly resolved. This effect may be enhanced when the narrator or focalizer is a character with 'thin boundaries'.

---

[236] Freud (1919), 18.
[237] Freud (1919), 18.
[238] Freud (1919), 18.
[239] Freud (1919), 18–19.

As Hartmann's research on his concept of 'boundaries in the mind' has shown, personality types differ with regard to their permeability of boundaries, for instance between themselves and others, waking and dreaming, past and present, thought and feeling. While most of us have a mixture of thin and thick boundaries, at the opposite ends of the spectrum we find the extreme case of people characterized by either very thick or very thin boundaries. The first case would include those personality types generally referred to as 'thick-skinned': 'people who strike us as very solid and very organized [...] well defended [...] rigid, even armored'.[240] At the other extreme of the spectrum we find 'people who are especially sensitive, open, or vulnerable. In their minds, things are relatively fluid; they experience thoughts and feelings—often many different feelings—at the same time. Such people have particularly thin boundaries'.[241] Such thin boundary types will also 'often experience states of being half-awake and half-asleep, or will become deeply immersed in daydreaming and reverie, so that sometimes the boundary between real life and fantasy may be unclear'.[242] This is, for instance, the case if a story is focalized through a young child, whose perspective allows for the simultaneous perception and acceptance of bizarreness. A child's psychological boundaries are not yet fully formed; they are thin boundaries, allowing for easier blurring of inside/outside realities, which is precisely what dreamers experience in their malleable, unstable dream environment.[243] The child's perspective also contributes to making the dreamlike effect plausible to the reader without casting serious doubt on the story's reality status. Thus, as Urs Margolin points out:

> Both science and common sense distinguish between standard and nonstandard modes of perception and resultant mental images. Nonstandard modes, resulting in a disproportionate or distorted visual image, are associated in literature with the defamiliarization effect on the reader, and are realistically motivated by the perception of an infant or small child.[244]

---

[240] Hartmann (1991b), 4.
[241] Hartmann (1991b), 4.
[242] Hartmann (2011), 89–90.
[243] See Hartmann (1991a), 120.
[244] Margolin (2003), 291.

It is important to note that, regardless of the narrator's reliability, dream narratives often disrupt and complicate categories defined against mimetic reality because dreams are themselves an unstable category; even though they are natural nightly occurrences, they can be imbued with supernatural meaning or render the dreamer vulnerable to foreign influences. A dream can be explained away as 'unreal', but it can also be understood as providing a message from another world or a door into an unknown second reality, in which case 'dreamers are only finding portals to other worlds, not creating them'.[245] Realizing that it was 'only' a dream, then, does not necessarily rule out 'fantastic' explanations or moments of hesitation. In reality dreams or false awakenings, it may be all but impossible for the dreamer to differentiate between waking and sleeping reality, resulting in an unsettling lack of certainty which can engender ontological doubt. Accordingly, it is important to note that dreamlike narratives are ideally suited to disrupting or questioning our established perception of reality, which, as Cynthia Duncan reminds us, 'is a cultural construct [...] that can vary across cultures and historical periods'.[246] A good case in point is Nathanial Hawthorne's tale 'Young Goodman Brown' (1835) in which the protagonist either dreams or perceives a Witches' Sabbath, celebrated in the nightly woods by pious local men and women including his wife Faith, an experience that will shatter his own 'faith' forever. The narrator's question at the end of the story—'Had Goodman Brown fallen asleep in the forest and only dreamed a wild dream of a witch meeting?'[247]—is ultimately irrelevant because the impact of the experience—whether real or dreamed—has shaken Goodman Brown's faith in humanity so profoundly that his life will never be the same: 'Be it so, if you will; but, alas! it was a dream of evil omen for young Goodman Brown. A stern, a sad, a darkly meditative, a distrustful, if not a desperate, man did he become from the night of that fearful dream.'[248]

---

[245] Wolf (2012), 236.
[246] Duncan (2010), 16.
[247] Hawthorne, 'Young Goodman Brown', 199.
[248] Hawthorne, 'Young Goodman Brown', 95. In this context, it is important to note that during the early modern period, in which Hawthorne's story is set, sleep was considered to be 'a state in which people's moral defenses were at their weakest and the mind most vulnerable to diabolic interference and deception' (Davies [2007], 144).

At least from Calderón's *Life Is a Dream* (1635) onward, authors have played with the ambiguity of waking and dreaming, deliberately tapping into deep-rooted ontological doubt and fears. In Lewis Carroll's *Through the Looking-Glass* (1871), Alice breaks into tears when Tweedledee and Tweedledum try to convince her that she is only a figment in the Red King's dream: '"Well, it's no use *your* talking about waking him," said Tweedledum, "when you're only one of the things in his dream. You know very well you're not real." "I *am* real!" said Alice, and began to cry.'[249] In the final chapter, after Alice has woken up from the dream, she is still not sure 'who it was that dreamed it all. [...] You see, Kitty, it *must* have been either me or the Red King. He was part of my dream, of course—but then I was part of his dream, too!'[250] Another case in point is Borges' famous story 'The Circular Ruins' (1940) which, incidentally, nods towards Carroll's dream narrative by means of its epigraph. In Borges' story, a wise old shaman dreams up a human being so real that only he, the creator, and the God named Fire know about his 'son's' dream origin. The story comes full circle when in the end the wise old man seeks death in the flames devouring his holy site only to find that the fire does not harm him: 'With relief, with humiliation, with terror, he realized that he, too, was but appearance, that another man was dreaming him.'[251]

A variation of this theme is found in Kingsley Amis' more recent short story 'Mason's Life' (1972), in which the protagonist, Mason, is approached by an excited stranger in a bar, who claims that he is experiencing a lucid dream and is trying to make contact with a potential fellow lucid dreamer. Mason takes pains to convince the stranger that neither is he immersed in his own nor a figment in another man's dream. Eventually, however, Mason's 'life' crumbles to dust when the stranger begins to blur and fade before his eyes—and Mason, in vain trying to grab the vanishing man's arm, realizes 'with difficulty' that 'the hand that had done the grabbing, his own hand [...] likewise no longer had fingers,

---

[249] Carroll, *Through the Looking-Glass*, 57.
[250] Carroll, *Through the Looking-Glass*, 136.
[251] Borges, 'The Circular Ruins', 100.

or front or back, or skin, or anything at all'.²⁵² In these stories, the age-old theme that life is a dream is taken literally and the moment of surprise and ontological doubt is created precisely by means of the reality sense characteristic of many dreams. This effect is heightened by the fact that the characters concerned are not even entrapped in their own dreams but figments in someone else's. In these deliberately short stories, then, it is not so much the blurring of boundaries or the creation of dreamlike strangeness that holds the reader's attention but the moment of shock triggered by a surprising and unexpected ending. One might perhaps argue that these stories work towards and dramatize the moment of waking rather than 'translating' the dream itself.

As I will argue in the following, some literary genres are particularly conducive to the creation of a dreamlike effect in the reader. In the remainder of this chapter, without laying any claim to completeness, I will focus on the ballad, the gothic novel and the short story as representative examples. In doing so, I will not only outline the ways in which these genres lend themselves to the creation of dreamlikeness but I will also analyse the strategies employed by individual writers to create a sense of dream in their texts. More specifically, Samuel Taylor Coleridge's ballad 'The Rime of the Ancient Mariner' (1798), the first chapter of Bram Stoker's novel *Dracula* (1897) and Katherine Mansfield's short story 'Sun and Moon' (1920) will be analysed in some depth not only in terms of their generic characteristics but also in regard to the texts' specific dreamlike features.

The Ballad: Samuel Taylor Coleridge, 'The Rime of the Ancient Mariner' (1798)

The idea of 'literary single-mindedness' is at least as old as Coleridge's *Biographia Literaria* (1817) in which the poet and philosopher puts forward his famous theory about the reader's 'suspension of disbelief for the moment, which constitutes poetic faith',²⁵³ a state of illusion akin to, but differing in degree from, the dream state. According to Coleridge,

---

²⁵² Amis, 'Mason's Life', 4.
²⁵³ Coleridge, *Biographia Literaria*, vol. 2, 6.

'[t]he poet does not require us to be awake and believe; he solicits us only to yield ourselves to a dream; and thus, too, with our eyes open, and our judgment *perdue* behind the curtain, ready to awaken us at the first motion of our will: and meantime, only not to *dis*believe'.[254] In other words, the poet aims to create a 'waking dream',[255] a dream that, though narrating improbable or even supernatural events, is still coherent enough and presented in such a way that the reader's waking judgement is not provoked. There is thus always a precarious balance between the fictional dream created and the reader's suspended judgement that may at any time shatter the dream if the illusion is not powerful and convincing enough. One way of creating and sustaining the reader's dreamlike state is by employing vivid images that are commonly shared by readers, at once universal and yet leaving room for differing personal interpretation, and not so unusual as to evoke exceeding surprise—a reaction which might easily and unduly arouse the reader's critical faculties and should thus be avoided. A further way to achieve this aim is to 'produce a trance-like state through a kind of physical rocking motion akin to a musical rhythm or chant'.[256] Coleridge employed both strategies in his arguably most famous poem 'The Rime of the Ancient Mariner'.

Highlighting the origins of poetic metre in the chanting of religious ritual, Anthony Stevens suggests that its effect on the neuronal systems of the brain might be comparable to that produced by REM sleep:

> By combining semantic meaning with an acoustic, felt rhythm, the recital of poetry brings into synchrony the activities of both left and right cerebral hemispheres and the deeper, older structures of the brain. It is likely that narrative poetry is particularly effective in bringing this about, and in this it resembles the cerebral events associated with dreaming.[257]

It is thus no coincidence that Coleridge gave this ballad the subtitle 'A Poet's Reverie'. As Patricia Adair aptly notes, the poem's 'fluid brilliance has the strange logic of a waking dream or reverie, only partly

---

[254] Coleridge, *Biographia Literaria*, vol. 2, 217–218.
[255] Coleridge, *Lectures on Literature*, vol. 2, 425.
[256] Massey (2009), 74.
[257] Stevens (1995), 155.

controlled by the conscious mind'.²⁵⁸ The ballad form with its soothing repetitions, alliterations and internal rhyme is particularly suited to the creation of such a dreamlike effect. To convey this dreamlike state to the reader, then, Coleridge employs what Daniel Robinson terms a 'prosody of dreams', using 'poetic form and metrical experimentation to explore in verse the unfathomed depths of the unconscious mind and the creative potentialities of dreaming'.²⁵⁹ More precisely, he employs the 'ancient Anglo-Saxon ballad stanza of untraceable origin but popularly revived in England', incorporating just enough 'interesting variations'²⁶⁰ to create a mesmerizing, dreamlike effect. This type of accentual non-syllabic verse provides the poet with a 'rougher, more irregular line [which] better captures the experience of dreaming in all its mystery and daemonic expression', loosening 'the unconscious experience from the more formal eighteenth-century line'.²⁶¹ However, despite this 'metrical experimentation', there is still a prevalence of regularity in the recurrence of the metre, which 'corresponds with the absence of surprise in the fantastic dream'.²⁶² The reader finds herself drawn into a dreamlike state of uncritical acceptance, the poem's form helping to 'break down conceptual resistance to its affective power'.²⁶³ What is more, as Leadbetter notes: 'The liberating impersonality of the form—accentuated by authorial anonymity in 1798—disperses the authorial self in sound and imagery, allowing the poem to operate without the poet's mediation as a character in his own work.'²⁶⁴ The directness of the form thus allows 'the images presented to work by their own force, without either denial or affirmation of their real existence by the judgement'.²⁶⁵

The emphasis on vision in the poem as indicated by numerous verbs of seeing—'beheld' (147), 'watched' (278), 'viewed' (443), 'see' (167, 334, 445, 465, 503, 508, 568, 588), 'saw' (261, 444, 487), 'peered'

---

[258] Adair (1967), 52.
[259] D. Robinson (1997), 121.
[260] D. Robinson (1997), 129.
[261] D. Robinson (1997), 132.
[262] D. Robinson (1997), 130.
[263] Leadbetter (2011), 166.
[264] Leadbetter (2011), 166.
[265] Coleridge, *Biographia Literaria*, vol. 2, 134.

(179), 'peer' (186), 'looked' (203, 240, 244, 255, 444)—as well as adjectives and nouns referring to vision—'glittering eye' (3, 13, 228), 'bright-eyed' (20), 'evil looks' (139), 'weary eye' (146, 251), 'eye' (215, 260, 618), 'eyes' (241, 332, 440, 486, 567), 'stony eyes' (436), 'look' (255, 538), 'bright eye' (416), 'sight' (493)—facilitates the reader's visualization of the content, thus increasing both the dreamlike effect and the sense of subjectivity. The latter becomes particularly obvious when, halfway through the poem, the Mariner recalls how he 'closed [his] lids and kept them close' (248) so that the ensuing vivid descriptions of dead bodies and water snakes 'seen' by the Mariner may well be read as images occurring before his inner eye in a dreamlike state. As Jennifer Ford points out:

> The mariner is unable to distinguish between subjective and objective sights and sounds: a distinction which, if weak, Coleridge strongly believed could account for the existence of many visions and otherwise supernatural phenomena. Much of the mariner's experience can be seen as this integration of all things seen and heard into a 'delirious Vision'.[266]

The events of the ship journey can be read in terms of a dream narrative in which the Mariner/dreamer is continually at the mercy of capricious oneiric forces. The 'STORM-BLAST' that takes the ship is personified as 'tyrannous and strong', as a 'foe' (47) chasing the ship along with his 'o'ertaking wings' (43) towards the South Pole, full of 'mist and snow' (51) and 'ice, mast-high' (53) and later into an uncharted ocean, below a 'hot and copper sky' (111), of which the Mariner recalls: 'We were the first that ever burst/Into that silent sea' (105–106). The image of a ship on its course through unknown, dangerous oceans, at the mercy of volatile winds is certainly well-suited to the representation of the dreamer's condition. What is more, it draws from the conceptual metaphor 'life is a journey', intuitively grasped by the reader and at the heart of many dreams. Accordingly, the setting appears as a dreamscape reflecting the Mariner's own state of psychological and physical torment as expressed by the extremes of unbearable heat, cold, silence and isolation. The reader

---

[266] Ford (1998), 127.

senses that the vividly painted images such as the albatross or the water snakes are imbued with strong symbolic, possibly religious, meaning and yet, as the divergent critical readings of the poem show, they are ambivalent enough to resist clear-cut symbolic interpretations—just like dreams do. The Mariner's dream, then, is not unlike Lessing's dream series about Kate's journey northward, but the effect is quite different because the reader is made to share the experience of the dream from the inside, unable to tell apart objective from subjective, outer from inner reality; and yet there is no choice for her but to succumb to the Mariner's story, enthralled by the same 'strange power of speech' (587) that also puts the Wedding-Guest under its spell.

The Mariner's shipmates appear like dream characters who violently turn against him in scenes that resonate with Coleridge's actual dreams recorded in his notebook, in which he finds himself 'in chains, or in rags, shunned or passed by, with looks of horror blended with sadness, by friends and acquaintance', certain that, in some 'alienation of mind [he] must have perpetrated some crime'[267]:

> Ah! well-a-day! What evil looks
> Had I from old and young!
> Instead of the cross, the Albatross
> About my neck was hung. (139–142)

Just like the geographical scenery, then, the dream characters reflect the Mariner's emotional state, suffused with guilt and remorse for a deed casually and irrationally committed. This is also why the crew members fail to display an identity of their own, but only serve to reflect the Mariner's own internal state, variously blaming or hailing him, fixing him with their dead stare or working the ship like a troop of zombies:

> They groaned, they stirred, they all uprose,
> nor spake, nor moved their eyes;
> It had been strange, even in a dream,
> To have seen those dead men rise. (331–334)

---

[267] Coleridge, *Collected Letters*, vol. 6, 716.

Edward E. Bostetter aptly sketches their existence as mere dream extras: 'Like the figures in a dream, they have no identity apart from the dreamer. We have no awareness of them as living human beings; we watch their deaths without surprise and without feeling, except insofar as they affect the Mariner.'[268] Even though one of the 'bodies' working side by side with the Mariner is referred to as that 'of my brother's son' (341), his identity has been erased at that stage in the poem; he has been turned into a mindless body, a lifeless, mechanical zombie, transmuted in the same way that nightmares transform friendly daytime acquaintances into strangers, friends into enemies or loved ones into monsters. This also explains why the game of dice played by Nightmare and DEATH is not about the crew or the ship itself, but solely about the Mariner, who is trapped in his solipsistic dreamworld, where everything refers back to the dreamer. Even though the other 200 crew members die, so that in terms of quantity DEATH might be regarded as winner, Nightmare rejoices in having won the game. The reason for this is that the Mariner is of necessity at the centre of his dream, or, more precisely, he *is* the dream, which is why every deed and image reflects and refracts his own emotional state, the ship mates' deaths being relevant only in so far as they contribute to his own sense of increasing isolation, horror and guilt.

Similarly, the nameless Mariner himself lacks a personality of his own, a circumstance noted by Charles Lamb, who claimed that the Mariner's condition was 'like the state of a man in a *Bad dream*, one terrible peculiarity of which is, that all consciousness of personality is *gone*'.[269] As Fulford notes, Coleridge's poetry aimed to reproduce

> the state of mind experienced in dreams and sought to recreate that state in its readers. For this to be achieved the social and historical details that gave the narrator a realistic personality or character had to be omitted. Deprived of his anchor in a carefully reproduced familiar world, the reader, like the mariner himself, is rendered vulnerable to extremes of emotion which he is unable to relate to ordinary experience.[270]

---

[268] Bostetter (1975), 111.
[269] Lamb quoted in Fulford (1997), 87.
[270] Fulford (1997), 87.

Like a dreamer, the Mariner, and by implication the reader, is adrift on an open sea, passively suffering rather than acting. His only notable deed is that of shooting the albatross. But for this act, no reason at all is given and the Mariner seems to have committed the deed as if in a trance. The deed itself is never described in any detail, but summed up retrospectively and rather matter-of-factly: 'With my cross-bow/I shot the ALBATROSS' (82–83). Compared to the very detailed description of the events preceding and following the deed, this recollection appears dreamlike in its pointed lack of causality or motivation, the focus instead being on the guilt he suffers for the 'hellish thing' (91) he has done. The Mariner's nightmarish dream, then, shows many characteristics of an existential dream, not least of all the fact that guilt is the dominant emotion or driving force to which all images are connected. Even the dying mates' souls pass the Mariner by '[l]ike the whizz of my crossbow' (223) and the lifeless bodies will go on haunting and cursing him after their deaths: 'But oh! More horrible than that/Is the curse in a dead man's eye!' (259–260). Kuiken, who briefly analyses the poem in conjunction with a matching existential dream, sees a moment of insight effected by the Mariner's close observation of the water snakes. According to Kuiken, the Mariner's ability to truly perceive the water snakes causes his experience of an 'unusual depth of feeling'[271] and provides the poem's turning point. However, although experiencing a moment of grace when (285) blessing the water snakes 'unaware', the Mariner's transformation does not last; he will forever be 'cursed': trapped by his irrational guilt, never questioning his own responsibility for his mates' destruction: 'I could not draw my eyes from theirs,/Nor turn them up to pray' (444–445). Even though this 'spell' (442) is lifted shortly after, the Mariner is still condemned to relive his nightmare 'at an uncertain hour' (582).

It is precisely because the Mariner remains under the spell of his supposed guilt that he himself turns into a walking nightmare, inflicting others with the same kind of spell that has befallen him. The dreamer's passivity and lack of control are aptly demonstrated by the spell under which the Wedding-Guest in 'The Ancient Mariner' finds himself:

---

[271] Kuiken (1995), 131.

> He holds him with his glittering eye –
> The Wedding-Guest stood still,
> And listens like a three years' child:
> The Mariner hath his will. (13–16)

The Wedding-Guest's will is suspended, his body paralysed like that of a dreamer. At the end of the poem, we learn that he turns 'from the bridegroom's door' (621) and returns home 'like one that hath been stunned,/ And is of sense forlorn' (622–623). The poem's last two lines are particularly crucial, as here the link between the Mariner's story and the Wedding-Guest's clearly impactful dream is once more confirmed: 'A sadder and a wiser man,/He rose the morrow morn' (624–625). It is for the reader to decide whether the encounter with the Mariner has taken place in waking reality or in the Wedding-Guest's dream. In the latter reading, the Mariner himself comes to represent the nightmare under whose spell the Wedding-Guest lives through an 'unfathomable hell'[272] that, upon his waking and rising 'the morrow morn', is to leave its lasting mark on him. Of course, the Mariner here resembles the poet whose curse or blessing it is to compulsively retell his tale and mesmerize his audience:

> Since then, at an uncertain hour,
> That agony returns:
> And till my ghastly tale is told,
> This heart within me burns. (582–585)

Ultimately, then, poet, Mariner, Wedding-Guest and reader all share the same dream, suffering its lasting impact in varying degree. The 'moral' retrospectively provided by the Mariner—'He prayeth well, who loveth well/Both man and bird and beast' (612–613)—has often been criticized as being too simplistic to do justice to the complexities of the poem. Reading 'The Ancient Mariner' as a dream poem might suggest that the Mariner and/or poet attempt to hold at bay more unsettling insights by means of this rather straightforward dream interpretation. Both the

---

[272] See Coleridge (1974d), 184.

poem's glossary summarizing the narrative and the Mariner's occasional attempts at interpretation serve the similar function of endowing the tale with daytime meaning, causality and morality, thereby attempting retrospectively to domesticate and control the dream. This is the case, for instance, when in the glossary, the ALBATROSS is called 'the pious bird of good omen' whose death is revenged by the 'Polar Spirit' or when the Mariner explains that the dead shipmates were animated by 'a troop of spirits blest' (349). In retrospect, Coleridge himself regretted what he called 'the obtrusion of the moral sentiment so openly on the reader as a principle or cause of action in a work of pure imagination'.[273] The very fact that these straightforward interpretations fail to do full justice to the dream narrative, as has been noted not only by Coleridge himself but by critics throughout the poem's reception history, reinforces the sense of deeper psychological and creative forces defying rational and causal explanation.

The Gothic Novel: Harker's Nightmare Journey in Bram Stoker's *Dracula* (1897)

Blurred boundaries are to a large extent responsible for the sense of strangeness and instability of the dream world in which the malleable dreamscape refracts the dreamer's own psychic concerns and the characters encountered are simultaneously 'Other' and creations of the dreamer's own dreaming imagination. These general dream characteristics are particularly unsettling when the dream in question is a nightmare in which hostile strangers or monsters chase the dreamer through dark labyrinthine passages, presenting a threat to the dreamer's sense of self in often palpably physical terms. Such nightmares have a particularly real feel to them or, to use Nielsen's term, they bear a heightened reality sense, blurring the boundaries between waking and sleeping, as repeatedly experienced by Jonathan Harker in *Dracula*: 'I suppose I must have fallen asleep; I hope so, but I fear, for all that followed was startingly real—so real that now, sitting here in the broad, full sunlight

---

[273] Coleridge, *Table Talk*, 149.

of the morning, I cannot in the least believe that it was all sleep' (68). As James B. Twitchell puts it: 'Horror art is, indeed, so informed by the dynamics of the nightmare that it may finally only be understood as "dreaming with one's eyes open", as dreamwork made real, the cinéma vérité of the psyche'.[274] The horror images giving us *the creeps*, then, 'are not drawn from the "real" world but from the "land of dreams"'.[275] This is the reason why horror fiction often sports monsters that have no existence in waking reality but may well have sprung from dream-like distortions or the hallucinations generated during sleep paralysis. Like our nightmare creations, these monsters 'are never totally non-human. Instead, they usually combine some major human attribute with some truly bizarre element',[276] thereby effectively disabling 'our attempts to classify, categorize, and hence control them'.[277] The monster encountered in horror fiction is thus the epitome of Otherness, the stranger within the self, the enemy within, the part of ourselves we fear to acknowledge and therefore repress. Here, Freud's concept of 'the uncanny' or *das Unheimliche* comes into play, as the monsters encountered in dreams are self-created in the same way that, for instance, Frankenstein has created the creature he recoils from.

Patrick McNamara notes that 'nightmares contain the "unfamiliar"'.[278] However, the strangers or monsters pursuing the dreamer have, of course, sprung from the dreamer's own imaginative consciousness; they have been given birth by the dreamer, have been patched together from a myriad of fears, anxieties, personal and cultural memories, myths and stories. In this sense, they are part of the dreamer, at once unfamiliar and intimately familiar, in short: uncanny. They belong to 'that class of the terrifying which leads back to something long known to us, once very familiar',[279] the return of the repressed. In his essay 'The Uncanny' (1919), Freud famously teases out the meanings of the German term

---

[274] Twitchell (1985), 16.
[275] Twitchell (1985), 18.
[276] Twitchell (1985), 23–24.
[277] Twitchell (1985), 24.
[278] McNamara (2008), 46.
[279] Freud (1919), 1–2.

das Unheimliche, which can mean at once *no longer familiar* and, in a less commonly used sense, *no longer secret/hidden*. The uncanny, then, 'is in reality nothing new or foreign, but something familiar and old—established in the mind that has been estranged only by the process of repression'.[280]

While Freud's theory of wish-fulfilment fails to do justice to the nightmare experience, his concept of the uncanny perfectly captures this particular type of dream even though the concept was not developed in the context of, or directly applied to, dream analysis. Arguably, the reason it fits so well is not simply because the hostile intruders in our nightmares have sprung from our own minds but because these creations, no matter how supernatural, otherworldly or monstrous they may appear, inevitably bear resemblance to persons and situations familiar to us from waking life. Thus, if the demonic pursuer bears traces of a person intimately known to us in waking life, the nightmarish effect will most likely be heightened rather than alleviated. What is more, the sense of the uncanny fits the nightmare experience because the nightmare is closer to the threshold of waking, often blurring the boundaries between the sleep and the wake state. This is especially the case with regard to the experience of Felt Presence, in which dream content is carried over into the waking world. Felt Presence, 'the vivid sensation that someone or something animate is present in the vicinity of a person' can occur in 'a variety of ways ranging from the most intense and realistic hallucinations, e.g., during sleep paralysis attacks or sensory deprivation, to the most subtle and fleeting sensations that "someone is there"'.[281] As Solomonova et al. point out: 'Possible "visitors" frequently include demonic malevolent entities, aliens, ghosts, witches, stalkers, intruders in the home and more'.[282] In such cases, then, an internally generated 'apparition' appears to us while we are seemingly awake and no longer subject to the dream realm. If dream figments come to 'haunt' the waking realm in this way, they turn into

---

[280] Freud (1919), 13.
[281] Solomonova et al. (2011), 171.
[282] Solomonova et al. (2011), 171.

truly uncanny experiences, unsettling the boundaries between self and other as well as between dreaming and waking. As Nicholas Royle explains:

> The uncanny has to do with the sense of a secret encounter: it is perhaps inseparable from an apprehension, however fleeting, of something that should have remained secret and hidden but has come to light. But it is not 'out there', in any simple sense: as a crisis of the proper and natural, it disturbs any straightforward sense of what is inside and what is outside. The uncanny has to do with a strangeness of framing and borders, an experience of liminality.[283]

Transgression and blurring of boundaries are central to both the nightmare and the Gothic. Matthew C. Brennan notes that from its earliest beginnings in the mid-eighteenth century, 'the Gothic has been an aesthetics of nightmare, an aesthetics of the liminal and of crossed or open boundaries'.[284] Accordingly, studying the Gothic mode in conjunction with dream psychology helps explain the fascination Gothic texts hold for many readers, since, as Elizabeth MacAndrew notes, 'the effects of "terror" in Gothic tales refer to something beyond the fictional devices that produce them. [...] These tales make use of the realization that monsters in fiction frighten because they are already the figments of our dreaming imaginations'.[285] According to MacAndrew, the Gothic 'conjures up beings—mad monks, vampires, and demons—and settings—forbidding cliffs and glowering buildings, stormy seas and the dizzying abyss—that have literary significance and the properties of dream symbolism as well'.[286] Transformations, say from human to animal, not only occur in nocturnal dreams, but constitute 'also a common Gothic motif [which] is a figurative crossing of boundaries'.[287] What is more, both nightmares and Gothic writings focus 'the spotlight on the self under [...] threat'.[288]

---

[283] Royle (2003), 1–2.
[284] Brennan (1998), 6.
[285] McAndrew (1979), 8.
[286] McAndrew (1979), 3.
[287] DeLamotte (1990), 21.
[288] McNamara (2008), 86.

'the driving motive [being] the striving [...] of the dreamer to protect the self'.[289] On the one hand, this is suggested by the loosening of ego boundaries that might endanger the dreamer's or protagonist's sense of self. On the other hand, it is suggested by the stock feature of the hostile intruder, in many cases consisting of humanoid 'creatures'[290] or predominantly male strangers.[291] The bizarreness evoked by Count Dracula precisely inheres in his combination of human and animalistic features, tapping into the characters'—and readers'—primal fears; these include his sharp pointed teeth, his hairy palms and his habit of crawling along his castle's walls like a lizard as much as his ability to metamorphose into non-human creatures such as a bat, a wolf or a dog.

The plots of gothic tales tend to resemble journeys into increasingly disorienting interior nightmare landscapes of the self. This becomes particularly obvious in Jonathan Harker's '[u]nremembered dream-journey'[292] at the beginning of Stoker's novel. As on repeated occasions during his sojourn in Transylvania, Harker, upon reaching Count Dracula's castle, finds himself retrospectively unsure whether he was awake or asleep: 'I must have been asleep, for certainly if I had been fully awake I must have noticed the approach to such a remarkable place' (45). Transylvania is a realm associated with the dangers of night and sleep, since it is the place in which Count Dracula, the epitome of Otherness, originates and resides. His castle is indeed situated 'in the extreme east of the country, just on the borders of three states, Transylvania, Moldavia, and Bukovina, in the midst of the Carpathian mountains; one of the wildest and least known portions of Europe' (32). Referring to the flourishing superstitions of the place, Harker describes it as 'the centre of some sort of imaginative whirlpool' (32) and further informs us that there exist 'no maps of this country' (32). His journey towards Count Dracula's castle is thus truly a journey into the unknown, where boundaries blur and natural laws fail to apply. The fact that Harker records his adventures in a private diary in shorthand (cf. 31) even heightens the sense of dreamlike solip-

---

[289] McNamara (2008), 84.
[290] See McNamara (2008), 47.
[291] See McNamara (2008), 137.
[292] Schleifer (1980), 301.

sism, self-referentiality and privacy in this strange, uncharted world that draws him in. After the castle's doors have closed behind him, Harker is caught in the epicentre of his nightmare, paralysed with terror and fear: 'I feel the dread of this horrible place overpowering me; I am in fear— in awful fear—and there is no escape for me; I am encompassed about with terrors that I dare not think of...' (66). His entrapment within the nightmare is visualized in very real spatial and architectural terms: '[D]oors, doors, doors everywhere, and all locked and bolted. In no place save from the windows in the castle walls is there an available exit. The castle is a veritable prison, and I am a prisoner!' (57).

From the beginning of his journey onwards, Harker mentions his sleeping disorders, accompanied by disturbing dreams: 'I did not sleep well, though my bed was comfortable enough, for I had all sorts of queer dreams' (32). Even though he tries to account for these bad dreams rationally, blaming the food or outside noises, he is soon affected by the peasants' irrational and superstitious warnings and rituals (cf. 36). When the 'strange driver' (41), who turns out to be Count Dracula himself, picks him up to take him to the castle, Harker, left behind by his fellow travellers, is overcome by 'a strange chill, and a lonely feeling' (41). Shortly after, he notes: 'I felt a little strangely, and not a little frightened' (41). Much later, when trapped in Dracula's castle, Harker places the crucifix a well-meaning peasant had given him over his bed, imagining 'that my rest is thus freer from dreams' (65). However, his waking imagination, too, becomes increasingly active as his stay in the castle progresses: 'I am beginning to feel this nocturnal existence tell on me. It is destroying my nerve. I start at my own shadow, and am full of all sorts of horrible imaginings' (65).

The circular journey on which the 'strange driver' takes him before reaching the castle resembles a nightmare journey in which the passenger is completely helpless and at the driver's mercy. As Day aptly puts it: 'As when in a dream we find ourselves powerless to act, so in the Gothic we intuitively recognize that action is hopeless'.[293] Thus, Harker remains silent even when he realizes that 'we were simply going over and over the same ground again' (41). Later, he notes that 'I think I must have fallen

---

[293] Day (1985), 45.

asleep and kept dreaming of the incident, for it seemed to be repeated endlessly, and now looking back, it is like a sort of awful nightmare [...]' (43). Finally, the strange blue flames in the forest and the 'ring of wolves, with white teeth and lolling red tongues' (43) surrounding him result in a 'paralysis of fear' (43) on Harker's part. At one point he notes: 'This was all so strange and uncanny that a dreadful fear came upon me, and I was afraid to speak or move' (44). These passages resonate with allusions to sleep paralysis accompanied by frightful visions. The repeated references to nightmares, dreams and (sleep) paralysis thus prepare the way for Harker's nightmarish sojourn in Dracula's castle. The fact that dreaming and waking increasingly blur in the course of Harker's stay bears testimony to Dracula's powers.

Trapped in the lion's den, Harker has no choice but to resign himself to the Count's terms, 'this strange night-existence' (56), so as to at least enjoy a temporary illusion of safety. Thus, Dracula warns him not to fall asleep anywhere else in the castle but his own rooms so as to avoid dangerous 'dreams': 'Let me advise you, my dear young friend—nay, let me warn you with all seriousness, that should you leave these rooms you will not by any chance go to sleep in any other part of the castle. It is old, and has many memories, and there are bad dreams for those who sleep unwisely' (64). When Harker fails to heed Dracula's advice—doubting 'whether any dream could be more terrible than the unnatural, horrible net of gloom and mystery which seemed closing around me' (64)—he faces the consequences in the form of an erotic and almost fatal encounter with what he later refers to as 'those weird sisters' (80). Having explored an uninhabited wing of the castle, Harker seems to fall asleep on a couch in a richly decorated, old-fashioned chamber. The reality sense of the vision he experiences is repeatedly emphasized. Harker 'suppose[s]' he 'must have fallen asleep', but while he 'hope[s] so', he 'fear[s]' it may not have been the case 'for all that followed was startlingly real'. Ultimately, he 'cannot in the least believe that it was all sleep' (68).

In contrast to the uncertainty displayed here, Harker's account of this 'startlingly real' encounter with the three vampire ladies is given in very detailed and straightforward terms, even though he recalls a moment of doubt based on his own rational realization that the three ladies throw no shadow despite the moonlight. And yet, his description reads like a typical Felt Presence experience:

> I was not alone. The room was the same, unchanged in any way since I came into it; I could see along the floor, in the brilliant moonlight, my own footsteps marked where I had disturbed the long accumulation of dust. In the moonlight opposite me were three young women, ladies by their dress and manner. (68)[294]

The sense of dream is heightened by one of the ladies' uncanny familiarity: 'I seemed somehow to know her face, and to know it in connection with some dreamy fear, but I could not recollect at the moment how or where' (69). The fair vampire, 'with great, wavy masses of golden hair and eyes like pale sapphires' (69) is clearly reminiscent of Lucy Westenra, the attractive best friend of Harker's fiancée Mina, which may well suggest some unacknowledged desire for Lucy on Harker's part. The wake–sleep boundary is further blurred when Dracula informs the three vampire ladies that he 'must awaken him [Harker]' (71), who, however, seems to be fully aware of all that is happening, including the women's greedy reception of Dracula's prey—a 'half-smothered child' (71)—and their mysterious disappearance: 'They simply seemed to fade into the rays of the moonlight and pass out through the window, for I could see outside the dim, shadowy forms for a moment before they entirely faded away' (71). It is only then that Harker passes out and eventually awakes on his own bed, surmising that either the Count must have carried him there or that he must have dreamed after all (cf. 72). Weighing all the evidence, Harker is unable to 'arrive at any unquestionable result' (72), though he intuitively senses that he was not dreaming: 'I fear it was no dream, and must act on this surmise' (72).

Harker's resolve to actively face the danger surrounding him is what ultimately saves him. He even comes face to face with the Count sleep-

---

[294] Count Dracula, too, repeatedly appears to the female characters Lucy and Mina as such a Felt Presence precisely at those transitional times when the characters are asleep or in the hypnagogic stages bordering on sleep.

ing in his coffin, although his attempt to destroy Dracula is doomed to failure. Instead, he feels paralysed by the vampire's eyes and 'their blaze of basilisk horror' (84).[295] One reason for Harker's resolve, thanks to which he manages to leave the castle against all odds, may well be the vampire's waning presence as Dracula prepares to leave for London. If Dracula represents the nightmare holding Harker in its thrall, his departure takes away Harker's paralysis and allows him to act. It could be argued that by confronting his fears, he eventually overcomes them. However, his nightmares continue in the delirious fever dreams Harker suffers during his long recovery. As Sister Agatha informs Mina in a letter: 'He has had some fearful shock—so says our doctor—and in his delirium his ravings have been dreadful; of wolves and poison and blood; of ghosts and demons; and I fear to say of what' (134). Having survived his 'brain fever' (140), Harker is determined to leave behind the horrors experienced in Transylvania, even suggesting that they may not have been real after all. As he tells Mina: 'I do not know if it was all real or the dreaming of a madman' (140). When he later recognizes the now young and dark-haired Count in the middle of London, he is at first transfixed, then, when Mina leads him to 'a comfortable seat in a shady place' (210), he falls asleep only to remember nothing of the event upon awaking. As Mina puts it: 'He had evidently forgotten all about the dark stranger, as in his illness he had forgotten all that this episode had reminded him of' (210). Encountering Dracula is like a dream that slips into oblivion and only shows in the physical and psychological impact he has on his victims. Infiltrating England 'as the embodiment of *fin-de-siècle* anxieties of degeneration and ethnic impurity',[296] it is by means of dreams that the Count gains control over his victims—and by means of dreams that he will ultimately face his defeat.

---

[295] For an analysis of *Dracula* in terms of mesmerism and fascination, see Baumbach (2015), 168–189.
[296] Baumbach (2015), 170.

The Short Story: Katherine Mansfield's 'Sun and Moon' (1920)

The third genre particularly suited to the creation of literary dreamlikeness is arguably the short story. As David Mitchell aptly puts it, 'at least when described from outside the sleeper's mind brevity is another quality of dreams'.[297] This quality obviously links dreams to short narrative forms. More crucially, Clare Hanson notes that the '"open" quality of the short story'[298] mirrors the often incomplete or fragmented dream experience. Another similarity is that both the dream and the short story tend to be image-dominated as well as elliptical. As Adrian Hunter argues, in contrast to the novel, the short story tends to cut away 'the kind of material we normally depend upon for narrative continuity and coherence, [...] working with these tactical omissions to *suggest* and *imply* meaning, rather than stating it directly'.[299] While the short story typically depends on images to retain a sense of narrative continuity and coherence, these images 'tend to resist such interpenetration and integration [as takes place in the novel], which is why they disturb us in a particular, a distinctive and distinctly non-novelistic way'.[300]

Besides 'disturbing' us, these images can also provide us with moments of psychological or existential insight: moments of being, to use Virginia Woolf's term, or epiphanies, to use James Joyce's—fleeting, intense and dreamlike. According to Hanson, the short story is thus often fuelled by 'images from the unconscious mind' which can be presented 'in the text in a relatively *untranslated* state. Such images retain an air of mystery and impenetrability, an air of dream'.[301] Another similarity is the typical self-absorption of both dreamers and short story characters as well as the dream's and short story's typical focus on the present. As Nadine Gordimer succinctly puts it: 'Short story writers see by the light of the flash; theirs is the art of the only thing one can be sure of—the present moment'.[302]

---

[297] Mitchell (2008), 436.
[298] Hanson (1989), 23.
[299] Hunter 2.
[300] Hanson (1989), 24.
[301] Hanson (1989), 25.
[302] Gordimer (1969), 459, quoted in Hunter (2007), 2.

Finally, in a similar way to the dream, in which the dream environment is often a projection of the dreamer's emotions and mood, short stories, too, tend to reflect their focalizing characters' feelings and psychological concerns. Accordingly, both dreams and short stories blur clear-cut boundaries between inner and outer reality, self and other, reality and fantasy.

Katherine Mansfield's short story 'Sun and Moon' (1920) is a particularly good example of a short story that blurs the boundaries between waking and dreaming by employing a child's point of view. As mentioned before, Mansfield claimed that she dreamed the story. In a letter to John Middleton Murry in 1918, she wrote:

> I *dreamed* a short story last night, even down to its name, which was *Sun and Moon*. It was very light. I dreamed it all—about children. I got up at 6.30 and wrote a note or two because I knew it would fade. I'll send it some time this week. It's so nice. I didn't dream that I read it. No, I was in it, part of it, and it played round invisible me. But the hero is no more than 5. In my dream I saw a supper table with the eyes of 5. It was awfully queer—especially a plate of half-melted ice-cream...[303]

The dream's 'awfully queer' quality originates from the child's point of view, as the dreamer sees 'a supper table with the eyes of 5'. The resultant 'touch of strangeness'[304] is preserved in the short story that emerged from the dream. 'Sun and Moon' tells the story of a young boy called Sun, who, together with his younger sister Moon, is witnessing the preparations for a party their parents will have later that day. From beginning to end the short story is focalized through Sun; all events and perceptions are filtered through his perspective. While at one point in the story, Sun prides himself in being able to know 'the difference between real things and not real ones' (154), in the course of the story this difference repeatedly blurs, suggesting a gap between objective reality and the boy's subjective experience.

Some of the dreamlike transformations have a benign *Alice in Wonderland* quality, for instance when Sun 'stared down from the balcony at the people carrying' the flowers and 'the flower pots looked like

---

[303] Mansfield, *Letters*, 161, original italics.
[304] Meier (1993), 64.

awfully nice hats nodding up the path' (153–154) or 'men in black with funny tails on their coats [look] like beetles' (157). Later, he admires a dinner table that seems to be transformed into a landscaped garden: 'Red ribbons and bunches of roses tied up the table at the corner. In the middle was a lake with rose petals floating on it. [...] Two silver lions with wings had fruit on their backs and the salt cellars were tiny birds drinking out of basins' (155). However, not unlike the world behind the looking-glass, Sun's world, too, is infused with a potentially more sinister and disturbing quality. The environment, idyllic as it may seem, is ultimately one hostile to the children. Their mother harshly tells them to keep out of the way and Sun is surprised at Cook's *unusual* kindness. When his father contradicts his mother, Sun is certain that 'Mother would have been dreadfully cross' (159). Similarly, he repeatedly expresses his surprise at 'this jolly Father' (159), which suggests that this is not the kind of father he ordinarily knows. Being a child, he is constantly faced with situations beyond his control and comprehension so that the apparent lightness of the story is undermined. The subjectively experienced brutality with which the children are treated becomes obvious when they are briefly presented to the party guests, fondled like pets or objects, especially when 'a skinny old lady with teeth that clicked said: "Such a serious little poppet", and rapped him [Sun] on the head with something hard' (157). What is more, animate and inanimate objects continually blur in the story, as when food is humanized—'almond finger' (154), 'collar on the ham' (155), 'fishes, with their heads and eyes' (155)—and the children objectified (as suggested by the passive voice indicating the way in which they are being 'handled', 'unbuttoned', 'dressed', 'picked up'). This helps create what Bardolph calls 'a Hansel-and-Gretel atmosphere' in which 'desire and eating seem to be of a cannibal order, and the intimacy of the parents aggressive and threatening, as when Father 'pretended to bite [Mother's] white shoulder'.[305]

The story hinges on two central images that turn the relatively simple plot into an emotionally and symbolically rich story. These central images both contextualize Sun's emotional concerns and provide the sense of bizarreness that makes the story 'shimmer with instability and

---

[305] Bardolph (1994), 166.

otherness'.[306] The first is the ice pudding that the children are allowed to admire while it is still in the fridge: 'Oh! Oh! Oh! It was a little house. It was a little pink house with white snow on the roof and green windows and a brown door and stuck in the house was a nut for a handle' (155). The sight of the miniature house has a strong emotional effect on Sun. At first, 'when Sun saw the nut he felt quite tired and had to lean against Cook' (155). Later in the story, when the children are allowed to look at the magnificently transformed and decorated dining room, Sun asks, to the adults' amusement, 'Are people going to eat the food?' (55). This worried question foreshadows the ending, when Sun is quite upset at the sight of the ruined dinner table and the melted house. The second image is a grey-haired stranger that Sun spots among the party guests. This 'little grey man, with long grey whiskers, who walked about by himself' is the only 'man that Sun really liked' (157). He is also the only one that takes a genuine interest in Sun:

> He came up to Sun and rolled his eyes in a very nice way and said: 'Hullo, my lad.' Then he went away. But soon he came back again and said: 'Fond of dogs?' Sun said: 'Yes.' But then he went away again, and though Sun looked for him everywhere he couldn't find him. He thought perhaps he'd gone outside to fetch in a puppy. (157–158)

After an abrupt change of scene, the children, having woken up in their beds, decide to go out on the landing to watch the party guests stroll over to the dining room:

> Then that door was shut; there was a noise of 'pops' and laughing. Then that stopped and Sun saw them all walking round and round the lovely table with their hands behind their backs like he had done. Round and round they walked, looking and staring. The man with the grey whiskers liked the little house best. When he saw the nut for a handle he rolled his eyes like he did before and said to Sun: 'Seen the nut?' (158)

The subtle change of consciousness is easy to miss but in fact Sun is dreaming this scene. After all, it is not possible for the children to witness

---

[306] States (1993), 25.

what the grown-ups are doing in the dining room since 'that door was shut'. So Sun must be imagining their childlike amazement, projecting his own sense of wonder onto the party guests, who most likely are not as deeply impressed with the decorations as Sun was earlier that day. He also dreams about the mysterious man with grey whiskers, who shares Sun's own particular fascination with the little nut serving as handle to the little house's door. When the children, having fallen asleep on the landing, are discovered by their parents after the guests have left, they are allowed to briefly come down and 'have some pickings' of the leftovers. Sun is shocked to find a scene of destruction instead of 'the beautiful dining room' he had expected: 'And the little pink house with the snow roof and the green windows was broken—broken—half melted away in the centre of the table' (159). The shock that Sun feels at the sight of the ruined dinner table, and the broken little house in particular, is deepened by his father's 'smashing in some more of the roof' as well as his sister's careless way as she picks the little nut 'out of the door and scrunched it up, biting hard and blinking' (160). His reaction of starting to wail and cry—'I think it's horrid—horrid—horrid!' (160)—is in line with this shock but totally incomprehensible to his parents, who angrily send him back to the nursery.

The emotional significance attached to the miniature house and what Sun perceives as its cruel destruction, lends the story a dreamlike quality. To Sun, the little fragile house made of ice cream is real. It is not just food, but represents an ideal little world, with the nut as handle providing entry. He is not at all able, then, to tell 'the difference between real things and not real ones' (154) because in his dreamlike world things keep shifting and transforming. In this world of dreamlike transformations, the solitary little man with grey whiskers who, alone of all the characters in the story, seems genuinely interested in Sun, able to mind-read his wishes and sharing his particular fascination with the house and the nut, assumes a symbolic quality which is often inherent in dream and fairy tale characters.[307] He seems rather out of place in the party

---

[307] The 'little grey man' is a popular character in various fairy tales, e.g. in the Grimm Brothers' 'The Golden Goose', where he functions as disguised helper. An even earlier story by Sophie Albrecht, titled 'Graumännchen oder die Burg Rabenbühl' ['The Little Grey Man or the Castle Rabenbühl']

surroundings; walking by himself, talking with no one, he has seemingly vanished when Sun goes in search of him. By emphasizing his part in the short dream scene, Mansfield casts doubt upon his overall reality status within the story. The reader begins to wonder whether Sun has dreamed up his presence from the beginning.

The 'little grey man' provides the element of bizarreness in the storyworld, precisely because his behaviour deviates from that of all the other grown-up characters and he seems out of place within the storyworld. For instance, he takes an interest in Sun rather than in Moon, and he notices the little nut that is ignored and unappreciated by the other adults. Especially his seemingly unmotivated question—'Fond of dogs?' (157)— contributes to this impression. This question seems to mirror Sun's secret longing for a dog and suggests that the 'little grey man' is really a dreamlike projection of his own wish to be taken notice of. The ending of the story, in which the disappointed and disillusioned little boy 'stumped off to the nursery' (160), may well signal something like the end of childhood: the little house's door and its handle have been destroyed and the 'little grey man' with his eyes rolling 'in a very nice way' may have disappeared for good. The reader, identifying with Sun, experiences the ending as the harsh awakening from a dream in which something initially beautiful and innocent has undergone a transformation into something 'horrid'. According to Pamela Dunbar, '[b]eyond its apparent slightness the sketch is another rite-of-passage tale; a fable about the inevitable spoiling of perfection and of the child's primal sense of contentment. The notion of the house's ideal nature, here a figure of family happiness, has lasted only as long as the dream'.[308]

(1799), can be considered as one of the predecessors of the more famous Grimm Brothers' fairy tale 'Rumpelstilskin'.
[308] Dunbar (1997), 150.

5

Conjuring Up the Dream: Three Literary Case Studies

Writing a Dream: Kazuo Ishiguro's *The Unconsoled* (1995)

> To write a dream, which shall resemble the real course of a dream, with all its inconsistency, its strange transformations, which are all taken as a matter of course, its eccentricities and aimlessness—with nevertheless a leading idea running through the whole. Up to this old age of the world, no such thing ever has been written.[1]

This claim was made by Nathaniel Hawthorne roughly 150 years prior to the publication of Kazuo Ishiguro's *The Unconsoled* (1995). It would be interesting to know Hawthorne's response to this novel, in which the first-person narrator is trapped in a 500-page exploration of the maze of his own psyche. With its incongruities, discontinuities of time, place and characters as well as its single-minded protagonist taking all 'its inconsistency, its strange transformations [...] as a matter of course', the fictional world depicted in the novel indeed resembles that of a dream: full of 'eccentricities and aimlessness—with nevertheless a leading idea running

---

[1] Hawthorne, *American Notebooks*, 99.

through the whole'. Accordingly, in what follows I will read Ishiguro's novel as an extended dream narrative emerging from the mental life of one single consciousness, that of its protagonist Mr Ryder. As I will argue, *The Unconsoled* is an oneiric text *par excellence* because it 'translates' the dream experience into a literary narrative by imitating the single-mindedness of the dreamer and keeping the mediating and guiding role of the narrator to a minimum. Readers willing to accompany Ryder on his Kafkaesque quest are thus forced to share the autodiegetic narrator's highly subjective and uncritical point of view, resigning themselves to the same sense of dreamlike acceptance.[2] Thanks to this narrative technique, the reader experiences Ryder's 'dream' from the inside rather than from the outside.

The novel is set in an unnamed city, with the locals' names suggesting a German-speaking country, possibly Austria. However, the precise setting is left deliberately open and the description of the city is kept unspecific, providing only a few pointers such as 'the Old Town', the 'Hungarian Café' or the 'medieval chapel'. As Richard Robinson rightly points out: 'Ishiguro's attempt to elude geographical (and thus, political, cultural, and historical) fixity is successful: it is clear that the city is not only unidentified but unidentifiable'.[3] This observation ties in with my reading of *The Unconsoled* as an oneiric fiction in which the setting is primarily a landscape of the mind rather than an actual place. What is more, the novel starts out *in medias res* and thus in the same way a dream begins: There cannot be a consciously experienced beginning since we always find ourselves right in the middle of the dream events. More specifically, Ryder enters a hotel lobby, accompanied by a taxi driver who 'seemed embarrassed to find there was no one—not even a clerk behind the reception desk—waiting to welcome me' (3). The purpose of his stay only gradually dawns on Ryder. It turns out that he, an internationally renowned concert pianist, has been invited to give both a concert and a speech on the following Thursday night. Over the course of his four-day stay, he is also expected to miraculously provide consolation for the unconsoled, to

---

[2] Quite obviously, the reader has the advantage of being able to re-read the text and reflect on its dreamlike features, unlike Ryder, who remains deeply immersed in his dreamlike state.
[3] R. Robinson (2006), 109.

save the community from falling into 'crisis' (99), from 'widespread misery' (99) and from turning into 'another cold, lonely city' (107). Besides thus catering to 'the cultural well-being of the city',[4] he is expected to tend to the private problems of numerous individuals who place their hopes in him, confide in him and keep asking for personal favours of various kinds. All this results in a tightly packed schedule whose precise contents not only remain vague but continually elude and overwhelm Ryder. What is more, it becomes increasingly clear to the reader (if not to Ryder) that the protagonist is trapped within the landscape of his mind, in 'a cage [constructed] of the past from which [he] cannot escape'.[5] One of the 'leading ideas' of the novel seems to be Ryder's utter inadequacy in performing the roles assigned to him combined with his failure to become lucid or 'double-minded', that is to critically reflect upon his past and present life and change the course of events accordingly.

While Ryder is roused from sleep at the beginning of each of the four parts subdividing the novel, these instances are like false awakenings after which the dream continues regardless, thereby reinforcing the sense that Ryder is caught up in a relentlessly ongoing nightmare. In part one of the novel, the awakening occurs at the beginning of Chap. 2; the three following parts all start out with Ryder awakening from sleep. This is what Green and McCreery write about the phenomenon of repeated false awakenings:

> One of the most dramatic forms of false awakening is that in which the person seems to awaken repeatedly, but without actually doing so. Some subjects report waking up in their bedrooms several times in succession, and seemingly setting off for work and beginning their normal day each time, before being aroused to apparent wakefulness by some discrepancy in the dream content and finding themselves back in their bedroom thinking, 'Oh, that was a dream.'[6]

In contrast to this, Ryder never even suspects that he may have dreamed the preceding events, which, however, could well be classified as a case

---
[4] R. Robinson (2006), 123.
[5] Adelman (2001), 167.
[6] Green and McCreary (1999), 65.

of 'unidentified false awakening'.[7] In any case it is telling that Ishiguro uses Ryder's awakenings—false or real—as a structural device in a novel so clearly informed by the dream state. Even though the novel does not literally narrate a dream, then, it simulates the dream state and employs a range of typical dream elements and scenarios. In analysing these oneiric devices, I will also discuss the strategies used by Ishiguro to adapt and manipulate these features so as to make Ryder's dreamlike journey accessible and readable.[8]

Discussing his undeniable departure from realism in *The Unconsoled*, Ishiguro himself confirms that in the novel he 'did consciously refer to dream a lot of the time'.[9] However, he immediately qualifies this statement by pointing out that the novel is still governed by its own laws: 'They are different rules from the ones that govern realistic fiction, but I wanted the reader to feel, after the initial period of confusion, that there were new laws.'[10] While Ishiguro seems to suggest that the adherence to a set of rules might render the text less dreamlike, I would argue that precisely the opposite is the case. Dreams, too, are governed by laws and do not generally ramble on in utter randomness. As States rightly notes, 'in the dream the prevailing emotion radiates to all parts of the dream world'.[11] This implies that all dream events occurring to the dreamer correspond to the prevailing emotion underlying the dream. Responding to Ishiguro's claim that it would break the storyworld's rules if any of the characters were suddenly to grow wings and fly away,[12] I would argue that flying would not be in accordance with the emotion underlying

---

[7] See Green and McCreery (1999), 89.
[8] The dreamlike quality of Ishiguro's text has been noticed by other critics, though mostly in passing. Thus, Carlos Villar Flor (2000), describing some of the novel's spatiotemporal discontinuities, notes that *The Unconsoled* has 'the consistency of a dream, and the whole context of the novel becomes oneiric or surrealistic' (162). Similarly, Gary Adelman (2001) claims that Ishiguro 'combines the fantastic realism of a dream narrative with the staginess of a theatrical farce' (167). Drag (2010) and Lewis (2000) read the novel through the lens of Freudian dream theory, with partly problematic results. Some critics, such as Walkowitz (2001) and Stamirowska (2002), though, completely disregard Ishiguro's use of dreamlike elements in the novel, rather surprisingly treating it as a piece of realist fiction, which it is clearly not.
[9] Krider (1998), 152.
[10] Krider (1998), 152.
[11] States (1993), 81.
[12] See Krider (1998), 152.

5 Conjuring Up the Dream: Three Literary Case Studies

the novel anyway. Firstly, though labelled as typical, flying dreams are not ones that average dreamers have on a regular basis. Instead, empirical evidence has shown that flying most often occurs in lucid dreams as the result of the dreamer's conscious decision and effort.[13] Even non-lucid dream flight, 'generally experienced as intensely pleasurable'[14] or 'exhilarating',[15] is not likely to occur in anxiety dreams but more typically takes place in transcendental dreams characterized by a serene, relaxed or elated mood.[16] However, Ryder's dream narrative is dominated by anxiety, disorientation, frustration and anger, with Ryder not achieving anything remotely close to serenity or lucidity throughout the entire course of the novel. Therefore, having him grow wings and fly away would indeed be against the laws governing his dream as much as it would be against the laws governing the novel. Instead, adhering to what Robinson aptly calls 'a pattern of destruction, incompletion and non-arrival',[17] the novel is replete with dream scenarios typical of what Kuiken terms alienation dreams, such as losing one's way in a labyrinthine city, finding oneself naked in public or getting side-tracked from pursuing one's goal by unexpected and increasingly absurd distractions and impediments.

Secondly, in order to facilitate the reader's immersion in the dreamlike state experienced by Ryder, it is important to establish certain rules the reader can grasp, become accustomed to and ultimately accept as given features of the storyworld—in the same way that Ryder, the protagonist, accepts these features with a dreamer's uncritical single-mindedness. As has been pointed out in the previous chapter, creating a dreamlike story is not about accumulating bizarre occurrences that strike the reader as being completely out of the ordinary, for, after all, in dreams 'bizarreness is the

---

[13] For the interconnectedness between flying dreams and lucid dreams, see Barrett (1991); LaBerge and Rheingold (1997), 95–96; Green and McCreery (1999).
[14] Hunt (1989), 197.
[15] States (1993), 89.
[16] Hunt (1989) defines lucid dreaming as a spontaneous state of meditation, during which the dreamer achieves 'a sense of clarity, exhilaration, and openness' (120). Likewise, Green and McCreery (1999) describe lucid dreams as having a 'tendency towards elation and exhilaration', with some lucid dreamers even describing the dream experience as '"mystical" or "transcendent"' (49).
[17] R. Robinson (2006), 123.

constant behavioural norm'[18] and as such largely accepted by the dreamer as ordinary. This is why bizarre events need to be described in such a way that the reader comes to accept them as the rules governing the story and ultimately comes to share 'the dreamer's complete conviction in the exclusivity of the dream *Umwelt*',[19] much as it might differ from our everyday world of waking reality. This is precisely what Ishiguro achieves in *The Unconsoled*, whose storyworld may be infused with dreamlike elasticity but is, at the same time, described with unwavering clarity and precision and whose global reality status is never called into question. In this regard, Ishiguro's approach may be even more radical than Kafka's, for, unlike Gregor Samsa, who, waking up from troubled dreams, comes to the conclusion that his metamorphosis into an insect is *not* a dream, Ryder never even comes close to considering such a possibility in the first place. While in Kafka's story dream elements intrude into the waking world, in Ishiguro's novel we get a faithful description of the dream state itself.

A dream is the product of a single consciousness, which is why the dream environment typically reflects the dreamer's personal situation, memories, feelings, fears and wishes. The same is true of the storyworld depicted in the novel; in Ishiguro's words: 'a world that is seen so much from the point of view of one consciousness that it very boldly appropriates things that it finds to serve its needs'—so much so that Ryder is able to 'bend and twist the whole world around into being some big expression of his feelings and emotions'.[20] Like a dreamer, Ryder has 'gained a capacity to rearrange the contents of the real world according to a nonhistorical, extratemporal, and subjective directive and at the same time to perceive this new content as being in every sense a reality in its own right'.[21] Conversely, just like a non-lucid dreamer, he lacks all critical awareness that the world he moves around in and interacts with is his own mind's creation. Therefore, I hesitate to agree with Adelman's suggestion that Ryder 'resembles the master of ceremonies in a cabaret'.[22]

---

[18] States (1993), 37.
[19] States (1993), 34.
[20] Krider (1998), 152.
[21] States (1993), 29.
[22] Adelman (2001), 167.

Even though Ryder is indeed the origin or 'author' of all the characters populating the story, he is, at the same time, anything but master of the dream plot, anything but master of the dream cast refracting his own anxieties and fears. Likewise, he appears to be utterly helpless in view of the numerous obstacles and distractions that continually keep him from fulfilling his commitments or from pursuing his own inclinations. This becomes obvious, for instance, when Mr Hoffmann, the hotel manager, wakes Ryder up in the middle of the night to make him deliver a speech at a dinner party (cf. 117–118) or when Ryder tries hard to speak up for a former childhood friend but can articulate nothing but 'a slightly strangled grunt' (239). We are clearly back here with the paradox of authorship: While everything that materializes in the dream/storyworld is Ryder's own creation and projection, his position is still that of a passive recipient, thrown into the world of his own making, with no critical awareness or volitional power to speak of. He is both writer and reader (as suggested by the amalgamated name 'Ryder') and yet he continually fails to make sense of his dream text or to even recognize it as his own.

Throughout the novel, Ryder's short-term memory seems to be seriously impaired as well. Even the purpose of his present sojourn in the city initially eludes him. As he puts it shortly after his arrival: 'Clearly, this city was expecting of me something more than a simple recital. But when I tried to recall some basic details about the present visit, I had little success' (15). It only gradually dawns on Ryder that he was provided with a schedule he vaguely recalls studying on his plane journey—however, 'try as I might, I could remember nothing of what had been written on that sheet' (15). During his sojourn in the city, childhood and other memories from his distant past continually resurface, while short-term plans and commitments tend to be forgotten in the blink of an eye. Even more peculiarly, time and again Ryder does not at first recognize characters and places that turn out to be intimately connected to him. To account for these apparent cognitive impairments, some critics have suggested that Ryder may suffer from some kind of—possibly alcohol-induced—amnesia.[23] However, such an explanation surely seems too realist for

---

[23] See Adelman (2001); Lewis (2000); Wong (2000), 73.

this decidedly non-realist novel. Ryder's partial 'amnesia' can be more convincingly accounted for by comparing his state to that of a dreamer. As Green and McCreery point out: 'In an ordinary dream [as opposed to a lucid dream] a person's memory of his waking life is very partial, although in a sense he clearly possesses some, since elements of his past waking experience, such as friends, relatives, or familiar places, may enter into the dream, and be recognized by the dreamer'.[24] The 'realist' explanation likewise fails to take account of the elasticity and unstableness of Ryder's surroundings in which strangers morph into relatives or friends and hotel rooms turn out to be childhood sanctuaries from days long past. These shifts and transformations are accepted and accounted for by Ryder in the same way that the dream's transmutations are accepted and accounted for by the dreamer.

Likewise, just like a single-minded dreamer, Ryder uncritically accepts all incongruities, uncertainties and discontinuities of place and time. Here, the first scenes of the novel may serve as an illustration. After his arrival at the hotel, Ryder is taking the elevator up to his room, accompanied by Gustav, the elderly porter. The dreamlike bizarreness of this scene is created in part by means of both temporal and spatial incongruity. Firstly, Ryder and Gustav get caught up in a lengthy conversation about the reputation of Gustav's profession, which allegedly depends on the porter's self-imposed rule of not putting the luggage down even for a moment. This intensely absurd conversation goes on for four pages, by far surpassing the duration of an average elevator ride. Even more bizarrely, at the end of these four pages, with the elevator still on its way up, Ryder—prompted by Gustav's repeated reference to 'Miss Hilde'—follows the porter's gaze to discover that a 'small young woman in a neat business suit was standing pressed into the corner behind me' (9). It is, of course, highly incongruous that, in the confined space of a hotel elevator, a third passenger could be overlooked in such a way. Miss Hilde, then, seems to materialize because her name has come up in the conversation—in the same way that a dreamer's thought often materializes as a dream image. Such incongruities do not give Ryder reason to pause and reflect though; like a dreamer he takes them in his stride. Even

---

[24] Green and McCreery (1999), 44.

5 Conjuring Up the Dream: Three Literary Case Studies

though he is slightly startled by Miss Hilde's unsuspected presence in the elevator, he neither doubts the reality status of his experience nor does he dwell on possible explanations. What is more, the detailed and pointedly factual descriptions of the characters and their actions contribute to the sense of realism informing even the most bizarre scenes. This is the case, for instance, when Miss Hilde admonishes Gustav for assuming that the local community does not hold their porters in sufficiently high regard:

> This was said in an unmistakably affectionate tone, but the porter seemed to feel real shame. He adjusted his posture away from us, the heavy cases thumping against his legs as he did so, and turned his gaze away sheepishly. […] While the young woman was speaking, Gustav must have continued to turn himself away, for when I next looked at him he was facing the opposite corner of the elevator with his back to us. The weight of the suitcases was making his knees sag and his shoulders quiver. His head was bent right down so as to be practically hidden from us behind him, but whether this was due to bashfulness or sheer physical exertion was hard to say. (9; 10)

While the narrator observes and registers Gustav's physical strain and speculates about the potential reasons—bashfulness, shame, physical exertion—behind the porter's body language, the global grotesqueness of the situation is glossed over by precisely these minute perceptions and serious speculations.

Another noteworthy example of Ryder's dreamlike lack of reflective awareness occurs in Chap. 2, when Mr Hoffmann picks up the pianist from the hotel to give him a lift to the dinner party. Despite the late hour and the fact that earlier that night the town had seemed asleep, they are now edging their way through heavy traffic. Eventually they leave the city, 'travelling on a long road with dark open spaces—perhaps farmland—to either side' (120). After what is described as a very long drive, they finally reach their destination, 'a substantial residence […] in a salubrious residential district' (123). The duration of their drive suggests that this district must be miles from the hotel. However, when the dinner party eventually draws to a close, one of the party guests, Stephan, offers to walk, rather than drive, Ryder back to his room:

> For a moment his words continued to puzzle me. Then, as I looked past the clusters of standing and seated dinner guests, past the waiters and the tables, to where the vast room disappeared into darkness, it suddenly dawned on me that we were in the atrium of the hotel. [...] I had no chance to dwell on this realisation, however, for Stephan was leading me away with surprising insistence. (147–148)

Even though Ryder is briefly puzzled by Stephan's words, this vague sense of hesitation is quickly superseded by a sense of comprehension (couched in the recurrent phrase 'it suddenly dawned on me'). While Ryder's realization that he is in the very same building he had departed from earlier that night constitutes an impossibility according to waking standards, he ultimately goes with the flow, displaying precisely the same lack of reflective awareness a non-lucid dreamer would. Linguistically, this lack of reflective awareness is emphasized by the placement of the adjective 'surprising'. Ryder, whose point of view filters the reader's perception, does not use this adjective to describe the realization of a completely impossible occurrence, but rather to describe the 'surprising insistence' with which Stephan leads him away. The reader is bound to be guided by such cues, focusing on the potential reasons for Stephan's unusual insistence rather than on explanations for an utterly implausible circumstance. Thus, sharing the first-person narrator's single-minded point of view, the reader, too, increasingly tends to go with the flow of the text, accepting its laws with less hesitation and surprise as the novel progresses.

The dinner party also serves as a good example for the various alienation dream elements scattered throughout the text. In this particular instance, Ishiguro draws on, and combines, two typical dream types that most readers will be familiar with in one way or another: the dream of being naked or inappropriately dressed in public and the public speaking dream. Not only does Ryder not have time to change into appropriate clothes before heading to the dinner party, instead entering a room full of smartly dressed strangers in only his dressing gown and slippers, but he—the special guest of honour—is more or less ignored and led 'around in slow circles' by the hostess, who makes 'no effort to introduce [him] to anyone' (125). All these are deviations from the dinner party script that even Ryder notes with some curiosity, without, however, questioning the scene's global reality status.

5 Conjuring Up the Dream: Three Literary Case Studies

Ryder is also expected to deliver a speech in front of the assembled guests, an occasion for which, needless to say, he is utterly unprepared. Ishiguro has the scene culminate in an anxiety/alienation dream scenario *par excellence* when Ryder believes to have been given the start signal even though everyone is still engaged in heated discussion about whether or not to erect a statue for the recently deceased dog of Mr Brodsky, the celebrated local musician supposed to conduct the orchestra on Thursday night:

> The room almost immediately fell silent and all eyes turned to me. The man who had objected to the statue broke off his argument and hurriedly took his seat. I cleared my throat a second time and was about to embark on my talk when I suddenly became aware that my dressing gown was hanging open, displaying the entire naked front of my body. Thrown into confusion, I hesitated for a second then sat back down again. (143)

There could hardly be a more straightforward reference to typical dream experience of which most readers will have either first- or second-hand knowledge. As is often the case in such dreams, the dinner guests seamlessly go on arguing without paying attention to Ryder's mishap. When Ryder eventually has a second go, this time making sure that his dressing gown is fastened, his intent is again thwarted and he fails to get beyond his opening line: 'Collapsing curtain rails! Poisoned rodents! Misprinted score sheets!' (145). At this point he is being unceremoniously interrupted by one of the other characters, Miss Collins, who addresses and engages him in an intensely personal conversation—with the other 100 dinner party guests presumably looking on or, again in dreamlike fashion, simply having faded out of the picture. At the semantic level, Ryder's lack of appropriate clothing metaphorically expresses his feeling of inadequacy, while his lack of preparation for the speech gestures towards his more general, deep-rooted fear of public failure or exposure. As Lewis notes, there is also a 'noticeable degree of wish fulfilment'[25] at work when on the following morning his eight-word speech is praised by Hoffmann for its supposed wittiness and brilliancy. The tension between Ryder's (fear of) inadequacy and exposure on the one hand and his desperate

---

[25] Lewis (2000), 107.

need for recognition and praise on the other, one of the leading themes of the novel, is brilliantly captured in this short 'dream' sequence.[26]

Another example for a typical dream scenario can be found towards the end of the novel when Ryder eventually sets out on his journey to the concert hall to give his long-expected concert. Because of heavy traffic Ryder is dropped off in sight of the concert hall building to cover the last part of the distance on foot. Preoccupied with worries about the upcoming evening he loses his way, straying through narrow unfamiliar side streets and being engulfed by a growing sense of panic. When he finally catches sight of the building again, 'no more than a block or two away' (386), he is stopped in his tracks by an unexpected obstacle: 'a brick wall running across my path—in fact, across the entire breadth of the street' (387). He realizes that there is no way to bypass the wall, described by a local woman as 'a folly' turned into a tourist attraction. As she explains, the wall was 'built by some eccentric person at the end of the last century […] it's rather odd, but it's been famous ever since' (388). While the reference to this odd obstacle might be thought to resonate with historical allusions to the Berlin Wall, the woman's explanation instead highlights the grotesque nature of a wall that was precisely *not* built for political reasons but apparently set up at a whim by 'some eccentric person'. It is like an unsurmountable dream wall barring the dreamer's path to his desired dream goal; despite the concert hall being a stone's throw away, there seems to be no easy way to reach it on foot. Interestingly though, at a later point in the novel, Ryder reaches the building without problems and with no further reference to the wall, which confirms that the obstacle is a projection of his present anxiety state.

The fact that Ryder is a complete stranger to the unnamed city reinforces the reader's sense of his disorientation and lack of autonomy. It is, of course, also in accordance with the fact that anxiety dreams are often set in an environment unknown to the dreamer. From the very first page of

---

[26] A similar scenario is repeated later in the novel when Ryder realizes shortly before the concert that he did not get a chance to practise the musical piece he is planning to recite. Accordingly, Hoffmann leads him to a room which turns out to be a toilet cubicle with a piano squeezed into it and, when this proves unsuitable, drives him to an isolated hut in the countryside. It is in line with dream logic that, similarly to the dinner party speech that Ryder never gives, his concert never actually takes place because by the time he makes it to the auditorium, after encountering countless other obstacles and getting involved in a number of tragicomic events, the audience has long left the building.

the novel, when the hotel lobby is described as 'gloomy' and as 'creating a slightly claustrophobic mood' (3), it becomes clear that the setting reflects Ryder's own feelings of anxiety, entrapment and disorientation. The incident with the wall outlined above is just the most drastic out of countless examples in the novel of Ryder getting lost, moving in circles or ending up in dead ends. As it were, the entire novel is made up of 'excursions that collapse back in on themselves'[27] and can perhaps best be viewed in terms of the extended conceptual metaphor 'life is a journey'. Ryder seems to be continually on the road, unable to provide a home either for himself or for his family. There is a lot of talk about the house Sophie wants to buy (with Ryder showing pointed lack of interest) as well as references to temporary 'homes' in the past such as Ryder's two-year childhood abode with his aunt or the 'old apartment' in which Sophie, Ryder and Boris appear to have lived. But in fact Ryder seems to be most at home in temporary and transitional 'dwellings' such as hotel rooms, public spaces, and even public means of transport. In the course of the novel Ryder hardly ever rests, doing full justice to the implications of his name. He seems to be always on the move to somewhere, riding on, however ineffectual his journeys may turn out to be. The recurrent motif of the circle is particularly striking. To give just a few examples: when he and Boris try to find their way to the 'old apartment', Ryder eventually realizes that they keep following a walkway leading round the vast housing estate and that it may be 'perfectly possible that we could walk in circles indefinitely' (212). Similarly, when Ryder loses his way in the brick wall scene, he feels that he is 'quite possibly going in circles' (386). Finally, as Lewis notes: 'The book even ends in a loop, with Ryder orbiting round the O-shaped suburbs of the town on a circular tram'.[28]

The metaphorical implications of the setting become particularly clear with regard to Ryder's relationship to Sophie. Early in the novel Ryder, Sophie and nine-year-old Boris head out for Sophie's apartment, which she claims is 'only a few minutes' walk from here, just past the medieval chapel' (38). They set out from a café in the city centre, stop for a while at a 'rather melancholy' (37) playground, and eventually leave via a 'deserted back street' (39). Leaving behind the Old Town, Sophie

---

[27] Lewis (2000), 108.
[28] Lewis (2000), 109.

increases her pace so that Ryder and Boris have difficulty keeping up and seem to be continually falling behind:

> Up ahead of us, Sophie's figure vanished around a corner and Boris's grip on my hand tightened. I had not until this moment appreciated how far in front we had allowed his mother to get and though we increased our pace, it seemed to take an inordinate time for us to reach the corner ourselves. Once we finally turned it, I saw to my annoyance that Sophie had gained even further on us. (40)

Ryder and Boris follow Sophie's lead through deserted, shabby districts, through 'a side alley, whose entrance was little more than a crack in the wall' (43), briefly catch up with her only to lose her again, are being joined by an old classmate of Ryder's on the way, reach an 'abandoned farmyard' (46) and watch Sophie in the distance disappear 'around the edge of some broken building' (46) until they finally lose sight of her for good, finding themselves 'at the edge of a vast grassy field' (48). Ryder recalls that Sophie's apartment, whose address he does not know, is supposed to be near the medieval chapel. Ryder's former classmate Saunders, in turn, informs them that the chapel is in the Old Town and advises them to take a bus, which, he assures them, will 'come in the end' (51). Needless to say it never does. As illustrated by this scene, the symbolically fraught spatial dimensions of Ryder's world often take conceptual metaphors literally in the same way that dreams do: the bleak impasse reached in Ryder's relationship with Sophie translates into a vast field, extending 'far beyond what could be seen by the moon' (48), with 'a harsh wind [sweeping] across the grass and on into the darkness' (48). From Saunders, Ryder's former classmate, Ryder learns that 'there's nothing that way. Nothing but emptiness. Only person living out there is that Brodsky fellow' (48). Brodsky, 'a has-been and a drunk',[29] in turn, happens to be the least desirable manifestation of one of Ryder's potential future selves.

Despite Ryder's unfamiliarity with the city, the places he finds there often turn into places familiar from both his recent and distant past. This is another dreamlike feature incorporated into the text. As has been

---

[29] Adelman (2001), 167.

5 Conjuring Up the Dream: Three Literary Case Studies

pointed out before, the dream 'cannot deal in flashbacks'[30] in the way that realist fiction would, which is why being reminded of your childhood home in a dream will in most cases transport this childhood home— or at least some composite version of it—into your dream present. In a realist novel, the narrator might switch back and forth between different levels of time, interspersing the plot with external analepses to the protagonist's childhood, or having the protagonist mentally relive a situation in the past in an interior monologue or in a dialogue with others. In contrast, as States points out: 'The dream would not really be flashing back to an earlier time or place but converting all time and place into an impacted extratemporal now, a trick that would get a novelist into quick trouble'.[31] Not so Ishiguro, who creates precisely such an 'extratemporal now', encompassing the protagonist's past, present and potential future. Admittedly, Ryder's memories do not always instantaneously conjure up different places, objects or characters from the past. For instance, when Ryder recalls having studied his schedule on a plane journey, he neither finds himself in an airplane nor does he suddenly hold the schedule in his hands. The most likely reason for this is that strict adherence to the dream law would render the text unreadable, requiring the reader to keep up with far too rapid and incomprehensible transformations of place and time. Indeed, one of the rules governing Ishiguro's text is that, throughout the novel, Ryder remains physically located in or around the unnamed city. However, this is not to say that the dream law of spatiotemporal transformations does not apply here. It is simply used in a modified and arguably more reader-friendly way whenever emotionally charged memories are evoked. Ishiguro himself has commented on this method as follows:

> Instead of using the more conventional methods like flashbacks, where you just learn about somebody's life from this point to that point, here, I thought, you could do it in a very different way, where someone apparently stumbles into this landscape in which everything is an expression of his past and his fears for the future.[32]

---

[30] States (1993), 24.
[31] States (1993), 24.
[32] Krider (1998), 152.

The city thus turns into a psychobiographical microcosm, a placeless place full of echoes from Ryder's past and mirrors refracting his present and potential future. It turns into a dreamscape in the sense that 'everything in the dream is the dreamer'.[33]

Lying on his bed in his anonymous hotel room, Ryder all of a sudden has an uncanny 'sense of recognition': 'The room I was now in, I realised, was the very room that had served as my bedroom during the two years my parents and I had lived at my aunt's house on the borders of England and Wales' (16). In a dream the outward features of the room would most likely morph into those of the remembered bedroom, with the dreamer stumbling upon his long-forgotten childhood toys and treasures. In Ryder's case, the transformation resembles an emotional sensing more than a visualization of the place from the past. In fact, Ryder's realization occurs while staring up at the ceiling, and it is the ceiling of all things that he apparently recognizes—despite the major changes he observes even here: 'It had been recently re-plastered and re-painted, its dimensions had been enlarged, the cornices had been removed, the decorations around the light fitting had been entirely altered. But it was unmistakably the same ceiling I had so often stared up at from my narrow creaking bed of those days' (16). Similarly, Ryder remains 'highly conscious of how all around the room features had been altered or removed' (17). Even though the room is not literally transformed then, Ryder is able to visually summon the features of what he calls his 'childhood sanctuary' in every small detail, experiencing 'a profound feeling of peace' in doing so:

> I closed my eyes and for a moment it was as though I were once more surrounded by all those old items of furniture. In the far corner to my right, the tall white wardrobe with the broken door knob. My aunt's painting of Salisbury Cathedral on the wall above my head. The bedside cabinet with its two small drawers filled with my little treasures and secrets. (17)

Tellingly, it is the hotel manager, a version of Ryder's own father, who soon after announces that Ryder will be moved to a different, more

---

[33] Van Dusen (1972), 103.

appropriate room whereas the present, supposedly unsuitable room will have to be demolished (cf. 122).

The hotel room is just one out of numerous other examples of unknown places becoming familiar or turning into places Ryder used to live in. More often than not these places are associated with England. Thus, when Ryder and Boris visit 'the old apartment', Ryder looks in through the window at a room 'looking steadily more familiar' (214) and full of objects that cause in him 'a poignant nudge of recognition' (214). He finds that the rear section of the room 'resembled exactly the back part of the parlour in the house my parents and I had lived in for several months in Manchester' (214). Here we have another temporary abode, in which Ryder, then precisely Boris' age, experienced 'the hope that a fresh, happier chapter was unfolding for us all' (214). When a neighbour informs them that the place is empty and that the previous tenants used to fight a lot, the man most certainly a heavy drinker, the reader gains insight at once into Ryder's and Boris' family situation.

Throughout the novel, then, there is a constant sense that Ryder has been 'there' before. This constant uncanny sense of *déjà vu* is reinforced by the fact that Ryder 'meets himself at every turn in characters and relationships that refract his history'.[34] Likewise, in a dream, 'the self always speaks to and of itself, though it might do so by converting itself into other dream characters'.[35] Essentially, the novel seems to be populated by three major types of characters all of which revolve around Ryder: firstly, those who imperceptibly turn from strangers into old acquaintances or friends of Ryder's; secondly, those who serve as ego projections, reflecting versions of Ryder at various stages in his life (boy, young adult, alter ego, and his potential future selves); and finally, those who impersonate aspects or character traits of Ryder's, at times carrying these to absurd extremes, thus holding up a mirror to his follies. As Adelman aptly sums up: 'The other characters exist only in reference to himself, as points of view on himself, as his stand-ins in a narrative he continuously relives'.[36]

---

[34] Adelman (2001), 167.
[35] States (1993), 89.
[36] Adelman (2001), 178.

The most important examples for the first group of characters are Fiona Roberts, an old childhood friend from England, and Sophie, Gustav's daughter and simultaneously Ryder's wife. Fiona first appears as a ticket inspector to whom Ryder tries to justify his lack of a valid tram ticket. Not in the least interested in his ticket, she unceremoniously reproaches him for having missed an important appointment with her the previous night. Needless to say, Ryder, though he remembers and recognizes Fiona, is not surprized about her presence, nor can he even recall having had an appointment with her or to what purpose. Though a minor character in the novel, Fiona is important as she provides the link to an emotionally critical time in Ryder's childhood, the two years spent at his aunt's house in Worcestershire with his parents before their ostensible separation. Having been a reliable and supportive friend back then, it is all the more crucial that throughout the novel she is continually let down by Ryder. When he eventually tries to make up for forgetting the appointment, he lets her down again by failing to reveal his identity and confirm their friendship in front of a circle of derisive local women. This scene culminates in Ryder's nightmarish transformation into a pig:

> 'Why don't you help me!' Fiona suddenly addressed me directly for the first time. 'What's the matter, why don't you do something?'
> In fact, all this time I had been continuing to strain. Now, just as Fiona turned to me, I caught a glimpse of myself in a mirror hung on the opposite wall. I saw that my face had become bright red and squashed into pig-like features, while my fists, clenched at chest level, were quivering along with the whole of my torso. Catching sight of myself in this condition took the wind right out of my sails and, losing heart, I collapsed back into the corner of the sofa, panting heavily. (240)

The reflection of a pig's face presented to Ryder in the mirror metaphorically captures his excessive self-contempt and sense of inadequacy. That such a transformation takes place precisely at this point of the novel may be related to the fact that the local women's committee has been formed to look after Ryder's parents during their imminent stay in the city. It is thus Fiona who reminds him—for the first time—that his parents are coming to town to attend his concert, a thought that will increasingly preoccupy and haunt him throughout the remainder of the novel.

Even more crucially, the hotel porter's daughter, and initially a complete stranger to Ryder, morphs into his wife Sophie. Early in the novel Ryder gives in to Gustav's urgent request to meet with her in order to 'find out what's troubling her' (34), this being one of the numerous favours Ryder finds himself obligated to provide. While his meeting with Sophie starts out as a meeting of strangers, at one point in their conversation Sophie suddenly adopts a familiar tone and starts talking about a house she is planning to buy for the family, that is herself, Ryder and nine-year-old Boris. This is how Ishiguro gives us the change from Ryder's perspective:

> She began to give me more details about the house. I remained silent, but only partly because of my uncertainty as to how I should respond. For the fact was, as we had been sitting together, Sophie's face had come to seem steadily more familiar to me, until now I thought I could even remember vaguely some earlier discussions about buying just such a house in the woods. (34)

Interestingly, Sophie's outward appearance is not described as changing. Much more subjectively, she comes 'to seem steadily more familiar' to Ryder, like a dream character recognized as a friend despite her different outward appearance. From this moment, Sophie is simultaneously the porter's daughter and Ryder's long-term partner. Similarly, Boris is both the porter's grandson and Ryder's (step-)son. In the course of the novel, Ryder goes through a number of conflict-laden situations with both Sophie and Boris, repeatedly demonstrating his own self-centredness and inability to live up to his role as partner and father and to provide a home for either himself or his family.

To even further complicate things, Boris is also one of Ryder's numerous ego projections. Roughly the same age that Ryder was during his formative time in Worcestershire, he relives similar situations, suffering under his parents' endless quarrels and Ryder's emotional neglect of his possibly non-biological son. At one level, Ryder has turned into a version of his own father, inflicting the same emotional wounds that were once inflicted on him. Conversely, a projection of Ryder's young adult self can be found in Stephan Hoffmann, the hotel manager's son. Stephan is supposed to perform at the same concert as Ryder and is eager to have Ryder's judgement on his performance. It becomes obvious that his greatest fear is that of failure and his greatest ambition to gain his parents' esteem.

Stephan, ostensibly a highly talented musician, has internalized the sense of being a failure unable to live up to his parents' expectations. He mirrors Ryder's own desire to gain his parents' praise and love, the driving force of Ryder's art and career. Geoffrey Saunders, the former classmate Ryder and Boris meet on their way to Sophie's apartment, seems like an alter ego of Ryder's, a version of what Ryder might have become save for his musical talent or what he might turn into without Sophie; he is possibly also a projection of Ryder's solipsistic self without the veneer of musical talent and success. Saunders is a lonely, frustrated bachelor, living in a tiny apartment and pining for his home in England like an exile. Finally, there are a number of projections of Ryder's possible future self, most importantly the other two musicians relevant to the plot: 'Christoph is the artist who has been rejected by the community; whereas Brodsky personifies the artist attempting to become reconciled with his audience.'[37] Brodsky is also an alcoholic, estranged from his ex-wife Miss Collins and nursing his mysterious war-time wound. According to Adelman, 'Brodsky, the ex-orchestra conductor, a has-been and a drunk, represents Ryder's future—the future ordained of him by his father—whereas a rehabilitated Brodsky courting Miss Collins (Brodsky's estranged wife) enacts Ryder's fantasy of changing the future' (167).[38]

The most important representative of the last group of characters is Gustav, the elderly porter, who serves as 'a mirror of Ryder, which parodies the artist's narcissistic obsession with the pain driving his art and with conferring the exalted dignity he must have'.[39] This 'narcissistic obsession' is demonstrated from the first chapter onwards, when Gustav explains to Ryder the importance of high standards in the profession of a porter, including his rule of never putting down the luggage, even while waiting in the elevator. The parody reaches its climax in Gustav's performance at the Porters' Dance, where, under the audience's cheerful applause, he lifts up more suitcases than he can possibly handle, the painful grimace on his face foreshadowing his death from exhaustion at the end of the novel. At the same time, Gustav has not spoken with his

---

[37] Lewis (2000), 111.
[38] Adelman (2001), 167.
[39] Adelman (2001), 176.

daughter Sophie since she was a child and seems quite incapable of dealing with this increasingly painful 'arrangement'. Quite obviously, Gustav reflects Ryder's own tendency to shoulder all the problems thrust upon him while conveniently ignoring the much more pressing ones of his own and his family's well-being. As he puts it early in the novel, justifying his frequent absences to Sophie: 'I arrive in a place and more often than not find terrible problems. Deep-seated, seemingly intractable problems, and people are so grateful I've come' (37). Ryder evidently fails to realize that the 'terrible', '[d]eep-seated', 'intractable' problems are indeed his own unresolved psychological issues, partly rooted in his unresolved childhood traumata and conflicted relationship with his parents.

Barry Lewis has argued that the novel cannot be read as Ryder's dream because 'the narration is refracted through what can only be called an omniscient/limited first-/third-person point of view, and resists easy focalisation. Ryder is not dreaming within his life; he is living within a dream. Whose dream it is, is not clear' (124). This is because on some occasions Ryder is miraculously aware of other characters' personal life-stories, is able to read their minds or to overhear conversations way out of his earshot. However, if we read *The Unconsoled* as Ryder's dream, then his partial omniscience is compatible with his dream authorship. Sartre has commented on 'that curious trait of the dream when everything is seen and known from both a superior point of view, which is that of the sleeper representing a world to himself, and from a relative and limited point of view, which is that of the imaginary me plunged into the world'.[40] While the limited point of view may be prevalent in most dreams, omniscience is not *per se* out of line with dream experience. As Adelman puts it: 'As dream-narrator, [Ryder] knows what characters are thinking; he knows their memories because they are his memories, and he knows what they are talking about when he is not present because their situations were, or, he fears, will be, his'.[41] There is not a single passage in the novel that does not emerge from his consciousness so that we might rephrase Wilson Van Dusen's statement that '[e]verything in the dream is the dreamer'[42] as: everything in the novel is Ryder. Giving Ryder

---

[40] Sartre (1972 [1940]), 202.
[41] Adelman (2001), 167.
[42] Van Dusen (1972), 103.

occasional omniscience, then, lays bare his dream authorship in a way that most dreams do not. However, Ryder cannot will this omniscience and ultimately he remains an unreliable narrator in an unreliable storyworld. This observation ties in with Lewis' claim that '[i]n many ways, Ryder is himself a kind of reader, struggling to make sense of the text in which he is trapped'.[43] Since he mostly 'reads' other dream characters' stories without recognizing them as his own projections, his attempts at making sense of the text are doomed to failure.

Ultimately, while many of the novel's features are reminiscent of dreaming, the purpose of the novel is perhaps not so much to faithfully render the dream experience than to show how waking life is dreamlike in various ways. As Ishiguro himself points out:

> We go through life rather like this guy goes through these four or five days. He's very aware of this patch [of light] as he's moving along, but it's an illusion to think that we carefully plan our lives. It's more that we blunder through, and every now and then we stop to take stock. We suddenly wonder, 'How did this happen? I'm here living in this place, working at this job, married to this person, but come to think of it, I've always lived like this.' You're pushed around by other people's agendas and accidents, all this time making an effort to say, 'Yes, I decided this consciously.' We tend to think we're in far more control than we are.[44]

At the end of his stay in the city Ryder has achieved nothing. He has gained no insight, no lucidity, and there is a strong sense that the same single-minded dream is going to repeat itself at his next destination, Helsinki (a colder climate, farther north). For the time being, however, Ryder is taking comfort in the affluent breakfast buffet served on the tram, finding momentary consolation in the prospect of 'pleasant talk' with his fellow travellers and in the unfaltering conviction that '[w]hatever disappointments this city had brought, there was no doubting that [his] presence had been greatly appreciated—just as it had been everywhere else [he] had ever gone' (534). Meanwhile, 'the tram [is] running a continuous circuit' (534) and Ryder is as much at home as he ever will

---

[43] Lewis (2000), 110.
[44] Krider (1998), 153.

be. If anyone experiences moments of insight and understanding, then, it is bound to be the reader, who, unlike Ryder, is mercifully allowed to wake up from the novel's relentlessly ongoing dream.

Dreaming of Wonderland: Clare Boylan's *Black Baby* (1988)

Towards the end of Clare Boylan's *Black Baby* the reader learns that large portions of the novel have taken place in the protagonist's mind—more precisely, in the dreamlike state into which the protagonist slips after falling into a coma halfway through the text. For the reader this shift from waking reality to dream happens imperceptibly. Even though the narration contains several incongruous passages and incidents, which might give the reader reason to pause and assess its reality status, such insight is ultimately suspended by means of various narrative techniques. The reader of Boylan's novel, then, accepts its reality status in much the same way that a non-lucid dreamer accepts that of his dream. The novel's dreamlike quality is gradually intensified over the course of the novel until it culminates in two bizarre—and truly dreamlike—scenes shortly *before* and *after* the truth is revealed to the reader. In what follows I will analyse how and to what effect the precarious balance between the reader's credulity in the 'reality' of the dream events and the dreamlike quality pervading the text is maintained in the novel. I will also argue that the dream state, facilitating broad connection-making, blurring of boundaries and deviation from waking categories of thinking, facilitates the protagonist's reimagining and rewriting of her own life story. This new narrative ultimately also blurs the boundaries of dream and reality for the reader so as to open up new vistas on the significance of the mind's interior life and a deeper truth that transcends waking standards of reality.

At the centre of the novel is Alice, an elderly 'spinster' in her mid-60s, who lives in her deceased parents' home in Dublin with only her cat for company. Her family boils down to 'the children', that is her two nephews and their respective wives, who routinely come to visit once a year at Christmas, and, to Alice's dismay, increasingly talk of having their aunt transferred to a home for the elderly. Besides this, Alice spends her time spying on her next-door neighbour's private life, secretly envying the widow's amorous adventures. After Alice is robbed and hospitalized, she and her neighbour befriend each other and it seems that the dullness of Alice's life will at last be broken. However, Mrs Willoughby drops dead on the very day Alice is released from hospital and, in her stead, a stranger enters Alice's life: a Black woman named Dinah, who, Alice believes, is the African baby she had 'bought' from the nuns with her First Communion money more than 50 years ago.[45] As the novel develops, Dinah moves in with Alice and utterly transforms her 'mother's' life. Increasingly, the timid elderly lady learns how to enjoy herself by letting go of her own late mother's overpowering influence. When a prostitute, temporarily given shelter in Alice's home, leaves behind her infant child, even Alice's innermost wish of mothering a real baby seems to come true. However, at this point the story unravels and the reader is forced to leave the inside perspective of Alice's dream for the outside perspective of hospital staff and relatives debating whether to switch off the machine that has been sustaining Alice since the stroke she suffered several weeks before. This realization is like a harsh awakening for the unsuspecting reader, who now witnesses a final increasingly bizarre dream sequence that ostensibly breaks off at the moment of Alice's death. The novel does not end here though. Instead, the focus shifts to Dinah, as we learn about her real life story as opposed to the one she made up for Alice. Dinah, actually Cora, was born in England, not Africa, and is, unsurprisingly, not the baby that Alice believes to have 'bought' from the nuns. We also learn that rather than searching out her supposed 'mother', she first shows up at Alice's house with the sinister intention of robbing the elderly lady, a plan she never puts into action. In the world of waking reality Alice and Dinah meet only on three occasions, the third and final one occurring in the hospital as Alice is recuperating from the actual robbery.

The narrative itself, told by a third-person omniscient narrator and partly focalized through Alice, is highly unreliable even before waking reality is superseded by Alice's dream. Thus, Alice is subject to a number

---

[45] Drawing on her own experience in a rural Catholic Irish school in the 1950s, Christine St. Peter (1997) explains that at Lent the children were indeed asked 'to bring our pennies and nickels to donate to a fund which would be sent to a foreign missionary […]. For $5 we could buy our own baby and give it a name' (36–37).

5 Conjuring Up the Dream: Three Literary Case Studies   231

of sense delusions and self-deceptions from the start. For instance, she mistakes the birthday gift of a gramophone for a coffin, which creates a sense of the surreal, even more so since her subjective impression is presented as objective fact. Even before Alice sees the gift, the narrator declares: 'The children had brought Alice a coffin for her birthday' (10). When the gift is unveiled a little later, the passage is focalized through Alice so that we get her unfiltered subjective impressions:

> They were all flanked defensively around the surprise. Andrea broke away from the group and crouched to lift a hem of the cloth, operating beneath it. All of a sudden Alice heard her father's voice. Father, who had been dead for years! His light tenor was muffled and weighted as if it clawed through the layers of earth which encased his body, to get to her. [...] And then Andrea whisked off the cloth and she found that she was staring at a coffin. (12)

Having been prepared for this revelation by the narrator's earlier statement as well as by the narrator's evocative description of the gift as 'long and solid and bulky' (8), the reader for a moment cannot help but wonder if 'the children' may indeed have played a macabre joke on their aunt, who 'stared at this cold wooden case which contained her father' (12). From Alice's perspective the idea that the box from which her late father's muffled singing voice emerges must be a coffin seems the only feasible explanation until she (and the reader) learns that the supposed coffin is really a gramophone on which to play her father's old recordings. However, even after the misunderstanding has been cleared up and 'the children' have left, Alice cannot quite rid herself of her initial suspicion: 'She walked over to the coffin and steeled herself to lift the lid. What if her father was there—what if he really was there?' (13). And even shortly afterwards, when Dinah shows up at her doorstep for the first time, she informs her: 'It's my birthday. [...] They gave me a coffin' (17). Given that 'the children' quite obviously cannot wait to lay their hands on Alice's worldly possessions, her insistence that they presented her with a coffin is not at all devoid of a sense of dreamlike psychological insight.

The first half of the novel abounds with other mildly bizarre moments, such as Alice's chance supermarket encounter with an unknown girl in wellingtons, who, after admonishing Alice for buying yellow lavatory paper and oranges from South Africa, invites her back 'to her bedsit to sample Bansha tea' (34), an invitation politely declined by Alice. Similarly, Alice enjoys a lengthy amiable conversation with a street prostitute, whom she provides with her address in case the girl should ever need help. While these encounters are part of the storyworld's waking reality, they pave the way for the even less likely occurrences to come. One of these is Alice's sudden realization that Dinah is the baby she named and bought with her First Communion money at the age of twelve. Interestingly, Alice calls the stranger 'Dinah' even before consciously remembering the 'black baby' and then has a dream the following night in which 'she was a little girl again in the playroom, rocking a cradle which would soon hold a baby' (25). This dream reminds Alice of the cradle she prepared for the baby that she thought the nuns would send to her, the same cradle she will later discover in the garden's undergrowth, where she hid and forgot about it more than 50 years ago. It is only then that '[t]he past swoop[s] in on her' and she 'remembers' (43). Most likely the attentive reader will be wary at this realization, not least because Alice is known to have just turned 67, while Dinah is described as being in her mid-30s. In this sense, Alice from the start is doing justice to her name by creating and living in her own make-believe wonderland. She conveniently explains away all incongruities, such as how Dinah would have been able to trace her and the fact that she looks 20 years younger than she ought to. Quite obviously, seeing in Dinah the baby she 'bought' as a child is a kind of wish-fulfilment on Alice's part, the new-found daughter being a miracle she chooses to believe in. Needless to say, none of Alice's assumptions are ever contradicted by Dinah, even though, on closer reading, they are never quite confirmed either. The reader thus either opts to believe the unlikely story constructed by Alice or, with more detachment, assumes that Alice is deceiving herself and/or is being deceived by Dinah, in short, that her unreliable make-believe tendencies colour the narrative.

There is a remarkable consistency to be found between the two parts of the novel. The dream continues seamlessly from Alice's waking life; there are no significant discontinuities of time and place, and the dream narrative is presented as a chronologically ordered sequence. Quite obviously, the author's aim here is not so much to faithfully render the dream state but to maintain the reader's credulity in the narrative's global reality,

5 Conjuring Up the Dream: Three Literary Case Studies 233

despite departing from it. On the other hand, the way in which characters and objects briefly introduced in the first half of the novel are absorbed into the second half suggests the dreamlike blending of day time residue with past experience. However, such dreamlike transformations and blurring of identity boundaries are only hinted at so as not to jeopardize the reader's 'willing suspension of disbelief'. In a similar vein, the omniscient perspective employed throughout the novel also serves to maintain the reader's credulity in the narrated events, more so than a story narrated solely from Alice's clearly unreliable point of view would. After all, since the story is partly focalized through Dinah, it follows that it cannot be entirely dreamed up by Alice.

The actual shift from waking reality to dream occurs in the transition from Chaps. 17 to 18. At the end of Chap. 17 Alice witnesses Mrs Willoughby's sudden death in a restaurant in which the two ladies celebrate Alice's release from hospital:

> There was a sharp rap on the table, which upset a glass and some cutlery. She [Alice] looked up quickly and was astonished to see that it was not Mrs Willoughby's hand which had struck the table, but her head. The vigilant glass eyes of the fox stared up from the bread plate, its dead paws flung out in alarm beside the dead head of its owner. (98)

The reference to the dead fox, characteristically worn around Mrs Willoughby's shoulders, will trigger later events at the deceased lady's funeral. However, at the beginning of chapter 18 we first learn that Alice is at home, cared for by the 'Meals people', and that something happened at Mrs Willoughby's funeral 'after which she would never be the same again' (99). This is a reference to Alice's stroke, which, as we learn in a flashback, occurred at her late neighbour's funeral, when Alice noticed that two of the mourners were wearing her late friend's clothes, including the fox collar she intimately associates with Mrs Willoughby. Striking out at the women in blind fury with her bunch of flowers, she witnesses how 'the helpless little fox [...] bounced forward from the usurper's shoulders. Alice watched it leaping into the grave, loyal as some trusty pet, and she realised it was what she herself should have done—flung herself in on top of the box to keep her neighbour company' (100–101). What follows is the concise description of Alice's recollection of her stroke: 'Her knees had turned to water and with a feeling of great foolishness she thumped on to the gravel' (101). As Maureen Reddy succinctly puts it, it is Mrs Willoughby's funeral, then, 'a precursor to and image of her own', which 'sends Alice down the rabbit hole'.[46]

The shift from waking reality to dream is thus imperceptible to the reader, who is bound to accept the narrator's claim that Alice is at home, recovering after her stroke, even though a number of subtle clues suggest that this might not be the case. Shortly after relating the scene at the funeral, the narrator tells us that '[s]ince her accident Alice found it hard to make her brain work. She appeared to exist in some atmosphere heavier than air and the people around her did not seem real' (101). Again, while on a second reading the reader comes to evaluate this statement differently—the people around Alice *are* quite literally not real but are hallucinated in her dreamlike state—on a first reading one is bound to view Alice's feeling of unreality as a symptom of the brain damage she has suffered (which in some sense it is). Crucially though, the very hint that Alice's brain may not be functioning as it used to also contributes to the reader's increased credulity in the global reality status of the events to come. After all, these are filtered through Alice's unreliable, partly impaired point of view, which in turn may easily account for certain instances of dreamlike bizarreness. Thus, any justified doubts about the narrative's global reality status on the reader's part are effectively precluded. What is more, the fact that Dinah is not only a character in, but a co-focalizer of, the second half of the novel likewise prevents the reader from suspecting a shift in the novel's reality status. It is here that an element of magic realism is most evident to the reader, if only with hindsight.

There are numerous hints that dream mechanisms may be at work in the novel, though mostly given in such a subtle way that the reader, prepared to accept incongruous occurrences, is not likely to suspect that waking reality has been superseded by Alice's dream. One of these is that characters appear in dreamlike fashion as though summoned by a mere thought. This, for instance, is the case with Dinah: 'As often happened

---

[46] Reddy (2014), 225.

when she [Alice] was thinking of Dinah, the black woman appeared, apparently from nowhere' (164). The most crucial of these generally very unobtrusive incidents is when 'the children', Andrea and Marjory, come to visit at the beginning of Chap. 18 to persuade Alice to move into a home for the elderly. Alice in vain tries to make them leave by claiming that she is expecting a visitor. To both Alice's and the two women's surprise, a visitor indeed materializes almost instantaneously: '"It's Dinah." Alice allowed herself to smile. The appearance of the black woman was like the sight of Noah to the last wingless animal as the flood foamed over its paws' (104). This is Dinah's first appearance in Alice's dream. Not only does she rescue Alice from the two younger women's bullying but she brings much-needed groceries and longed-for treats such as milk, bread, biscuits and vinegar chips as well as equally needed emotional sustenance.

In this respect, Alice's story narrated in the second half of the novel may read like a straightforward wish-fulfilment dream. In a sense, she creates her own inverted wonderland reality, a 'utopia of love, tolerance, and sensual freedom compared to the real one'.[47] Her loneliness is broken by Dinah, who moves in with her, looks after her and at the same time helps her emancipate herself both from her parents' still overpowering influence and from 'the children's' claim on herself and her belongings. Her presence provides Alice with a sense of safety: 'Dinah's snores rumbled amid the relics. She had the power to subdue ghosts, to disperse the clinging dust of their determination. The thought of her in the next room was comforting and disturbing' (108). At the same time, Dinah challenges Alice's inherited notions of morality, sexuality and race as well as making her face uncomfortable truths about herself. As Reddy rightly puts it, she saves Alice from her 'lifelong project of forgetting',[48] thereby enabling her to reimagine her own story. In true dream character fashion, Dinah is allowed to voice thoughts, insights and feelings repressed by Alice, for instance with regard to 'the children' or with regard to Alice's late parents. Dinah also ruthlessly transforms the house, turning it from a cold and musty mausoleum into a tolerably comfortable home. At one

---

[47] Shumaker (2006), 106.
[48] Reddy (2014), 219.

point, Alice, waking up after a nap, actually senses she may be dreaming as she takes in the change: 'The room had been transformed. Instead of the gaunt yellow light dripping down the walls there were gentle pools of radiance at elbow level. The curtains had been pulled, shutting out the gnashing wind. It reminded her of Mrs Willoughby's window when she had spied on it from her scullery' (114). Most importantly, Dinah recovers the garden, whose miraculous transformation metaphorically comes to represent Alice's own late flowering.

At one point in the novel Dinah, working in the garden, jokes that she may be 'some kind of gravedigger [...] sent here to dig up your past' (114). The past thus dug up is very closely related to Alice's late parents, whose hold on Alice is ubiquitous both in the house and in her mind. Their influence is symbolized by her father's 13 clocks in the hallway, which Alice obediently winds up every night (a duty she begins to neglect in the course of the novel) and by her mother's notions of gender, sexuality, race and morality, inherited, though never fully internalized by Alice. One of these is that 'family came first, however badly they behaved' (50) along with her mother's mantra that '[s]trangers were dangerous. They poked their noses into your business and then stabbed you in the back' (34). By opening up her home to 'strangers' and turning one of them, Dinah, into her own 'daughter', Alice increasingly challenges and ultimately rejects her mother's unwritten law. Such insight on Alice's part, however, is arguably facilitated by the dreaming mind's connection-making abilities, which, in turn, manifest themselves through the blending of characters.

Alice's mother appears in her dream in the shape of Verity, the street prostitute she met and provided with her address in the first half of the novel. To the reader (if not to Alice) it is obvious that it was Verity who passed Alice's address on to the two men who brutally robbed her on the night immediately after their first encounter. Now, however, shortly before Christmas, Verity knocks on Alice's door as she has no other place to go and Alice is delighted to take her in, thinking that 'Dinah would be pleased that she had captured such an exotic' (175). However, Verity's presence soon feels like a nightmare to Alice and, furthermore, lets the suspicion that she might indeed be dreaming take shape in Alice's mind for the very first time:

5 Conjuring Up the Dream: Three Literary Case Studies

She climbed back into bed, wishing she could undo the episode or wake up to Dinah's cheerful bustle and discover that it had all been a dream. The thought occurred then: perhaps it was a dream. It had the unpleasant, unmalleable qualities of a nightmare. She pinched herself but she was too numb with cold to feel anything. 'I don't know where I am,' she thought in sudden panic. 'Oh, Dina! Oh, Papa!' (176–177)

On Christmas Day, Verity (derisively called Ferrety by Dinah) dresses in the clothes of Alice's deceased mother as she owns no clothes of her own:

When she saw her mother waiting for her in the churchyard, her [Alice's] smile fell off. She looked disgusted, tall and bony in her grey lisle stockings and lace-up shoes, her rat-grey dress, watching Alice making a fool of herself. [...] Of course she had known it was Ferrety [sic] after a second or two, but the realisation brought no relief. How had the girl assembled the exact outfit with which Mother, for many years, had renounced life? Where had she found the grey stockings and how did her feet adjust themselves so neatly to Mother's brittle shoes? She came towards them with that stiff, remembered walk and looked over Alice in exasperation. 'You look like a teacosy in that jumper,' she said. She laughed then, her cat's laugh. (187–188)

Even though Alice tolerates Verity in her home, she cannot rid herself of the impression that her own mother has somehow returned to haunt her and, more important, spoil the fun she is having. On the other hand, the uncanny effect Verity clearly has on Alice is also therapeutic or in some sense cathartic. By recognizing her own mother in Verity, Alice is able to voice criticism of her mother's way of life for the first time. Conversely, Verity does justice to her name and speaks the truth by holding a mirror up to Alice: "'There's a photograph of your mother in the drawing room, dressed like this. I knew it was your mother. She's the spit of you.' "No!" Alice clung to Dinah's arm. "Take me home"' (188). During the Christmas Day meal in Alice's house there is only one other moment in which her mother's presence haunts Alice in the shape of Verity:

There was a moment, after they had eaten, when a thick, digestive silence fell and Alice became aware that Ferrety was watching her, that old look of derisive assessment that she knew so well from her mother. She jumped up and began to clear the table and when she came back with the pudding, sweating alcohol beneath its blazing twig, the instant was safely past and Ferrety cheered along with everyone else. (189)

After this, Verity, though still not pleasant company, is no longer associated with Alice's mother, a restrictive force that Alice seems to have overcome eventually, a presence exorcized from her life. Obviously, the connection between Verity, a prostitute, and her mother is not one that Alice would have easily made in waking life. As Reddy notes: 'When Verity puts on Alice's mother's clothes, we see that Verity *is* the mother; harsh, judgemental, racist, and angry, accepting precisely the patriarchal precepts Alice's mother upheld'.[49] By blending the two characters, Alice's dream captures the similarities that waking consciousness would not allow her to make. These are partly of a socio-cultural nature, as rightly noted by Reddy, who points out that both Verity and Alice's mother are ultimately victims of the same patriarchal system that turns them into commodities on the one hand and into asexual mothers on the other.[50] It is telling that Verity, though looking after her child out of a sense of duty, ultimately leaves the baby behind. By blending Verity and her mother, Alice's dream self becomes able to see her mother's negatives sides more clearly but ultimately also to understand the socio-cultural forces shaping her behaviour. In a sense, she is also able to liberate her mother:

> After that the events of the day grew hazy. She was aware of intense happiness. She was awed by life's capacity for transformation, swift and unpredictable as the seasons. She was impressed by a similar facility in Ferrety, the fallen woman. From time to time in the midst of her drinking and singing, Alice would catch her mother looking at her from a corner of the room and for an instant she would feel fraudulent and abashed.
>
> In other moments she became aware of a cluster of men buzzing in some part of the room but, when she came over for a closer look, she saw that it was Ferrety they enclosed; Ferrety in her plain grey dress, but now laughing and teasing in a scornful manner so that men were drawn to her as a pin to a magnet. (193–194)

---

[49] Reddy (2014), 226.
[50] See Reddy (2014), 226.

5 Conjuring Up the Dream: Three Literary Case Studies

When Alice, in the penultimate chapter, is reunited with her father, he asks: '"Is she gone?"' (206). This reference is to Alice's mother/Verity. When Alice confirms his question, his reaction betrays relief: '"That's all right, then"' (206).

Unsurprisingly, Alice's father is associated with Dinah. This becomes obvious especially in those instances in which Alice's senses momentarily delude her and she mistakes Dinah for her father. While these sense deceptions are soon cleared up, they are still narrated in such a way that a dreamlike blurring of identities is suggested. The most crucial incident is the following:

> She [Alice] was putting away her good plates when she saw Father striding past the scullery window in the dusk. Her heart gave a warning thump and she clutched at it, almost dropping a piece of china. She squinted at the pane. Teasing, it flung back a picture of her ugly scullery. Now she could make out the ghost again and she saw with astonishment that death had adorned his bald pate with a fine crop of black curls. But of course it was Dinah, sensibly kitted out in Father's old gardening clothes which were preserved, along with everything else, in the giant wardrobe. (126)

A little later, when Alice and Dinah make a bonfire so that Alice can roast sausages over an open fire for the first time in her life, Dinah's presence again evokes that of Alice's father, intensified by the sound of one of his recordings: 'The figure poking at the fire, the frail, damaged tenor voice floating out over smoke and woodspark, made her feel that her father was very close to her. She was at peace' (129).

It is significant that Dinah recovers the garden once planted by Alice's father and now so overgrown that at the beginning of the novel it 'would not let her [Alice] in' (42). In the course of the novel, the garden metaphorically comes to represent Alice's own late flowering. Despite the winter season, the garden begins to bloom:

> It was a phenomenon. Flowers did not bloom in the depths of December. Maybe they did. Maybe the foolish ones were lured out by the unseasonal spell of mild weather. Surely there would have to be something there already in the earth to lure. It was only a month since Dinah had begun her reclamation of the garden, since she had pushed in the tiny onions with their graveyard markers, the seeds as unpromising as mouse droppings. (163)

When towards the end of the novel Alice is reunited with her father, he asks to be shown the garden, where the ultimate wish-fulfilment is achieved in form of his praise: '"You've done all right, Ally." He patted her arm and led her outside' (207). The garden is now truly a dream garden, effusing the 'dizzy humming scents of summer roses, the pepper of nasturtium and the violet's whispering aura of romance. She sensed the high, pure tone of lavender and the swooning breath of honeysuckle' (207).

While the actual shift from waking reality to dream occurs in the transition from Chaps. 17 to 18, for the reader this becomes obvious only with hindsight, at the transition from Chaps. 31 to 32. In Chap. 31, Dinah and Alice discover the baby left behind by Verity and the chapter is becoming increasingly surreal, especially after Alice has fallen asleep, dreaming about the garden and waking up to find Dinah gone. The thought of holding the baby occurs to her, as she imagines 'the feathery feel of a new human, still fluttery from prehensile wings left over from its recent angel state' (199). However, the actual experience is disappointing and turns into what can best be described as an anxiety dream: the baby, '[i]ts stoic unappeal [being] a mirror to Alice's earliest past' (199), begins to remind her of, and therefore turns into, a pig:

> The child's face began to change. Its features drew together and its snout wrinkled up and its eyes vanished into folds of flesh. It [sic] complexion turned the bright unwholesome ruby of a monkey's behind. It grunted. It actually grunted.
>
> 'Dinah!' Alice was becoming increasingly uncomfortable. 'I think it's done something!'
>
> 'Dinah?' The silence that followed was an answer. Alice strained every fibre into that carrying blackness. 'Dinah!' She cried out in panic. She began to understand. The pig bucked and squealed in her arms as she ran from room to room, calling. (199–200)

What is it that Alice begins to understand? Simply that Dinah has left? That she has been dreaming? Or that the 'silence' and 'blackness' are the prelude to the end of her dream? Is she waking up? Or sinking into some deeper, final sleep?

What is certain is that, as readers, we are shocked into an understanding at the beginning of Chap. 32 when we leave Alice's mind for the outside perspective of the hospital room. The 'children' speculate about what Alice may be thinking and their conclusion that '[s]he's thinking nothing at all' (201) is, of course, highly ironic in view of the turbulent dream narrative we have just witnessed. However, we also learn that 'Alice had taken a turn in the night. The long sleep that followed her stroke had become the final stage of coma. He [the doctor] was sorry, but she was now technically dead' (202). The doctor further confirms that Alice had been living in a world of her own for the month following her seizure and that 'she seemed happy. Now and then the nurses heard her laughing. On the night before Christmas she sang a verse of "Silent Night" and, before her final collapse, she seemed to imagine she had a baby' (202). Believing the doctor's claim that '[t]here's nothing going on any more' (203) and that switching off the machine is 'just a formality' (203), the 'children' give their consent to do so—in 15 minutes' time. It is Alice's final 15 minutes, then, that the reader witnesses in the next chapter, which picks up from where we left Alice, running through the house and looking for Dinah, who, as Alice herself knows very well, 'has gone' (205). The baby, too, has vanished when she looks inside the green cradle and all of a sudden Alice is no longer sure if there ever was a baby: '"Baby?" she said aloud. "What made me think of a baby? We never had a baby in this house. I must be dreaming"' (205–206). Scared of the silence and sensing her impending death, for which she is '"[…] not ready"' (206), Alice decides to play one of her father's records, opens the gramophone and finds her father inside: 'Father was lying in the box, his hands folded on his chest, one corner of his mouth lifted in a little smirk, as if he was playing a joke. She started back when he opened an eye and winked at her' (206). What in waking life was only imagined now literally comes into being.

A sense of irony pervades the end of the chapter, when Alice and her father step out into the blooming garden, described in flamboyant detail, the magnolia petals spinning down 'satin and cream, pallor and blush, twirling and touching, piling up on the path like dancer's slippers in a dressing room' (207). As readers we are now fully aware that we are inside Alice's dream, that we witness her imaginative creation so that the narrator's reference to Alice's 'imagination failing her as usual' (207) is highly ironic. Having lived through her eventful and vibrant dream, we know better than this. And yet, when the only thing that comes to Alice's mind as she looks at the Edenic garden is '"it's ... heavenly"' (207), the reader cannot help but be in two minds about Alice's end. Is she still dreaming? Has she entered another sphere or, to put it differently, is she in Heaven? The reader's doubt remains unresolved, especially since the novel deliberately ends with Dinah/Cora continuing her involuntary magic. Thus, at the end of the novel Dinah, about to leave Dublin and determined to finally visit her mother's homeland in Africa, accidentally meets another elderly lady with unresolved issues in the park. As Dinah is following her new 'mother', the reader begins to suspect that she may not be an ordinary woman after all but possibly some kind of spiritual saviour; an angel who has somehow been sent to transform the final weeks of Alice's life, and who, despite herself, may well go on performing similar miracles for others, if only in their dreams. This note of magic realism, on which the novel ends, ironically raises questions about the reality status of Alice's dream, a dream which was, after all, lived more (joy)fully than the preceding 67 years of Alice's waking life.

Maureen Reddy writes that 'Alice think[s] through her life as she lies in a coma'.[51] Another critic refers to her 'comatose fantasy'.[52] However, it is not *thinking* or *fantasizing* but *dreaming* that enables Alice to reimagine her story; the loosening of boundaries and the making of new and broader connections is facilitated by the dream state in which her mind is increasingly freed from the standard categories of ordinary waking thinking. The dreaming Alice is able to see connections that she would never have 'dreamed' of making, such as between Verity and her mother or between Dinah and her father. Thanks to the subversive potential inherent in dreams, Alice gradually revises her inherited notions of gender, race and family and she contradicts waking perceptions about herself as unimaginative, rigid and fearful. Her dream narrative may be utopian and not realizable in the waking world as Alice can neither communicate her new-found knowledge nor change her waking life based on the insight gleaned in her dream. The dream's impact can only be on the reader's life as it emphasizes the 'potential richness and power of the usu-

---

[51] Reddy (2014), 218.
[52] Shumaker (2006), 103.

ally ignored subjectivity of a completely ordinary—and therefore culturally silenced and invisible—older woman'[53] by letting the reader share in her extraordinary dream.

Dreaming Up the Past: John Banville's *The Sea* (2005)

In a lecture entitled 'Fiction and the Dream', John Banville reveals that he sometimes incorporates his own dreams into his novels. By way of an example, he refers to a dream included in his Man Booker Prize-winning novel *The Sea* (2005):

> One night I dreamt a dream of myself as a boy, embarked on a mysterious journey, which affected me profoundly, and haunted my days for long afterwards, and which even still I still recall with a prescient shiver. So strong and so mysteriously meaningful did it seem that I could not resist putting it into the book.[54]

In the novel, this dream is related in considerably richer detail by the first-person narrator, Max Morden, a recent widower in his 60s, who seeks to come to terms with the grief over his wife's death by retreating into the supposed shelter of his distant past. His nocturnal dream of 'walking along a country-road [...] in winter, at dusk', at once 'the age I am now' and 'a boy as well' (24), sparks memories of a particularly formative time in his childhood, the transitional period from boyhood to early adolescence, as well as the place and people associated with it:

> I thought of Ballyless and the house there on Station Road, and the Graces, and Chloe Grace, I cannot think why, and it was as if I had stepped suddenly out of the dark into a splash of pale, salt-washed sunlight. It endured only a minute, less than a minute, that happy lightsomeness, but it told me what to do, and where I must go. (26)

---

[53] Reddy (2014), 218.
[54] Banville, 'Fiction and the Dream', 26–27.

The dream thus prompts his journey to the Irish seaside resort of his childhood summers, where he now becomes a lodger in the Cedars, the house in which the Graces, a family consisting of Carlo and Constance Grace, the twins Chloe and Myles, and their young governess Rose, used to stay one summer more than 50 years ago.

Banville's insistence that the dream included in the book is a 'novelised description'[55] of his own dream, rather than a purposely contrived fiction, is interesting for a number of reasons. For one, in a novel concerned with the themes of identity and authenticity, his avowal serves to blur the line between the autobiographical and the fictional, an impression reinforced by the fact that the narrator's childhood vacations resonate with details of Banville's own repeated summers spent in a Southern Irish seaside resort.[56] In his lecture, Banville resists any interpretation of his dream either in autobiographical or in fictional terms: 'I have no idea what this dream was about, either when I had dreamed it, or when I put it into the book; nor can I say what its function in the narrative might be. It just felt right to incorporate it into the action, such as it was, at that point'.[57] Evidently, the term 'novelised description' implies that, contrary to the author's claim, the dream was not simply incorporated into the novel 'such as it was' but in doing so was inevitably fictionalized and literalized. Be that as it may, it is, of course, not at all unusual for writers to intersperse their fictional works with their characters' clearly demarcated dreams which may or may not be based on their own. The functions of such literary dreams are various: they can provide insight into the characters' psyches; lend the novel psychological credibility or symbolic depth; or simply echo or reinforce its themes. While Banville refrains from commenting on these functions, he nevertheless emphasizes the strong emotional impact the dream had not only on himself but on various readers who told him 'how deeply they were affected by that particular passage'.[58]

The dream revolves around the notion of home, a word that occurs seven times in the comparatively short dream report provided by the nov-

---

[55] Banville, 'Fiction and the Dream', 28.
[56] See Facchinello (2010), 37.
[57] Banville, 'Fiction and the Dream', 28.
[58] Banville, 'Fiction and the Dream', 28.

el's narrator, Max Morden. Sketching a long, lonely, snowy country road in winter, either at nightfall or in 'a strange sort of dimly radiant night, the sort of night that there is only in dreams' (24), the narrator describes how he was 'determinedly on [his] way somewhere, going home, it seemed, although [he] did not know what or where exactly home might be' (24). Besides the characteristic vagueness of time and place, the dream contains some further elements of incongruity: The trees are full of leaves and yet covered in snow; the dreamer experiences a curious sense of a composite self, at once adult and child; and finally there is a dreamlike elusiveness shrouding the circumstances of his dream self's journey. The narrator has a vague recollection that '[s]omething had broken down, a car, no, a bicycle, a boy's bicycle' (24), and that he was 'on [his] way home, it must have been home, or somewhere that had been home, once, and that [he] would recognise again, when [he] got there' (24). As to the journey's purpose, it was 'of surpassing but inexplicable importance, one that I must make and was bound to complete' (24–25). The journey, then, is a quest that only the narrator/dreamer can accomplish: 'I was calm in myself, quite calm, and confident, too, despite not knowing rightly where I was going except that I was going home. I was alone on the road. The snow which had been slowly drifting down all day was unmarked by tracks of any kind, tyre, boot or hoof, for no one had passed this way and no one would' (25). What is noteworthy here, besides clear connotations of the conceptual metaphor 'life is a journey', is the dreamer's split sense of self; he is adult dreamer and dreamed child at the same time and he feels a curiously detached sense of compassion for his younger self, who is walking on fearlessly, unaware of what life has in store for him: 'I felt compassion for myself, that is to say the dreamer that I was felt compassion for the self being dreamed, this poor lummox going along dauntlessly in the snow at fall of day with only the road ahead of him and no promise of homecoming' (25). While the purpose and destination of the journey remain unclear within the dream, upon awakening the dreamer immediately feels 'that something had been achieved, or at least initiated' (25–26) and experiences a sense of clarity as to where his journey must lead him. Besides sparking the impulse to embark on the physical journey to Ballyless, then, this impactful dream reflects psychological and existential concerns at the heart of the novel in which the narrator sets out on an 'exploratory journey into the slippery realms of identity, authenticity, home and belonging'.[59]

As shown in the previous chapter, one of the effects of such clearly demarcated dreams in longer works of fiction is to provide a clear-cut line between waking and dreaming reality. John Banville's *The Sea*, however, is a novel of the mind and several reviewers have remarked on its dreamlike quality. The dream related in the early pages of the book not only impacts the narrator's mood and actions but seamlessly blends in with his relentless stream of consciousness, which consists of layers of memories as inward, subjective and portentous as the remembered dream itself. In other words, the dream is as 'real' and as subjectively filtered as all the other memories, which in turn always verge on the dreamlike. The sea provides an apt metaphor for this constant wavelike closing in and receding, this ceaseless blurring and overlapping of the different layers of consciousness as well as the unstable boundaries between present and past, inner and outer reality, self and other, fiction and truth, memory and dream.

The novel is subdivided into two parts, which in turn consist of unnumbered paragraphs of variable length. Like the waves of the incoming tide, these paragraphs carry the reader in and out of distant and more recent memories, interspersed with the narrator's reflections and daydreams about his past, present and future. Occasionally, the novel's main time levels—present (his stay at the Cedars), recent past (the year of his wife Anna's slow process of dying), distant past (the childhood summer with the Graces more than 50 years ago)—are curiously convoluted, for instance when the narrator recalls how, as a boy, he imagined the future in terms of an idealized version of the past: '[W]hat I foresaw for the future was in fact, if fact comes into it, a picture of what could only be an imagined past' (96). Likewise, revisiting the haunts of his childhood summers, Morden is at once confronted with the physical remains (or absence) of his multilayered memories which, in turn, are characteristically preserved and merged in his dreams. Thus, he remembers how, as a boy, the sound of the creaking 'sign over the Strand Café' reminded him of the gate of the Cedars on which he had seen another boy, Myles, swinging some time before. The gate is still there today while the sign is

---

[59] Facchinello (2010), 34.

5 Conjuring Up the Dream: Three Literary Case Studies

not. In his dreams both merge: 'They creak, this present gate, that past sign, to this day, to this night, in my dreams' (13). Similarly, reminiscing the day, a year ago, on which his wife Anna learned she was terminally ill with cancer, he recalls how the sight of the doctor's folder containing her file caused his mind to drift back to his school days: 'the pale-pink cardboard of the folder made me think of those shivery first mornings back at school after the summer holidays, the feel of brand-new schoolbooks and the somehow bodeful smell of ink and pared pencils. How the mind wanders, even on the most concentrated of occasions' (15). The link between present and past is, of course, provided by the emotional association evoked by the folder, past and present linked by the word/ sensation 'shivery' and the neologism 'bodeful'.

However, often the associational shifts between different time levels and states of consciousness are less obvious; they deliberately blur and thus become more dreamlike. The following passage refers to the day on which Chloe and her brother Myles died drowning in the sea, witnessed from the beach by Max and their governess Rose. The passage starts out with a reference to Morden's revisiting the day in his dreams, and it is unclear whether the memories then described refer to these dreams, the actual experience, or both. Towards the end of the passage, the reality status of his memories is even further complicated by reference to Max' imaginings. Due to the rapid shifts between time levels and states of consciousness, the reader experiences the boundaries between memory, dream and daydream in constant flux:

> Often in my dreams I am back there again, wading through that sand that grows ever more resistant, so that it seems that my feet themselves are made of some massy, crumbling stuff. What did I feel? Most strongly, I think, a sense of awe, awe of myself, that is, who had known two living creatures that now were suddenly, astoundingly dead. But did I believe they were dead? In my mind they were held suspended in a vast bright space, upright, their arms linked and their eyes wide open, gazing gravely before them into illimitable depths of light. (246)

As the narrator himself puts it elsewhere: 'The truth is, it has all begun to run together, past and possible future and impossible present' (96). He describes how, in the weeks before Anna's death, he 'seemed to inhabit a twilit netherworld in which it was scarcely possible to distinguish dream from waking, since both waking and dreaming had the same penetrable, darkly velutinous texture' (96–97). At a later stage he recalls how, during that time,

> I could not rightly tell if I had been awake or just dreaming that I was. Those nights that I spent sprawled in the armchair beside her bed were rife with curiously mundane hallucinations, half dreams of preparing meals for her, or talking about her to people I had never seen before, or just walking along with her, through dim, nondescript streets, I walking, that is, and she lying comatose beside me and yet managing to move, and keep pace with me, somehow, sliding along on solid air, on her journey towards the Field of Reeds. (237–238)

While such liminal or 'thin boundary' states occur during particularly trying moments in the narrator's life, such as Anna's death or his alcohol-induced blackout towards the end of the novel, a similar blurring of boundaries is visible throughout the text. Arguably, Morden's crisis caused by the loss of his wife renders him a person characterized by what Hartmann describes as 'thin or permeable boundaries, by fluidity, by merging, in a number of different psychological senses'.[60] This includes the tendency to fluidly move between states of waking and dreaming,[61] a tendency visible in the narrator's increasingly evident attempts to dream things into being, which in turn leaves the reader with an increasing sense of the narrator's unreliability.

The unreliability of Morden's memory is repeatedly dealt with. Occasionally, the narrator revels in the power of his memory to conjure up the past in a vivid way: 'I am at the Strand Café, with Chloe, after the pictures and that memorable kiss. We sat at a plastic table drinking our favourite drink [...] Remarkable the clarity with which, when I concentrate, I can see us there. Really, one might almost live one's life over, if only one could make a sufficient effort of recollection' (160). However, despite this optimism, Morden soon comes to realize that his memory is full of errors, uncertainties and blanks. Recalling his first encounter with

---

[60] Hartmann (1991a), 17.
[61] Hartmann (1991a), 17.

the Graces, he writes: 'Later that day, the day the Graces came, or the following one, or the one following that, I saw the black car again [...]' (9). Elsewhere, he insists that he 'distinctly recall[s]' a particular incident, only to admit that '[p]erhaps that was another day' (236). Unable to recall the Café owner's name, he decides to 'call her Mrs Strand' and sardonically comments: '[S]o much for Memory's prodigious memory' (161). More crucially, going on to imagine Chloe's appearance at the plastic table, her hair 'pale as the sunlight on the floor at her foot' (162), he realizes that the scene does not match the facts, for '[w]hen we left the picture-house it was evening, an evening after rain, and now it is the middle of an afternoon, hence that soft sunlight, that meandering breeze' (162–163). It becomes increasingly obvious that some of the gaps in his memory are filled in. Other memories are coloured by his retrospective knowledge and emotional bias. Conjuring up the memory of Chloe shortly before she moves into the sea to drown, for instance, he notes: 'It is only my fancy, I know, but I see the little waves lapping hungrily at her heels' (243). The reader, then, increasingly experiences doubt as to the authenticity and accuracy of Morden's memories and yet remains captured by his story as though enthralled by a dream.

Banville himself has repeatedly likened the creation of fiction to a dream-like state but also, more crucially in the present context, he has described the writer's ambition to create a dream in the reader's mind: 'The novelist's aim is to make the reader *have the dream*—not just to read about it, but actually to experience it; to have the dream, to write the novel'.[62] From the first page onwards, the reader of *The Sea* is drawn into the narrator's mind, left at the mercy of his solipsistic, drifting and twisting journey inwards and backwards in time. The cadence of Banville's sentences, with their often-noted 'dream-like, lyrical density',[63] is instrumental in creating a trancelike state in the reader. As John Kenny puts it with reference to the novel's beginning: 'By his own intent, Banville's prose in his late period reads more and more like absolute music. Once the long sentence rolls in with its description of the "strange tide" of the titular sea, the reader is sunk,

---

[62] Banville, 'Fiction and the Dream', 23.
[63] Berensmeyer (2000), 247.

seduced even by sound alone'.[64] However, dreams are visual and spatial experiences whereas the novel is a predominantly temporal art form. As Kenny notes: 'Rather than being experienced in an instant of sensory perception, the effect of the work of literary art is cumulative and cannot have the same direct similitude as physical representation'.[65] This is why Hobson and Wohl suggest that the art form closest to the dream state is visual art. According to them, like works of visual art, '[d]reams, too, are sets of perceptions and related emotions which arise directly in the mind without the medium of language'.[66] In Banville criticism, it is a commonplace that the author is obsessed 'with stories of the eye'.[67] His narrators struggle to paint visual images as vividly as possible, his 'emphasis on directly optical images and metaphors [being] a component part of Banville's project of phenomenological realism'.[68] His aim, then, is to 'generate vivid visual images and powerful physical sensations' in an attempt to capture the '"thereness of the world"'.[69] This 'thereness of the world', however, includes the world of imagination alongside that of physical reality, as illustrated by the following passage:

> That grass needs cutting, once more will suffice, for this year. I should offer to do it. The thought occurs and at once there I am, in shirt-sleeves and concertina trousers, stumbling sweat-stained behind the mower, grass-haulms in my mouth and the flies buzzing about my head. Odd, how often I see myself like this these days, at a distance, being someone else and doing things that only someone else would do. (43)

Given the importance of visuality in the novel, it is thus no coincidence that Morden is an art historian, working on a critical study of the French Modernist painter Pierre Bonnard (1867–1947). Interestingly, Bonnard's paintings, including domestic interiors, landscapes, still lifes, nudes and portraits, are often described as dreamlike. Rather than painting objects

---

[64] Kenny (2012), 177–178.
[65] Kenny (2006), 52–53.
[66] Hobson and Wohl (2005), 16.
[67] Kenny (2006), 54.
[68] Kenny (2006), 56.
[69] Facchinello (2010), 41.

5 Conjuring Up the Dream: Three Literary Case Studies

directly as they were in front of him, Bonnard preferred to paint from memory, after 'dreaming' over the notes, photographs and drawings on which his paintings were based. As the artist himself put it, '"I have all my subjects to hand. [...] I go back and look at them. I take notes. Then I go home. And before I start painting I reflect, I dream".'[70] Rather than direct reflections of the outside world, then, his paintings can be considered as imaginings based on memories. The same is true of Morden's visual recollections of the past, which, far from accurate, are a mixture of fiction and fact, dreamlike in both their vividness and their unstable elusiveness. They illustrate what Ricoeur, commenting on the difference between '"pure memory" and memory image',[71] calls 'the pitfalls of the imaginary, inasmuch as this putting-into-images, bordering on the hallucinatory function of the imagination, constitutes a sort of weakness, a discredit, a loss of reliability for memory'.[72] Thus, Morden's attempts to visually conjure up the past are not always successful. With regard to Chloe, for instance, he eventually admits: 'Try as I may, pretend as I may, I am unable to conjure her as I can her mother, say, or Myles, or even jug-eared Joe from the Field. I cannot, in short, see her. She wavers before my memory's eye at a fixed distance, always just beyond focus, moving backward at exactly the same rate as I am moving forward' (139). And about Anna he writes: 'I make myself think of her, I do it as an exercise. She is lodged in me like a knife and yet I am beginning to forget her. Already the image of her that I hold in my head is fraying, bits of pigments, flakes of gold leaf, are chipping off. Will the entire canvas be empty one day?' (215).

These gaps in Morden's visual memory are often filled in by resorting to the paintings of Bonnard and others, sometimes unconsciously so when, for instance, after describing Chloe's 'highly-domed, oddly convex forehead' he realizes that it looked 'remarkably like the forehead of that ghostly figure seen in profile hovering at the edge of Bonnard's painting *Table in Front of the Window*' (137). In fact, many details described in Morden's recollections of the past, in particular the interior scenes at the

---

[70] Whitfield and Elderfield (1998), 9.
[71] Ricoeur (1984), 52.
[72] Ricoeur (1984), 54.

Cedars, have been taken from Bonnard's domestic interiors (39). These include minor details like the sweet peas and a little black dog alluding to Bonnard's paintings *Sweetpeas* (1912) and *Woman and Dog* (1891) such as in the following scene in which Max comes face to face with Mrs Grace for the first time:

> So there I am, in that Edenic moment at what was suddenly the centre of the world, with that shaft of sunlight and those vestigial flowers—sweet pea? all at once I seem to see sweet pea—[…] Through an open doorway a small black woolly dog came skittering in from outside—somehow the action has shifted from the living room to the kitchen—[…]. (89–90)

Not only does the dog appear out of nowhere—as Morden later muses, 'By the way, that dog. I never saw it again. Whose can it have been?' (92)—but inexplicable scene shifts occur in dreamlike fashion: 'Mrs Grace was leaning against the table—the one with the sweet pea on it, for magically we are back in the living room again—smoking her cigarette in the way that women did in those days, one arm folded across her midriff and the elbow of the other cupped in a palm' (92). This vignette-like scene reads like the description of one of Bonnard's paintings. Facchinello links the evocations of Bonnard's paintings of his own home to Morden's state of homelessness, arguing that 'the presence of details from Bonnard's interiors in Morden's pictures of the Cedars signal [sic] an attempt to compensate for his homelessness, while at the same time it acts as a reminder for us of Morden's peculiar condition'.[73] As she rightly concludes, the sense of home he tries to create in his recollections with regard to what is a rented summer house occupied by another family is ultimately achieved 'at the expense of his selfhood, as those added details eloquently point to the home and self of another' (40).[74]

However, the intertextual allusions to Bonnard's paintings also serve a number of other functions. For one, they compensate for the gaps in Morden's memory and, by filling in the gaps with details from Bonnard's paintings, they help to create a sense of dreamlike vividness

---
[73] Facchinello (2010), 39–40.
[74] Facchinello (2010), 40.

and immediacy. They also compensate for Morden's own perceived inadequacy of visually re-creating his memories in contrast to a painter like Bonnard, who 'would have caught that texture exactly, the quiet sheen and shimmer of it' (43). At times, Morden's descriptions come close to this painterly ideal and he makes no bones about sacrificing what Ricoeur calls 'the faithfulness of memories'[75] to the 'visualizing function of imagination'.[76] The following passage, again about the narrator's first face-to-face encounter with Constance Grace, provides a good example:

> What was it she had been doing at the table? Arranging flowers in a vase—or is that too fanciful? There is a multi-coloured patch in my memory of the moment, a shimmer of variegated brightness where her hands hover. [...] How intensely that sunbeam glows. [...] Beyond the smouldering sunlight there is the placid gloom of indoors on a summer afternoon, where my memory gropes in search of details, solid objects, the components of the past. Mrs Grace, Constance, Connie, is still smiling at me in that unfocused way, which, now that I consider it, is how she looked at everything, as if she were not absolutely persuaded of the world's solidity and half expected it all at any moment to turn, in some outlandish and hilarious way, into something entirely different. (86–87)

The lack of persuasion 'of the world's solidity' is, of course, Morden's own; or as he puts it elsewhere: 'Everything seemed to be something else' (65). What point, then, in remaining 'faithful' to memories about objects, people and places that are anything but solid and real?

While the numerous intertextual references are obvious reminders that Morden's memory is biased, framed by and filtered through cultural texts that would not have been available to his 11-year-old self, they also serve to infuse the text with the uncanny presence of other characters and settings, the dreams of others that are subtly interwoven with the texture of Morden's own verbal–visual tapestry. This tapestry contains allusions not only to paintings but also to a myriad of literary works and myths which,

---

[75] Ricoeur (2006), 55.
[76] Ricoeur (2006), 52.

again, often take on a dreamlike quality, such as in the following almost mystical vision at the end of the novel's first part:

> Standing there in that white box of light I was transported for a moment to some far shore, real or imagined, I do not know which, although the details had a remarkable dreamlike definition, where I sat in the sun on a hard ridge of shaly sand holding in my hands a big flat smooth blue stone. The stone was dry and warm, I seemed to press it to my lips, it seemed to taste saltily of the sea's deeps and distances, far islands, lost places under leaning fronds, the frail skeletons of fishes, wrack and rot. (132)

The dreamlike, intensely visual quality of the description is even enhanced when the narrator goes on to describe the scene in the present tense, thereby intensifying the immediacy of the tangible experience of his memory/dream:

> The little waves before me at the water's edge speak with an animate voice, whispering eagerly of some ancient catastrophe, the sack of Troy, perhaps, or the sinking of Atlantis. [...] I see the black ship in the distance, looming imperceptibly nearer at every instant. I am there. I hear your siren's song. I am there, almost there. (132)

While evoking a number of vivid sense perceptions—hearing, tasting, touching and, most importantly, seeing—the dreamlike quality of this passage is retained by means of the sense of vagueness of time and place, the use of the verb 'seemed' and finally the mythical overtones reverberating with dreamlike echoes of apocalyptic portents: Troy, Atlantis, *The Odyssey*, *The Tempest*.

Morden also blurs the boundaries between himself and the fictional and mythical characters he conjures up by means of the numerous literary allusions with which the novel is riddled to such an extent that they 'transform Morden's narrative into a chorus of other voices'.[77] Facchinello uses the homecoming dream as a case in point, identifying sources that range from Elizabeth Bishop's poem 'Questions of Travel' to Beckett's *Molloy*.[78] Some of the novel's allusions to well-known fictions and myths

---

[77] Facchinello (2010), 37.
[78] See Facchinello (2010), 38.

5 Conjuring Up the Dream: Three Literary Case Studies   255

are provided directly, for instance when Morden describes himself as 'a lyreless Orpheus' (24) or refers to his 'journal of the plague year' (24). Others are more hidden and their impact, as with the sources identified by Facchinello, may depend on the reader's individual alertness and personal reading tastes. Nevertheless, these literary echoes resonate between the lines of Banville's novel and will be recognized and evoked to a varying degree by different readers, thereby causing a sense of the uncanny in their blurring of characters, identities and fictional worlds. As Nicholas Lezard aptly puts in a review of *The Sea*, it is '[n]ot that this is a book full of literary references, the kind ready to exclude those who don't get them. You don't need to be aware of them to feel the uncanny, haunting atmosphere'.[79] Far from being exhaustive, the following examples infused this particular reader's imagination with subtexts haunting the novel in such an uncanny way, thereby reinforcing its dreamlike qualities during the reading process.

The first is a discreet allusion to Daphne du Maurier's novel *Rebecca* (1938) evoked by the narrator's name Max Morden. Interestingly enough, in the course of the novel we learn that Max is not the narrator's real name but a name he chose for himself after meeting his wife Anna. Several critics have commented on the fact that *Max* is a recurring name in Banville's fictional universe and that characters called Max in his previous novels tended to be of a particularly nondescript personality.[80] This observation fits in with Morden's self-declared lack of identity which he partly tries to patch up by resorting to a variety of fictional predecessors. As he points out, 'I never had a personality, not in the way that others have, or think they have' (216). One of the reasons why Anna's death leaves him so utterly stranded is that she was 'the medium of [his] transmutation. She was the fairground mirror in which all [his] distortions would be made straight' (216). In other words, it was thanks to Anna that he could reinvent himself, by following her mantra '*Be anyone you like*' and thereby supposedly leaving behind 'the congeries of affects, inclinations, received ideas, class tics, that [his] birth and upbringing had bestowed on [him] in place of a personality' (216). Accordingly, the name Max may certainly also have been chosen to reflect Morden's newly acquired upper

---

[79] Lezard (2006), n. pag.
[80] See Facchinello (2010), 36.

middle-class identity. This is in line with the social position of his literary namesake in du Maurier's novel: Max de Winter—widowed husband of Rebecca, the absent *femme fatale* of the eponymous novel, who haunts both her husband's and his new young wife's minds and dreams. It is certainly no coincidence that the name 'de Winter' evokes Max Morden's snow-filled homecoming dream while the name 'Morden', German for *to murder*, evokes Max de Winter's unatoned deed of drowning his wife's body in the sea on another coast, during another 'strange tide', only to be haunted by her memory ever since. While Max Morden may not have killed Chloe by his own hand, in various complicated ways he feels responsible for her death by drowning, not least thanks to his secret wish of taking the twins' place in the Grace family. Incidentally, *Rebecca* also starts out with a dream, in which the now exiled/homeless narrator returns to Manderley and is thus prompted to relive and tell the story of the past. This causes a blurring of fictional identities—like Max de Winter, Max Morden is widowed and guilt-ridden; like de Winter's nameless new wife, he is drawn back into the past by a homecoming dream. He also shares her lower social origins, both having married up through their choice of partners, as well as her essentially homeless condition and her lack of identity. In fact, his own self-explanatory dream of 'trying to write [his] will on a machine that was lacking the word *I*. The letter *I*, that is, small and large' (71) is reminiscent of the young Mrs de Winter's dream at the end of *Rebecca*, in which she realizes that the notes she has been writing are not in her own 'small square handwriting' but in Rebecca's characteristic hand—'long, and slanting, with curious pointed strokes'.[81]

Another unobtrusive allusion provided by one of the character's names is to Henry James' *The Turn of the Screw* (1898). Chloe's mute twin is called Myles, which brings to mind Miles and Flora, the strange twins at the heart of James' novella. Like Max, the name Myles may well be another name invented by the narrator rather than the boy's actual name; there is a continual sense in the novel that the names of places (such as Ballymore and Ballyless) and characters (such as the Graces) are made up by Morden. Be that as it may, the literary echo of *The Turn of the Screw* triggered by the presence of twins, one of whom is called Myles, is unmistakable and opens up a welter of possible associations and *déjà vus* for the

---

[81] Du Maurier, *Rebecca*, 396.

5 Conjuring Up the Dream: Three Literary Case Studies

reader. *The Turn of the Screw* is, of course, another text haunted by the past, including Mrs Jessel's, the former governess's, death by drowning, which eerily evokes the twins' similar fate in Banville's text. The ghosts that come to haunt and tempt the children in James' novel may be actual ghosts or figments of the new governess's imagination, a question deliberately left open and up to the reader's interpretation. At any rate, the boundaries between reality and dream are deliberately blurred in this novel, just as they are in Banville's. While James' narrator experiences visions of Mrs Jessel and Mr Quint that are 'as definite as a picture in a frame',[82] Banville's narrator tries to conjure up the ghosts from his past in a similar way. The only ghost he 'hallucinates', however, is his own:

> I saw the scene as if from outside myself, the dining room half lit by two standard lamps, the ugly table with the whorled legs, Miss Vavasour absently at gaze and the Colonel stooped over his plate and baring one side of his upper dentures as he chewed, and I this big dark indistinct shape, like the shape that no one at the séance sees until the daguerreotype is developed. I think I am becoming my own ghost. (193–194)

If Chloe and Myles evoke Flora and Miles, whose part in *The Turn of the Screw* could be Morden's? Is he one of the ghosts, Mr Quint, marked by his lower social class, eager to move up in the hierarchy, an intruder dressing up in his master's clothes?[83] Or does he adopt the narrator's position, that of the new governess, jealous of the twins' unity and their closeness to the ghosts, eager to belong and become part of the family beyond her reach? At the same time, the Graces' governess, Rose, provides another link to James' novel. Not only does her name link her to Flora, but, like James' narrator, who daydreams about her absent employer, Rose, too, seems to harbour passionate feelings for Mr Grace—or so young Max mistakenly assumes, not realizing that it is in fact Constance Grace that Rose is pining for, a misunderstanding that may have led to an argument between Chloe and Rose, and ultimately to Chloe's and Myles' death.

Another novel tentatively evoked by *The Sea* is Emily Brontë's *Wuthering Heights* (1847), most obviously so when Morden seems momentarily to

---

[82] James, *The Turn of the Screw*, 171.
[83] See James, *The Turn of the Screw*, 180.

merge with Heathcliff in his boundless suffering and grief over the death of a passionately loved one. Thus, Morden addresses his late wife Anna as follows:

> Why have you not come back to haunt me? It is the least I would have expected of you. Why this silence day after day, night after interminable night? It is like a fog, this silence of yours. [...] Send back your ghost. Torment me, if you like. Rattle your chains, drag your cerements across the floor, keen like a banshee, anything. I would have a ghost. (247–248)

These words are clearly a milder echo of Heathcliff's savage outburst after Catherine's death: 'Catherine Earnshaw, may you not rest as long as I am living! You said I killed you—haunt me, then! [...] Be with me always—take any form—drive me mad! only *do* not leave me in this abyss, where I cannot find you!'[84] Inevitably, they also evoke the scene of Lockwood's dream during his brief sojourn at the Heights, in which Cathy's ghost requires entrance through the window of her old bedroom. There is clearly a stronger link between Cathy and Chloe (rather than Anna) as both are children haunting their now grown-up lovers' minds and both are described as wild, capricious and occasionally cruel, 'prone to sudden and unnerving flashes of violence' (170). While a similarly 'ghostly' dream scene does not occur in *The Sea*, the novel still evokes a sense of Morden trying to resurrect the dead, conjuring up their ghost-like presence in his mind as vividly as he can and by all means.

Raising ghosts, in turn, links Morden to Shakespeare's Prospero, the magician/playwright from *The Tempest*, another literary precursor from a text in which the motif of the sea plays a central role. However, in the scene in which Morden relives his memory (or fantasy?) of bringing the news of the twins' death to their parents, he likens himself to Ariel, Prospero's airy servant who, in obedience to his master's wishes, caused the storm and shipwreck at the start of the play:

> In the house all was tranquil and still. I moved among the rooms as if I were myself a thing of air, a drifting spirit, Ariel set free and at a loss. I found Mrs Grace in the living room. She turned to me, putting a hand to her mouth, the milky light of afternoon at her back. This all is silence, save

---

[84] Brontë, *Wuthering Heights*, 144.

for the drowsy hum of summer from without. Then Carlo Grace came in, saying, 'Damned thing, it seems to be...' and he stopped too, and so we stood in stillness, we three, at the end.

Was't well done? (247)[85]

Not only is this scene permeated with painterly and literary allusions but the phrase uttered by Carlo Grace brings the novel full circle in that it is the very same phrase overheard by the narrator when encountering Mr Grace for the first time, in a completely different context (cf. 7)—another uncanny echo. There are countless other instances in the text that might cause the reader to doubt its reality status. Thus, remembering the scene of Rose's and Chloe's final fight on the beach, the narrator wonders whether the disclosure of Rose's supposed passion for Mr Grace may have caused Chloe to walk into the sea. He then muses: 'After all, why should I be less susceptible than the next melodramatist to the tale's demand for a neat closing twist?' (235). Such a 'closing twist' is indeed provided at the end of the novel when the reader learns, in passing, that Morden's landlady Miss Vavasour is in fact Rose, whose passion was not focused on Mr Grace but on his wife, Constance (cf. 261–262).

What then is fact, what fiction? And does it really matter? As Nicholas Lezard puts it: 'The knowledge that everything is, or could be, contingent—on the facts, a faulty memory, the act of reading a book—is what, paradoxically, gives this story its weight and plausibility'.[86] This 'weight and plausibility', I would argue, is of the kind provided by dreams in which past and present events merge because they share the same emotional resonance and in which the central image (in this novel clearly the image of the sea) provides 'an *explanatory metaphor* for the dreamer's emotional state of mind'.[87] As Domhoff notes, 'past experiences are sometimes used as personal metaphors to express current conflicts that have similar emotions and feelings at their core',[88] which helps explain why Morden's helplessness vis-à-vis Anna's slow process of dying evokes

---

[85] This is, of course, a reference to Ariel's question in Shakespeare, *The Tempest*, 5.1, upon which Prospero sets him free.
[86] Lezard (2006), n. pag.
[87] Hartmann (1989), 4.
[88] Domhoff (2001b), n. pag.

childhood memories of helplessly witnessing Chloe's drowning from the beach. In fact, the novel ends with Morden's memory of the moment of Anna's death and his own sense of 'walking into the sea' (264). If *The Unconsoled* narrates Ryder's twisted journey through the labyrinthine passages of an unceasing REM-like dream, then *The Sea* provides us with an account of Morden's ceaseless mind-wandering, which occasionally deepens into a dreamlike state of consciousness. The novel also allows us glimpses of the author at work in 'the drama of the self, the theatrical ways in which the self imagines [or dreams] itself into uncertain being'.[89] Ultimately, then, it achieves Banville's declared ambition 'to make the reader *have the dream*—not just to read about it, but actually to experience it; to have the dream, to write the novel'.[90]

---

[89] Kenny (2012), 151.
[90] Banville, 'Fiction and the Dream', 23.

6

Conclusion

Aiming to lay the groundwork for an aesthetics of dreaming, this book has approached the intersections of dreaming and the literary imagination from various angles. The first part explored similarities between dreaming and waking imaginative states. Neurocognitive, empirical as well as phenomenological evidence corroborates the basic assumption at the heart of this book that dreaming and waking imaginative states share similar underlying physiological and mental processes. As researchers are beginning to explore more fully the implications of the recently discovered default mode network, it is likely that this hypothesis will be further solidified, confirming that dreaming is part of a continuum which 'runs roughly from focused-waking-thought at one end through looser thought or reverie to fantasy, daydreaming, and eventually to dreaming'.[1] It has been shown that dreams can be reduced neither to random neural firings nor to repressive mechanisms; on the contrary, the majority of contemporary researchers emphasize the creative, playful and aesthetic potential of dreaming, reminding us that dreams should be valued as 'the fair share of imaginative life we all inherit'.[2]

---

[1] Hartmann (2011), 31.
[2] States (1978/79), 571.

This empirically informed insight paved the way for a discussion of the potential evolutionary functions of dreaming and waking fictions in terms of each other. While such a discussion is bound to involve a good deal of speculation, there is ample evidence to suggest that both dreaming and waking imaginative states may serve as adaptive functions by enabling the dreamer to 'rehearse' threatening scenarios as well as to enhance their social skills, including empathy and theory of mind, in a realistic but safe mental simulation. Similarly, the dream's likely function of matching new and old experiences according to similar emotional categories finds its equivalent in what Keith Oatley terms 'appraisal patterns' in the reader, enabling him or her to relive remembered emotions in new fictional contexts. In more general terms, both dreaming and waking fictions involve broad connection-making, thus facilitating creative problem-solving as well as equipping us with the ability to deal with new situations and adapt to changes in the outside world. Ultimately, dreaming and waking imagination have been inextricably entwined from an early age, with the dream likely being 'the ur-form of all imaginative thought'.[3] In view of all evidence available, there is good reason to assume that they share not only similar creative processes but also similar, potentially adaptive, functions.

This book has deliberately chosen to focus on the *literary* imagination rather than on visual art forms such as painting or film. Initially, readers may well have been puzzled by this choice, given that dreams are predominantly visual and that film tends to be the medium traditionally likened to the dream state. However, it has become clear that the author's and reader's imaginative and creative processes are in many ways closer to the dream process, especially if the dreamer is viewed as simultaneously writer and reader of his or her dream. The 'paradox of authorship'—the puzzle how a dream can be simultaneously created and experienced—is not adequately captured by likening dreaming to the spectator's immersion in a finished film product that presents them with externally created percepts rather than with internally and spontaneously generated images. As amply corroborated by both empirical evidence and numerous writers' accounts, dreaming can more usefully be understood as an associative

---

[3] States (1993), 85.

process of spontaneous composition comparable to that of the fictional writer.

On the other hand, dreaming can be compared to a form of readerly immersion and thus can be usefully discussed in the context of reader response criticism. Especially recent approaches highlighting the active role of the reader in regard to mental simulation, visualization and spatiotemporal immersion have offered a number of fruitful insights. Conversely, dream research can shed new light on controversially debated problems such as the 'paradox of fiction' and concomitant questions concerning dream belief and identification. In this context, the state of lucid dreaming, in which the dreamer is immersed without being deceived as to the reality status of the dream, plays a particularly significant role. Most importantly, my approach to dreaming as a form of 'writingandreading'[4] highlights the often blurred boundaries between imaginative states, illuminating the ways in which the act of reading can easily shade into the activity of dreaming, how our conscious creative processes continue and intensify during the dream state, how waking and dreaming permeate each other and are linked by liminal states such as lucid dreaming, hypnagogia, readerly immersion and what has been called 'the writer's trance'.

After analysing dreaming as a process of imaginative creation and reception and in relation to waking imaginative states such as writing and reading, the second part of this book focused on the multiplicity of dream types and the 'language' of dreams. Despite some promising advances, most notably by Don Kuiken and his colleagues, much work still needs to be done in terms of empirical research on dream types and possible classificatory systems. The four impactful types of dream identified and studied by Kuiken and his team show interesting parallels to corresponding literary genres, modes and narrative techniques. However, further empirical research is needed before more far-reaching comparative generic studies can be attempted. My analysis of the more 'general' language of dreams highlighted the dream's narrative structure, its visual and metaphorical characteristics as well as the dreamer's typical 'single-mindedness'. It also explored the question if and how this 'language', in

---

[4] Oatley (2003).

the sense of the dreamer's subjective experience, can be translated into a literary language of dream. The basic argument was that, while we have to rely on dream reports in order to analyse the dream as aesthetically appreciated 'mental object', these dream reports are problematic in a number of ways and generally fail to adequately convey the elusive dream experience.

Accordingly, shifting the focus towards the more palpable 'aesthetic object' of the literary text, the various strategies and genres employed by writers to create a sense of dream were analysed and illustrated with examples spanning three centuries. Despite the challenges faced by the writer trying to 'translate' the sense of dream into language, it can be argued that narrative texts such as the ballad, the gothic novel or the short story are well-suited to the creation of a dreamlike effect. This is the case especially if the text, rather than presenting a clearly demarcated dream, either depicts the dream as part of the storyworld's waking reality or deliberately blurs the boundaries between dreaming and waking. The dreamlike effect on the reader is further facilitated by a text's high visuality and by means of narrative devices such as a trance-inducing rhythm. Expanding on and weaving together the findings from previous chapters, the final chapter of this book offered three in-depth case studies focusing on contemporary novels by Kazuo Ishiguro, Clare Boylan and John Banville, in all of which a sense of dreamlikeness is created in strikingly different ways and to different effect. The choice of texts purposely encompasses the broad range of dream experience from the use of typical dream scenarios and single-minded immersion in Ishiguro's *The Unconsoled* to the subtle and imperceptible supplanting of waking reality in Boylan's *Black Baby* to Banville's skilful blurring of the boundaries between memory, daydream and dream in *The Sea*.

It is important to note that relating the dream to waking states of imagination such as daydreaming and fictional immersion is not to deny its strangeness and otherness, which is precisely what writers and dreamers have been fascinated with throughout history. In fact, the dream may highlight precisely what is 'Other' in our everyday lives in the same way that literature can defamiliarize the ordinary or draw our attention to things easily overlooked. This includes moments of being such as, for instance, captured by short stories which have been found to bear a strong affinity to the dream. The same goes for the sense of *déjà vu* we sometimes experience in a city we have not visited before or the general 'touch of strangeness', at times verging on the grotesque, that we occasionally encounter in our daily lives but are too busy to notice or reflect about. This touch of strangeness or sense of dream is precisely what the writers discussed in this book try to capture and 'translate' into literary language. Literature, then, can bring us in touch with the elusive 'otherness' of the dream that is such an intimate, if undervalued, part of ourselves.

Even though this book has sought to outline some major strategies employed by writers to achieve this process of 'translation', it needs to be stressed that there cannot be *one* dream language or *one* oneiric style because the dream experience is far too diverse and multifaceted. The diversity of dreams necessitates more elaborate classifications than have hitherto been attempted. Further empirical studies on the typology of impactful dreams would facilitate and corroborate the first tentative insights on intersections between dream types and literary modes, genres and narrative techniques. Expanding the definition to include waking states of dreaming, moreover, highlights the fact that the boundaries between waking and dreaming are anything but clear-cut and that more time may be spent by many of us in a dreamlike or near-dreamlike state than we care to admit. It is precisely the blurring of dream–wake boundaries and the concomitant uncertainty, at times verging on ontological doubt, that many writers are interested in exploring. At the same time, they highlight the value of dreams as imaginatively, aesthetically and psychologically meaningful experiences.

Acknowledging the importance and value of the often marginalized dream experience has been an implicit concern running through the chapters of this book. In doing so, I have focused on the cross-cultural universality of dreaming both as imaginative experience and as aesthetic manifestation in literary works of fiction from three different centuries. Approaching works as diverse as Coleridge's 'The Rime of the Ancient Mariner' (1798) and John Banville's *The Sea* (2005) in terms of their dreamlikeness is to highlight the unchanging core of our emotional thinking as exemplified by the dream state and its metaphorical structures. For instance, the deeply ingrained conceptual metaphor 'life is a journey' informs the dreamlike journeys in many of the texts explored or referred to in this book, including the Ancient Mariner's ship voyage to the Arctic Sea, Harker's Transylvanian nightmare trip, Kate's archetypal journey northward, Ryder's restless travels to unnamed cities and Morden's homecoming dream prompting his journey into the past. What these texts further have in common is that the storyworlds, like dreamscapes, reflect and refract their characters' psychological and emotional concerns, including typical dream emotions such as guilt, fear and grief but also, occasionally, a sense of transcendence and elation as well as the potential for renewal, healing and liberation from the constraints of waking scripts, categories and cultural schemas. Dreams, just like literary narratives, present us with 'possible worlds', concerned with contingency rather than fact and occasionally with a sense of truth that transcends waking reality. At least this is what our dream life can achieve at its best, by means of broad connection-making, metaphorical playfulness and imaginal thinking, and this is what it shares with consciously created fictions which, in turn, enable us to aesthetically and consciously access our elusive dreamworld.

As has been emphasized time and again, dreaming is a solipsistic experience, revolving around the self and its emotional concerns, which constitutes a universal psychobiological constant connecting us across ages and cultures. It is this often noted universality of the dream which this book has highlighted. This is not to deny, however, that dreams can have culturally specific uses or culturally determined meanings and representations. As Susan Parman reminds us: 'The significations of dreams are cultural, and the study of such significations can serve as a kind of cultural key to help us understand Western cultural assumptions about humankind, social order, and so on'.[5] In this sense, the various cultural representations of dreams may yield new and fascinating insights by opening a window onto 'the mental life of a past culture'.[6] Thus, for instance, in the early modern period, dreams were often read as divinely inspired or prophetic and were put to religious and political uses accordingly, sometimes serving as powerfully subversive 'tools of change'.[7]

---

[5] Parman (1991), 4.
[6] McLuskie (1999), 167.
[7] Sobel (2000), 10.

For women in particular, they provided an opportunity to participate in public discourse or to vent their creative energies by hiding under the protective cover of a divinely inspired dream.[8] Janine Rivière, referring to the vibrant seventeenth-century intellectual debate on dreams, notes: 'The danger of dreams for many writers lay, as Thomas Hobbes noted in 1651, in their potential to incite civil war and religious dissent.'[9] Another good example is the cross-culturally experienced phenomenon of sleep paralysis, often accompanied by vivid hallucinations, a sense of pressure upon the chest and such an acute reality sense that the experience has given rise to various culturally specific and often supernatural explanations. In early modern Europe, for instance, this attack was frequently 'attributed to witchcraft'.[10] As Davies notes from a historian's perspective: 'Understanding sleep paralysis provides the historian […] with a unique sense of shared physical experience, a direct and very real link with the supernatural interpretations of past cultures'.[11]

Conversely, some of the approaches and research findings discussed in this book, such as McGinn's and States' models of dream authorship and Lakoff's concept of metaphor, partly echo previous findings, especially as regards the vibrant nineteenth-century dream discourse that was superseded by Freud's influential new school. This dream discourse mainly involved laypeople who recorded and analysed their own dreams, conducted introspective experiments and came to conclusions that are in many ways strikingly similar to those reached by researchers today.[12] The material available in form of dream diaries, articles and scientific studies has only just begun to be explored and promises a wealth of new discoveries to complement and enrich present-day research. It might also provide a reminder that, while not all of us may have access to a sleep lab or an fMRI scanner, we all have first-hand access to our own nightly dreams and should feel free to tap their potential for either pleasure or research.

---

[8] See Schrage-Früh (2012b).
[9] Rivière (2003), 120.
[10] Davies (2003), 181.
[11] Davies (2003), 199.
[12] See Groth and Lusty (2013).

There are, then, many possible avenues in which the neurocognitive and empirically informed approach to dreaming and the literary imagination might branch out to chart potentially undiscovered territory. I strongly concur with Patrick Colm Hogan though that 'the study of universals and the study of cultural and historical particularity are mutually necessary'.[13] Deepening our knowledge about the physiological and neurocognitive processes underlying our dreaming imagination will enrich our understanding of historical, cultural and literary approaches to dreaming. Thus, a reading of dream reports, literary dreams and dreamlike fictions in light of contemporary dream research may facilitate an understanding of a common core of unchanging human concerns as experienced and expressed in dream narratives dressed in culturally varied garb. As Carole Levin aptly puts it: 'Dreams indicate to us the ways in which we are fundamentally the same as peoples of earlier times and also the ways in which we are deeply different'.[14] To return to the initial claim made at the beginning of this book, our understanding of the human mind and its cultural and aesthetic creations can never be complete without including the volatile second reality inhabited each night by our nocturnal selves. To this end, the insights gleaned from neurocognitive and empirical dream research may be indispensable, but so are the cultural, literary and philosophical perspectives that challenge, complement and complete these findings. Above all, however, it is the literary text that allows us to aesthetically access and analyse the closed world of the dream beyond our own private, elusive and limited experience of dreaming.

---

[13] Hogan (2003), 10.
[14] Levin (2008), 1.

Bibliography

Primary Sources

Almansi, Guido and Claude Béguin, eds. 1986a. *Theatre of Sleep: An Anthology of Literary Dreams*. London: Pan Books.
Alvarez, Alfred. 1996. *Night: An Exploration of Night Life, Night Language, Sleep and Dreams*. London: Vintage.
Amis, Kingsley. 2001. Mason's Life. In *The Young Oxford Book of Nightmares*, ed. Dennis Pepper, 1–4. Oxford and New York: Oxford University Press.
Arnold-Forster, Mary. 1921. *Studies in Dreams*. London: George Allen & Unwin.
Bacon, Francis. 2011. The Advancement of Learning. In *The Works of Francis Bacon*, Philosophical Works 3, vol 3, eds. James Spedding et al., 253–492. Cambridge: Cambridge University Press.
Banville, John. 2005a. *The Sea*. Basingstoke and Oxford: Picador.
———. 2005b. Fiction and the Dream. In *Irish Studies in Brazil*, eds. Munira H. Mutran and Laura P.R. Izarra, 21–28. São Paulo: Associação Editorial Humanitas.
Borges, Jorge Luis. 1984. *Seven Nights*. New York: New Directions.
———. 1999. *Collected Fictions*. Trans. Andrew Hurley. London: Allen Lane.
———. The Circular Ruins. *Collected Fictions*, 96–100.

———. *Dreamtigers. Collected Fictions*, 294.
———. Foreword. *Brodie's Report. Collected Fictions*, 345–347.
———. 1999. Coleridge's Dream (1951). In *Selected Non-Fictions*, ed. Eliot Weinberger, 169–172. New York: Viking.
Boylan, Clare. 1988. *Black Baby*. London: Abacus.
Brook, Steven, ed. 1983. *The Oxford Book of Dreams*. Oxford: Oxford University Press.
Brontë, Emily. 1990. *Wuthering Heights and Poems*, ed. Philip Henderson. London: J. M. Dent and Sons.
Browne, Thomas. 1734. *Religio Medici* (1643). London: E. Curll.
———. 1835–36. On Dreams. In *Collected Works of Sir Thomas Browne*, ed. Simon Wilkin, 342–346. Norwich: Fletcher and Son.
Calvino, Italo. 1986. *If on a Winter's Night a Traveller*. Trans. William Weaver. Toronto: Lester and Orpen Dennys.
Carroll, Lewis. 1979. *Through the Looking-Glass and What Alice Found There* (1871). London: J. M. Dent and Sons.
Cobbe, Frances Power. 1872. Unconscious Cerebration: A Psychological Study (1870). In *Darwinism in Morals and Other Essays*, 305–334. London: Williams and Norgate.
———. 1872. Dreams, as Illustrations of Involuntary Cerebration (1871). In *Darwinism in Morals and Other Essays*, 336–338. London: Williams and Norgate.
Coleridge, Samuel Taylor. 1974. *The Portable Coleridge*, ed. Ian Richards. New York: The Viking Press.
———. Christabel. *The Portable Coleridge*, 105–127.
———. Kubla Khan. *The Portable Coleridge*, 156–158.
———. The Rime of the Ancient Mariner. *The Portable Coleridge*, 80–105.
———. The Pains of Sleep. *The Portable Coleridge*, 182–184.
———. 1835. *Specimens of the Table Talk*. 2 vols. vol 1. New York: Harper.
———. 1956–71. *Collected Letters of Samuel Taylor Coleridge*, ed. E.L. Griggs. 6 vols. London: Oxford University Press.
———. 1957–2002. *The Notebooks of Samuel Taylor Coleridge*, ed. Kathleen Coburn. 5 vols. Princeton, NJ: Princeton University Press.
———. 1969. *The Collected Works of Samuel Taylor Coleridge*, ed. Kathleen Coburn. London: Routledge.
———. 1969. *The Friend*, ed. B.E. Rooke. vol 4. *The Collected Works of Samuel Taylor Coleridge*, ed. Kathleen Coburn. London: Routledge.
———. 1983. *Biographia Literaria*, ed. James Engell and Walter Jackson Bate. 2 vols. *The Collected Works of Samuel Taylor Coleridge*, ed. Kathleen Coburn. London: Routledge.

———. 1987. *Lectures on Literature 1808–19*, ed. R.A. Foakes. 2 vols. *The Collected Works of Samuel Taylor Coleridge*, ed. Kathleen Coburn. London: Routledge.
De La Mare, Walter. 1984. *Behold This Dreamer! Of Reverie, Night, Sleep, Dream, Love-Dreams, Nightmare, Death, the Unconscious, the Imagination, Divination, the Artist, and Kindred Subjects* (1939). London and Boston: Faber and Faber.
Descartes, René. 1993. *Meditations on First Philosophy in Which the Existence of God and the Distinction of the Soul from the Body Are Demonstrated* (1641). Trans. Donald A. Cress. Indianapolis/Cambridge: Hacket Publishing Company.
Dickens, Charles. 1905. Early Coaches. In *Sketches by Boz*. vol 1 (1836). New York: Charles Scribner's Sons, 154–160.
———. 1964. Lying Awake. In *The Uncommercial Traveller* (1860). London: Oxford University Press, 431–437.
———. 1964. Night Walks. In *The Uncommercial Traveller* (1860). London: Oxford University Press, 127–135.
———. 2012. *The Selected Letters of Charles Dickens* (1851), ed. Jenny Hartley. Oxford: Oxford University Press.
Dostoyevsky, Fyodor. 1997. *Crime and Punishment*. Trans. David McDuff. London: Penguin.
Du Maurier, Daphne. 1975. *Rebecca* (1938). London: Pan Books.
———. 1988. The Pool (1959). In *The Blue Lenses and Other Stories*. London: Penguin, 128–158.
Ellis, Havelock. 1911. *The World of Dreams*. Boston, NY: Houghton Mifflin Company.
Epel, Naomi. 1993. *Writers Dreaming*. New York: Carol Southern Books.
Eliot, T.S. 2011. The Love Song of J. Alfred Prufrock. In *The Waste Land and Other Poems*. Toronto, ON: Broadview Press, 17–22.
Feltham, Owen. 2005. Of Dreams (1661). In *Great English Essays: From Bacon to Chesterton*, ed. Bob Blaisdell, 16–17. Mineola, NY: Dover Thrift Editions.
Gardner, John. 1978. *On Moral Fiction*. New York: Basic.
———. 1983. *The Art of Fiction*. New York: Vintage.
Gaskell, Elizabeth. 1997. *The Life of Charlotte Brontë* (1857). London: Penguin.
Gidion, Heidi. 2006. *Phantastische Nächte: Traumerfahrungen in Poesie und Prosa*. Göttingen: Vandenhoeck & Ruprecht.
Gordimer, Nadine. 1969. The International Symposium on the Short Story. *Kenyon Review* 30: 457–461.
Greenwood, Frederick. 1894. *Imagination in Dreams and Their Study*. London: John Lane.

Handke, Peter. 1990. *Absence*. Trans. Ralph Manheim. New York: Farrar, Straus, and Giroux.

Hawthorne, Nathaniel. 1932. *The American Notebooks of Nathaniel Hawthorne*, ed. Randall Stewart. New Haven, CT: Yale University Press.

———. 2013. Young Goodman Brown (1835). In *Nathaniel Hawthorne's Tales*, ed. James McIntosh, 84–96. New York and London: W.W. Norton & Company.

———. 2008. The Haunted Mind (1837). In *Twice-Told Tales*. Newcastle-upon-Tyne: Cambridge Scholars Publishing, 186–189.

Hill, Brian, ed. 1968. *Gates of Horn and Ivory: An Anthology of Dreams*. New York: Taplinger Publishing Company.

Hobbes, Thomas. 2005. *Leviathan, Part I: Of Man* (1651). Raleigh, NC: Hayes Barton Press.

Hustvedt, Siri. 2010. What Is Sleep? *The New York Times*, April 21, http://opinionator.blogs.nytimes.com/2010/04/21/what-is-sleep/?_r=0

Ishiguro, Kazuo. 1995. *The Unconsoled*. London: Faber and Faber.

James, Henry. 2010. *The Turn of the Screw and Other Tales*, ed. Kimberly S. Reid. Toronto, ON: Broadview Editions.

Jay, Clare. 2011. Dreamwriting. *Mslexia*, 13–15. http://www.clarejay.com/wordpress/wp-content/uploads/LucidDreamingFeature.pdf

Joyce, James. 2006. Araby. In *Dubliners* (1914), ed. Margot Norris, 20–26. New York and London: W.W. Norton & Company.

Kafka, Franz. 1990. Die Verwandlung (1915). In *Sämtliche Erzählungen*, ed. Paul Raabe, 56–99. Frankfurt: Fischer.

Lessing, Doris. 2002. *The Summer Before the Dark* (1973). London: Flamingo.

Levertov, Denise. 1998. Interweavings: Reflections on the Role of Dreams in the Making of Poems. In *Night Errands: How Poets Use Dreams*, ed. Roderick Townley, 105–119. Pittsburgh: University of Pittsburgh Press.

Lovecraft, H.P. 1994. *The H.P. Lovecraft Dream Book*, ed. S.T. Joshi, Will Murray and David E. Schultz. West Warwick: Necronomicon Press.

Macnish, Robert. 1830. *The Philosophy of Sleep*. Glasgow: W. R. M'Phun.

Mansfield, Katherine. 1981. Sun and Moon (1920). In *The Collected Stories of Katherine Mansfield*. London: Penguin, 153–160.

———. 1981. Bliss (1920). In *The Collected Stories of Katherine Mansfield*. London: Penguin, 91–105.

———. 1951. *Katherine Mansfield's Letters to John Middleton Murry, 1913–1922*, ed. John Middleton Murry. New York: Alfred A. Knopf.

Mitchell, David. 2008. What Use Are Dreams in Fiction? *Journal of European Studies* 38(4): 431–441.

Poe, Edgar Allan. 1963. Marginalia. In *The Works of Edgar Allan Poe*. vol 3. New York: W. J. Widdleton, 483–596.
———. 2004. The Fall of the House of Usher (1839). In *The Selected Writings of Edgar Allan Poe*, ed. G.R. Thompson, 199–215. New York and London: W.W. Norton and Company.
———. 2004. The Narrative of Arthur Gordon Pym (1838). In *The Selected Writings of Edgar Allan Poe*, ed. G.R. Thompson, 429–563. New York and London: W.W. Norton and Company.
Royle, Nicholas, ed. 1996. *The Tiger Garden: A Book of Writers' Dreams*. London and New York: Serpent's Tail.
Shakespeare, William. 2009. *The Tempest*, ed. Gerald Graff and James Phelan. Boston: Bedford/St. Martins.
Stevenson, Robert Louis. 2005. A Chapter on Dreams (1888). In *The Strange Case of Dr Jekyll and Mr Hyde*, ed. Martin A. Danahay, 95–105. Toronto, ON: Broadview Editions.
Stoker, Bram. 2000. *Dracula* (1897), ed. Glennis Byron. Toronto, ON: Broadview Press.
Townley, Roderick, ed. 1998. *Night Errands: How Poets Use Dreams*. Pittsburgh: University of Pittsburgh Press.
Wolf, Christa. 1988. *Cassandra: A Novel and Four Essays*. Trans. Jan Van Heurck. New York: Farrar, Straus, Giroux.
Woolf, Virginia. 1966. Reading. In *Collected Essays*, vol 2, 12–33. London: Hogarth Press.
———. 1969. *Between the Acts* (1941). New York: Harcourt Brace & Company.
———. 1976. A Sketch of the Past. In *Moments of Being: Unpublished Autobiographical Writings*, ed. Jeanne Schulkind, 61–137. London: Sussex University Press.
Whitman, Walt. 2002. Thoughts Under an Oak—A Dream (1875). In *The Oxford Book of Dreams*, ed. Stephen Brook, 116. Oxford: Oxford University Press.

Secondary Sources

Adair, Patricia M. 1967. *The Waking Dream: A Study of Coleridge's Poetry*. London: Arnold.
Adelman, Gary. 2001. Doubles on the Rocks: Ishiguro's *The Unconsoled*. *Critique: Studies in Contemporary Fiction* 42(2): 166–179.

Almansi, Guido and Claude Béguin. 1986b. Introduction. In *Theatre of Sleep: An Anthology of Literary Dreams*, eds. Guido Almansi and Claude Béguin, 3–11. London: Pan Books.

Alt, André. 2002. *Der Schlaf der Vernunft: Literatur und Traum in der Kulturgeschichte der Neuzeit*. München: C.H. Beck.

Andrade, Jackie, David Kavanagh and Alan Baddeley. 1997. Eye-Movements and Visual Imagery: A Working Memory Approach to the Treatment of Post-Traumatic Stress Disorder. *British Journal of Clinical Psychology* 36(2): 9–23.

Andrews-Hanna, Jessica, et al. 2010. Functional-Anatomic Fractionation of the Brain's Default Network. *Neuron* 65(4): 550–562.

Antrobus, John S. 1993. The Dreaming Mind/Brain: Understanding Its Processes with Connectionist Models. In *Dreaming as Cognition*, eds. Corrado Cavallero and David Foulkes, 77–92. New York: Harvester Wheatsheaf.

Antrobus, John S., Judith S. Antrobus and Jerome L. Singer. 1964. Eye Movements Accompanying Daydreaming, Visual Imagery, and Thought Suppression. *Journal of Abnormal and Social Psychology* 69(3): 244–252.

Aserinsky, Eugene and Nathanial Kleitman. 1953. Regularly Occurring Periods of Eye Motility and Concurrent Phenomena During Sleep. *Sleep Medicine Reviews* 118: 273–274.

Atchity, Kenneth and Vincent Atchity. 1990. Dreams, Literature, and the Arts. In *Dreamtime and Dreamwork: Decoding the Language of the Night*, ed. Stanley Krippner, 101–110. Los Angeles: Jeremy Tarcher.

Barcaro, Umberto and Marco Paoli. 2015. Dreaming and Neuroesthetics. In Neuroscience: Neuroscience and Aesthetics. *Frontiers in Human Neuroscience*. doi:10.3389/fnhum.2015.00348

Bardolph, Jacqueline. 1994. The French Connection. Bandol. In *Katherine Mansfield: In from the Margin*, ed. Roger Robinson, 158–172. Baton Rouge: Louisiana State University Press.

Baron-Cohen, Simon. 2007. The Biology of the Imagination. *Entelechy: Mind and Culture* 9, http://www.entelechyjournal.com/simonbaroncohen.htm

Barrett, Deirdre. 1991. Flying Dreams and Lucidity: An Empirical Study of Their Relationship. *Dreaming* 1(2): 129–134.

———. 2001. *The Committee of Sleep: How Artists, Scientists, and Athletes Use Their Dreams for Creative Problem-Solving and How You Can Too*. Oneiroi Press.

———. 2007. An Evolutionary Theory of Dreams and Problem-Solving. Cultural and Theoretical Perspectives. In *The New Science of Dreaming*,

vol 3, eds. Deirdre Barrett and Patrick McNamara, 133–153. Westport: Praeger.
Baumbach, Sibylle. 2015. *Literature and Fascination*. Basingstoke: Palgrave Macmillan.
Berensmeyer, Ingo. 2000. *John Banville: Fictions of Order. Authority, Authorship, Authenticity*. Heidelberg: Universitätsverlag C. Winter.
Blagrove, M., L. Farmer and E. Williams. 2004. The Relationship of Nightmare Frequency and Nightmare Distress to Well-Being. *Journal of Sleep Research* 13: 129–136.
Blanchot, Maurice. 1982. *The Space of Literature*. Trans. Ann Smock. Lincoln: University of Nebraska Press.
Bosnak, Robert. 2007. *Embodiment: Creative Imagination in Medicine, Art and Travel*. London: Routledge.
Bostetter, Edward E. 1975. *The Romantic Ventriloquists: Wordsworth, Coleridge, Keats, Shelley, Byron*. Seattle: University of Washington Press.
Brann, Eva T.H. 1991. *The World of the Imagination: Sum and Substance*. Lanham, MD: Rowman & Littlefield.
Brennan, Matthew C. 1997. *The Gothic Psyche: Disintegration and Growth in Nineteenth-Century English Literature*. New York: Camden House.
Brosch, Renate. 2013. Reading and Visualisation. *Anglistik* 24(4): 169–179.
Brown, Peter, ed. 1999. *Reading Dreams: The Interpretation of Dreams from Chaucer to Shakespeare*, 147–167. Oxford: Oxford University Press.
Buckner, R.L. 2011. The Serendipitous Discovery of the Brain's Default Network. *NeuroImage*, 1–9.
Buckner, R.L., J.R. Andrews-Hannah and D.L. Schacter. 2008. The Brain's Default Network: Anatomy, Function and Relevance to Disease. *Annals of the New York Academy of Sciences* 1124: 1–38.
Bulkeley, Kelly. 1999. *Visions of the Night: Dreams, Religion, and Psychology*. Albany: State University of New York Press.
———. 2010. Dreaming as Inspiration: Evidence from Religion, Philosophy, Literature, and Film. *International Review of Neurobiology* 92: 31–46.
Carroll, Joseph. 2004. *Literary Darwinism: Evolution, Human Nature, and Literature*. New York: Routledge.
———. 2012. The Adaptive Function of the Arts: Alternative Evolutionary Hypothesis. In *Telling Stories: Literature and Evolution/Evolution of Literature*, eds. Carsten Gansel and Dirk Vanderbeke, 50–63. Berlin: De Gruyter.
Cartwright, Rosalind D. 2010. *The Twenty-Four-Hour Mind: The Role of Sleep and Dreaming in Our Emotional Lives*. Oxford: Oxford University Press.

Castle, Terry. 1988. Phantasmagoria: Spectral Technology and the Metaphorics of Modern Reverie. *Critical Inquiry* 15(1): 26–61.

Cavallero, Corrado and David Foulkes, eds. 1993a. *Dreaming as Cognition*. New York: Harvester Wheatsheaf.

———. 1993b. Introduction. *Dreaming as Cognition*. New York: Harvester Wheatsheaf.

Chow, H.M., et al. 2013. Rhythmic Alternating Patterns of Brain Activity Distinguish Rapid Eye Movement Sleep from Other States of Consciousness. *Proceedings of the National Academy of Science of the United States of America* 110(25): 10300–10305.

Cipolli, C. and D. Poli. 1992. Story Structure in Verbal Reports of Mental Sleep Experience After Awakening in REM Sleep. *Sleep* 15: 133–142.

Cipolli, C., et al. 2015. Time-of-Night Variations in the Story-Like Organization of Dream Experience Developed During Rapid Eye Movement Sleep. *Journal of Sleep Research* 24(2): 234–240.

Cooke, Brandon. 2012. Research Methods and Problems in Aesthetics. In *The Continuum Companion to Aesthetics*, ed. Anna Christina Ribeiro, 14–38. London and New York: Continuum.

Cosmides, Leda and John Tooby. 2001. Does Beauty Build Adapted Minds? Toward an Evolutionary Theory of Aesthetics, Fiction and the Arts. *SubStance* 30(1/2): 6–27.

Craig, P. Erik. 1987. The Realness of Dreams. In *Dreams Are Wiser Than Men*, ed. Richard A. Russo, 34–57. Berkeley: North Atlantic.

Davies, Owen. 2003. The Nightmare Experience, Sleep Paralysis and Witchcraft Accusations. *Folklore* 114(2): 181–203.

———. 2007. *The Haunted: A Social History of Ghosts*. Basingstoke: Palgrave Macmillan.

Dawes, James. 2004. Fictional Feeling: Philosophy, Cognitive Science, and the American Gothic. *American Literature* 76(3): 437–466.

Day, William Patrick. 1985. *In the Circles of Fear and Desire: A Study of Gothic Fantasy*. Chicago: Chicago University Press.

DeLamotte, Eugenia C. 1990. *Perils of the Night: A Feminist Study of Nineteenth-Century Gothic*. Oxford: Oxford University Press.

Dement, William C. 1993. REM Sleep, Discovery of. In *Encyclopedia of Sleep and Dreaming*, ed. Mary A. Carskadon, 505–507. New York: Macmillan.

———. 1999. *The Promise of Sleep: A Pioneer in Sleep Medicine Explores the Vital Connection Between Health, Happiness, and a Good Night's Sleep*. New York: Delacorte Press.

Dennett, Daniel C. 1976. Are Dreams Experiences? *Philosophical Review* 85: 151–171.
Dieterle, Bernard, ed. 1998. *Träumungen: Traumerzählung in Film und Literatur*. St. Augustin: Gardez! Verlag.
Domhoff, G. William. 2001a. Why Did Empirical Dream Researchers Reject Freud? A Critique of Historical Claims by Mark Solms. *Dreaming* 14: 3–17.
———. 2001b. A New Neurocognitive Theory of Dreams. *Dreaming* 11(1): 13–33. http://www2.ucsc.edu/dreams/Library/domhoff_2001a.html
———. 2003. *The Scientific Study of Dreams: Neural Networks, Cognitive Development, and Content Analysis*. Washington, DC: American Psychological Association.
Domhoff, G. William and Kieran Fox. 2015. Dreaming and the Default Network: A Review, Synthesis, and Counterintuitive Research Proposal. *Consciousness and Cognition* 33: 342–353.
Drag, Wojciech. 2010. Elements of the Dreamlike and the Uncanny in Kazuo Ishiguro's *The Unconsoled*. *Styles of Communication* 2: 31–40.
Dreisbach, Christopher. 2000. Dreams in the History of Philosophy. *Dreaming* 10(1): 31–41.
Dunbar, Pamela. 1997. *Radical Mansfield: Double Discourse in Katherine Mansfield's Short Stories*. Basingstoke: Macmillan Press.
Duncan, Cynthia. 2010. *Unraveling the Real: The Fantastic in Spanish-American Ficciones*. Philadelphia: Temple University Press.
Eberwein, Robert T. 1980. The Filmic Dream and Point of View. *Literature/Film Quarterly* 8(3): 197–203.
———1984. *Film and the Dream Screen*. Princeton, NJ: Princeton University Press.
Edelman, Gerald M. 1989. *The Remembered Present: A Biological Theory of Consciousness*. New York: Basic Books.
Engel, Manfred. 2004. Jeder Träumer ein Shakespeare? Zum poetogenen Potential des Traumes. In *Anthropologie der Literatur: Poetogene Strukturen und ästhetisch-soziale Handlungsfelder*, eds. Rüdiger Zymner and Manfred Engel, 102–117. Paderborn: Mentis.
Esrock, Ellen J. 1994. *The Reader's Eye: Visual Imaging as Reader's Response*. Baltimore, MD: John Hopkins University Press.
Facchinello, Monica. 2010. "The Old Illusion of Belonging": Distinctive Style, Bad Faith and John Banville's *The Sea*. *Estudios Irlandeses* 5: 33–44.
Farbman, Herschel. 2008. *The Other Night: Dreaming, Writing, and Restlessness in Twentieth-Century Literature*. New York: Fordham University.
Felski, Rita. 2008. *Uses of Literature*. Malden, MA and Oxford: Blackwell.

Flanagan, Owen. 2000. *Dreaming Souls: Sleep, Dreams, and the Evolution of the Conscious Mind*. Oxford: Oxford University Press.
Ford, Jennifer. 1998. *Coleridge on Dreaming: Romanticism, Dreams and the Medical Imagination*. Cambridge: Cambridge University Press.
———. 1999. Samuel Taylor Coleridge and the Pains of Sleep. *History Workshop Journal* 48: 169–189.
Foulkes, David. 1974. How Do Hypnagogic Dreams Differ from REM Dreams? In *The New World of Dreams: An Anthology*, eds. Ralph L. Woods and Herbert B. Greenhouse, 319–325. New York: Macmillan Publishing.
———. 1978. *A Grammar of Dreams*. New York: Basic Books.
———. 1990. Dreaming and Consciousness. *European Journal of Cognitive Psychology* 2(1): 39–55.
———. 1993. Children's Dreaming. In *Dreaming as Cognition*, eds. Corrado Cavallero and David Foulkes, 114–132. New York: Harvester Wheatsheaf.
Foulkes, David and Gerald Vogel. 1965. Mental Activity at Sleep Onset. *Journal of Abnormal Psychology*, 231–243.
Fox, K.C.R., S. Nijeboer, E. Solomonova, G.W. Domhoff and K. Christoff. 2013. Dreaming as Mind Wandering: Evidence from Functional Neuroimaging and First-Person Content Reports. *Frontiers in Human Neuroscience* 7: 412.
Fraiberg, Selma. 1956. Kafka and the Dream. *The Partisan Review*, 47–69.
Franklin, Michael S. and Michael J. Zyphur. 2005. The Role of Dreams in the Evolution of the Human Mind. *Evolutionary Psychology* 3: 59–78.
Freud, Sigmund. 1953 (1900). The Interpretation of Dreams. In *The Standard Edition of the Complete Psychological Works of Sigmund Freud*. Trans. James Strachey. vols IV and V. London: The Hogarth Press, 1–715.
———. 1914. *On Dreams*. Rebman Company: Trans. M. D. Eder. New York.
———. 1919. The Uncanny. http://web.mit.edu/allanmc/www/freud1.pdf, 1–19.
———. 1962 (1922). Dreams and Telepathy. In *The Standard Edition of the Complete Psychological Works of Sigmund Freud*. Trans. James Strachey. vol XVIII (1920–1922). London: The Hogarth Press, 197–220.
———. 1992 (1933). Revision of the Theory of Dreams. In *Essential Papers on Dreams*, ed. Melvin R. Lansky, 32–52. New York: New York University Press.
Fulford, Tim. 1997. Dreams and the Egotistical Sublime: Coleridge and Wordsworth. *Dreaming* 7(2): 85–98.
Globus, Gordon. 1987. *Dream Life, Wake Life: The Human Condition through Dreams*. Albany: State University of New York Press.
Goumegou, Susanne and Marie Guthmüller, eds. 2011. *Traumwissen und Traumpoetik: Onirische Schreibweisen von der literarischen Moderne bis zur Gegenwart*. Würzburg: Königshausen & Neumann.

Goumegou, Susanne. 2011. Surrealistisch oder Kafkaesk? Zur Traumpoetik Roger Caillois' und dem Problem literarischer Traumhaftigkeit im 20. Jahrhundert. In *Traumwissen und Traumpoetik: Onirische Schreibweisen von der literarischen Moderne bis zur Gegenwart*, eds. Susanne Goumegou and Marie Guthmüller, 195–226. Würzburg: Königshausen & Neumann.

Gover, Tzivia and David Kahn. 2010. Consciousness in Dreams. *International Review of Neurobiology* 92: 181–195.

Green, Celia and Charles McCreery. 1999. *Lucid Dreaming: The Paradox of Consciousness During Sleep*. London: Routledge.

Greenfield, Thelma. 1998. Our Nightly Madness: Shakespeare's *Dream* Without *The Interpretation of Dreams*. In *A Midsummer Night's Dream: Critical Essays*, ed. Dorothea Kehler, 331–344. New York: Garland.

Gregor, Thomas. 1981. A Content Analysis of Mehinaku Dreams. *Ethos* 9: 353–390.

Griffith, Richard M., Otoya Miyagi and Akira Tago. 1958. The Universality of Typical Dreams: Japanese Versus Americans. *American Anthropologist* 68: 1173–1179.

Groth, Helen and Natalya Lusty. 2013. *Dreams and Modernity: A Cultural History*. New York: Routledge.

Haas, Henriette, Inge Strauch and Hayim Guitar-Amsterdamer. 1988. Die Erfassung bizarrer Elemente im Traum. *Schweizerische Zeitschrift für Psychologie* 47(4): 237–247.

Hacking, Ian. 2001. Dreams in Place. *The Journal of Aesthetics and Art Criticism* 59(3): 245–260.

Hall, Calvin S. 1953. A Cognitive Theory of Dreams. *The Journal of General Psychology* 49: 273–282.

———1968. Foreword. In *The Gates of Horn and Ivory: An Anthology of Dreams*, ed. Brian Hill, xvii–xxix. New York: Taplinger Publishing Company.

Hall, Calvin S. and Robert van de Castle. 1966. *The Content Analysis of Dreams*. New York: Appleton-Century-Crofts.

Hall, Calvin S. and Richard E. Lind. 1970. *Dreams, Life and Literature: A Study of Franz Kafka*. Chapel Hill: University of North Carolina Press.

Hanson, Clare. 1989. "Things Out of Words": Towards a Poetics of Short Fiction. In *Re-Reading the Short Story*, ed. Clare Hanson, 22–33. New York: St. Martin's Press.

Hartmann, Ernest. 1991a. *Boundaries in the Mind: A New Psychology of Personality*. New York: Basic Books.

———. 1991b. Thin and Thick Boundaries: Personality, Dreams, and Imagination. In *Mental Imagery*, ed. Robert G. Kunzendorf, 71–78. New York: Plenum.

———. 1998. *Dreams and Nightmares: The Origin and Meaning of Dreams.* Cambridge, MA: Perseus.

———. 2000a. We Do Not Dream of the Three R's: Implications for the Nature of Dreaming Mentation. *Dreaming* 10(2): 103–110.

———. 2000b. The Psychology and Physiology of Dreaming: A New Synthesis. In *Dreams 1900–2000: Science, Art, and the Unconscious Mind*, ed. Lynn Gamwell, 61–76. New York: Cornell University Press.

———. 2010. The Underlying Emotion and the Dream: Relating Dream Imagery to the Dreamer's Underlying Emotion Can Help Elucidate the Nature of Dreaming. *International Review of Neurobiology* 92: 297–214.

———. 2011. *The Nature and Functions of Dreaming.* Oxford and New York: Oxford University Press.

Hartmann, Ernest, Robert Harrison and Michael Zborowski. 2001. Boundaries in the Mind: Past Research and Future Directions. *North American Journal of Psychology* 3(3): 347–368.

Hayter, Alethea. 1969. *Opium and the Romantic Imagination.* London: Faber and Faber.

Hillman, James. 1979. *The Dream and the Underworld.* New York: Harper and Row.

Hobson, John Allan. 1988. *The Dreaming Brain.* New York: Basic Books.

———. 1992. The Brain as a Dream Machine: An Activation-Synthesis Hypothesis of Dreaming. In *Essential Papers on Dreams*, ed. Melvin R. Lansky, 452–473. New York: New York University Press.

———. 1999. *Dreaming as Delirium: How the Brain Goes Out of Its Mind.* Cambridge, MA: MIT Press.

———. 2002. The New Neuropsychology of Sleep: Implications for Psychoanalysis. In *Dreams: A Reader on the Religious, Cultural, and Psychological Dimensions of Dreaming*, ed. Kelly Bulkeley, 321–332. New York: Palgrave.

Hobson, John Allan and Hellmut Wohl. 2005. *From Angels to Neurones: Art and the New Science of Dreaming.* Parma: Mattioli.

Hobson, John Allan, and Robert McCarley. 1977. The Brain as a Dreamstate Generator: An Activation-Synthesis Hypothesis of the Dream Process. *American Journal of Psychiatry* 134: 1335–1348.

Hodgkin, Katharine, Michelle O'Callaghan, and Susan J. Wiseman (ed). 2008. *Reading the Early Modern Dream: The Terrors of the Night.* New York: Routledge.

Hogan, Patrick Colm. 2003. *The Mind and Its Stories: Narrative Universals and Human Emotion.* Cambridge: Cambridge University Press.

Hunt, Harry T. 1989. *The Multiplicity of Dreams: Memory, Imagination, and Consciousness*. New Haven: Yale University Press.
Hunter, Adrian. 2007. Introduction. In *The Cambridge Introduction to the Short Story in English*, ed. Adrian Hunter, 1–4. Cambridge: Cambridge University Press.
Ichikawa, Jonathan. 2009. Dreaming and Imagination. *Mind and Language* 24(1): 103–121.
Immordino-Yang, M.H., J.A. Christodoulou and V. Singh. 2012. Rest Is Not Idleness: Implications of the Brain's Default Mode for Human Development and Education. *Perspectives Psychological Science* 7: 352–364.
Iser, Wolfgang. 1980. *The Act of Reading: A Theory of Aesthetic Response*. Baltimore, MD: John Hopkins University Press.
Jacobs, Arthur M. and Roel M. Willems. 2016. Caring About Dostoyevsky: The Untapped Potential of Studying Literature. *Trends in Cognitive Sciences* 20(4): 243–245.
Kaplan, Jonas T., et al. 2016. Processing Narratives Concerning Protected Values: A Cross-Cultural Investigation of Neural Correlates. *Cerebral Cortex*: 1–11.
Kenny, John. 2006. Well Said Well Seen: The Pictorial Paradigm in John Banville's Fiction. *Irish University Review* 36(1): 52–67.
———. 2009. *John Banville*. Dublin: Irish Academic Press.
Kerr, Nancy H. 1993. Mental Imagery, Dreams, and Perception. In *Dreaming as Cognition*, eds. Corrado Cavallero and David Foulkes, 18–37. New York: Harvester Wheatsheaf.
Kilroe, Patricia. 2000. The Dream as Text, the Dream as Narrative. *Dreaming* 10(3): 125–137.
Kivy, Peter, ed. 2004. *The Blackwell Guide to Aesthetics*. Oxford: Blackwell Publishing.
Kosslyn, Stephen and Oliver Koenig. 1992. *Wet Mind: The New Cognitive Neuroscience*. New York: Free Press.
Kreuzer, Stefanie. 2014. *Traum und Erzählen in Literatur, Film und Kunst*. Paderborn: Wilhelm Fink.
Krider, Dylan Otto. 1998. Rooted in a Small Space: An Interview with Kazuo Ishiguro. *The Kenyon Review* 20(2): 146–154.
Kuiken, Don. 1991a. Interdisciplinary Studies of Dreams: Finding a Common Ground. In *Dream Images: A Call to Mental Arms*, eds. Jayne Gackenbach and Anees A. Sheikh, 185–202. Baywood: Farmingale, NY.
———. 1991b. Dreams and Self-Knowledge. In *Sleep and Dreams: A Source Book*, ed. Jayne Gackenbach, 225–250. New York: Garland.
———. 1995. Dreams and Feeling Realization. *Dreaming* 5(3): 129–157.

Kuiken, Don and Shelley Sikora. 1993. The Impact of Dreams on Waking Thoughts and Feelings. In *Functions of Dreaming*, eds. Alan Moffitt, Milton Kramer and Robert Hoffmann, 419–476. Albany: State University of New York Press.

Kuiken, Don and Ria Busink. 1996. Identifying Types of Impactful Dreams. *Dreaming* 6(2): 97–119.

Kuiken, Don and David Miall. 2002. A Feeling for Fiction: Becoming What We Behold. *Poetics* 30: 221–241.

Kuiken, Don, et al. 2004. Locating Self-Modifying Feelings Within Literary Reading. *Discourse Processes* 38(2): 267–286.

Kumar, Niven. 2009. The Poetics of Dreaming in Borges, Coleridge, and Kafka. In *Literature and Sensation*, eds. Anthony Uhlmann, Helen Groth, Paul Sheehan and Stephen McLaren, 122–132. Newcastle upon Tyne: Cambridge Scholars Publishing.

Kuzmičová, Anežka. 2013. The Words and Worlds of Literary Narratives: The Trade-Off Between Verbal Presence and Direct Presence in the Activity of Reading. In *Stories and Minds: Cognitive Approaches to Literary Narratives*, eds. Lars Bernaerts, Dirk De Geest, Luc Herman and Bart Vervaeck, 107–128. Lincoln and London: University of Nebraska Press.

LaBerge, Stephen. 1988. The Psychophysiology of Lucid Dreaming. In *Conscious Mind, Sleeping Brain: Perspectives on Lucid Dreaming*, eds. Jayne Gackenbach and Stephen LaBerge, 135–153. New York: Plenum Press.

———. 1993. Lucid Dreaming. In *Encyclopedia of Sleep and Dreaming*, ed. Mary A. Carskadon, 338–341. New York: Macmillan.

LaBerge, Stephen and Howard Rheingold. 1997. *Exploring the World of Lucid Dreaming*. New York: Ballantine.

LaBerge, Stephen and Donald J. DeGracia. 2000. Varieties of Lucid Dreaming Experience. In *Individual Differences in Consciousness Experience*, eds. R.G. Kunzendorf and B. Wallace, 269–307. Amsterdam: John Benjamins.

Lakoff, George. 2001. How Metaphor Structures Dreams: The Theory of Conceptual Metaphor Applied to Dream Analysis. In *Dreams: A Reader on the Religious, Cultural, and Psychological Dimensions of Dreaming*, ed. Kelly Bulkeley, 265–284. New York: Palgrave.

Lakoff, George and Mark Johnson. 1980. *Metaphors We Live By*. Chicago and London: The University of Chicago Press.

———. 1999. *Philosophy in the Flesh: The Embodied Mind and Its Challenge to Western Thought*. New York: Basic Books.

Lamarque, Peter and Stein Haugom Olsen. 2004. The Philosophy of Literature: Pleasure Restored. In *The Blackwell Guide to Aesthetics*, ed. Peter Kirvy, 195–214. Oxford: Blackwell Publishing.

Leadbetter, Gregory. 2011. *Coleridge and the Daemonic Imagination*. New York: Palgrave Macmillan.

Levin, Carole. 2008. *Dreaming the English Renaissance: Politics and Desire in Court and Culture*. Basingstoke: Palgrave Macmillan.

Levin, Ross, Jodi Galin and Bill Zywiak. 1991. Nightmares, Boundaries and Creativity. *Dreaming* 1(1): 63–74.

Levin, Ross and Tore Nielsen. 2007. Nightmares: A New Neurocognitive Model. *Sleep Medicine* 11(4): 295–310.

Levinson, Jerrold. 1997. Emotion in Response to Art: A Survey of the Terrain. In *Emotion and the Arts*, eds. Mette Hjort and Sue Laver, 1–34. New York: Oxford University Press.

Lewis, Barry. 2000. *Kazuo Ishiguro*. Manchester: Manchester University Press.

Lezard, Nicholas. 2006. A Strange Kind of Remembering. Review of *The Sea*, by John Banville. *The Guardian*. http://www.theguardian.com/books/2006/may/06/fiction.johnbanville

Llinás, Rodolfo R. and Denis Paré. 1991. Of Dreaming and Wakefulness. *Neuroscience* 44(3): 521–535.

Lowes, John L. 1957. *The Road to Xanadu: A Study in the Ways of the Imagination*. Princeton, NJ: Princeton University Press.

Mageo, Jeanette Marie, ed. 2003. *Dreaming and the Self: New Perspectives on Subjectivity, Identity, and Emotion*. Albany: State University of New York Press.

Margolin, Uri. 2003. Cognitive Science, the Thinking Mind, and Literary Narrative. In *Narrative Theory and the Cognitive Sciences*, ed. David Herman, 271–294. Stanford: CSLI.

Mar, Raymond A. 2004. The Neuropsychology of Narrative: Story Comprehension, Story Production and Their Interrelation. *Neuropsychologia* 42: 1414–1434.

Mars, Rogier B., et al. 2012. On the Relationship Between the "Default Mode Network" and the "Social Brain." *Frontiers of Human Neuroscience* 6: 189.

Massey, Irving. 2009. *The Neural Imagination: Aesthetic and Neuroscientific Approaches to the Arts*. Austin: University of Texas Press.

Mavromatis, Andreas. 1991. *Hypnagogia: The Unique State of Consciousness Between Wakefulness and Sleep*. London: Routledge.

McAndrew, Elizabeth. 1979. *The Gothic Tradition in Fiction*. New York: Columbia University.
McGinn, Colin. 2004. *Mindsight: Image, Dream, Meaning*. Cambridge: Harvard University Press.
———. 2005. *The Power of Movies: How Screen and Mind Interact*. New York: Vintage.
McLuskie, Kathleen. 1999. The "Candy-Colored Clown": Reading Early Modern Dreams. In *Reading Dreams: The Interpretation of Dreams from Chaucer to Shakespeare*, ed. Peter Brown, 147–167. Oxford: Oxford University Press.
McNamara, Patrick. 2008. *Nightmares: The Science and Solution of Those Frightening Visions During Sleep*. Westport: Praeger.
McNamara, Patrick, et al. 2010. REM and NREM Sleep and Mentation. *International Review of Neurobiology* 92: 69–86.
Meier, Barbara. 1993. Speech and Thinking in Dreams. In *Dreaming as Cognition*, eds. Corrado Cavallero and David Foulkes, 58–76. New York: Harvester Wheatsheaf.
Metz, Christian. 1977. *Psychoanalysis and Cinema: The Imaginary Signifier*. Trans. Celia Britton, Annwyl Williams, Ben Brewster and Alfred Guzzetti. London: Macmillan.
Miller, Patricia Cox. 1994. *Dreams in Late Antiquity: Studies in the Imagination of a Culture*. Princeton, NJ: Princeton University Press.
Montangero, Jacques. 1993. Dream, Problem-Solving, and Creativity. In *Dreaming as Cognition*, eds. Corrado Cavallero and David Foulkes, 93–113. New York: Harvester Wheatsheaf.
Montangero, Jacques and Corrado Cavallero. 2015. What Renders Dreams More or Less Narrative? A Microstructural Study of REM and Stage 2 Dreams Reported Upon Morning Awakening. *International Journal of Dream Research* 8(2): 105–119.
Nell, Victor. 1988. *Lost in a Book: The Psychology of Reading for Pleasure*. New Haven: Yale University Press.
Nielsen, Tore A. 1991. Reality Dreams and Their Effects on Spiritual Belief: A Revision of Animism Theory. In *Dream Images: A Call to Mental Arms*, eds. Jayne Gackenbach and A.A. Sheikh, 233–264. Amityville: Baywood Publishing.
———. 2010. Dream Analysis and Classification: The Reality Simulation Perspective. In *Principles and Practice of Sleep Medicine*, eds. Meir H. Kryger, Thomas Roth and William C. Dement, 595–603. New York: Elsevier.

Nielsen, Tore, Don Kuiken, Robert Hoffman and Alan Moffitt. 2001. REM and NREM Sleep Mentation Differences: A Question of Story Structure? *Sleep and Hypnosis* 3(1): 9–17.

Nir, Y. and G. Tononi. 2010. Dreaming and the Brain. *Trends in Cognitive Science* 14(2): 88–100.

Oatley, Keith. 2003. Writingandreading: The Future of Cognitive Poetics. In *Cognitive Poetics in Practice*, eds. G.J. Steen and J. Gavins, 161–173. London: Routledge.

———. 2011. *Such Stuff as Dreams: The Psychology of Fiction*. Oxford: Wiley-Blackwell.

Ostby, Y., et al. 2012. Mental Time Travel and Default-Mode Network Functional Connectivity in the Developing Brain. *Proceedings of the National Academy of Science of the United States of America* 109: 16800–16804.

Pace-Schott, Edward F. 2013. Dreaming as a Story-Telling Instinct. *New Frontiers in Psychology* 4: 159.

Palombo, Stanley R. 1980. The Cognitive Act in Dream Construction. *The Journal of the American Academy of Psychoanalysis* 8: 185–201.

———. 1983. The Genius of the Dream. *American Journal of Psychoanalysis* 43(4): 301–313.

Parman, Susan. 1991. *Dream and Culture: An Anthropological Study of the Western Intellectual Tradition*. New York: Praeger.

Payne, Jennifer. 2004. Memory Consolidation, the Diurnal Rhythm of Cortisol, and the Nature of Dreams: A New Hypothesis. *International Review of Neurobiology* 94: 103–134.

Pick, Daniel and Lyndal Roper, eds. 2004. *Dreams and History: The Interpretation of Dreams from Ancient Greece to Modern Psychoanalysis*. London and New York: Routledge.

Porter, Laurence M. 1993. Real Dreams, Literary Dreams, and the Fantastic in Literature. In *The Dream and the Text: Essays on Literature and Language*, ed. Carol Schreier Rupprecht, 32–47. Albany: State University of New York Press.

Poulet, Georges. 1969. Phenomenology of Reading. *New Literary History* 1(1): 53–68.

Primm, Ross D. 1987. *The Dream Poem and Sixteenth-Century English Poetry*. Ann Arbor: UMI.

Prince, Morton. 1921. Foreword. In: *Studies in Dreams*. By Mary Arnold-Forster. London: George Allen & Unwin, n. pag.

Raichle, M.E., A.M. Snyder and A.Z. Snyder. 2007. A Default Mode of Brain Function: A Brief History of an Evolving Idea. *Neuroimage* 37: 1083–1090.

Rechtschaffen, Allan. 1978. The Single-Mindedness and Isolation of Dreams. *Sleep: Journal of Sleep and Sleep Disorders Research* 1: 97–109.

Reddy, Maureen. 2014. Towards a Multiracial Ireland: *Black Baby*'s Revision of Irish Motherhood. In *Literary Visions of Multicultural Ireland: The Immigrant in Contemporary Irish Culture*, ed. Pilar Villar-Argáiz, 217-229. Manchester: Manchester University Press.

Revonsuo, Antti. 2000. The Reinterpretation of Dreams: An Evolutionary Hypothesis of the Function of Dreaming. *Behavioral and Brain Sciences* 23: 877–901.

Richardson, Alan. 1999. Cognitive Science and the Future of Literary Studies. *Philosophy and Literature* 23(1): 157–173.

———. 2001. *British Romanticism and the Science of the Mind*. Cambridge: Cambridge University Press.

Ricoeur, Paul. 1984. *Time and Narrative*. Trans. Kathleen McLaughlin and David Pellauer. 2 vols. Chicago: University of Chicago Press.

———. 2006. *Memory, History, Forgetting*. Trans. Kathleen Blamey and David Pellauer. Chicago and London: The University of Chicago Press.

Rivière, Janine. 2003. "Visions of the Night": The Reform of Popular Dream Beliefs in Early Modern England. *Parergon* 20(1): 109–138.

Robinson, Richard. 2006. Nowhere, in Particular: Kazuo Ishiguro's *The Unconsoled* and Central Europe. *Critical Quarterly* 48(4): 107–130.

Robinson, Daniel. 1997. Coleridge, Mary Robinson, and the Prosody of Dreams. *Dreaming* 7(2): 119–140.

Royle, Nicholas. 2003. *The Uncanny*. Manchester: Manchester University Press.

Rupprecht, Carol Schreier. 1991. Dreams and Literature: A Reader's Guide. In *Sleep and Dreams: A Source Book*, ed. Jayne Gackenbach, 359–377. New York: Garland.

———, ed. 1993. *The Dream and the Text: Essays on Literature and Language*. Albany: State University of New York Press.

———. 1999. Dreaming and the Impossible Art of Translation. *Dreaming* 9(1): 71–99.

———. 2007. Dreaming, Language, Literature. In *The New Science of Dreaming: Volume III. Cultural and Theoretical Perspectives on Dreaming*, eds. Deirdre Barrett and Patrick McNamara, 1–34. Westport: Praeger Perspectives.

Rupprecht, Carol Schreier, and Kelly Bulkeley. 1993. Reading Yourself to Sleep: Dreams in/and/as Texts. In *The Dream and the Text: Essays on Literature and*

Language, ed. Carol Schreier Rupprecht, 1–10. Albany: State University of New York Press.

Ryan, Marie-Laure. 2010. Narratology and Cognitive Science: A Problematic Relation. *Style* 44(4): 469–495.

Rycroft, Charles. 1979. *The Innocence of Dreams*. London: Hogarth.

Sacks, Oliver. 2012. *Hallucinations*. London: Picador.

Sartre, Jean-Paul. 1972 (1940). *The Psychology of Imagination*. London: Methuen.

Scarry, Elaine. 2001. *Dreaming by the Book*. Princeton, NJ: Princeton University Press.

Schacter, Daniel L. 1976. The Hypnagogic State: A Critical Review of the Literature. *Psychological Bulletin* 83(3): 452–481.

Schleifer, Ronald. 1980. The Trap of the Imagination: The Gothic Tradition, Fiction and "The Turn of the Screw". *Criticism* 22(4): 297–319.

Schmidt-Hannisa, Hans-Walter. 1998. Die Kunst der Seele: Poetologie und Psychologie des Traums bei Hermann Hesse. In *Träumungen: Traumerzählung in Film und Literatur*, ed. Bernard Dieterle, 203–231. St. Augustin: Gardez! Verlag.

———. 2001a. "Der Träumer vollendet sich im Dichter": Die ästhetische Emanzipation der Traumaufzeichnung. In *Hundert Jahre 'Die Traumdeutung': Kulturwissenschaftliche Perspektiven in der Traumforschung*, ed. Burkhard Schnepel, 83–106. Köln: Köppe.

———. 2001b. "Der Traum ist unwillkürliche Dichtkunst": Traumtheorie und Traumaufzeichnung bei Jean Paul. *Jahrbuch der Jean-Paul-Gesellschaft* 35(36): 93–113.

Schönhammer, Rainer. 2004. *Fliegen, Fallen, Flüchten: Psychologie Intensiver Träume*. Tübingen: dgvt.

Schrage-Früh, Michaela. 2009. "Transforming That Past": The Healing Power of Dreams in Paula Meehan's Poetry. *An Sionnach: A Journal of Literature, Culture, and the Arts* 5(1/2): 114–126.

———. 2012a. "The Roots of Art Are in the Dream": Dreams, Literature and Evolution. In *Telling Stories: Literature and Evolution/Evolution of Literature*, eds. Carsten Gansel and Dirk Vanderbeke, 156–171. Berlin: De Gruyter.

———. 2012b. (Un-)Writing the Self: Authorial Strategies in Seventeenth-Century Women's Religious Prophecy. In *Anglistentag 2011 Freiburg: Proceedings*, 111–127. Trier: WVT.

Schredl, Michael. 2010. Dream Content Analysis: Basic Principles. *International Journal of Dream Research* 3(1): 65–73.

Schredl, Michael and Daniel Erlacher. 2007. Self-Reported Effects of Dreams on Waking-Life Creativity: An Empirical Study. *Journal of Psychology* 141(1): 35–46.

———. 2008. Do REM (Lucid) Dreamed and Executed Actions Share the Same Neural Substrate? *International Journal of Dream Research* 1(1): 7–14.

Schwartz, Sophie. 2000. A Historical Loop of One Hundred Years: Similarities Between 19th Century and Contemporary Dream Research. *Dreaming* 10(1): 55–66.

———. 2004. What Dreaming Can Reveal About Cognitive and Brain Functions During Sleep: A Lexico-Statistical Analysis of Dream Reports. *Psychologica Belgica* 44(1–2): 5–42.

Schwenger, Peter. 1999. *Fantasm and Fiction: On Textual Envisioning*. Stanford: Stanford University Press.

———. 2012. *At the Borders of Sleep: On Liminal Literature*. Minneapolis: University of Minnesota Press.

Shafton, Anthony. 1995. *Dream Reader: Contemporary Approaches to the Understanding of Dreams*. Albany: State University of New York Press.

Shumaker, Jeanette Roberts. 2006. Accepting the Grotesque Body: Bildungs by Clare Boylan and Eilis Ni Dhuibhne. *Estudios Irlandeses* 1: 103–111.

Siegel, Jerome M. 1993. REM Sleep, Function of. In *Encyclopedia of Sleep and Dreaming*, ed. Mary A. Carskadon, 507–510. New York: Macmillan.

Sobel, Mechal. 2000. Introduction. *Teach Me Dreams: The Search for Self in the Revolutionary Era*. Princeton and Oxford: Princeton University Press, 3–16.

Solms, Mark and Oliver Turnbull. 2002. *The Brain and the Inner World: An Introduction to the Neuroscience of Subjective Experience*. New York: Other Press.

Solomonova, Elizaveta, Elena Frantova and Tore Nielsen. 2011. Felt Presence: The Uncanny Encounters with the Numinous Other. *AI & Soc* 26: 171–178.

Southey, Robert and Caroline Bowles. 1881. *Correspondence with Caroline Bowles, to Which Are Added: Correspondence with Shelley, and Southey's Dreams*, ed. Edward Dowden. Dublin: Hodges, Figgis, and Co.

Speer, Nicole, et al. 2009. Reading Stories Activates Neural Representations of Visual and Motor Experience. *Psychological Science* 20: 989–999.

Spolsky, Ellen. 2001. *Satisfying Skepticism: Embodied Knowledge in the Early Modern World*. Aldershot: Ashgate.

St. Peter, Christine. 1997. Black Baby Takes Us Back: Dreaming the Postcolonial Mother. *Canadian Woman Studies/Les Cahiers de la Femme* 17(3): 36–38.

Stamirowska, Krystyna. 2002. Revisiting a Foreign Land: *The Unconsoled* and *When We Were Orphans* by Kazuo Ishiguro. In *Studies in Literature and Culture*, ed. Maria Edelson, 218–226. Wydaw. Uniw.

States, Bert O. 1978–79. The Art of Dreaming. *Hudson Review* 31(4): 571–586.

———. 1987. *The Rhetoric of Dreams*. Ithaca: Cornell University Press.

———. 1993. *Dreaming and Storytelling*. Ithaca: Cornell University Press.

———. 1994. Authorship in Dreams and Fictions. *Dreaming* 4(4): 237–254.

———. 1997. *Seeing in the Dark: Reflections on Dreams and Dreaming*. New Haven and London: Yale University Press.

———. 2001. Dreams: The Royal Road to Metaphor. *SubStance* 30(1/2): 104–118.

Stephen, Michele. 2003. Memory, Emotion and the Imaginal Mind. In *Dreaming and the Self: New Perspectives on Subjectivity, Identity, and Emotion*, ed. Jeannette Marie Mageo, 97–129. Albany: State University of New York Press.

Stevens, Anthony. 1995. *Private Myths: Dreams and Dreaming*. Cambridge: Harvard University Press.

Strauch, Inge and Barbara Meier. 1996. *In Search of Dreams: Results of Experimental Dream Research*. Trans. M. Ebon. Albany: State University of New York Press.

Taylor, Laewrence J., Shiri Lev-Ari and Rolf A. Zwaan. Inferences About Action Engage Acton Systems. *Brain and Language* 107(1): 62–67.

Tedlock, Barbara. 1991. The New Anthropology of Dreaming. *Dreaming* 1: 161–178.

Thomas, Nigel J.T. 2014. The Multidimensional Spectrum of Imagination: Images, Dreams, Hallucinations, and Active, Imaginative Perception. *Humanities* 3: 132–184.

Thomas, Ronald R. 1990. *Dreams of Authority: Freud and the Fictions of the Unconscious*. Ithaca and London: Cornell University Press.

Todorov, Tzvetan. 1975. *The Fantastic: A Structural Approach to a Literary Genre*. Ithaca: Cornell University Press.

Turner, Mark. 1996. *The Literary Mind*. Oxford: Oxford University Press.

———. 2003. Double-Scope Stories. In *Narrative Theory and the Cognitive Sciences*, ed. David Herman, 117–142. Stanford, CA: CSLI Publications.

Twitchell, James B. 1985. *Dreadful Pleasures: An Anatomy of Modern Horror*. Oxford: Oxford University Press.

Ullman, Montague. 1969. Dreaming as Metaphor in Motion. *Archives in General Psychiatry* 21: 696–703, http://siivola.org/monte/papers_grouped/copyrighted/Dreams/Dreaming_as_Metaphor_in_Motion.htm

Valli, Katja and Antti Revonsuo. 2007. Evolutionary Psychological Approaches to Dream Content. Cultural and Theoretical Perspectives. In *The New Science of Dreaming*, vol 3, eds. Deirdre Barrett and Patrick McNamara, 95–116. Westport: Praeger.

Van Dusen, Wilson. 1972. *The Natural Depth in Man*. New York: Harper and Row.

Villar Flor, Carlos. 2000. Unreliable Selves in an Unreliable World: The Multiple Projections of the Hero in Kazuo Ishiguro's *The Unconsoled*. *Journal of English Studies* 2: 159–169.

Vogel, Gerald W. 1993. Activation-Synthesis Hypothesis. In *Encyclopedia of Sleep and Dreaming*, ed. Mary A. Carskadon, 2–6. New York: Macmillan.

Walkowitz, Rebecca L. 2001. Ishiguro's Floating Worlds. *ELH* 68: 1049–1076.

Walsh, Richard. 2007. *The Rhetoric of Fictionality: Narrative Theory and the Idea of Fiction*. Columbus: The Ohio State University Press.

———. 2010. Dreaming and Narrative Theory. In *Toward a Cognitive Theory of Narrative Acts*, ed. Frederick Luis Aldama, 141–158. Austin: University of Texas Press.

Weidhorn, Manfred. 1970. *Dreams in Seventeenth-Century English Literature*. The Hague: Mouton.

White-Lewis, Jane. 1993. In Defense of Nightmares: Clinical and Literary Cases. In *The Dream and the Text: Essays on Literature and Language*, ed. Carol Schreier Rupprecht, 48–70. Albany: State University of New York Press.

Whitfield, Sarah, and John Elderfield. 1998. *Bonnard*. New York: Harry N. Abrams.

Windt, Jennifer M. 2013. Reporting Dream Experience: Why (Not) to Be Sceptical About Dream Reports. *Frontiers in Human Neuroscience* 7: 708. doi:10.3389/fnhum.2013.00708.

———. 2015. *Dreaming: A Conceptual Framework for Philosophy of Mind and Empirical Research*. Cambridge, MA and London: MIT Press.

Wolf, Mark J.P. 2012. *Building Imaginary Worlds: The Theory and History of Subcreation*. New York: Routledge.

Wong, Cynthia F. 2000. *Kazuo Ishiguro*. Plymouth: Northcote House.

Woods, Ralph L. and Herbert B. Greenhouse, eds. 1974. *The New World of Dreams: An Anthology*. New York: Macmillan Publishing.

Index

A

absorption. *See* immersion
activation-synthesis model, 31, 34
Aeschylus, 110
aesthetic feeling, 125. *See also* literary feelings; rasa
aesthetics, 9–11, 14, 17, 21–57, 194, 261
agency in dreams, 72, 81, 82. *See also* dream control
Alice in Wonderland (Carroll), 201
alienation dream. *See* dream types
Alvarez, Alfred, 8, 29, 29n45, 105, 105n197, 149n97, 171n202
Amis, Kingsley, 182, 183n252
   'Mason's Life,' 182, 183n252
Angelou, Maya, 86
animal dreaming, 71, 117, 194, 235
anxiety dream, 65, 131, 138, 144, 144n73, 146, 211, 218, 240. *See also* dream types
'Araby' (Joyce), 143, 143n67
archetypal dream. *See* dream types
Aristotle, 6, 137
Arnold-Foster, Mary
   and criticism of Freud, 131
   on dream diversity, 131, 132
   and dream reports, 75, 75n60, 170
art, 1, 10, 16, 17, 19, 26, 33, 41, 52, 54, 55, 64, 66, 87, 98, 99n166, 103n183, 137, 141, 157, 167, 171, 192, 200, 226, 250, 262
Aserinsky, Eugene, 3n16, 27
Atkins, Peter, 161

Note: Page numbers followed by n denote footnotes.

B

Bacon, Francis, 6, 6n29
ballad, 18, 183–91, 264. *See also*
    Coleridge, 'The Rime of the
    Ancient Mariner'
Banville, John, 171, 171n203,
    171n204, 172, 172n205, 243,
    243n53, 244, 244n54,
    244n56, 244n57, 249,
    249n61, 250, 260n88, 264
    The Sea, 18, 173, 243–60,
        264, 265
Barnes, Djuna, 98
Baron-Cohen, Simon, 66, 66n25
Barrett, Deirdre, 15, 42, 42n111, 44,
    44n121, 49, 49n150, 135,
    211n13
Barth, John, 86, 154
belief, 5, 17, 63, 67, 73, 76, 76n63,
    82, 95, 120–5, 128, 176,
    178, 263
bizarreness
    Barbara Meier on, 44n119, 83
    Bert O. States on, 14, 15, 17,
        18, 25, 52, 81, 84, 136,
        166, 168
    characteristics of, 31n56, 133
    Don Kuiken on, 9, 14, 15, 18,
        26, 263
    in dreams, 136, 158
    Harry T. Hunt on, 14, 18, 37,
        66, 132
    John Allan Hobson on, 8, 28
    in literature, 180
    Owen Flanagan on, 135
Blanchot, Maurice, 8, 8n37, 15
blending, 17, 53, 54, 104, 233, 236,
    238
'Bliss' (Mansfield), 142, 142n55

body, 6, 11, 27, 56, 113–15, 117,
    130, 188, 190, 215, 217, 231,
    256
Bonnard, Pierre, 250, 251, 253
Borges, Jorge Luis, 2, 2n8, 75,
    75n61, 89, 89n125, 98n161,
    111, 182, 182n251
    Brodie's Report, 98n161
    'Coleridge's Dream,' 111,
        111n222
    'Dreamtigers,' 75, 75n61
    'The Circular Ruins,' 182,
        182n251
Bosnak, Robert, 3n15, 113n232,
    114, 114n235, 114n236
boundaries in the mind, 180. *See also*
    thick boundaries; thin
    boundaries
Boylan, Clare, 264
    Black Baby, 18, 229–43, 264
brain, 8, 11, 12, 27, 28, 31–4, 36,
    38, 40, 40n101, 41–3, 45, 54,
    55, 62, 76, 79, 82, 84, 88, 92,
    96, 114, 114n236, 149, 184,
    199, 234
Brodie's Report (Borges), 98n161
Brontë, Charlotte, 126, 126n279
Brontë, Emily, 109, 257, 258n82
    Wuthering Heights, 109, 257,
        258n82
Brosch, Renate, 100, 100n171,
    101n175, 103, 103n185, 104,
    104n187, 120n258
Browne, Thomas, 6, 6n30, 79,
    79n81
Bulkeley, Kelly, 4n20, 9, 9n40,
    49n152, 56n188, 109,
    109n212
Byron, George Gordon, 3, 3n18

C

Calvino, Italo, 102n178
  If on a Winter's Night a Traveler, 101
Cardano, Girolamo, 1
Carroll, Joseph, 11n49, 45, 45n127
Carroll, Lewis
  Alice in Wonderland, 201
  Through the Looking-Glass, 182, 182n249
Cartwright, Rosalind, 20, 27n32, 28n41, 46n136, 47, 47n137–40, 48, 129, 130n297, 130n298, 149, 149n99
Kassandra (Wolf), 110
central image, 48, 149, 202, 259
'Chapter on Dreams, A' (Stevenson), 78, 78n75, 78n76, 79n77, 79n78, 80n83
children's dreams, 35, 67
'Christabel' (Coleridge), 87
'Circular Ruins, The' (Borges), 182, 182n251
Clark, Andy, 50n156
Cobbe, Frances Power, 79n78, 153, 153n118
cognitive narratology, 16
cognitive sciences, 11–14, 151n112
Coleridge, Samuel Taylor, 2, 79, 183–91
  Biographia Literaria, 123n264, 183, 183n253, 183n254, 184n265
  'Christabel,' 87
  'Kubla Khan,' 110, 111, 111n221
  'The Rime of the Ancient Mariner,' 144, 183–91, 265

'Coleridge's Dream' (Borges), 111, 111n222
Commentary on the Dream of Scipio (Macrobius), 7
conceptual metaphor, 150–4, 186, 219, 220, 245, 265. *See also* metaphor
consciousness, 8, 12, 14, 18, 23, 24, 34, 50, 51, 60, 62n9, 63, 70, 75, 82, 85–7, 90, 96n153, 97, 97n153, 98, 101, 104, 107, 109, 111, 114, 116, 123, 130, 134, 136, 147, 151, 151n112, 163, 164, 166, 167, 169, 188, 192, 203, 208, 212, 227, 238, 246, 247, 260
Cosmides, Leda, 52, 53, 53n172, 55, 55n181–3
creativity. *See also under* dreaming
  and bizarreness, 134, 157
  and boundary types, 180
cultural determinism, 12
culture pattern dream. *See* dream types

D

Damasio, Antonio, 12
Darwin, Erasmus, 122, 122n262
daydreaming, 17, 37, 38, 40, 41, 55, 68, 69, 76, 82, 86, 97, 98, 100, 109, 180, 261, 264. *See also* default mode network; mind-wandering
daymare, 72
defamiliarization, 53, 180

294 Index

default mode network, 17, 38, 39, 39n99, 76, 77, 261. *See also* mind-wandering
Dement, William, 5, 5n22, 27n35, 27n36, 61
Dennett, Daniel, 83n95
Descartes, René, 59, 60, 60n2, 60n3, 66
Dickens, Charles, 19, 19n71, 60, 60n4, 61, 70, 70n41, 72, 72n49, 95, 95n145, 119
Domhoff, G. W., 11n49, 15, 38n93–38n95, 39, 39n97, 39n99, 42
Dostoyevsky, Fyodor, 13, 79, 79n82
Dracula (Bram Stoker), 144, 183, 191, 195–9, 199n295
dramatic dream. *See* dream types
dream authorship, 78, 81, 227, 228, 267. *See also* 'paradox of authorship'
dream beliefs, 6, 168
dream characters, 4, 24, 88, 95, 104, 113, 116, 119, 128, 144, 160, 163, 164, 187, 223, 228
dream content, 8, 9, 23, 24n14, 31, 39, 43, 49, 75, 163, 167n186, 193, 209. *See also* Hall-Van de Castle system of content analysis
dream control, 71, 191. *See also* agency in dreams
dream deception, 73
dream delusion. *See* dream deception
dream diversity, 18, 131–46, 265. *See also* dream types
dreaming
  in antiquity, 6, 133
  connection-making in, 17, 47, 48, 229, 236, 262, 266
  and creativity, 57
  as cross-cultural activity, 3, 53, 265, 267
  evolutionary approaches to, 17, 43
  experience of, 2, 9, 10, 16, 56, 114n236, 168, 169, 176, 185
  and imagination, 59
  in Judeo-Christian tradition, 6
  and latent content, 23
  and manifest content, 23, 27, 30, 167
  and memory consolidation, 46
  as mental activity, 13, 16, 34, 34n73, 36, 42, 94
  as metaphor, 147
  narrative structure of, 155
  phenomenology of, 101
  physiology of (*see* dream physiology)
  as play, 173, 241
  and prophecy, 51
  single-mindedness of, 68, 94n141, 175, 208
dream journey, 8, 174, 195
dream 'language'
  diversity of, 131–46, 265
  translation of, 10, 18, 146, 167, 167n186, 167n191, 170, 177, 265
  universality of, 3n15, 265, 266
dreamlikeness in fiction, 10, 18, 177, 200, 264, 265

dream lucidity, 125, 140, 140n50.
See also dream types, lucid
dream
dream phenomenology, 8, 18,
147n85
dream physiology
NREM sleep, 3n16, 27, 34,
35n78, 36, 38, 46
REM sleep, 3n16, 17, 27, 27n35,
28, 28n39, 32–40, 40n101,
41, 42, 42n110, 44, 45,
45n124, 47, 50, 69, 76,
107, 121, 134, 149, 184
sleep cycle, 28
sleep phases, 7, 34, 36, 37
dream recall, 48, 99, 156n135, 172
dream recollection. See dream recall
dream reports, 4, 8, 18, 19n67, 30,
31n36, 35, 36, 68n35, 75,
83n95, 116, 145n79, 147n88,
158, 170, 171, 264, 268
dream-self, 79, 116–19, 161, 162, 174
'Dreamtigers' (Borges), 75, 75n61
dream types. See also dream diversity
archetypal dream, 139 (see also
Jungian dream theory)
Bert O. States on, 14–18, 25, 52,
81, 84, 136, 166
Charles Dickens on, 19, 60, 70,
72, 95
culture pattern dream, 139
Don Kuiken on, 9, 14, 15, 18,
26, 263
falling dream, 150, 151, 209,
220, 229
flying dream, 75, 138, 150, 151,
211, 211n13

Frederick Greenwood on, 107, 131
Harry T. Hunt on, 14, 18, 37, 66,
132
impactful dream
alienation dream, 138, 144,
145, 211, 216, 217
anxiety dream, 65, 131, 138,
144n73, 146, 211, 218, 240
(see also nightmare)
existential dream, 138, 142–4,
144n73, 145, 146, 189
transcendent dream, 138, 140,
142, 146
lucid dream, 4n19, 131, 182, 214
Mary Arnold-Forster on, 131
mundane dream, 133–5, 145,
156, 158
nightmare, 8, 29, 30n49, 56, 69,
131, 133, 144, 144n73,
188–99, 209, 236, 237, 266
(see also anxiety dream; Felt
Presence; hallucinatory sleep
paralysis)
reality dream, 73, 138, 181
S. T. Coleridge on, 87n117, 110,
119, 123, 144
typical dream, 19, 150, 162, 210,
216–18, 264, 266 (see also
dream types, falling dream;
dream types, flying dream)
wish-fulfilment dream, 131, 235
(see also Freudian dream
theory)
dream-wake boundaries, 265
blurring of, 265
dream-work, 11, 26, 62, 79. See also
Freudian dream theory

Du Maurier, Daphne
   Rebecca, 255, 256, 256n79
   'The Pool,' 65, 65n23
Dürer, Albrecht, 2n3

E
Edelman, Gerald, 7, 7n33, 12
Eliot, T.S.
   'The Love-Song of J. Alfred Prufrock,' 177n228
Ellis, Havelock, 70, 93, 132n5, 162, 165, 166
embodied mind, 11, 115
emotion, 17, 28, 31, 33, 44n119, 47, 48, 53, 78, 106, 122, 125, 128–30, 137, 139–41, 145, 149, 150, 159, 188, 189, 210. *See also* aesthetic feeling; literary feelings
   in dreams, 35, 44n119, 127, 266
   in fiction, 14, 17, 18, 41, 44, 46, 50, 52–4, 72, 76, 81, 92, 102, 116, 118, 119, 122, 124–206, 210, 249, 259, 262, 265, 266
emotional memory system, 50
empathy, 17, 46, 116, 128, 262. *See also* identification
Engel, Manfred, 15, 94n142, 147n85, 168n191
enjoyment, 50, 55
epic dream. *See* dream types
Epic of Gilgamesh, The, 56
epiphany, 143. *See also* moment of being
Erlacher, Daniel, 57n193
Esrock, Ellen J., 18, 99, 99n168, 99n169, 100n170

evolution, 41–57
existential dream. *See* dream types

F
falling dream. *See* dream types
'Fall of the House of Usher, The' (Poe), 109, 109n213, 175, 175n220
fantastic, the, 61, 185, 210n8
fascination, 123, 153, 194, 199n295, 204
fear, 4, 31, 44, 44n119, 124–8, 143–5, 191, 192, 196–9, 217, 225, 266
Felski, Rita, 127, 127n284
Feltham, Owen, 54n180
Felt Presence, 193, 198, 198n294
fiction, 1–3, 7, 9, 14, 17, 18, 44–6, 46n134, 50, 52, 53n171, 54, 62, 85, 87, 91, 92, 96, 98, 99, 99n166, 116, 120n258, 122, 124–6, 128–30, 141, 145, 148, 160, 170, 171, 171n203, 172n205, 173, 175, 176, 178, 179, 192, 194, 208, 210, 210n8, 221, 243, 243n53, 244, 244n54, 244n56, 246, 249, 249n61, 251, 259, 260n88, 263, 265
film, 15, 16, 82, 83, 101–3, 103n183, 113, 114n237, 126, 128, 129, 162, 262
Finnegans Wake (Joyce), 98
Flanagan, Owen, 42, 42n110, 92, 92n137, 135, 135n21, 162
flying dream. *See* dream types

Foulkes, David, 8, 25, 80, 105n193
Freud, Sigmund, 21. *See also* Freudian dream theory
Die Traumdeutung, 21, 27
on dream as disguised wish-fulfilment, 7, 29, 131, 193, 232, 235, 240
on dream as guardian of sleep, 27n35, 29
on dream-work, 11, 26, 62, 79
on nightmares, 30, 30n49, 44, 48, 192, 193
'On Dreams,' 6n30, 24n14, 25n17
'Revision of the Theory of Dreams,' 25n17
on the uncanny, 176, 178, 179, 192–4, 237, 253, 255
Freudian dream theory
criticism of, 32, 131
impact of, 22, 210
functions of dreaming, 41, 262
Fuseli, Henri
The Nightmare (painting), 144

G

Gardner, John, 85, 85n105, 98, 99n166
Gaskell, Elizabeth, 126n278
gates of horn and ivory, 5, 6. *See also* Homer, *The Odyssey*
Globus, Gordon, 140, 140n51, 141, 166, 166n179
Gordimer, Nadine, 200, 200n302
Gordon, John, 91, 140
Gothic, The, 15, 18, 144, 183, 191–9, 264

Gover, Tzivia, 5, 5n23, 8, 8n38, 28n39, 28n40, 51n162, 113, 114n233, 114n234
Greenwood, Frederick, 107, 107n204, 131, 131n1

H

Hacking, Ian, 168, 168n189
Hall, Calvin, 19, 19n68, 30, 31, 31n57, 43, 44n119, 145n79, 148, 148n95, 148n96, 218
Hall, James W., 86
hallucinations, 5, 22, 24, 29, 42, 51, 60–2, 62n9, 64, 68, 69, 110, 192, 193, 248, 267
hallucinatory sleep paralysis, 69
Hall-Van de Castle system of content analysis, 30, 31, 31n57. *See also* dream content
Handke, Peter, 127, 127n285
Hartmann, Ernest
on boundary types, 180 (*see also* thick boundaries; thin boundaries)
on central image of dream, 149, 259
on connection-making in dreams, 17, 47, 48, 229, 236, 262, 266
on creativity, 34, 37, 41, 49, 51, 57, 57n193, 91, 134, 157
on dreams as *explanatory metaphors*, 47, 259

Hawthorne, Nathaniel, 169,
   170n194, 181n247, 181n248,
   207, 207n1
  'Young Goodman Brown,' 181,
   181n247, 181n248
Hesse, Hermann, 171
Hobbes, Thomas, 6, 60n3, 267
  Leviathan, 6n28, 60
Hobson, John Allan, 3n17, 8,
   8n34, 28, 28n39, 29n43,
   30n55, 31, 31n59, 31n60,
   32, 32n64, 33, 33n67–9, 34,
   34n70, 34n71, 34n73, 61,
   61n5–8, 62n9, 64, 64n19,
   65n20, 114n237, 122,
   136n25, 250, 250n65. *See
   also* activation-synthesis
   model
  on auto-creativity, 33
  on dream bizarreness, 32, 60,
   135, 136
  on dream delusion, 61, 63, 122
  on REM sleep, 28, 31, 31n59,
   32–4
Hogan, Patrick Colm
  on literary feelings, 18, 125,
   268
  on literary universals, 19
Homer, 5, 6
  The Odyssey, 5, 6, 254
horror, 44, 65, 124–6, 144, 163,
   187, 188, 192, 199
Hunt, Harry T.
  on dream bizarreness, 156, 157,
   157n140
  on dream diversity, 131–46
Hustvedt, Siri, 69, 69n38
hypnagogia, 29, 105, 107,
   120, 263

Ichikawa, Jonathan, 62, 71, 71n46,
   72n47, 73, 73n51, 124,
   124n268
identification, 78, 95, 116, 118, 122,
   129, 263
If on a Winter's Night a Traveler
   (Calvino), 101
imagery, 63, 64, 66, 71, 73, 75, 76,
   87, 89, 105–8, 110, 113, 115,
   134, 135, 147, 149, 150, 152,
   156–8, 185
imaginal memory register, 88. *See
   also* memory
imaginal mind, 50
imagination
  versus delusion, 4, 61, 63, 67,
   122, 125, 176, 231
  dreaming, 1, 4, 5, 7–11, 13, 14,
   16–57, 59–205, 207–62,
   264, 266, 268
  multidimensional spectrum of
   imagination, 68, 87, 97
  versus perception, 69 (*see also*
   perception)
  visual, 110
  waking, 9, 10, 22, 25, 42, 57,
   59–130, 196, 262
imaginative perception, 68, 70
immersion
  readerly, 17, 78, 81, 93, 114, 117,
   118, 127, 263
  spatiotemporal, 95, 113, 114,
   127, 128, 263
  writerly, 17, 78
impactful dream. *See* dream types
Inception, 7
inspiration, 1, 4, 25, 34, 56, 110
interdisciplinarity, 9–11, 14

Iser, Wolfgang, 18, 94n143, 96, 96n148, 102, 103, 103n182, 103n184, 103n186, 104, 104n188, 121, 121n259, 123, 123n266, 123n267, 129, 190, 209
Ishiguro, Kazuo, 18, 145, 207–29, 264
The Unconsoled, 18, 145, 207–29, 260, 264

J

James, Henry, 109, 109n214–16, 110n197, 110n198, 121, 122, 256, 257n80, 257n81
Jay, Clare, 87, 87n115
Jean Paul, 2, 18
Joyce, James
 'Araby,' 143, 143n67
 Finnegans Wake, 98
Jung, Carl Gustav, 15, 19n67, 49n151, 133, 139, 154. *See also* Jungian dream theory
Jungian dream theory, 154

K

Kafka, Franz
 'Metamorphosis,' 65, 89, 90, 145, 176, 177, 212
Kassandra (Wolf). *See* Cassandra (Wolf)
Keaton, Buster, 161, 162
Kerr, Nancy, 63, 64, 64n16, 64n17
Khan, David, 51
King, Stephen, 85, 86, 91, 92, 92n134, 182
Kleitmann, Nathaniel, 3n16, 27, 169, 207

Kreuzer, Stefanie, 15, 103n183, 135n22, 178n232
'Kubla Khan' (Coleridge), 110, 111, 111n221
Kuiken, Don
 on dream bizarreness, 32, 60, 135, 136, 156, 157, 157n140, 159, 162
 on impactful dreams, 14, 137, 138, 140n50, 144–6, 155, 158, 265
 on interdisciplanarity, 9–11, 14
 on literary feelings, 54, 116, 125, 136, 138, 140, 142, 146, 180, 212, 219, 235, 257, 259
 on script-theory, 155

L

LaBerge, Stephen, 4n19, 7n32, 72, 72n48, 84n97, 164, 164n171, 211n13
Lakoff, George, 18, 150, 150n107, 151, 151n109, 151n110, 151n112, 152, 152n113–17, 153, 153n119, 154n121
Lessing, Doris
 The Summer Before the Dark, 142, 173, 174n211–14
Levertov, Denise, 167, 167n183–5
Leviathan (Hobbes), 6, 6n28, 60n3
literary feelings, 116, 136, 146, 259. *See also* aesthetic feeling
literary mind, 3, 172
Lovecraft, H. P., 80
'Love-Song of J. Alfred Prufrock, The' (Eliot), 177n228
lucid dream. *See* dream types
lyric dream. *See* dream types

Index

M
Macnish, Robert, 2, 2n7
Marcrobius, 7n31
madness, 4, 121, 122
make-belief emotions, 125, 127. *See also* aesthetic feeling; emotion; literary feelings
Mansfield, Katherine, 80, 108
 'Bliss,' 142, 142n55–8
 'Sun and Moon,' 120, 183, 200–5
marvelous, the, 179
'Mason's Life' (Kingsley), 182, 183
Massey, Irving, 9, 10n46, 14, 52, 52n167, 52n168, 184n256
Mavromatis, Andreas, 29, 29n46–8, 34n74, 37, 37n87, 42n112, 55, 55n184, 55n185, 74, 74n58, 105n195, 106, 106n200–106n203, 107, 107n205, 107n206, 132n7
McGinn, Colin, 14, 17, 62, 63, 63n12, 68, 68n35, 69, 70n39, 81, 81n88–91, 82, 82n92–4, 83, 83n95, 84, 89, 100, 103n183, 126, 126n280, 126n281, 127n282, 127n283, 267
McNamara, Patrick, 14n61, 16n63, 19, 30n49, 35, 35n78, 35n79, 36n82–36n84, 56, 56n189, 56n190, 94, 95n144, 133, 133n11, 192, 192n278, 194n288, 197n289–91
Meehan, Paula, 51n161
Meier, Barbara, 30n55, 44n119, 83, 83n96, 135, 136n23, 148n92, 163, 163n165, 163n166, 165, 165n175, 165n176, 175, 175n218, 201n304

memory, 7n31, 10, 18, 28, 28n39, 38, 46–8, 50, 51, 53, 54, 62, 76, 83, 83n95, 88, 105, 108, 114n236, 129, 130, 134, 141, 145, 155, 157, 168–72, 213, 214, 246–9, 251–4, 256, 258–60, 264
'Metamorphosis' (Kafka), 65, 89, 90, 145, 176, 177, 212
metaphor, 1, 2, 19, 23–5, 47, 49, 50, 67, 113, 133, 147, 147n85, 150–4, 157, 159, 170, 177, 186, 219, 245, 246, 259, 265, 267
Metz, Christian, 101, 101n176, 101n177, 103n183
Midsummer Night's Dream, A (Shakespeare), 128
mind, 3, 5, 6, 8, 10–14, 17, 20, 22, 25, 32, 33, 38, 39, 46, 47, 50, 50n156, 52, 54, 55, 62n9, 63, 68, 72, 76, 77, 80, 81, 86, 88, 90, 92, 94, 94n141, 95, 97–100, 102, 104, 109, 111, 112, 115, 118, 119, 122, 126, 129, 132, 139, 153, 154, 156, 159, 170n194, 172, 177, 178, 180, 181n248, 185, 187, 188, 193, 200, 204, 208, 209, 229, 236, 240, 242, 246, 247, 249, 250, 256, 258–60, 262, 268. *See also* embodied mind; imaginal mind; literary mind
mind-wandering, 38, 39, 76, 77, 88, 104, 260. *See also* daydreaming; default mode network

mirroring, 128
mirror neurons, 43, 96. *See also* mirroring
Mitchell, David, 53, 53n171, 200, 200n297
moment of being, 141, 142. *See also* epiphany
monsters, 4, 65, 139, 188, 191, 192, 194
movie. *See* film
Mukherjee, Bharati, 91, 92, 92n134
mundane dream. *See* dream types

N

The Narrative of Arthur Gordon Pym, 65
narrative perspective, 120
narrativity, 14, 62, 169. *See also under* dreaming
Nell, Victor, 18, 95, 95n146, 97, 97n154–7, 97n158, 98, 98n159, 98n160, 98n163–5
neurcognitive theory of dreams, 39, 153
neuroimaging, 10, 28, 43, 61, 76, 96
Nielsen, Tore, 15, 36, 37n85, 48n145, 73, 73n52–5, 73n57, 127n286, 133n12, 136n26, 147n89, 191
nightmare. *See* dream types
Nightmare, The (painting, Fuseli), 144
NREM sleep, 3n16, 27, 34–6, 38, 46. *See also* REM sleep; sleep cycle; sleep physiology

O

Oatley, Keith, 2, 2n9–11, 3, 3n12, 14, 18, 38, 38n92, 43, 43n117, 45n126, 46, 46n129–32, 46n133, 46n134, 50, 52n154, 52n156, 53, 53n173–5, 54, 54n178, 54n179, 56n186, 88, 88n119, 90, 90n129, 96, 96n149, 96n150, 96n152, 96n153, 98, 98n162, 116, 116n247, 128, 128n291, 129, 129n292–5, 129n296, 130, 130n299, 159n152, 262, 263n4
  on dream as 'model world,' 2
  on emotions, 53, 54, 116, 128, 129, 262
  on metaphor, 2, 50, 159
  on mirroring, 128, 128n291
Odyssey, The (Homer), 5, 6, 254
oneirogenic effects, 73
Ovid, 65, 113

P

Palombo, Stanley, 26, 26n29, 46n136, 48, 48n146, 49n147, 49n148
Paracelsus, 1, 2n3
'paradox of authorship,' 17, 80, 84, 213, 262. *See also* dream authorship
'paradox of fiction,' 17, 122, 124, 128, 263. *See also* belief; emotion; identification

perception, 11, 17, 35, 43, 60, 61, 63–71, 95, 99–101, 103n183, 114, 120, 146, 168, 170, 175, 177, 178, 180, 181, 216, 250. *See also* imaginative perception
versus imagination, 11, 17, 61, 63–71, 101, 103n183, 114, 178, 241, 250
pleasure. *See* enjoyment
Poe, Edgar Allan, 107, 107n207, 109n213, 175n220, 176
'The Fall of the House of Usher,' 109, 109n213, 175, 175n220
The Narrative of Arthur Gordon Pym, 65
poetry, 2, 51n161, 87n117, 107, 141, 149, 184, 188
'Pool, The' (du Maurier), 65, 65n23, 195, 236
Poulet, Georges, 96n153
Prince, Morton, 132, 132n6

R

rasa, 53, 125. *See also* aesthetic feeling; literary feelings
reader, 10, 14, 16, 18, 19, 44, 76n63, 78, 87, 93–130, 160, 167, 171, 175–7, 179, 180, 183, 185–91, 205, 208–13, 216, 221, 223, 228–32, 234, 236, 240–3, 246–9, 257, 259, 260, 262–4
reader response criticism, 14, 263
reading, 10, 15, 17, 43, 47, 57, 77, 93, 94n141, 95, 96, 96n153, 97–9, 99n167, 100–5, 108–11, 115, 118, 121–4, 126, 127, 129, 130, 187, 190, 208, 232, 234, 255, 259, 263, 268
reality dream. *See* dream types
Rebecca (du Maurier), 255, 256, 256n79
Rechtschaffen, Alan, 94n141, 164, 164n169
reductionism, 8, 32
REM sleep, 3n16, 17, 27, 27n35, 28, 28n39, 31–40, 40n101, 41, 42, 42n110, 44, 45, 45n124, 47, 50, 69, 76, 107, 121, 134, 149, 184. *See also* NREM sleep; sleep cycle; sleep physiology
Revonsuo, Antti, 42n110, 43, 43n114. *See also* threat rehearsal theory
Rice, Anne, 86
Richardson, Alan, 11n50, 12, 12n54, 12n55
Ricoeur, Paul, 251, 251n70, 251n71, 253, 253n73, 253n74
'Rime of the Ancient Mariner, The' (Coleridge), 144, 183–91, 265
Rimmer, Dave, 74
Romanticism, 2
Rupprecht, Carol Schreier, 1, 3n14, 49n151, 56, 56n187, 56n188, 56n191, 57, 57n194, 109, 167n186, 170, 170n198
Ryan, Marie-Laure, 16, 16n64, 113n227

S

Sacks, Oliver, 62n9
Sartre, Jean Paul, 18, 63, 63n11, 90, 90n126–8, 94, 94n143, 112, 112n224–6, 115, 115n244, 116, 116n245, 116n246, 117, 117n249, 117n250, 119, 119n254, 120, 120n255, 120n256, 120n258, 123, 123n265, 227, 227n39
Scarry, Elaine, 85n104, 100, 100n173
schema, 51, 66, 112, 129, 130, 266
Schmidt-Hannisa, Hans-Walter, 2n3, 2n4, 2n6, 15, 171, 171n200
Schredl, Michael, 30n55, 43n115, 57n193, 59n1, 84n97, 96n151
Schwartz, Sophie, 8n39, 22, 22n2, 27n31, 30, 30n52–30n54, 46n136, 147n88
Schwenger, Peter, 101, 102, 102n178–81, 104, 104n189, 104n190, 110, 110n219, 110n220, 130, 130n300, 172n209
script, 109, 136, 155, 167n186, 216
Sea, The (Banville), 18, 173, 243–60, 264, 265
self, 16, 19, 23, 27, 28, 33, 39, 47, 66, 67, 79, 92, 105, 116–19, 121, 122, 125, 130, 133, 139–42, 146, 148, 157, 161, 162, 165, 173, 174, 176, 185, 191, 192, 194–6, 200, 201, 214, 223–6, 231, 238, 245, 246, 252, 253, 255, 256, 260, 266. *See also* dream-self
self-knowledge
and dreams, 256
and literature, 1, 153
Shakespeare, William
A Midsummer Night's Dream, 128
The Tempest, 254, 258, 259
short story, 18, 56, 65, 80, 120, 142, 143, 182, 183, 200–5
theory, 81, 183
simulation, 43n115, 59, 95, 96, 115, 136, 159, 262, 263
single-mindedness, 68, 94n141, 164, 175, 177, 178, 183, 208, 211, 263
sleep cycle, 28
sleep paralysis, 69, 192, 193, 197, 267
sleep physiology, 28
Solms, Mark, 12, 12n52, 12n53, 28n37, 28n38, 32n63, 40, 40n101
Southey, Robert, 94n141
speech acts, 26, 52, 147n85
in dreams, 26, 52, 147n85
Spolsky, Ellen, 12n54
States Bert, O., 14, 15, 17, 18, 25, 52
on bizarreness, 136
on dream authorship, 81
on dream types, 18, 136
on metaphors, 50, 83
on single-mindedness, 164, 164n170, 175, 211, 263
Stephen, Michelle, 50, 50n133, 51, 51n157–60, 51n161, 68, 72, 85, 91, 92n134

Stevenson, Robert Louis
  'A Chapter on Dreams,' 78,
    78n75, 78n76, 79n77,
    79n78, 80n83
  *The Strange Case of Dr. Jekyll and
    Mr. Hyde*, 78
Stoker, Bram, 144
  Dracula, 144, 183, 191–9,
    199n295
storytelling
  dreaming, 10, 17, 19, 56, 81, 84,
    92, 95, 97
  waking, 10, 17, 20, 56, 81, 84,
    92, 97
*Strange Case of Dr. Jekyll and Mr.
  Hyde, The* (Stevenson), 78
Summer Before the Dark, The
  (Lessing), 142, 173,
  174n211–14
'Sun and Moon' (Mansfield), 120,
  183, 200–5
supernatural, the, 6, 179, 267

T

Tan, Amy, 86, 91, 92
Tempest, The (Shakespeare), 254,
  258, 259n83
theory of mind (TOM), 17, 46, 54,
  262
thick boundaries, 180
thin boundaries, 57, 57n193,
  179, 180
Thomas, Nigel T., 64n18, 68, 68n34,
  69, 69n36, 71, 71n42–6, 79,
  87, 95n147, 267
threat rehearsal theory, 44
Through the Looking Glass (Carroll),
  182, 182n249, 182n250

Todorov, Tzvetan, 178n231,
  178n233, 179
Tolstoy, Leo, 109
Tooby, John, 52, 53n170, 53n172,
  55, 55n181–3
trance, 65, 86, 87, 117, 120, 189,
  263, 264
transcendent dream. *See* dream
  types
trauma, 48, 48n144, 149
Turner, Mark, 3n13, 53, 54,
  54n176, 54n177, 172n208
Turn of the Screw, The (James),
  109n214–16, 110n197,
  110n198, 257n80,
  257n81

U

Ullman, Montague, 50, 50n123,
  147, 147n87, 147n88
unconscious, the, 12, 15, 22, 32, 33,
  72, 79n78, 81, 83n95, 87,
  150, 151, 151n112, 152–4,
  170, 185, 200, 251
Unconsoled, The (Ishiguro), 18, 145,
  207–29, 260, 264

V

Van de Castle, Robert, 30, 31,
  31n56, 31n57, 43
verbal memory system, 51
'Verwandlung, Die' (Kafka). *See*
  'Metamorphosis' (Kafka)
visual imagery, 64, 76, 107, 147
visualization, 17, 95, 98, 100,
  101, 104, 105, 112, 186,
  222, 263

W

Walsh, Richard, 14, 18, 62, 62n10, 77n73, 124, 125n273, 125n274, 164
wandering viewpoint, 104
Whitman, Walt, 65, 65n21
Windt, Jennifer, 14, 18, 63, 63n13, 72n48, 73n56, 75, 76, 76n62, 76n64, 83n96, 84n98, 113, 113n231, 114, 115n238, 117, 117n248
wish-fulfilment dream. *See* dream types
Wolf, Christa, 110, 110n220, 181n245, 195
  Kassandra, 110
Woolf, Virginia, 99, 99n167, 141, 141n52–4
Wordsworth, Dorothy, 166
writer, 16, 51, 56, 68n35, 74, 78, 80n84, 85–7, 92n134, 94, 96, 107, 130, 161, 171, 179, 213, 262–4
writing, 3, 15, 57, 77, 80n84, 84–6, 88, 91, 93, 95, 97, 131–205, 207–29, 256, 263
Wuthering Heights (Brontë), 109, 257, 258n82

Y

Yeats, William Butler, 80, 80n85
'Young Goodman Brown' (Hawthorne), 181, 181n247, 181n248

The manufacturer's authorised representative in the EU is Springer Nature Customer Service Centre GmbH, Europaplatz 3, 69115 Heidelberg, Germany. If you have any concerns regarding our products, please contact ProductSafety@springernature.com

Printed and bound by CPI Group (UK) Ltd, Croydon, CR0 4YY

23/03/2026

02076662-0009